Butterworths St
Intellectual P

Butterworths Student Statutes

Intellectual Property Law

Paul Torremans, Licentiaat in de Rechten (KU Leuven),
Licentiaat in het Notariaat (Examencommissie van de Staat, Leuven),
Geaggregeerde voor het HSO in de Rechten (KU Leuven),
LLM (Leicester)
Lecturer in Law, University of Leicester

Jon Holyoak, BA (Cantab), Barrister
Senior Lecturer in Law, University of Leicester

Butterworths
London, Dublin, Edinburgh
1996

United Kingdom	Butterworths a Division of Reed Elsevier (UK) Ltd, Halsbury House, 35 Chancery Lane, LONDON WC2A 1EL and 4 Hill Street, EDINBURGH EH2 3JZ
Australia	Butterworths, SYDNEY, MELBOURNE, BRISBANE, ADELAIDE, PERTH, CANBERRA and HOBART
Canada	Butterworth Canada Ltd, TORONTO and VANCOUVER
Ireland	Butterworth (Ireland) Ltd, DUBLIN
Malaysia	Malayan Law Journal Sdn Bhd, KUALA LUMPUR
New Zealand	Butterworths of New Zealand Ltd, WELLINGTON and AUCKLAND
Singapore	Reed Elsevier (Singapore) Pte Ltd, SINGAPORE
South Africa	Butterworths Publishers (Pty) Ltd, DURBAN
USA	Michie, CHARLOTTESVILLE, Virginia

Crown copyright material is reproduced with the permission of the Controller of Her Majesty's Stationery Office

A CIP catalogue record for this book is available from the British Library.

ISBN 0 406 99376 9

Printed and bound in Great Britain by Clays Ltd, St Ives plc

Preface

Intellectual property law continues to fascinate an increasing number of students. They are no doubt attracted by the diversity which this challenging topic offers them. Inventions and technology lead to patents, artistic works lead to copyright, and trade marks, designs, passing-off etc are all situated between these two extremes.

The diversity of the subject is reflected in the legislation that covers it. International Conventions are supplemented by a string of EC Directives and Regulations and together they underpin our own statutes, forming the textual foundations for any intellectual property law course. This book gives students easy access to these foundations, providing them with an invaluable selection of source materials. Of course, it does not replace a textbook with its detailed analysis of both the case law and the statutory provisions, and it is recommended that the two should be used together.

It was unfortunately not possible to include all statutory provisions which apply to intellectual property. We are however convinced that this book contains all the essential material which students will need. Our selection of international, EC and UK materials is based upon the provisions to which we refer in Holyoak and Torremans *Intellectual Property Law* (Butterworths, 1995), but it can also be used in conjunction with any other intellectual property law textbook.

We also wish to use this opportunity to thank all those at Butterworths for their commitment and encouragement in assisting us to prepare this book.

The contents are reproduced as amended to 5 April 1996.

Paul Torremans and Jon Holyoak
Leicester, April 1996

Contents

PART IV DESIGNS

PART V TRADE MARKS

PART VI MISCELLANEOUS

PART I
INTERNATIONAL FOUNDATIONS

PARIS CONVENTION FOR THE PROTECTION OF INDUSTRIAL PROPERTY

(20 March 1883)

(As revised at Brussels on 14 December 1900, at Washington on 2 June 1911, at the Hague on 6 November 1925, at London on 2 June 1934, at Lisbon on 31 October 1958, and at Stockholm on 14 July 1967, and as amended on 28 September 1979.)

NOTES

Articles have been given titles to facilitate their identification. There are no titles in the signed (French) text.

Article 1 [Establishment of the Union; Scope of Industrial Property]

(1) The countries to which this Convention applies constitute a Union for the protection of industrial property.

(2) The protection of industrial property has as its object patents, utility models, industrial designs, trademarks, service marks, trade names, indications of source or appellations of origin, and the repression of unfair competition.

(3) Industrial property shall be understood in the broadest sense and shall apply not only to industry and commerce proper, but likewise to agricultural and extractive industries and to all manufactured or natural products, for example, wines, grain, tobacco leaf, fruit, cattle, minerals, mineral waters, beer, flowers, and flour.

(4) Patents shall include the various kinds of industrial patents recognised by the laws of the countries of the Union, such as patents of importation, patents of improvement, patents and certificates of addition, etc.

Article 2 [National Treatment for Nationals of Countries of the Union]

(1) Nationals of any country of the Union shall, as regards the protection of industrial property, enjoy in all the other countries of the Union the advantages that their respective laws now grant, or may hereafter grant, to nationals; all without prejudice to the rights specially provided for by this Convention. Consequently, they shall have the same protection as the latter, and the same legal remedy against any infringement of their rights, provided that the conditions and formalities imposed upon nationals are complied with.

(2) However, no requirement as to domicile or establishment in the country where protection is claimed may be imposed upon nationals of countries of the Union for the enjoyment of any industrial property rights.

(3) The provisions of the laws of each of the countries of the Union relating to judicial and administrative procedure and to jurisdiction, and to the designation of an address for service or the appointment of an agent, which may be required by the laws on industrial property are expressly reserved.

Article 3 [Same Treatment for Certain Categories of Persons as for Nationals of Countries of the Union]

Nationals of countries outside the Union who are domiciled or who have real and effective industrial or commercial establishments in the territory of one of the countries of the Union shall be treated in the same manner as nationals of the countries of the Union.

Article 4   [A to I. Patents, Utility Models, Industrial Designs, Marks, Inventors' Certificates: Right of Priority.—G. Patents: Division of the Application]

A—(1)   Any person who has duly filed an application for a patent, or for the registration of a utility model, or of an industrial design, or of a trademark, in one of the countries of the Union, or his successor in title, shall enjoy, for the purpose of filing in the other countries, a right of priority during the periods hereinafter fixed.

(2)   Any filing that is equivalent to a regular national filing under the domestic legislation of any country of the Union or under bilateral or multilateral treaties concluded between countries of the Union shall be recognised as giving rise to the right of priority.

(3)   By a regular national filing is meant any filing that is adequate to establish the date on which the application was filed in the country concerned, whatever may be the subsequent fate of the application.

B   Consequently, any subsequent filing in any of the other countries of the Union before the expiration of the periods referred to above shall not be invalidated by reason of any acts accomplished in the interval, in particular, another filing, the publication or exploitation of the invention, the putting on sale of copies of the design, or the use of the mark, and such acts cannot give rise to any third-party right or any right of personal possession. Rights acquired by third parties before the date of the first application that serves as the basis for the right of priority are reserved in accordance with the domestic legislation of each country of the Union.

C—(1)   The periods of priority referred to above shall be twelve months for patents and utility models, and six months for industrial designs and trademarks.

(2)   These periods shall start from the date of filing of the first application; the day of filing shall not be included in the period.

(3)   If the last day of the period is an official holiday, or a day when the Office is not open for the filing of applications in the country where protection is claimed, the period shall be extended until the first following working day.

(4)   A subsequent application concerning the same subject as a previous first application within the meaning of paragraph (2), above, filed in the same country of the Union, shall be considered as the first application, of which the filing date shall be the starting point of the period of priority, if, at the time of filing the subsequent application, the said previous application has been withdrawn, abandoned, or refused, without having been laid open to public inspection and without leaving any rights outstanding, and if it has not yet served as a basis for claiming a right of priority. The previous application may not thereafter serve as a basis for claiming a right of priority.

D—(1)   Any person desiring to take advantage of the priority of a previous filing shall be required to make a declaration indicating the date of such filing and the country in which it was made. Each country shall determine the latest date on which such declaration must be made.

(2)   These particulars shall be mentioned in the publications issued by the competent authority, and in particular in the patents and the specifications relating thereto.

(3)   The countries of the Union may require any person making a declaration of priority to produce a copy of the application (description, drawings, etc) previously filed. The copy, certified as correct by the authority which received such application,

shall not require any authentication, and may in any case be filed, without fee, at any time within three months of the filing of the subsequent application. They may require it to be accompanied by a certificate from the same authority showing the date of filing, and by a translation.

(4) No other formalities may be required for the declaration of priority at the time of filing the application. Each country of the Union shall determine the consequences of failure to comply with the formalities prescribed by this Article, but such consequences shall in no case go beyond the loss of the right of priority.

(5) Subsequently, further proof may be required.

Any person who avails himself of the priority of a previous application shall be required to specify the number of that application; this number shall be published as provided for by paragraph (2), above.

E—(1) Where an industrial design is filed in a country by virtue of a right of priority based on the filing of a utility model, the period of priority shall be the same as that fixed for industrial designs.

(2) Furthermore, it is permissible to file a utility model in a country by virtue of a right of priority based on the filing of a patent application, and vice versa.

F No country of the Union may refuse a priority or a patent application on the ground that the applicant claims multiple priorities, even if they originate in different countries, or on the ground that an application claiming one or more priorities contains one or more elements that were not included in the application or applications whose priority is claimed, provided that, in both cases, there is unity of invention within the meaning of the law of the country.

With respect to the elements not included in the application or applications whose priority is claimed, the filing of the subsequent application shall give rise to a right of priority under ordinary conditions.

G—(1) If the examination reveals that an application for a patent contains more than one invention, the applicant may divide the application into a certain number of divisional applications and preserve as the date of each the date of the initial application and the benefit of the right of priority, if any.

(2) The applicant may also, on his own initiative, divide a patent application and preserve as the date of each divisional application the date of the initial application and the benefit of the right of priority, if any. Each country of the Union shall have the right to determine the conditions under which such division shall be authorised.

H Priority may not be refused on the ground that certain elements of the invention for which priority is claimed do not appear among the claims formulated in the application in the country of origin, provided that the application documents as a whole specifically disclose such elements.

I—(1) Applications for inventors' certificates filed in a country in which applicants have the right to apply at their own option either for a patent or for an inventor's certificate shall give rise to the right of priority provided for by this Article, under the same conditions and with the same effects as applications for patents.

(2) In a country in which applicants have the right to apply at their own option either for a patent or for an inventor's certificate, an applicant for an inventor's certificate shall, in accordance with the provisions of this Article relating to patent applications, enjoy a right of priority based on an application for a patent, a utility model, or an inventor's certificate.

Article 4bis [Patents: Independence of Patents Obtained for the Same Invention in Different Countries]

(1)   Patents applied for in the various countries of the Union by nationals of countries of the Union shall be independent of patents obtained for the same invention in other countries, whether members of the Union or not.

(2)   The foregoing provision is to be understood in an unrestricted sense, in particular, in the sense that patents applied for during the period of priority are independent, both as regards the grounds for nullity and forfeiture, and as regards their normal duration.

(3)   The provision shall apply to all patents existing at the time when it comes into effect.

(4)   Similarly, it shall apply, in the case of the accession of new countries, to patents in existence on either side at the time of accession.

(5)   Patents obtained with the benefit of priority shall, in the various countries of the Union, have a duration equal to that which they would have, had they been applied for or granted without the benefit of priority.

Article 4ter [Patents: Mention of the Inventor in the Patent]

The inventor shall have the right to be mentioned as such in the patent.

Article 4^{quater} [Patents: Patentability in Case of Restrictions of Sale by Law]

The grant of a patent shall not be refused and a patent shall not be invalidated on the ground that the sale of the patented product or of a product obtained by means of a patented process is subject to restrictions or limitations resulting from the domestic law.

Article 5   [A. Patents: Importation of Articles; Failure to Work or Insufficient Working; Compulsory Licenses.—B. Industrial Designs: Failure to Work; Importation of Articles.—C. Marks: Failure to Use; Different Forms; Use by Co-proprietors.—D. Patents, Utility Models, Marks, Industrial Designs: Marking]

A—(1)   Importation by the patentee into the country where the patent has been granted of articles manufactured in any of the countries of the Union shall not entail forfeiture of the patent.

(2)   Each country of the Union shall have the right to take legislative measures providing for the grant of compulsory licenses to prevent the abuses which might result from the exercise of the exclusive rights conferred by the patent, for example, failure to work.

(3)   Forfeiture of the patent shall not be provided for except in cases where the grant of compulsory licenses would not have been sufficient to prevent the said abuses. No proceedings for the forfeiture or revocation of a patent may be instituted before the expiration of two years from the grant of the first compulsory license.

(4)   A compulsory license may not be applied for on the ground of failure to work or insufficient working before the expiration of a period of four years from the date of filing of the patent application or three years from the date of the grant of the patent, whichever period expires last; it shall be refused if the patentee justifies his

inaction by legitimate reasons. Such a compulsory license shall be non-exclusive and shall not be transferable, even in the form of the grant of a sub-license, except with that part of the enterprise or goodwill which exploits such license.

(5)   The foregoing provisions shall be applicable, mutatis mutandis, to utility models.

B   The protection of industrial designs shall not, under any circumstance, be subject to any forfeiture, either by reason of failure to work or by reason of the importation of articles corresponding to those which are protected.

C—(1)   If, in any country, use of the registered mark is compulsory, the registration may be cancelled only after a reasonable period, and then only if the person concerned does not justify his inaction.

(2)   Use of a trademark by the proprietor in a form differing in elements which do not alter the distinctive character of the mark in the form in which it was registered in one of the countries of the Union shall not entail invalidation of the registration and shall not diminish the protection granted to the mark.

(3)   Concurrent use of the same mark on identical or similar goods by industrial or commercial establishments considered as co-proprietors of the mark according to the provisions of the domestic law of the country where protection is claimed shall not prevent registration or diminish in any way the protection granted to the said mark in any country of the Union, provided that such use does not result in misleading the public and is not contrary to the public interest.

D   No indication or mention of the patent, of the utility model, of the registration of the trademark, or of the deposit of the industrial design, shall be required upon the goods as a condition of recognition of the right to protection.

Article 5bis   [All Industrial Property Rights: Period of Grace for the Payment of Fees for the Maintenance of Rights; Patents: Restoration]

(1)   A period of grace of not less than six months shall be allowed for the payment of the fees prescribed for the maintenance of industrial property rights, subject, if the domestic legislation so provides, to the payment of a surcharge.

(2)   The countries of the Union shall have the right to provide for the restoration of patents which have lapsed by reason of non-payment of fees.

Article 5ter   [Patents: Patented Devices Forming Part of Vessels, Aircraft, or Land Vehicles]

In any country of the Union the following shall not be considered as infringements of the rights of a patentee—

1. the use on board vessels of other countries of the Union of devices forming the subject of his patent in the body of the vessel, in the machinery, tackle, gear and other accessories, when such vessels temporarily or accidentally enter the waters of the said country, provided that such devices are used there exclusively for the needs of the vessel;

2. the use of devices forming the subject of the patent in the construction or operation of aircraft or land vehicles of other countries of the Union, or of accessories of such aircraft or land vehicles, when those aircraft or land vehicles temporarily or accidentally enter the said country.

Article 5^{quater}   [Patents: Importation of Products Manufactured by a Process Patented in the Importing Country]

When a product is imported into a country of the Union where there exists a patent protecting a process of manufacture of the said product, the patentee shall have all the rights, with regard to the imported product, that are accorded to him by the legislation of the country of importation, on the basis of the process patent, with respect to products manufactured in that country.

Article 5^{quinquies}   [Industrial Designs]

Industrial designs shall be protected in all the countries of the Union.

Article 6   [Marks: Conditions of Registration; Independence of Protection of Same Mark in Different Countries]

(1)   The conditions for the filing and registration of trademarks shall be determined in each country of the Union by its domestic legislation.

(2)   However, an application for the registration of a mark filed by a national of a country of the Union may not be refused, nor may a registration be invalidated, on the ground that filing, registration, or renewal, has not been effected in the country of origin.

(3)   A mark duly registered in a country of the Union shall be regarded as independent of marks registered in the other countries of the Union, including the country of origin.

Article 6bis   [Marks: Well–Known Marks]

(1)   The countries of the Union undertake, ex officio if their legislation so permits, or at the request of an interested party, to refuse or to cancel the registration, and to prohibit the use, of a trademark which constitutes a reproduction, an imitation, or a translation, liable to create confusion, of a mark considered by the competent authority of the country of registration or use to be well known in that country as being already the mark of a person entitled to the benefits of this Convention and used for identical or similar goods. These provisions shall also apply when the essential part of the mark constitutes a reproduction of any such well-known mark or an imitation liable to create confusion therewith.

(2)   A period of at least five years from the date of registration shall be allowed for requesting the cancellation of such a mark. The countries of the Union may provide for a period within which the prohibition of use must be requested.

(3)   No time limit shall be fixed for requesting the cancellation or the prohibition of the use of marks registered or used in bad faith.

Article 6ter   [Marks: Prohibitions concerning State Emblems, Official Hallmarks, and Emblems of Intergovernmental Organisations]

(1)   (a)   The countries of the Union agree to refuse or to invalidate the registration, and to prohibit by appropriate measures the use, without authorisation by the competent authorities, either as trademarks or as elements of trademarks, of armorial bearings, flags, and other State emblems, of the countries of the Union, official signs and hallmarks indicating control and warranty adopted by them, and any imitation from a heraldic point of view.

(b)   The provisions of subparagraph (a), above, shall apply equally to armorial bearings, flags, other emblems, abbreviations, and names, of international intergovernmental organisations of which one or more countries of the Union are members, with the exception of armorial bearings, flags, other emblems, abbreviations, and names, that are already the subject of international agreements in force, intended to ensure their protection.

(c)   No country of the Union shall be required to apply the provisions of subparagraph (b), above, to the prejudice of the owners of rights acquired in good faith before the entry into force, in that country, of this Convention. The countries of the Union shall not be required to apply the said provisions when the use or registration referred to in subparagraph (a), above, is not of such a nature as to suggest to the public that a connection exists between the organisation concerned and the armorial bearings, flags, emblems, abbreviations, and names, or if such use or registration is probably not of such a nature as to mislead the public as to the existence of a connection between the user and the organisation.

(2)   Prohibition of the use of official signs and hallmarks indicating control and warranty shall apply solely in cases where the marks in which they are incorporated are intended to be used on goods of the same or a similar kind.

(3)   (a)   For the application of these provisions, the countries of the Union agree to communicate reciprocally, through the intermediary of the International Bureau, the list of State emblems, and official signs and hallmarks indicating control and warranty, which they desire, or may hereafter desire, to place wholly or within certain limits under the protection of this Article, and all subsequent modifications of such list. Each country of the Union shall in due course make available to the public the lists so communicated.

    Nevertheless such communication is not obligatory in respect of flags of States.

(b)   The provisions of subparagraph (b) of paragraph (1) of this Article shall apply only to such armorial bearings, flags, other emblems, abbreviations, and names, of international intergovernmental organisations as the latter have communicated to the countries of the Union through the intermediary of the International Bureau.

(4)   Any country of the Union may, within a period of twelve months from the receipt of the notification, transmit its objections, if any, through the intermediary of the International Bureau, to the country or international intergovernmental organisation concerned.

(5)   In the case of State flags, the measures prescribed by paragraph (1), above, shall apply solely to marks registered after 6 November 1925.

(6)   In the case of State emblems other than flags, and of official signs and hallmarks of the countries of the Union, and in the case of armorial bearings, flags, other emblems, abbreviations, and names of intergovernmental organisations, these provisions shall apply only to marks registered more than two months after receipt of the communication provided for in paragraph (3), above.

(7)   In cases of bad faith, the countries shall have the right to cancel even those marks incorporating State emblems, signs, and hallmarks, which were registered before 6 November 1925.

(8) Nationals of any country who are authorised to make use of the State emblems, signs, and hallmarks, of their country may use them even if they are similar to those of another country.

(9) The countries of the Union undertake to prohibit the unauthorised use in trade of the State armorial bearings of the other countries of the Union, when the use is of such a nature as to be misleading as to the origin of the goods.

(10) The above provisions shall not prevent the countries from exercising the right given in paragraph (3) of Article 6^{quinqies}, Section B, to refuse or to invalidate the registration of marks incorporating, without authorisation, armorial bearings, flags, other State emblems, or official signs and hallmarks adopted by a country of the Union, as well as the distinctive signs of international intergovernmental organisations referred to in paragraph (1), above.

Article 6^{quater} [Marks: Assignment of Marks]

(1) When, in accordance with the law of a country of the Union, the assignment of a mark is valid only if it takes place at the same time as the transfer of the business or goodwill to which the mark belongs, it shall suffice for the recognition of such validity that the portion of the business or goodwill located in that country be transferred to the assignee, together with the exclusive right to manufacture in the said country, or to sell therein, the goods bearing the mark assigned.

(2) The foregoing provision does not impose upon the countries of the Union any obligation to regard as valid the assignment of any mark the use of which by the assignee would, in fact, be of such a nature as to mislead the public, particularly as regards the origin, nature, or essential qualities, of the goods to which the mark is applied.

Article 6^{quinquies} [Marks: Protection of Marks Registered in One Country of the Union in the Other Countries of the Union]

A—(1) Every trademark duly registered in the country of origin shall be accepted for filing and protected as is in the other countries of the Union, subject to the reservations indicated in this Article. Such countries may, before proceeding to final registration, require the production of a certificate of registration in the country of origin, issued by the competent authority. No authentication shall be required for this certificate.

(2) Shall be considered the country of origin the country of the Union where the applicant has a real and effective industrial or commercial establishment, or, if he has no such establishment within the Union, the country of the Union where he has his domicile, or, if he has no domicile within the Union but is a national of a country of the Union, the country of which he is a national.

B Trademarks covered by this Article may be neither denied registration nor invalidated except in the following cases—

1. when they are of such a nature as to infringe rights acquired by third parties in the country where protection is claimed;
2. when they are devoid of any distinctive character, or consist exclusively of signs or indications which may serve, in trade, to designate the kind, quality, quantity, intended purpose, value, place of origin, of the goods, or the time of production, or have become customary in the current language or in the bona fide and established practices of the trade of the country where protection is claimed;

3.   when they are contrary to morality or public order and, in particular, of such a nature as to deceive the public. It is understood that a mark may not be considered contrary to public order for the sole reason that it does not conform to a provision of the legislation on marks, except if such provision itself relates to public order.

This provision is subject, however, to the application of Article 10bis.

C—(1)   In determining whether a mark is eligible for protection, all the factual circumstances must be taken into consideration, particularly the length of time the mark has been in use.

(2)   No trademark shall be refused in the other countries of the Union for the sole reason that it differs from the mark protected in the country of origin only in respect of elements that do not alter its distinctive character and do not affect its identity in the form in which it has been registered in the said country of origin.

D   No person may benefit from the provisions of this Article if the mark for which he claims protection is not registered in the country of origin.

E   However, in no case shall the renewal of the registration of the mark in the country of origin involve an obligation to renew the registration in the other countries of the Union in which the mark has been registered.

F   The benefit of priority shall remain unaffected for applications for the registration of marks filed within the period fixed by Article 4, even if registration in the country of origin is effected after the expiration of such period.

Article 6^{sexies} [Marks: Service Marks]

The countries of the Union undertake to protect service marks. They shall not be required to provide for the registration of such marks.

Article 6^{septies} [Marks: Registration in the Name of the Agent or Representative of the Proprietor Without the Latter's Authorisation]

(1)   If the agent or representative of the person who is the proprietor of a mark in one of the countries of the Union applies, without such proprietor's authorisation, for the registration of the mark in his own name, in one or more countries of the Union, the proprietor shall be entitled to oppose the registration applied for or demand its cancellation or, if the law of the country so allows, the assignment in his favour of the said registration, unless such agent or representative justifies his action.

(2)   The proprietor of the mark shall, subject to the provisions of paragraph (1), above, be entitled to oppose the use of his mark by his agent or representative if he has not authorised such use.

(3)   Domestic legislation may provide an equitable time limit within which the proprietor of a mark must exercise the rights provided for in this Article.

Article 7   [Marks: Nature of the Goods to which the Mark is Applied]

The nature of the goods to which a trademark is to be applied shall in no case form an obstacle to the registration of the mark.

Article 7bis [Marks: Collective Marks]

(1)   The countries of the Union undertake to accept for filing and to protect collective marks belonging to associations the existence of which is not contrary to

the law of the country of origin, even if such associations do not possess an industrial or commercial establishment.

(2)   Each country shall be the judge of the particular conditions under which a collective mark shall be protected and may refuse protection if the mark is contrary to the public interest.

(3)   Nevertheless, the protection of these marks shall not be refused to any association the existence of which is not contrary to the law of the country of origin, on the ground that such association is not established in the country where protection is sought or is not constituted according to the law of the latter country.

Article 8   [Trade Names]

A trade name shall be protected in all the countries of the Union without the obligation of filing or registration whether or not it forms part of a trademark.

Article 9   [Marks, Trade Names: Seizure, on Importation, etc, of Goods Unlawfully Bearing a Mark or Trade Name]

(1)   All goods unlawfully bearing a trademark or trade name shall be seized on importation into those countris of the Union where such mark or trade name is entitled to legal protection.

(2)   Seizure shall likewise be effected in the country where the unlawful affixation occurred or in the country into which the goods were imported.

(3)   Seizure shall take place at the request of the public prosecutor, or any other competent authority, or any interested party, whether a natural person or a legal entity, in conformity with the domestic legislation of each country.

(4)   The authorities shall not be bound to effect seizure of goods in transit.

(5)   If the legislation of a country does not permit seizure on importation, seizure shall be replaced by prohibition of importation or by seizure inside the country.

(6)   If the legislation of a country permits neither seizure on importation nor prohibition of importation nor seizure inside the country, then, until such time as the legislation is modified accordingly, these measures shall be replaced by the actions and remedies available in such cases to nationals under the law of such country.

Article 10   [False Indications: Seizure, on Importation, etc, of Goods Bearing False Indications as to their Source or the Identity of the Producer]

(1)   The provisions of the preceding Article shall apply in cases of direct or indirect use of a false indication of the source of the goods or the identity of the producer, manufacturer, or merchant.

(2)   Any producer, manufacturer, or merchant, whether a natural person or a legal entity, engaged in the production or manufacture of or trade in such goods and established either in the locality falsely indicated as the source, or in the region where such locality is situated, or in the country falsely indicated, or in the country where the false indication of source is used, shall in any case be deemed an interested party.

Article 10bis [Unfair Competition]

(1)   The countries of the Union are bound to assure to nationals of such countries effective protection against unfair competition.

(2)   Any act of competition contrary to honest practices in industrial or commercial matters constitutes an act of unfair competition.

(3)   The following in particular shall be prohibited—

1.   all acts of such a nature as to create confusion by any means whatever with the establishment, the goods, or the industrial or commercial activities, of a competitor;

2.   false allegations in the course of trade of such a nature as to discredit the establishment, the goods, or the industrial or commercial activities, of a competitor;

3.   indications or allegations the use of which in the course of trade is liable to mislead the public as to the nature, the manufacturing process, the characteristics, the suitability for their purpose, or the quantity, of the goods.

Article 10ter   [Marks, Trade Names, False Indications, Unfair Competition: Remedies, Right to Sue]

(1)   The countries of the Union undertake to assure to nationals of other countries of the Union appropriate legal remedies effectively to repress all the acts referred to in Articles 9, 10, and 10bis.

(2)   They undertake, further, to provide measures to permit federations and associations representing interested industrialists, producers, or merchants, provided that the existence of such federations and associations is not contrary to the laws of their countries, to take action in the courts or before the administrative authorities, with a view to the repression of the acts referred to in Articles 9, 10, and 10bis, in so far as the law of the country in which protection is claimed allows such action by federations and associations of that country.

Article 11   [Inventions, Utility Models, Industrial Designs, Marks: Temporary Protection at Certain International Exhibitions]

(1)   The countries of the Union shall, in conformity with their domestic legislation, grant temporary protection to patentable inventions, utility models, industrial designs, and trademarks, in respect of goods exhibited at official or officially recognised international exhibitions held in the territory of any of them.

(2)   Such temporary protection shall not extend the periods provided by Article 4. If, later, the right of priority is invoked, the authorities of any country may provide that the period shall start from the date of introduction of the goods into the exhibition.

(3)   Each country may require, as proof of the identity of the article exhibited and of the date of its introduction, such documentary evidence as it considers necessary.

Article 19   [Special Agreements]

It is understood that the countries of the Union reserve the right to make separately between themselves special agreements for the protection of industrial property, in so far as these agreements do not contravene the provisions of this Convention.

[1]

(This Convention is reproduced with the permission of the International Bureau of the World Intellectual Property Organisation (WIPO).)

BERNE CONVENTION FOR THE PROTECTION OF LITERARY AND ARTISTIC WORKS

(Paris Act, 24 July 1971)

NOTES

Each article and the Appendix have been given titles to facilitate their identification. There are no titles in the signed (English) text.

Article 1   [Establishment of a Union]

The countries to which this Convention applies constitute a Union for the protection of the rights of authors in their literary and artistic works.

Article 2   [Protected Works: 1. "Literary and artistic works"; 2. Possible requirement of fixation; 3. Derivative works; 4. Official texts; 5. Collections; 6. Obligation to protect; beneficiaries of protection; 7. Works of applied art and industrial designs; 8. News]

(1)   The expression "literary and artistic works" shall include every production in the literary, scientific and artistic domain, whatever may be the mode or form of its expression, such as books, pamphlets and other writings; lectures, addresses, sermons and other works of the same nature; dramatic or dramatico-musical works; choreographic works and entertainments in dumb show; musical compositions with or without words; cinematographic works to which are assimilated works expressed by a process analogous to cinematography; works of drawing, painting, architecture, sculpture, engraving and lithography; photographic works to which are assimilated works expressed by a process analogous to photography; works of applied art; illustrations, maps, plans, sketches and three-dimensional works relative to geography, topography, architecture or science.

(2)   It shall, however, be a matter for legislation in the countries of the Union to prescribe that works in general or any specified categories of works shall not be protected unless they have been fixed in some material form.

(3)   Translations, adaptations, arrangements of music and other alterations of a literary or artistic work shall be protected as original works without prejudice to the copyright in the original work.

(4)   It shall be a matter for legislation in the countries of the Union to determine the protection to be granted to official texts of a legislative, administrative and legal nature, and to official translations of such texts.

(5)   Collections of literary or artistic works such as encyclopaedias and anthologies which, by reason of the selection and arrangement of their contents, constitute intellectual creations shall be protected as such, without prejudice to the copyright in each of the works forming part of such collections.

(6)   The works mentioned in this Article shall enjoy protection in all countries of the Union. This protection shall operate for the benefit of the author and his successors in title.

(7)   Subject to the provisions of Article 7(4) of this Convention, it shall be a matter for legislation in the countries of the Union to determine the extent of the

application of their laws to works of applied art and industrial designs and models, as well as the conditions under which such works, designs and models shall be protected. Works protected in the country of origin solely as designs and models shall be entitled in another country of the Union only to such special protection as is granted in that country to designs and models; however, if no such special protection is granted in that country, such works shall be protected as artistic works.

(8)   The protection of this Convention shall not apply to news of the day or to miscellaneous facts having the character of mere items of press information.

Article 2bis [Possible Limitation of Protection of Certain Works: 1. Certain speeches; 2. Certain uses of lectures and addresses; 3. Right to make collections of such works]

(1)   It shall be a matter for legislation in the countries of the Union to exclude, wholly or in part, from the protection provided by the preceding Article political speeches and speeches delivered in the course of legal proceedings.

(2)   It shall also be a matter for legislation in the countries of the Union to determine the conditions under which lectures, addresses and other works of the same nature which are delivered in public may be reproduced by the press, broadcast, communicated to the public by wire and made the subject of public communication as envisaged in Article 11bis(1) of this Convention, when such use is justified by the informatory purpose.

(3)   Nevertheless, the author shall enjoy the exclusive right of making a collection of his works mentioned in the preceding paragraphs.

Article 3   [Criteria of Eligibility for Protection: 1. Nationality of author; place of publication of work; 2. Residence of author; 3. "Published" works; 4. "Simultaneously published" works]

(1)   The protection of this Convention shall apply to—
    (a)   authors who are nationals of one of the countries of the Union, for their works, whether published or not;
    (b)   authors who are not nationals of one of the countries of the Union, for their works first published in one of those countries, or simultaneously in a country outside the Union and in a country of the Union.

(2)   Authors who are not nationals of one of the countries of the Union but who have their habitual residence in one of them shall, for the purposes of this Convention, be assimilated to nationals of that country.

(3)   The expression "published works" means works published with the consent of their authors, whatever may be the means of manufacture of the copies, provided that the availability of such copies has been such as to satisfy the reasonable requirements of the public, having regard to the nature of the work. The performance of a dramatic, dramatico-musical, cinematographic or musical work, the public recitation of a literary work, the communication by wire or the broadcasting of literary or artistic works, the exhibition of a work of art and the construction of a work of architecture shall not constitute publication.

(4)   A work shall be considered as having been published simultaneously in several countries if it has been published in two or more countries within thirty days of its first publication.

Article 4 [Criteria of Eligibility for Protection of Cinematographic Works, Works of Architecture and Certain Artistic Works]

The protection of this Convention shall apply, even if the conditions of Article 3 are not fulfilled, to—

(a) authors of cinematographic works the maker of which has his headquarters or habitual residence in one of the countries of the Union;

(b) authors of works of architecture erected in a country of the Union or of other artistic works incorporated in a building or other structure located in a country of the Union.

Article 5 [Rights Guaranteed: 1. and 2. Outside the country of origin; 3. In the country of origin; 4. "Country of origin"]

(1) Authors shall enjoy, in respect of works for which they are protected under this Convention, in countries of the Union other than the country of origin, the rights which their respective laws do now or may hereafter grant to their nationals, as well as the rights specially granted by this Convention.

(2) The enjoyment and the exercise of these rights shall not be subject to any formality; such enjoyment and such exercise shall be independent of the existence of protection in the country of origin of the work. Consequently, apart from the provisions of this Convention, the extent of protection, as well as the means of redress afforded to the author to protect his rights, shall be governed exclusively by the laws of the country where protection is claimed.

(3) Protection in the country of origin is governed by domestic law. However, when the author is not a national of the country of origin of the work for which he is protected under this Convention, he shall enjoy in that country the same rights as national authors.

(4) The country of origin shall be considered to be—

(a) in the case of works first published in a country of the Union, that country; in the case of works published simultaneously in several countries of the Union which grant different terms of protection, the country whose legislation grants the shortest term of protection;

(b) in the case of works published simultaneously in a country outside the Union and in a country of the Union, the latter country;

(c) in the case of unpublished works or of works first published in a country outside the Union, without simultaneous publication in a country of the Union, the country of the Union of which the author is a national, provided that—

(i) when these are cinematographic works the maker of which has his headquarters or his habitual residence in the country of the Union, the country of origin shall be that country, and

(ii) when these are works of architecture erected in a country of the Union or other artistic works incorporated in a building or other structure located in a country of the Union, the country of origin shall be that country.

Article 6 [Possible Restriction of Protection in Respect of Certain Works of Nationals of Certain Countries Outside the Union: 1. In the country of the first publication and in other countries; 2. No retroactivity; 3. Notice]

(1) Where any country outside the Union fails to protect in an adequate manner the works of authors who are nationals of one of the countries of the Union, the

latter country may restrict the protection given to the works of authors who are, at the date of the first publication thereof, nationals of the other country and are not habitually resident in one of the countries of the Union. If the country of first publication avails itself of this right, the other countries of the Union shall not be required to grant to works thus subjected to special treatment a wider protection than that granted to them in the country of first publication.

(2)   No restrictions introduced by virtue of the preceding paragraph shall affect the rights which an author may have acquired in respect of a work published in a country of the Union before such restrictions were put into force.

(3)   The countries of the Union which restrict the grant of copyright in accordance with this Article shall give notice thereof to the Director-General of the World Intellectual Property Organisation (hereinafter designated as "the Director-General") by a written declaration specifying the countries in regard to which protection is restricted, and the restrictions to which rights of authors who are nationals of those countries are subjected. The Director-General shall immediately communicate this declaration to all the countries of the Union.

Article 6bis   [Moral Rights: 1. To claim authorship; to object to certain modifications and other derogatory actions; 2. After the author's death; 3. Means of redress]

(1)   Independently of the author's economic rights, and even after the transfer of the said rights, the author shall have the right to claim authorship of the work and to object to any distortion, mutilation or other modification of, or other derogatory action in relation to, the said work, which would be prejudicial to his honour or reputation.

(2)   The rights granted to the author in accordance with the preceding paragraph shall, after his death, be maintained, at least until the expiry of the economic rights, and shall be exercisable by the persons or institutions authorised by the legislation of the country where protection is claimed. However, those countries whose legislation, at the moment of their ratification of or accession to this Act, does not provide for the protection after the death of the author of all the rights set out in the preceding paragraph may provide that some of these rights may, after his death, cease to be maintained.

(3)   The means of redress for safeguarding the rights granted by this Article shall be governed by the legislation of the country where protection is claimed.

Article 7   [Term of Protection: 1. Generally; 2. For cinematographic works; 3. For anonymous and pseudonymous works; 4. For photographic works and works of applied art; 5. Starting date of computation; 6. Longer terms; 7. Shorter terms; 8. Applicable law; "comparison" of terms]

(1)   The term of protection granted by this Convention shall be the life of the author and fifty years after his death.

(2)   However, in the case of cinematographic works, the countries of the Union may provide that the term of protection shall expire fifty years after the work has been made available to the public with the consent of the author, or, failing such an event within fifty years from the making of such a work, fifty years after the making.

(3)   In the case of anonymous or pseudonymous works, the term of protection granted by this Convention shall expire fifty years after the work has been lawfully

made available to the public. However, when the pseudonym adopted by the author leaves no doubt as to his identity, the term of protection shall be that provided in paragraph (1). If the author of an anonymous or pseudonymous work discloses his identity during the above-mentioned period, the term of protection applicable shall be that provided in paragraph (1). The countries of the Union shall not be required to protect anonymous or pseudonymous works in respect of which it is reasonable to presume that their author has been dead for fifty years.

(4)   It shall be a matter for legislation in the countries of the Union to determine the term of protection of photographic works and that of works of applied art in so far as they are protected as artistic works; however, this term shall last at least until the end of a period of twenty-five years from the making of such a work.

(5)   The term of protection subsequent to the death of the author and the terms provided by paragraphs (2), (3) and (4) shall run from the date of death or of the event referred to in those paragraphs, but such terms shall always be deemed to begin on the first of January of the year following the death or such event.

(6)   The countries of the Union may grant a term of protection in excess of those provided by the preceding paragraphs.

(7)   Those countries of the Union bound by the Rome Act of this Convention which grant, in their national legislation in force at the time of signature of the present Act, shorter terms of protection than those provided for in the preceding paragraphs shall have the right to maintain such terms when ratifying or acceding to the present Act.

(8)   In any case, the term shall be governed by the legislation of the country where protection is claimed; however, unless the legislation of that country otherwise provides, the term shall not exceed the term fixed in the country of origin of the work.

Article 7[bis]   [Term of Protection for Works of Joint Authorship]

The provisions of the preceding Article shall also apply in the case of a work of joint authorship, provided that the terms measured from the death of the author shall be calculated from the death of the last surviving author.

Article 8   [Right of Translation]

Authors of literary and artistic works protected by this Convention shall enjoy the exclusive right of making and of authorising the translation of their works throughout the term of protection of their rights in the original work.

Article 9   [Right of Reproduction: 1. Generally; 2. Possible exceptions; 3. Sound and visual recordings]

(1)   Authors of literary and artistic works protected by this Convention shall have the exclusive right of authorising the reproduction of these works, in any manner or form.

(2)   It shall be a matter for legislation in the countries of the Union to permit the reproduction of such works in certain special cases, provided that such reproduction does not conflict with a normal exploitation of the work and does not unreasonably prejudice the legitimate interests of the author.

(3)   Any sound or visual recording shall be considered as a reproduction for the purposes of this Convention.

Article 10   **[Certain Free Uses of Works: 1. Quotations; 2. Illustrations for teaching; 3. Indication of source and author]**

(1)   It shall be permissible to make quotations from a work which has already been lawfully made available to the public, provided that their making is compatible with fair practice, and their extent does not exceed that justified by the purpose, including quotations from newspaper articles and periodicals in the form of press summaries.

(2)   It shall be a matter for legislation in the countries of the Union, and for special agreements existing or to be concluded between them, to permit the utilisation, to the extent justified by the purpose, of literary or artistic works by way of illustration in publications, broadcasts or sound or visual recordings for teaching, provided such utilisation is compatible with fair practice.

(3)   Where use is made of works in accordance with the preceding paragraphs of this Article, mention shall be made of the source, and of the name of the author if it appears thereon.

Article 10bis   **[Further Possible Free Uses of Works: 1. Of certain articles and broadcast works; 2. Of works seen or heard in connection with current events]**

(1)   It shall be a matter for legislation in the countries of the Union to permit the reproduction by the press, the broadcasting or the communication to the public by wire of articles published in newspapers or periodicals on current economic, political or religious topics, and of broadcast works of the same character, in cases in which the reproduction, broadcasting or such communication thereof is not expressly reserved. Nevertheless, the source must always be clearly indicated; the legal consequences of a breach of this obligation shall be determined by the legislation of the country where protection is claimed.

(2)   It shall also be a matter for legislation in the countries of the Union to determine the conditions under which, for the purpose of reporting current events by means of photography, cinematography, broadcasting or communication to the public by wire, literary or artistic works seen or heard in the course of the event may, to the extent justified by the informatory purpose, be reproduced and made available to the public.

Article 11   **[Certain Rights in Dramatic and Musical Works: 1. Right of public performance and of communication to the public of a performance; 2. In respect of translations]**

(1)   Authors of dramatic, dramatico-musical and musical works shall enjoy the exclusive right of authorising—
    (i)   the public performance of their works, including such public performance by any means or process;
    (ii)   any communication to the public of the performance of their works.

(2)   Authors of dramatic or dramatico-musical works shall enjoy, during the full term of their rights in the original works, the same rights with respect to translations thereof.

Article 11bis   **[Broadcasting and Related Rights: 1. Broadcasting and other wireless communications, public communication of broadcast by wire or rebroadcast, public communication of broadcast by loudspeaker or analogous instruments; 2. Compulsory licences; 3. Recording; ephemeral recordings]**

(1)   Authors of literary and artistic works shall enjoy the exclusive right of authorising—

(i)   the broadcasting of their works or the communication thereof to the public by any other means of wireless diffusion of signs, sounds or images;

(ii) any communication to the public by wire or by rebroadcasting of the broadcast of the work, when this communication is made by an organisation other than the original one;

(iii) the public communication by loudspeaker or any other analogous instrument transmitting, by signs, sounds or images, the broadcast of the work.

(2)   It shall be a matter for legislation in the countries of the Union to determine the conditions under which the rights mentioned in the preceding paragraph may be exercised, but these conditions shall apply only in the countries where they have been prescribed. They shall not in any circumstances be prejudicial to the moral rights of the author, nor to his right to obtain equitable remuneration which, in the absence of agreement, shall be fixed by competent authority.

(3)   In the absence of any contrary stipulation, permission granted in accordance with paragraph (1) of this Article shall not imply permission to record, by means of instruments recording sounds or images, the work broadcast. It shall, however, be a matter for legislation in the countries of the Union to determine the regulations for ephemeral recordings made by a broadcasting organisation by means of its own facilities and used for its own broadcasts. The preservation of these recordings in official archives may, on the ground of their exceptional documentary character, be authorised by such legislation.

Article 11ter   [Certain Rights in Literary Works: 1. Right of public recitation and of communication to the public of a recitation; 2. In respect of translations]

(1)   Authors of literary works shall enjoy the exclusive right of authorising—
   (i)   the public recitation of their works, including such public recitation by any means or process;
   (ii) any communication to the public of the recitation of their works.

(2)   Authors of literary works shall enjoy, during the full term of their rights in the original works, the same rights with respect to translations thereof.

Article 12   [Right of Adaptation, Arrangement and Other Alteration]

Authors of literary or artistic works shall enjoy the exclusive right of authorising adaptations, arrangements and other alterations of their works.

Article 13   [Possible Limitation of the Right of Recording of Musical Works and Any Words Pertaining Thereto: 1. Compulsory licences; 2. Transitory measures; 3. Seizure on importation of copies made without the author's permission]

(1)   Each country of the Union may impose for itself reservations and conditions on the exclusive right granted to the author of a musical work and to the author of any words, the recording of which together with the musical work has already been authorised by the latter, to authorise the sound recording of that musical work, together with such words, if any; but all such reservations and conditions shall apply only in the countries which have imposed them and shall not, in any circumstances, be prejudicial to the rights of these authors to obtain equitable remuneration which, in the absence of agreement, shall be fixed by competent authority.

(2)   Recordings of musical works made in a country of the Union in accordance with Article 13(3) of the Conventions signed at Rome on 2 June 1928, and at Brussels on 26 June 1948, may be reproduced in that country without the permission of the author of the musical work until a date two years after that country becomes bound by this Act.

(3)   Recordings made in accordance with paragraphs (1) and (2) of this Article and imported without permission from the parties concerned into a country where they are treated as infringing recordings shall be liable to seizure.

Article 14   [Cinematographic and Related Rights: 1. Cinematographic adaptation and reproduction; distribution; public performance and public communication by wire of works thus adapted or reproduced; 2. Adaptation of cinematographic productions; 3. No compulsory licences]

(1)   Authors of literary or artistic works shall have the exclusive right of authorising—
   (i)   the cinematographic adaptation and reproduction of these works, and the distribution of the works thus adapted or reproduced;
   (ii)   the public performance and communication to the public by wire of the works thus adapted or reproduced.

(2)   The adaptation into any other artistic form of a cinematographic production derived from literary or artistic works shall, without prejudice to the authorisation of the author of the cinematographic production, remain subject to the authorisation of the authors of the original works.

(3)   The provisions of Article 13(1) shall not apply.

Article 14bis   [Special Provisions Concerning Cinematographic Works: 1. Assimilation to "original" works; 2. Ownership; limitation of certain rights of certain contributors; 3. Certain other contributors]

(1)   Without prejudice to the copyright in any work which may have been adapted or reproduced a cinematographic work shall be protected as an original work. The owner of copyright in a cinematographic work shall enjoy the same rights as the author of an original work, including the rights referred to in the preceding Article.

(2)   (a)   Ownership of copyright in a cinematographic work shall be a matter for legislation in the country where protection is claimed.
   (b)   However, in the countries of the Union which, by legislation, include among the owners of copyright in a cinematographic work authors who have brought contributions to the making of the work, such authors, if they have undertaken to bring such contributions, may not, in the absence of any contrary or special stipulation, object to the reproduction, distribution, public performance, communication to the public by wire, broadcasting or any other communication to the public, or to the subtitling or dubbing of texts, of the work.
   (c)   The question whether or not the form of the undertaking referred to above should, for the application of the preceding subparagraph (b), be in a written agreement or a written act of the same effect shall be a matter for the legislation of the country where the maker of the cinematographic work has his headquarters or habitual residence. However, it shall be a matter for the legislation of the country of the Union where protection is

claimed to provide that the said undertaking shall be in a written agreement or a written act of the same effect. The countries whose legislation so provides shall notify the Director-General by means of a written declaration, which will be immediately communicated by him to all the other countries of the Union.

(d) By "contrary or special stipulation" is meant any restrictive condition which is relevant to the aforesaid undertaking.

(3) Unless the national legislation provides to the contrary, the provisions of paragraph (2)(b) above shall not be applicable to authors of scenarios, dialogues and musical works created for the making of the cinematographic work, or to the principal director thereof. However, those countries of the Union whose legislation does not contain rules providing for the application of the said paragraph (2)(b) to such director shall notify the Director-General by means of a written declaration, which will be immediately communicated by him to all the other countries of the Union.

Article 14ter ["Droit de suite" in Works of Art and Manuscripts: 1. Right to an interest in resales; 2. Applicable law; 3. Procedure]

(1) The author, or after his death the persons or institutions authorised by national legislation, shall, with respect to original works of art and original manuscripts of writers and composers, enjoy the inalienable right to an interest in any sale of the work subsequent to the first transfer by the author of the work.

(2) The protection provided by the preceding paragraph may be claimed in a country of the Union only if legislation in the country to which the author belongs so permits, and to the extent permitted by the country where this protection is claimed.

(3) The procedure for collection and the amounts shall be matters for determination by national legislation.

Article 15 [Right to Enforce Protected Rights: 1. Where author's name is indicated or where pseudonym leaves no doubt as to author's identity; 2. In the case of cinematographic works; 3. In the case of anonymous and pseudonymous works; 4. In the case of certain unpublished works of unknown authorship]

(1) In order that the author of a literary or artistic work protected by this Convention shall, in the absence of proof to the contrary, be regarded as such, and consequently be entitled to institute infringement proceedings in the countries of the Union, it shall be sufficient for his name to appear on the work in the usual manner. This paragraph shall be applicable even if this name is a pseudonym, where the pseudonym adopted by the author leaves no doubt as to his identity.

(2) The person or body corporate whose name appears on a cinematographic work in the usual manner shall, in the absence of proof to the contrary, be presumed to be the maker of the said work.

(3) In the case of anonymous and pseudonymous works, other than those referred to in paragraph (1) above, the publisher whose name appears on the work shall, in the absence of proof to the contrary, be deemed to represent the author, and in this capacity he shall be entitled to protect and enforce the author's rights. The provisions of this paragraph shall cease to apply when the author reveals his identity and establishes his claim to authorship of the work.

(4)   (a)   In the case of unpublished works where the identity of the author is unknown, but where there is every ground to presume that he is a national of a country of the Union, it shall be a matter for legislation in that country to designate the competent authority which shall represent the author and shall be entitled to protect and enforce his rights in the countries of the Union.

(b)   Countries of the Union which make such designation under the terms of this provision shall notify the Director-General by means of a written declaration giving full information concerning the authority thus designated. The Director-General shall at once communicate this declaration to all other countries of the Union.

Article 16   [Infringing Copies: 1. Seizure; 2. Seizure on importation; 3. Applicable law]

(1)   Infringing copies of a work shall be liable to seizure in any country of the Union where the work enjoys legal protection.

(2)   The provisions of the preceding paragraph shall also apply to reproductions coming from a country where the work is not protected, or has ceased to be protected.

(3)   The seizures shall take place in accordance with the legislation of each country.

Article 17   [Possibility of Control of Circulation, Presentation and Exhibition of Works]

The provisions of this Convention cannot in any way affect the right of the Government of each country of the Union to permit, to control, or to prohibit, by legislation or regulation, the circulation, presentation, or exhibition of any work or production in regard to which the competent authority may find it necessary to exercise that right.

[2]

(This Convention is reproduced with the permission of the International Bureau of the World Intellectual Property Organisation (WIPO).)

MADRID AGREEEMENT CONCERNING THE INTERNATIONAL REGISTRATION OF MARKS

(14 April 1891)

(As revised at Brussels on 14 December 1900, at Washington on 2 June 1911, at The Hague on 6 November 1923, at London on 2 June 1934, at Nice on 15 June 1957, and at Stockholm on 14 July 1967, and as amended on 28 September 1979)

NOTES

Articles have been given titles to facilitate their identification. There are no titles in the signed, French text.

Article 1   [Establishment of a Special Union. Filing of Marks at International Bureau. Definition of Country of Origin]

(1)   The countries to which this Agreement applies constitute a Special Union for the International registration of marks.

(2) Nationals of any of the contracting countries may, in all the other countries party to this Agreement, secure protection for their marks applicable to goods or services, registered in the country of origin, by filing the said marks at the International Bureau of Intellectual Property (hereinafter designated as "the International Bureau") referred to in the Convention establishing the World Intellectual Property Organisation (hereinafter designated as "the Organisation"), through the intermediary of the Office of the said country of origin.

(3) Shall be considered the country of origin the country of the Special Union where the applicant has a real and effective industrial or commercial establishment; if he has no such establishment in a country of the Special Union, the country of the Special Union where he has his domicile; if he has no domicile within the Special Union but is a national of a country of the Special Union, the country of which he is a national.

Article 2 [Reference to Article 3 of Paris Convention (Same Treatment for Certain Categories of Persons as for Nationals of Countries of the Union)]

Nationals of countries not having acceded to this Agreement who, within the territory of the Special Union constituted by the said Agreement, satisfy the conditions specified in Article 3 of the Paris Convention for the Protection of Industrial Property shall be treated in the same manner as nationals of the contracting countries.

Article 3 [Contents of Application for International Registration]

(1) Every application for international registration must be presented on the form prescribed by the Regulations; the Office of the country of origin of the mark shall certify that the particulars appearing in such application correspond to the particulars in the national register, and shall mention the dates and numbers of the filing and registration of the mark in the country of origin and also the date of the application for international registration.

(2) The applicant must indicate the goods or services in respect of which protection of the mark is claimed and also, if possible, the corresponding class or classes according to the classification established by the Nice Agreement concerning the International Classification of Goods and Services for the Purposes of the Registration of Marks. If the applicant does not give such indication, the International Bureau shall classify the goods or services in the appropriate classes of the said classification. The indication of classes given by the applicant shall be subject to control by the International Bureau, which shall exercise the said control in association with the national Office. In the event of disagreement between the national Office and the International Bureau, the opinion of the latter shall prevail.

(3) If the applicant claims color as a distinctive feature of his mark, he shall be required—
    1.   to state the fact, and to file with his application a notice specifying the color or the combination of colors claimed;
    2.   to append to his application copies in color of the said mark, which shall be attached to the notification given by the International Bureau. The number of such copies shall be fixed by the Regulations.

(4) The International Bureau shall register immediately the marks filed in accordance with Article 1. The registration shall bear the date of the application for international registration in the country of origin, provided that the application has been received by

the International Bureau within a period of two months from that date. If the application has not been received within that period, the International Bureau shall record it as at the date on which it received the said application. The International Bureau shall notify such registration without delay to the Offices concerned. Registered marks shall be published in a periodical journal issued by the International Bureau, on the basis of the particulars contained in the application for registration. In the case of marks comprising a figurative element or a special form of writing, the Regulations shall determine whether a printing block must be supplied by the applicant.

(5)   With a view to the publicity to be given in the contracting countries to registered marks, each Office shall receive from the International Bureau a number of copies of the said publication free of charge and a number of copies at a reduced price, in proportion to the number of units mentioned in Article 16(4)(a) of the Paris Convention for the Protection of Industrial Property, under the conditions fixed by the Regulations. Such publicity shall be deemed in all the contracting countries to be sufficient, and no other publicity may be required of the applicant.

Article 3bis ["Territorial Limitation"]

(1)   Any contracting country may, at any time, notify the Director General of the Organisation (hereinafter designated as "the Director General") in writing that the protection resulting from the international registration shall extend to that country only at the express request of the proprietor of the mark.

(2)   Such notification shall not take effect until six months after the date of the communication thereof by the Director General to the other contracting countries.

Article 3ter [Request for "Territorial Extension"l

(1)   Any request for extension of the protection resulting from the international registration to a country which has availed itself of the right provided for in Article 3bis must be specially mentioned in the application referred to in Article 3(1).

(2)   Any request for territorial extension made subsequently to the international registration must be presented through the intermediary of the Office of the country of origin on a form prescribed by the Regulations. It shall be immediately registered by the International Bureau, which shall notify it without delay to the Office or Offices concerned. It shall be published in the periodical journal issued by the International Bureau. Such territorial extension shall be effective from the date on which it has been recorded in the International Register; it shall cease to be valid on the expiration of the international registration of the mark to which it relates.

Article 4   [Effects of International Registration]

(1)   From the date of the registration so effected at the International Bureau in accordance with the provisions of Articles 3 and 3ter, the protection of the mark in each of the contracting countries concerned shall be the same as if the mark had been filed therein direct. The indication of classes of goods or services provided for in Article 3 shall not bind the contracting countries with regard to the determination of the scope of the protection of the mark.

(2)   Every mark which has been the subject of an international registration shall enjoy the right of priority provided for by Article 4 of the Paris Convention for the Protection of Industrial Property, without requiring compliance with the formalities prescribed in Section D of that Article.

Article 4bis [Substitution of International Registration for Earlier National Registrations]

(1)   When a mark already filed in one or more of the contracting countries is later registered by the International Bureau in the name of the same proprietor or his successor in title, the international registration shall be deemed to have replaced the earlier national registrations, without prejudice to any rights acquired by reason of such earlier registrations.

(2)   The national Office shall, upon request, be required to take note in its registers of the international registration.

Article 5 [Refusal by National Offices]

(1)   In countries where the legislation so authorises, Offices notified by the International Bureau of the registration of a mark or of a request for extension of protection made in accordance with Article 3ter shall have the right to declare that protection cannot be granted to such mark in their territory. Any such refusal can be based only on the grounds which would apply, under the Paris Convention for the Protection of Industrial Property, in the case of a mark filed for national registration. However, protection may not be refused, even partially, by reason only that national legislation would not permit registration except in a limited number of classes or for a limited number of goods or services.

(2)   Offices wishing to exercise such right must give notice of their refusal to the International Bureau, together with a statement of all grounds, within the period prescribed by their domestic law and, at the latest, before the expiration of one year from the date of the international registration of the mark or of the request for extension of protection made in accordance with Article 3$^{ter.}$

(3)   The International Bureau shall, without delay, transmit to the Office of the country of origin and to the proprietor of the mark, or to his agent if an agent has been mentioned to the Bureau by the said Office, one of the copies of the declaration of refusal so notified. The interested party shall have the same remedies as if the mark had been filed by him direct in the country where protection is refused.

(4)   The grounds for refusing a mark shall be communicated by the International Bureau to any interested party who may so request.

(5)   Offices which, within the aforesaid maximum period of one year, have not communicated to the International Bureau any provisional or final decision of refusal with regard to the registration of a mark or a request for extension of protection shall lose the benefit of the right provided for in paragraph (1) of this Article with respect to the mark in question.

(6)   Invalidation of an international mark may not be pronounced by the competent authorities without the proprietor of the mark having, in good time, been afforded the opportunity of defending his rights. Invalidation shall be notified to the International Bureau.

Article 5bis [Documentary Evidence of Legitimacy of Use of Certain Elements of Mark]

Documentary evidence of the legitimacy of the use of certain elements incorporated in a mark, such as armorial bearings, escutcheons, portraits, honorary distinctions, titles, trade names, names of persons other than the name of the applicant, or other like inscriptions, which might be required by the Offices of the contracting countries shall be exempt from any legalisation or certification other than that of the Office of the country of origin.

Article 5ᵗᵉʳ   [Copies of Entries in International Register. Searches for Anticipation. Extracts from International Register]

(1)   The International Bureau shall issue to any person applying therefor, subject to a fee fixed by the Regulations, a copy of the entries in the Register relating to a specific mark.

(2)   The International Bureau may also, upon payment, undertake searches for anticipation among international marks.

(3)   Extracts from the International Register requested with a view to their production in one of the contracting countries shall be exempt from all legalisation.

Article 6   [Period of Validity of International Registration, Independence of International Registration. Termination of Protection in Country of Origin]

(1)   Registration of a mark at the International Bureau is effected for twenty years, with the possibility of renewal under the conditions specified in Article 7.

(2)   Upon expiration of a period of five years from the date of the international registration, such registration shall become independent of the national mark registered earlier in the country of origin, subject to the following provisions.

(3)   The protection resulting from the international registration, whether or not it has been the subject of a transfer, may no longer be invoked, in whole or in part, if, within five years from the date of the international registration, the national mark, registered earlier in the country of origin in accordance with Article 1, no longer enjoys, in whole or in part, legal protection in that country. This provision shall also apply when legal protection has later ceased as the result of an action begun before the expiration of the period of five years.

(4)   In the case of voluntary or ex officio cancellation, the Office of the country of origin shall request the cancellation of the mark at the International Bureau, and the latter shall effect the cancellation. In the case of judicial action, the said Office shall send to the International Bureau, ex officio or at the request of the plaintiff, a copy of the complaint or any other documentary evidence that an action has begun, and also of the final decision of the court; the Bureau shall enter notice thereof in the International Register.

Article 7   [Renewal of International Registration]

(1)   Any registration may be renewed for a period of twenty years from the expiration of the preceding period, by payment only of the basic fee and, where necessary, of the supplementary and complementary fees provided for in Article 8(2).

(2)   Renewal may not include any change in relation to the previous registration in its latest form.

(3)   The first renewal effected under the provisions of the Nice Act of 15 June 1957, or of this Act, shall include an indication of the classes of the International Classification to which the registration relates.

(4)   Six months before the expiration of the term of protection, the International Bureau shall, by sending an unofficial notice, remind the proprietor of the mark and his agent of the exact date of expiration.

(5)   Subject to the payment of a surcharge fixed by the Regulations, a period of grace of six months shall be granted for renewal of the international registration.

PROTOCOL RELATING TO THE MADRID AGREEMENT CONCERNING THE INTERNATIONAL REGISTRATION OF MARKS

(Adopted at Madrid on 27 June 1989)

Article 1   Membership in the Madrid Union

The States party to this Protocol (hereinafter referred to as "the Contracting States"), even where they are not party to the Madrid Agreement Concerning the International Registration of Marks as revised at Stockholm in 1967 and as amended in 1979 (hereinafter referred to as "the Madrid (Stockholm) Agreement"), and the organisations referred to in Article 14(1)(b) which are party to this Protocol (hereinafter referred to as "the Contracting Organisations") shall be members of the same Union of which countries party to the Madrid (Stockholm) Agreement are members. Any reference in this Protocol to "Contracting Parties" shall be construed as a reference to both Contracting States and Contracting Organisations.

Article 2   Securing Protection through International Registration

(1)   Where an application for the registration of a mark has been filed with the Office of a Contracting Party, or where a mark has been registered in the register of the Office of a Contracting Party, the person in whose name that application (hereinafter referred to as "the basic application") or that registration (hereinafter referred to as "the basic registration") stands may, subject to the provisions of this Protocol, secure protection for his mark in the territory of the Contracting Parties, by obtaining the registration of that mark in the register of the International Bureau of the World Intellectual Property Organisation (hereinafter referred to as "the international registration," "the International Register," "the International Bureau" and "the Organisation," respectively), provided that—

    (i)   where the basic application has been filed with the Office of a Contracting State or where the basic registration has been made by such an Office, the person in whose name that application or registration stands is a national of that Contracting State, or is domiciled, or has a real and effective industrial or commercial establishment, in the said Contracting State,

    (ii)   where the basic application has been filed with the Office of a Contracting Organisation or where the basic registration has been made by such an Office, the person in whose name that application or registration stands is a national of a State member of that Contracting Organisation, or is domiciled, or has a real and effective industrial or commercial establishment, in the territory of the said Contracting Organisation.

(2)   The application for international registration (hereinafter referred to as "the international application") shall be filed with the International Bureau through the intermediary of the Office with which the basic application was filed or by which the basic registration was made (hereinafter referred to as "the Office of origin"), as the case may be.

(3)   Any reference in this Protocol to an "Office" or an "Office of a Contracting Party" shall be construed as a reference to the office that is in charge, on behalf of a

Contracting Party, of the registration of marks, and any reference in this Protocol to "marks" shall be construed as a reference to trademarks and service marks.

(4)   For the purposes of this Protocol, "territory of a Contracting Party" means, where the Contracting Party is a State, the territory of that State and, where the Contracting Party is an intergovernmental organisation, the territory in which the constituting treaty of that intergovernmental organisation applies.

Article 3   International Application

(1)   Every international application under this Protocol shall be presented on the form prescribed by the Regulations. The Office of origin shall certify that the particulars appearing in the international application correspond to the particulars appearing, at the time of the certification, in the basic application or basic registration, as the case may be. Furthermore, the said Office shall indicate—

(i)   in the case of a basic application, the date and number of that application,

(ii)   in the case of a basic registration, the date and number of that registration as well as the date and number of the application from which the basic registration resulted.

The Office of origin shall also indicate the date of the international application.

(2)   The applicant must indicate the goods and services in respect of which protection of the mark is claimed and also, if possible, the corresponding class or classes according to the classification established by the Nice Agreement Concerning the International Classification of Goods and Services for the Purposes of the Registration of Marks. If the applicant does not give such indication, the International Bureau shall classify the goods and services in the appropriate classes of the said classification. The indication of classes given by the applicant shall be subject to control by the International Bureau, which shall exercise the said control in association with the Office of origin. In the event of disagreement between the said Office and the International Bureau, the opinion of the latter shall prevail.

(3)   If the applicant claims color as a distinctive feature of his mark, he shall be required—

(i)   to state the fact, and to file with his international application a notice specifying the color or the combination of colors claimed;

(ii)   to append to his international application copies in color of the said mark, which shall be attached to the notifications given by the International Bureau; the number of such copies shall be fixed by the Regulations.

(4)   The International Bureau shall register immediately the marks filed in accordance with Article 2. The international registration shall bear the date on which the international application was received in the Office of origin, provided that the international application has been received by the International Bureau within a period of two months from that date. If the international application has not been received within that period, the international registration shall bear the date on which the said international application was received by the International Bureau. The International Bureau shall notify the international registration without delay to the Offices concerned. Marks registered in the International Register shall be published in a periodical gazette issued by the International Bureau, on the basis of the particulars contained in the international application.

(5)   With a view to the publicity to be given to marks registered in the International Register, each Office shall receive from the International Bureau a number of copies

of the said gazette free of charge and a number of copies at a reduced price, under the conditions fixed by the Assembly referred to in Article 10 (hereinafter referred to as "the Assembly"). Such publicity shall be deemed to be sufficient for the purposes of all the Contracting Parties, and no other publicity may be required of the holder of the international registration.

Article 3bis Territorial Effect

The protection resulting from the international registration shall extend to any Contracting Party only at the request of the person who files the international application or who is the holder of the international registration. However, no such request can be made with respect to the Contracting Party whose Office is the Office of origin.

Article 3ter Request for "Territorial Extension"

(1)   Any request for extension of the protection resulting from the international registration to any Contracting Party shall be specially mentioned in the international application.

(2)   A request for territorial extension may also be made subsequently to the international registration. Any such request shall be presented on the form prescribed by the Regulations. It shall be immediately recorded by the International Bureau, which shall notify such recordal without delay to the Office or Offices concerned. Such recordal shall be published in the periodical gazette of the International Bureau. Such territorial extension shall be effective from the date on which it has been recorded in the International Register; it shall cease to be valid on the expiry of the international registration to which it relates.

Article 4   Effects of International Registration

(1)   (a)   From the date of the registration or recordal effected in accordance with the provisions of Articles 3 and 3ter, the protection of the mark in each of the Contracting Parties concerned shall be the same as if the mark had been deposited direct with the Office of that Contracting Party. If no refusal has been notified to the International Bureau in accordance with Article 5(1) and (2) or if a refusal notified in accordance with the said Article has been withdrawn subsequently, the protection of the mark in the Contracting Party concerned shall, as from the said date, be the same as if the mark had been registered by the Office of that Contracting Party.

(b)   The indication of classes of goods and services provided for in Article 3 shall not bind the Contracting Parties with regard to the determination of the scope of the protection of the mark.

(2)   Every international registration shall enjoy the right of priority provided for by Article 4 of the Paris Convention for the Protection of Industrial Property, without it being necessary to comply with the formalities prescribed in Section D of that Article.

Article 4bis Replacement of a National or Regional Registration by an International Registration

(1)   Where a mark that is the subject of a national or regional registration in the Office of a Contracting Party is also the subject of an international registration and both registrations stand in the name of the same person, the international registration

is deemed to replace the national or regional registration, without prejudice to any rights acquired by virtue of the latter, provided that—

(i)   the protection resulting from the international registration extends to the said Contracting Party under Article 3ter(1) or (2),

(ii) all the goods and services listed in the national or regional registration are also listed in the international registration in respect of the said Contracting Party,

(iii) such extension takes effect after the date of the national or regional registration.

(2)   The Office referred to in paragraph (1) shall, upon request, be required to take note in its register of the international registration.

Article 5   Refusal and Invalidation of Effects of International Registration in Respect of Certain Contracting Parties

(1)   Where the applicable legislation so authorises, any Office of a Contracting Party which has been notified by the International Bureau of an extension to that Contracting Party, under Article 3ter(1) or (2), of the protection resulting from the international registration shall have the right to declare in a notification of refusal that protection cannot be granted in the said Contracting Party to the mark which is the subject of such extension. Any such refusal can be based only on the grounds which would apply, under the Paris Convention for the Protection of Industrial Property, in the case of a mark deposited direct with the Office which notifies the refusal. However, protection may not be refused, even partially, by reason only that the applicable legislation would permit registration only in a limited number of classes or for a limited number of goods or services.

(2)   (a)   Any Office wishing to exercise such right shall notify its refusal to the International Bureau, together with a statement of all grounds, within the period prescribed by the law applicable to that Office and at the latest, subject to subparagraphs (b) and (c), before the expiry of one year from the date on which the notification of the extension referred to in paragraph (1) has been sent to that Office by the International Bureau.

(b)   Notwithstanding subparagraph (a), any Contracting Party may declare that, for international registrations made under this Protocol, the time limit of one year referred to in subparagraph (a) is replaced by 18 months.

(c)   Such declaration may also specify that, when a refusal of protection may result from an opposition to the granting of protection, such refusal may be notified by the Office of the said Contracting Party to the International Bureau after the expiry of the 18-month time limit. Such an Office may, with respect to any given international registration, notify a refusal of protection after the expiry of the 18-month time limit, but only if—

(i)   it has, before the expiry of the 18-month time limit, informed the International Bureau of the possibility that oppositions may be filed after the expiry of the 18-month time limit, and

(ii) the notification of the refusal based on an opposition is made within a time limit of not more than seven months from the date on which the opposition period begins; if the opposition period expires before this time limit of seven months, the notification must be made within a time limit of one month from the expiry of the opposition period.

(d)   Any declaration under subparagraphs (b) or (c) may be made in the instruments referred to in Article 14(2), and the effective date of the declaration shall be the same as the date of entry into force of this Protocol with respect to the State or intergovernmental organisation having made the declaration. Any such declaration may also be made later, in which case the declaration shall have effect three months after its receipt by the Director General of the Organisation (hereinafter referred to as "the Director General"), or at any later date indicated in the declaration, in respect of any international registration whose date is the same as or is later than the effective date of the declaration.

(e) Upon the expiry of a period of ten years from the entry into force of this Protocol, the Assembly shall examine the operation of the system established by subparagraphs (a) to (d). Thereafter, the provisions of the said subparagraphs may be modified by a unanimous decision of the Assembly.

(3) The International Bureau shall, without delay, transmit one of the copies of the notification of refusal to the holder of the international registration. The said holder shall have the same remedies as if the mark had been deposited by him direct with the Office which has notified its refusal. Where the International Bureau has received information under paragraph (2)(c)(i), it shall, without delay, transmit the said information to the holder of the international registration.

(4) The grounds for refusing a mark shall be communicated by the International Bureau to any interested party who may so request.

(5) Any Office which has not notified, with respect to a given international registration, any provisional or final refusal to the International Bureau in accordance with paragraphs (1) and (2) shall, with respect to that international registration, lose the benefit of the right provided for in paragraph (1).

(6) Invalidation, by the competent authorities of a Contracting Party, of the effects, in the territory of that Contracting Party, of an international registration may not be pronounced without the holder of such international registration having, in good time, been afforded the opportunity of defending his rights. Invalidation shall be notified to the International Bureau.

Article 5bis   Documentary Evidence of Legitimacy of Use of Certain Elements of the Mark

Documentary evidence of the legitimacy of the use of certain elements incorporated in a mark, such as armorial bearings, escutcheons, portraits, honorary distinctions, titles, trade names, names of persons other than the name of the applicant, or other like inscriptions, which might be required by the Offices of the Contracting Parties shall be exempt from any legalisation as well as from any certification other than that of the Office of origin.

Article 5ter   Copies of Entries in International Register; Searches for Anticipations; Extracts from International Register

(1) The International Bureau shall issue to any person applying therefor, upon the payment of a fee fixed by the Regulations, a copy of the entries in the International Register concerning a specific mark.

(2) The International Bureau may also, upon payment, undertake searches for anticipations among marks that are the subject of international registrations.

(3) Extracts from the International Register requested with a view to their production in one of the Contracting Parties shall be exempt from any legalisation.

Article 6   Period of Validity of International Registration; Dependence and Independence of International Registration

(1)   Registration of a mark at the International Bureau is effected for ten years, with the possibility of renewal under the conditions specified in Article 7.

(2)   Upon expiry of a period of five years from the date of the international registration, such registration shall become independent of the basic application or the registration resulting therefrom, or of the basic registration, as the case may be, subject to the following provisions.

(3)   The protection resulting from the international registration, whether or not it has been the subject of a transfer, may no longer be invoked if, before the expiry of five years from the date of the international registration, the basic application or the registration resulting therefrom, or the basic registration, as the case may be, has been withdrawn, has lapsed, has been renounced or has been the subject of a final decision of rejection, revocation, cancellation or invalidation, in respect of all or some of the goods and services listed in the international registration. The same applies if—

    (i)   an appeal against a decision refusing the effects of the basic application,

    (ii)   an action requesting the withdrawal of the basic application or the revocation, cancellation or invalidation of the registration resulting from the basic application or of the basic registration, or

    (iii)   an opposition to the basic application

results, after the expiry of the five-year period, in a final decision of rejection, revocation, cancellation or invalidation, or ordering the withdrawal, of the basic application, or the registration resulting therefrom, or the basic registration, as the case may be, provided that such appeal, action or opposition had begun before the expiry of the said period. The same also applies if the basic application is withdrawn, or the registration resulting from the basic application or the basic registration is renounced, after the expiry of the five-year period, provided that, at the time of the withdrawal or renunciation, the said application or registration was the subject of a proceeding referred to in item (i), (ii) or (iii) and that such proceeding had begun before the expiry of the said period.

(4)   The Office of origin shall, as prescribed in the Regulations, notify the International Bureau of the facts and decisions relevant under paragraph (3), and the International Bureau shall, as prescribed in the Regulations, notify the interested parties and effect any publication accordingly. The Office of origin shall, where applicable, request the International Bureau to cancel, to the extent applicable, the international registration, and the International Bureau shall proceed accordingly.

Article 7   Renewal of International Registration

(1)   Any international registration may be renewed for a period of ten years from the expiry of the preceding period, by the mere payment of the basic fee and, subject to Article 8(7), of the supplementary and complementary fees provided for in Article 8(2).

(2)   Renewal may not bring about any change in the international registration in its latest form.

(3)   Six months before the expiry of the term of protection, the International Bureau shall, by sending an unofficial notice, remind the holder of the international registration and his representative, if any, of the exact date of expiry.

(4)   Subject to the payment of a surcharge fixed by the Regulations, a period of grace of six months shall be allowed for renewal of the international registration.

[4]

(This Agreement and Protocol are reproduced with the permission of the International Bureau of the World Intellectual Property Organisation (WIPO).)

INTERNATIONAL CONVENTION FOR THE PROTECTION OF PERFORMERS, PRODUCERS OF PHONOGRAMS AND BROADCASTING ORGANISATIONS

(Rome, 26 October 1961)

NOTES

Articles have been given titles to facilitate their identification. There are no titles in the signed text.

Article 1   [Safeguard of copyright proper]

Protection granted under this Convention shall leave intact and shall in no way affect the protection of copyright in literary and artistic works. Consequently, no provision of this Convention may be interpreted as prejudicing such protection.

Article 2   [Protection given by the Convention]

1.   For the purposes of this Convention, national treatment shall mean the treatment accorded by the domestic law of the Contracting State in which protection is claimed—
    (a)   to performers who are its nationals, as regards performance taking place, broadcast, or first fixed, on its territory;
    (b)   to producers of phonograms who are its nationals, as regards phonograms first fixed or first published on its territory;
    (c)   to broadcasting organisations which have their headquarters on its territory, as regards broadcasts transmitted from transmitters situated on its territory.

2.   National treatment shall be subject to the protection specifically guaranteed, and the limitations specifically provided for, in this Convention.

Article 3   [Definitions]

For the purposes of this Convention—
    (a)   "performers" means actors, singers, musicians, dancers, and other persons who act, sing, deliver, declaim, play in, or otherwise perform literary or artistic works;
    (b)   "phonogram" means any exclusively aural fixation of sounds of a performance or of other sounds;
    (c)   "producer of phonograms" means the person who, or the legal entity which, first fixes the sounds of a performance or other sounds;
    (d)   "publication" means the offering of copies of a phonogram to the public in reasonable quantity;
    (e)   "reproduction" means the making of a copy or copies of a fixation;
    (f)   "broadcasting" means the transmission by wireless means for public reception of sounds or of images and sounds;
    (g)   "rebroadcasting" means the simultaneous broadcasting by one broadcasting organisation of the broadcast of another broadcasting organisation.

Article 4   [Performances protected]

Each Contracting State shall grant national treatment to performers if any of the following conditions is met—
    (a)   the performance takes place in another Contracting State;
    (b)   the performance is incorporated in a phonogram which is protected under Article 5 of this Convention;
    (c)   the performance, not being fixed on a phonogram, is carried by a broadcast which is protected by Article 6 of this Convention.

Article 5   [Protected phonograms]

1.   Each Contracting State shall grant national treatment to producers of phonograms if any of the following conditions is met—
    (a)   the producer of the phonogram is a national of another Contracting State (criterion of nationality);
    (b)   the first fixation of the sound was made in another Contracting State (criterion of fixation);
    (c)   the phonogram was first published in another Contracting State (criterion of publication).

2.   If a phonogram was first published in a non–Contracting State but if it was also published, within thirty days of its first publication, in a Contracting State (simultaneous publication), it shall be considered as first published in the Contracting State.

3.   By means of a notification deposited with the Secretary-General of the United Nations, any Contracting State may declare that it will not apply the criterion of publication or, alternatively, the criterion of fixation. Such notification may be deposited at the time of ratification, acceptance or accession, or at any time thereafter; in one last case, it shall become effective six months after it has been deposited.

Article 6   [Protected broadcasts]

1.   Each Contracting State shall grant national treatment to broadcasting organisations if either of the following conditions is met—
    (a)   the headquarters of the broadcasting organisation is situated in another Contracting State;
    (b)   the broadcast was transmitted from a transmitter situated in another Contracting State.

2.   By means of a notification deposited with the Secretary-General of the United Nations, any Contracting State may declare that it will protect broadcasts only if the headquarters of the broadcasting organisation is situated in another Contracting State and the broadcast was transmitted from a transmitter situated in the same Contracting State. Such notification may be deposited at the time of ratification, acceptance or accession, or at any time thereafter; in the last case, it shall become effective six months after it has been deposited.

Article 7   [Minimum protection for performers]

1.   The protection provided for performers by this Convention shall include the possibility of preventing—
    (a)   the broadcasting and the communication to the public, without their consent, of their performance, except where the performance used in the

broadcasting or the public communication is itself already a broadcast performance or is made from a fixation;

(b)   the fixation, without their consent, of their unfixed performance;

(c)   the reproduction, without their consent, of a fixation of their performance—

(i)   if the original fixation itself was made without their consent;

(ii)   if the reproduction is made for purposes different from those for which the performers gave their consent;

(iii)   if the original fixation was made in accordance with the provisions of Article 15, and the reproduction is made for purposes different from those referred to in those provisions.

2.—(1)   If broadcasting was consented to by the performers, it shall be a matter for the domestic law of the Contracting State where protection is claimed to regulate the protection against rebroadcasting, fixation for broadcasting purposes and the reproduction of such fixation for broadcasting purposes.

(2)   The terms and conditions governing the use by broadcasting organisations of fixations made for broadcasting purposes shall be determined in accordance with the domestic law of the Contracting State where protection is claimed.

(3)   However, the domestic law referred to in sub-paragraphs (1) and (2) of this paragraph shall not operate to deprive performers of the ability to control, by contract, their relations with broadcasting organisations.

Article 8   [Performers acting jointly]

Any Contracting State may, by its domestic laws and regulations, specify the manner in which performers will be represented in connection with the exercise of their rights if several of them participate in the same performance.

Article 9   [Variety and circus artists]

Any Contracting State may, by its domestic laws and regulations, extend the protection provided for in this Convention to artists who do not perform literary or artistic works.

Article 10   [Right of reproduction for phonogram producers]

Producers of phonograms shall enjoy the right to authorise or prohibit the direct or indirect reproduction of their phonograms.

Article 11   [Formalities for phonograms]

If, as a condition of protecting the rights of producers of phonograms, or of performers, or both, in relation to phonograms, a Contracting State, under its domestic law, requires compliance with formalities, these shall be considered as fulfilled if all the copies in commerce of the published phonogram or their containers bear a notice consisting of the symbol ℗, accompanied by the year date of the first publication, placed in such a manner as to give reasonable notice of claim of protection; and if the copies or their containers do not identify the producer or the licensee of the producer (by carrying his name, trade mark or other appropriate designation), the notice shall also include the name of the owner of the rights of the producer; and, furthermore, if the copies or their containers do not identify the principal performers, the notice shall also include the name of the person who, in the country in which the fixation was effected, owns the rights of such performers.

Article 12   [Secondary uses of phonograms]

If a phonogram published for commercial purposes, or a reproduction of such phonogram, is used directly for broadcasting or for any communication to the public, a single equitable remuneration shall be paid by the user to the performers, or to the producers of the phonograms, or to both. Domestic law may, in the absence of agreement between these parties, lay down the conditions as to the sharing of this remuneration.

Article 13   [Minimum rights for broadcasting organisations]

Broadcasting organisations shall enjoy the right to authorise or prohibit—
- (a)   the rebroadcasting of their broadcasts;
- (b)   the fixation of their broadcasts;
- (c)   the reproduction—
    - (i)   of fixations, made without their consent, of their broadcasts;
    - (ii)   of fixations, made in accordance with the provisions of Article 15, of their broadcasts, if the reproduction is made for purposes different from those referred to in those provisions;
- (d)   the communication to the public of their television broadcasts if such communication is made in places accessible to the public against payment of an entrance fee; it shall be a matter for the domestic law of the State where protection of this right is claimed to determine the conditions under which it may be exercised.

Article 14   [Minimum duration of protection]

The term of protection to be granted under this Convention shall last at least until the end of a period of twenty years computed from the end of the year in which—
- (a)   the fixation was made—for phonograms and for performances incorporated therein;
- (b)   the performance took place—for performances not incorporated in phonograms;
- (c)   the broadcast took place—for broadcasts.

Article 15   [Permitted exceptions]

1.   Any Contracting State may, in its domestic laws and regulations, provide for exceptions to the protection guaranteed by this Convention as regards—
- (a)   private use;
- (b)   use of short excerpts in connection with the reporting of current events;
- (c)   ephemeral fixation by a broadcasting organisation by means of its own facilities and for its own broadcasts;
- (d)   use solely for the purposes of teaching or scientific research.

2.   Irrespective of paragraph 1 of this Article, any Contracting State may, in its domestic laws and regulations, provide for the same kinds of limitations with regard to the protection of performers, producers of phonograms and broadcasting organisations, as it provides for, in its domestic laws and regulations, in connection with the protection of copyright in literary and artistic works. However, compulsory licences may be provided for only to the extent to which they are compatible with this Convention.

[5]

(This Convention is reproduced with the permission of the International Bureau of the World Intellectual Property Organisation (WIPO).)

CONVENTION ON THE GRANT OF EUROPEAN PATENTS (EUROPEAN PATENT CONVENTION)

(Munich, 5 October 1973)

[The Convention has been ratified by the United Kingdom]

PART I
GENERAL AND INSTITUTIONAL PROVISIONS

CHAPTER I. GENERAL PROVISIONS

Article 1   European law for the grant of patents

A system of law, common to the Contracting States, for the grant of patents for invention is hereby established.

Article 2   European patent

(1)   Patents granted by virtue of this Convention shall be called European patents.

(2)   The European patent shall, in each of the Contracting States for which it is granted, have the effect of and be subject to the same conditions as a national patent granted by that State, unless otherwise provided in this Convention.

Article 3   Territorial effect

The grant of a European patent may be requested for one or more of the Contracting States.

[6]

PART II
SUBSTANTIVE PATENT LAW

CHAPTER I. PATENTABILITY

Article 52   Patentable inventions

(1)   European patents shall be granted for any inventions which are susceptible of industrial application, which are new and which involve an inventive step.

(2)   The following in particular shall not be regarded as inventions within the meaning of paragraph 1—
    (a)   discoveries, scientific theories and mathematical methods;
    (b)   aesthetic creations;
    (c)   schemes, rules and methods for performing mental acts, playing games or doing business, and programs for computers;
    (d)   presentations of information.

(3)   The provisions of paragraph 2 shall exclude patentability of the subject-matter or activities referred to in that provision only to the extent to which a European patent application or European patent relates to such subject-matter or activities as such.

(4) Methods for treatment of the human or animal body by surgery or therapy and diagnostic methods practised on the human or animal body shall not be regarded as inventions which are susceptible of industrial application within the meaning of paragraph 1. This provision shall not apply to products, in particular substances or compositions, for use in any of these methods.

Article 53   Exceptions to patentability

European patents shall not be granted in respect of—
- (a) inventions the publication or exploitation of which would be contrary to "ordre public" or morality, provided that the exploitation shall not be deemed to be so contrary merely because it is prohibited by law or regulation in some or all of the Contracting States;
- (b) plant or animal varieties or essentially biological processes for the production of plants or animals; this provision does not apply to microbiological processes or the products thereof.

Article 54   Novelty

(1) An invention shall be considered to be new if it does not form part of the state of the art.

(2) The state of the art shall be held to comprise everything made available to the public by means of a written or oral description, by use, or in any other way, before the date of filing of the European patent application.

(3) Additionally, the content of European patent applications as filed, of which the dates of filing are prior to the date referred to in paragraph 2 and which were published under Article 93 on or after that date, shall be considered as comprised in the state of the art.

(4) Paragraph 3 shall be applied only insofar as a Contracting State designated in respect of the later application, was also designated in respect of the earlier application as published.

(5) The provisions of paragraphs 1 to 4 shall not exclude the patentability of any substance or composition, comprised in the state of the art, for use in a method referred to in Article 52, paragraph 4, provided that its use for any method referred to in that paragraph is not comprised in the state of the art.

Article 55   Non-prejudicial disclosures

(1) For the application of Article 54 a disclosure of the invention shall not be taken into consideration if it occurred no earlier than six months preceding the filing of the European patent application and if it was due to, or in consequence of—
- (a) an evident abuse in relation to the applicant or his legal predecessor, or
- (b) the fact that the applicant or his legal predecessor has displayed the invention at an official, or officially recognised, international exhibition falling within the terms of the Convention on international exhibitions signed at Paris on 22 November 1928 and last revised on 30 November 1972.

(2) In the case of paragraph 1(b), paragraph 1 shall apply only if the applicant states, when filing the European patent application, that the invention has been so displayed and files a supporting certificate within the period and under the conditions laid down in the Implementing Regulations.

Article 56   Inventive step

An invention shall be considered as involving an inventive step if, having regard to the state of the art, it is not obvious to a person skilled in the art. If the state of the art also includes documents within the meaning of Article 54, paragraph 3, these documents are not to be considered in deciding whether there has been an inventive step.

Article 57   Industrial application

An invention shall be considered as susceptible of industrial application if it can be made or used in any kind of industry, including agriculture.

CHAPTER II. PERSONS ENTITLED TO APPLY FOR AND OBTAIN EUROPEAN PATENTS—MENTION OF THE INVENTOR

Article 58   Entitlement to file a European patent application

A European patent application may be filed by any natural or legal person, or any body equivalent to a legal person by virtue of the law governing it.

Article 59   Multiple applicants

A European patent application may also be filed either by joint applicants or by two or more applicants designating different Contracting States.

Article 60   Right to a European patent

(1)   The right to a European patent shall belong to the inventor or his successor in title. If the inventor is an employee the right to the European patent shall be determined in accordance with the law of the State in which the employee is mainly employed; if the State in which the employee is mainly employed cannot be determined, the law to be applied shall be that of the State in which the employer has his place of business to which the employee is attached.

(2)   If two or more persons have made an invention independently of each other, the right to the European patent shall belong to the person whose European patent application has the earliest date of filing; however, this provision shall apply only if this first application has been published under Article 93 and shall only have effect in respect of the Contracting States designated in that application as published.

(3)   For the purposes of proceedings before the European Patent Office, the applicant shall be deemed to be entitled to exercise the right to the European patent.

Article 61   European patent applications by persons not having the right to a European patent

(1)   If by a final decision it is adjudged that a person referred to in Article 60, paragraph 1, other than the applicant, is entitled to the grant of a European patent, that person may, within a period of three months after the decision has become final, provided that the European patent has not yet been granted, in respect of those Contracting States designated in the European patent application in which the decision has been taken or recognised, or has to be recognised on the basis of the Protocol on Recognition annexed to this Convention—
    (a) prosecute the application as his own application in place of the applicant,
    (b) file a new European patent application in respect of the same invention, or
    (c) request that the application be refused.

(2)   The provision of Article 76, paragraph 1, shall apply *mutatis mutandis* to a new application filed under paragraph 1.

(3)   The procedure to be followed in carrying out the provisions of paragraph 1, the special conditions applying to a new application filed under paragraph 1 and the time limit for paying the filing, search and designation fees on it are laid down in the Implementing Regulations.

Article 62   Right of the inventor to be mentioned

The inventor shall have the right, *vis-à-vis* the applicant for or proprietor of a European patent, to be mentioned as such before the European Patent Office.

CHAPTER III. EFFECTS OF THE EUROPEAN PATENT AND THE EUROPEAN PATENT APPLICATION

Article 63   Term of the European patent

(1)   The term of the European patent shall be 20 years as from the date of filing of the application.

(2)   Nothing in the preceding paragraph shall limit the right of a Contracting State to extend the term of a European patent under the same conditions as those applying to its national patents, in order to take into account a state of war or similar emergency conditions affecting that State.

Article 64   Rights conferred by a European patent

(1)   A European patent shall, subject to the provisions of paragraph 2, confer on its proprietor from the date of publication of the mention of its grant, in each Contracting State in respect of which it is granted, the same rights as would be conferred by a national patent granted in that State.

(2)   If the subject-matter of the European patent is a process, the protection conferred by the patent shall extend to the products directly obtained by such process.

(3)   Any infringement of a European patent shall be dealt with by national law.

Article 65   Translation of the specification of the European patent

(1)   Any Contracting State may prescribe that if the text, in which the European Patent Office intends to grant a European patent or maintain a European patent as amended for that State, is not drawn up in one of its official languages, the applicant for or proprietor of the patent shall supply to its central industrial property office a translation of this text in one of its official languages at his option or, where that State has prescribed the use of one specific official language, in that language. The period for supplying the translation shall be three months after the start of the time limit referred to in Article 97, paragraph 2(b), or Article 102, paragraph 3(b), unless the State concerned prescribes a longer period.

(2)   Any Contracting State which has adopted provisions pursuant to paragraph 1 may prescribe that the applicant for or proprietor of the patent must pay all or part of the costs of publication of such translation within a period laid down by that State.

(3)   Any Contracting State may prescribe that in the event of failure to observe the provisions adopted in accordance with paragraphs 1 and 2, the European patent shall be deemed to be void *ab initio* in that State.

Article 66   Equivalence of European filing with national filing

A European patent application which has been accorded a date of filing shall, in the designated Contracting States, be equivalent to a regular national filing, where appropriate with the priority claimed for the European patent application.

Article 67   Rights conferred by a European patent application after publication

(1)   A European patent application shall, from the date of its publication under Article 93, provisionally confer upon the applicant such protection as is conferred by Article 64, in the Contracting States designated in the application as published.

(2)   Any Contracting State may prescribe that a European patent application shall not confer such protection as is conferred by Article 64. However, the protection attached to the publication of the European patent application may not be less than that which the laws of the State concerned attach to the compulsory publication of unexamined national patent applications. In any event, every State shall ensure at least that, from the date of publication of a European patent application, the applicant can claim compensation reasonable in the circumstances from any person who has used the invention in the said State in circumstances where that person would be liable under national law for infringement of a national patent.

(3)   Any Contracting State which does not have as an official language the language of the proceedings, may prescribe that provisional protection in accordance with paragraphs 1 and 2 above shall not be effective until such time as a translation of the claims in one of its official languages at the option of the applicant or, where that State has prescribed the use of one specific official language, in that language—

> (a)   has been made available to the public in the manner prescribed by national law, or
>
> (b)   has been communicated to the person using the invention in the said State.

(4)   The European patent application shall be deemed never to have had the effects set out in paragraphs 1 and 2 above when it has been withdrawn, deemed to be withdrawn or finally refused. The same shall apply in respect of the effects of the European patent application in a Contracting State the designation of which is withdrawn or deemed to be withdrawn.

Article 68   Effect of revocation of the European patent

The European patent application and the resulting patent shall be deemed not to have had, as from the outset, the effects specified in Articles 64 and 67, to the extent that the patent has been revoked in opposition proceedings.

Article 69   Extent of protection

(1)   The extent of the protection conferred by a European patent or a European patent application shall be determined by the terms of the claims. Nevertheless, the description and drawings shall be used to interpret the claims.

(2)   For the period up to grant of the European patent, the extent of the protection conferred by the European patent application shall be determined by the latest filed claims contained in the publication under Article 93. However, the European patent as granted or as amended in opposition proceedings shall determine retroactively the protection conferred by the European patent application, insofar as such protection is not thereby extended.

Article 70   Authentic text of a European patent application or European patent

(1)   The text of a European patent application or a European patent in the language of the proceedings shall be the authentic text in any proceedings before the European Patent Office and in any Contracting State.

(2)   However, in the case referred to in Article 14, paragraph 2, the original text shall, in proceedings before the European Patent Office, constitute the basis for determining whether the subject-matter of the application or patent extends beyond the content of the application as filed.

(3)   Any Contracting State may provide that a translation, as provided for in this Convention, in an official language of that State, shall in that State be regarded as authentic, except for revocation proceedings, in the event of the application or patent in the language of the translation conferring protection which is narrower than that conferred by it in the language of the proceedings.

(4)   Any Contracting State which adopts a provision under paragraph 3—
- (a)   must allow the applicant for or proprietor of the patent to file a corrected translation of the European patent application or European patent. Such corrected translation shall not have any legal effect until any conditions established by the Contracting State under Article 65, paragraph 2, and Article 67, paragraph 3, have been complied with *mutatis mutandis*;
- (b)   may prescribe that any person who, in that State, in good faith is using or has made effective and serious preparations for using an invention the use of which would not constitute infringement of the application or patent in the original translation may, after the corrected translation takes effect, continue such use in the course of his business or for the needs thereof without payment.

CHAPTER IV. THE EUROPEAN PATENT APPLICATION AS AN OBJECT OF PROPERTY

Article 71   Transfer and constitution of rights

A European patent application may be transferred or give rise to rights for one or more of the designated Contracting States.

Article 72   Assignment

An assignment of a European patent application shall be made in writing and shall require the signature of the parties to the contract.

Article 73   Contractual licensing

A European patent application may be licensed in whole or in part for the whole or part of the territories of the designated Contracting States.

Article 74   Law applicable

Unless otherwise specified in this Convention, the European patent application as an object of property shall, in each designated Contracting State and with effect for such State, be subject to the law applicable in that State to national patent applications.

PART III
APPLICATION FOR EUROPEAN PATENTS

CHAPTER I. FILING AND REQUIREMENTS OF THE EUROPEAN PATENT APPLICATION

Article 75   Filing of the European patent application

(1)   A European patent application may be filed—
- (a) at the European Patent Office at Munich or its branch at The Hague, or
- (b) if the law of the Contracting State so permits, at the central industrial property office or other competent authority of that State. An application filed in this way shall have the same effect as if it had been filed on the same date at the European Patent Office.

(2)   The provisions of paragraph 1 shall not preclude the application of legislative or regulatory provisions which, in any Contracting State—
- (a) govern inventions which, owing to the nature of their subject-matter may not be communicated abroad without the prior authorisation of the competent authorities of that State, or
- (b) prescribe that each application is to be filed initially with a national authority or make direct filing with another authority subject to prior authorisation.

(3)   No Contracting State may provide for or allow the filing European divisional applications with an authority referred to in paragraph 1(b).

Article 76   European divisional applications

(1)   A European divisional application must be filed directly with the European Patent Office at Munich or its branch at The Hague. It may be filed only in respect of subject-matter which does not extend beyond the content of the earlier application as filed; insofar as this provision is complied with, the divisional application shall be deemed to have been filed on the date of filing of the earlier application and shall have the benefit of any right to priority.

(2)   The European divisional application shall not designate Contracting States which were not designated in the earlier application.

(3)   The procedure to be followed in carrying out the provisions of paragraph 1, the special conditions to be complied with by a divisional application and the time limit for paying the filing, search and designation fees are laid down in the Implementing Regulations.

Article 77   Forwarding of European patent applications

(1)   The central industrial property office of a Contracting State shall be obliged to forward to the European Patent Office, in the shortest time compatible with the application of national law concerning the secrecy of inventions in the interests of the State, any European patent applications which have been filed with that office or with other competent authorities in that State.

(2)   The Contracting States shall take all appropriate steps to ensure that European patent applications, the subject of which is obviously not liable to secrecy by virtue of the law referred to in paragraph 1, shall be forwarded to the European Patent Office within six weeks after filing.

(3)   European patent applications which require further examination as to their liability to secrecy shall be forwarded in such manner as to reach the European Patent Office within four months after filing, or, where priority has been claimed, fourteen months after the date of priority.

(4)   A European patent application, the subject of which has been made secret, shall not be forwarded to the European Patent Office.

(5)   European patent applications which do not reach the European Patent Office before the end of the fourteenth month after filing or, if priority has been claimed, after the date of priority, shall be deemed to be withdrawn. The filing, search and designation fees shall be refunded.

Article 78   Requirements of the European patent application

(1)   A European patent application shall contain—
   (a)   a request for the grant of a European patent;
   (b)   a description of the invention;
   (c)   one or more claims;
   (d)   any drawings referred to in the description or the claims;
   (e)   an abstract.

(2)   A European patent application shall be subject to the payment of the filing fee and the search fee within one month after the filing of the application.

(3)   A European patent application must satisfy the conditions laid down in the Implementing Regulations.

Article 79   Designation of Contracting States

(1)   The request for the grant of a European patent shall contain the designation of the Contracting State or States in which protection for the invention is desired.

(2)   The designation of a Contracting State shall be subject to the payment of the designation fee. The designation fees shall be paid within twelve months after filing the European patent application or, if priority has been claimed, after the date of priority; in the latter case, payment may still be made up to the expiry of the period specified in Article 78, paragraph 2, if that period expires later.

(3)   The designation of a Contracting State may be withdrawn at any time up to the grant of the European patent. Withdrawal of the designation of all the Contracting States shall be deemed to be a withdrawal of the European patent application. Designation fees shall not be refunded.

Article 80   Date of filing

The date of filing of a European patent application shall be the date on which documents filed by the applicant contain—
   (a)   an indication that a European patent is sought;
   (b)   the designation of at least one Contracting State;
   (c)   information identifying the applicant;
   (d)   a description and one or more claims in one of the languages referred to in Article 14, paragraphs 1 and 2, even though the description and the claims do not comply with the other requirements of this Convention.

Article 81   Designation of the inventor

The European patent application shall designate the inventor. If the applicant is not the inventor or is not the sole inventor, the designation shall contain a statement indicating the origin of the right to the European patent.

Article 82   Unity of invention

The European patent application shall relate to one invention only or to a group of inventions so linked as to form a single general inventive concept.

Article 83   Disclosure of the invention

The European patent application must disclose the invention in a manner sufficiently clear and complete for it to be carried out by a person skilled in the art.

Article 84   The claims

The claims shall define the matter for which protection is sought. They shall be clear and concise and be supported by the description.

Article 85   The abstract

The abstract shall merely serve for use as technical information; it may not be taken into account for any other purpose, in particular not for the purpose of interpreting the scope of the protection sought nor for the purpose of applying Article 54, paragraph 3.

Article 86   Renewal fees for European patent applications

(1)   Renewal fees shall be paid to the European Patent Office in accordance with the Implementing Regulations in respect of European patent applications. These fees shall be due in respect of the third year and each subsequent year, calculated from the date of filing of the application.

(2)   When a renewal fee has not been paid on or before the due date, the fee may be validly paid within six months of the said date, provided that the additional fee is paid at the same time.

(3)   If the renewal fee and any additional fee have not been paid in due time the European patent application shall be deemed to be withdrawn. The European Patent Office alone shall be competent to decide this.

(4)   The obligation to pay renewal fees shall terminate with the payment of the renewal fee due in respect of the year in which the mention of the grant of the European patent is published.

CHAPTER II. PRIORITY

Article 87   Priority right

(1)   A person who has duly filed in or for any State party to the Paris Convention for the Protection of Industrial Property, an application for a patent or for the registration of a utility model or for a utility certificate or for an inventor's certificate, or his successors in title, shall enjoy, for the purpose of filing a European patent application in respect of the same invention, a right of priority during a period of twelve months from the date of filing of the first application.

(2)   Every filing that is equivalent to a regular national filing under the national law of the State where it was made or under bilateral or multilateral agreements, including this Convention, shall be recognised as giving rise to a right of priority.

(3)   By a regular national filing is meant any filing that is sufficient to establish the date on which the application was filed, whatever may be the outcome of the application.

(4)   A subsequent application for the same subject–matter as a previous first application and filed in or in respect of the same State shall be considered as the first application for the purposes of determining priority, provided that, at the date of filing the subsequent application, the previous application has been withdrawn, abandoned or refused, without being open to public inspection and without leaving any rights outstanding, and has not served as a basis for claiming a right of priority. The previous application may not thereafter serve as a basis for claiming a right of priority.

(5)   If the first filing has been made in a State which is not a party to the Paris Convention for the Protection of Industrial Property, paragraphs 1 to 4 shall apply only insofar as that State, according to a notification published by the Administrative Council, and by virtue of bilateral or multilateral agreements, grants on the basis of a first filing made at the European Patent Office as well as on the basis of a first filing made in or for any Contracting State and subject to conditions equivalent to those laid down in the Paris Convention, a right of priority having equivalent effect.

Article 88   Claiming priority

(1)   An applicant for a European patent desiring to take advantage of the priority of a previous application shall file a declaration of priority, a copy of the previous application and, if the language of the latter is not one of the official languages of the European Patent Office, a translation of it in one of such official languages. The procedure to be followed in carrying out these provisions is laid down in the Implementing Regulations.

(2)   Multiple priorities may be claimed in respect of a European patent application, notwithstanding the fact that they originated in different countries. Where appropriate, multiple priorities may be claimed for any one claim. Where multiple priorities are claimed, time limits which run from the date of priority shall run from the earliest date of priority.

(3)   If one or more priorities are claimed in respect of a European patent application, the right of priority shall cover only those elements of the European patent application which are included in the application or applications whose priority is claimed.

(4)   If certain elements of the invention for which priority is claimed do not appear among the claims formulated in the previous application, priority may nonetheless be granted, provided that the documents of the previous application as a whole specifically disclose such elements.

Article 89   Effect of priority right

The right of priority shall have the effect that the date of priority shall count as the date of filing of the European patent application for the purposes of Article 54, paragraphs 2 and 3, and Article 60, paragraph 2.

PART IV
PROCEDURE UP TO GRANT

Article 90   Examination on filing

(1)   The Receiving Section shall examine whether—
    (a)   the European patent application satisfies the requirements for the accordance of a date of filing;
    (b)   the filing fee and the search fee have been paid in due time;
    (c)   in the case provided for in Article 14, paragraph 2, the translation of the European patent application in the language of the proceedings has been filed in due time.

(2)   If a date of filing cannot be accorded, the Receiving Section shall give the applicant an opportunity to correct the deficiencies in accordance with the Implementing Regulations. If the deficiencies are not remedied in due time, the application shall not be dealt with as a European patent application.

(3)   If the filing fee and the search fee have not been paid in due time or, in the case provided for in Article 14, paragraph 2, the translation of the application in the language of the proceedings has not been filed in due time, the application shall be deemed to be withdrawn.

Article 91   Examination as to formal requirements

(1)   If a European patent application has been accorded a date of filing, and is not deemed to be withdrawn by virtue of Article 90, paragraph 3, the Receiving Section shall examine whether—
    (a)   the requirements of Article 133, paragraph 2, have been satisfied;
    (b)   the application meets the physical requirements laid down in the Implementing Regulations for the implementation of this provision;
    (c)   the abstract has been filed;
    (d)   the request for the grant of a European patent satisfies the mandatory provisions of the Implementing Regulations concerning its content and, where appropriate, whether the requirements of this Convention concerning the claim to priority have been satisfied;
    (e)   the designation fees have been paid;
    (f)   the designation of the inventor has been made in accordance with Article 81;
    (g)   the drawing referred to in Article 78, paragraph 1(d), were filed on the date of filing of the application.

(2)   Where the Receiving Section notes that there are deficiencies which may be corrected, it shall give the applicant an opportunity to correct them in accordance with the Implementing Regulations.

(3)   If any deficiencies noted in the examination under paragraph 1(a) to (d) are not corrected in accordance with the Implementing Regulations, the application shall be refused; where the provisions referred to in paragraph 1(d) concern the right of priority, this right shall be lost for the application.

(4)   Where, in the case referred to in paragraph 1(e), the designation fee has not been paid in due time in respect of any designated State, the designation of that State shall be deemed to be withdrawn.

(5)   Where, in the case referred to in paragraph 1(f), the omission of the designation of the inventor is not, in accordance with the Implementing Regulations and subject

to the exceptions laid down therein, corrected within 16 months after the date of filing of the European patent application or, if priority is claimed, after the date of priority, the application shall be deemed to be withdrawn.

(6)   Where, in the case referred to in paragraph 1(g), the drawings were not filed on the date of filing of the application and no steps have been taken to correct the deficiency in accordance with the Implementing Regulations, either the application shall be re-dated to the date of filing of the drawings or any reference to the drawings in the application shall be deemed to be deleted, according to the choice exercised by the applicant in accordance with the Implementing Regulations.

Article 92   The drawing up of the European search report

(1)   If a European patent application has been accorded a date of filing and is not deemed to be withdrawn by virtue of Article 90, paragraph 3, the Search Division shall draw up the European search report on the basis of the claims, with due regard to the description and any drawings, in the form prescribed in the Implementing Regulations.

(2)   Immediately after it has been drawn up, the European search report shall be transmitted to the applicant together with copies of any cited documents.

Article 93   Publication of a European patent application

(1)   A European patent application shall be published as soon as possible after the expiry of a period of eighteen months from the date of filing or, if priority has been claimed, as from the date of priority. Nevertheless, at the request of the applicant the application may be published before the expiry of the period referred to above. It shall be published simultaneously with the publication of the specification of the European patent when the grant of the patent has become effective before the expiry of the period referred to above.

(2)   The publication shall contain the description, the claims and any drawings as filed and, in an annex, the European search report and the abstract, insofar as the latter are available before the termination of the technical preparations for publication. If the European search report and the abstract have not been published at the same time as the application, they shall be published separately.

Article 94   Request for examination

(1)   The European Patent Office shall examine, on written request, whether a European patent application and the invention to which it relates meet the requirements of this Convention.

(2)   A request for examination may be filed by the applicant up to the end of six months after the date on which the European Patent Bulletin mentions the publication of the European search report. The request shall not be deemed to be filed until after the examination fee has been paid. The request may not be withdrawn.

(3)   If no request for examination has been filed by the end of the period referred to in paragraph 2, the application shall be deemed to be withdrawn.

Article 95   Extension of the period within which requests for examination may be filed

(1)   The Administrative Council may extend the period within which requests for examination may be filed if it is established that European patent applications cannot be examined in due time.

(2)   If the Administrative Council extends the period, it may decide that third parties will be entitled to make requests for examination. In such cases, it shall determine the appropriate rules in the Implementing Regulations.

(3)   Any decision of the Administrative Council to extend the period shall apply only in respect of applications filed after the publication of such decision in the Official Journal of the European Patent Office.

(4)   If the Administrative Council extends the period, it must lay down measures with a view to restoring the original period as soon as possible.

Article 96   Examination of the European patent application

(1)   If the applicant for a European patent has filed the request for examination before the European search report has been transmitted to him, the European Patent Office shall invite him after the transmission of the report to indicate, within a period to be determined, whether he desires to proceed further with the European patent application.

(2)   If the examination of a European patent application reveals that the application or the invention to which it relates does not meet the requirements of this Convention, the Examining Division shall invite the applicant, in accordance with the Implementing Regulations and as often as necessary, to file his observations within a period to be fixed by the Examining Division.

(3)   If the applicant fails to reply in due time to any invitation under paragraph 1 or paragraph 2, the application shall be deemed to be withdrawn.

Article 97   Refusal or grant

(1)   The Examining Division shall refuse a European patent application if it is of the opinion that such application or the invention to which it relates does not meet the requirements of this Convention, except where a different sanction is provided for by this Convention.

(2)   If the Examining Division is of the opinion that the application and the invention to which it relates meet the requirements of this Convention, it shall decide to grant the European patent for the designated Contracting States provided that—

(a)   it is established, in accordance with the provisions of the Implementing Regulations, that the applicant approves the text in which the Examining Division intends to grant the patent;

(b)   the fees for grant and printing are paid within the time limit prescribed in the Implementing Regulations;

(c)   the renewal fees and any additional fees already due have been paid.

(3)   If the fees for grant and printing are not paid in due time, the application shall be deemed to be withdrawn.

(4)   The decision to grant a European patent shall not take effect until the date on which the European Patent Bulletin mentions the grant. This mention shall be published at least 3 months after the start of the time limit referred to in paragraph 2(b).

(5)   Provision may be made in the Implementing Regulations for the applicant to file a translation, in the two official languages of the European Patent Office other than the language of the proceedings, of the claims appearing in the text in which the Examining Division intends to grant the patent. In such case, the period laid down in paragraph 4 shall be at least five months. If the translation has not been filed in due time, the application shall be deemed to be withdrawn.

Article 98   Publication of a specification of the European patent

At the same time as it publishes the mention of the grant of the European patent, the European Patent Office shall publish a specification of the European patent containing the description, the claims and any drawings.

[9]

PART V
OPPOSITION PROCEDURE

Article 99   Opposition

(1)   Within nine months from the publication of the mention of the grant of the European patent, any person may give notice to the European Patent Office of opposition to the European patent granted. Notice of opposition shall be filed in a written reasoned statement. It shall not be deemed to have been filed until the opposition fee has been paid.

(2)   The opposition shall apply to the European patent in all the Contracting States in which that patent has effect.

(3)   An opposition may be filed even if the European patent has been surrendered or has lapsed for all the designated States.

(4)   Opponents shall be parties to the opposition proceedings as well as the proprietor of the patent.

(5)   Where a person provides evidence that in a Contracting State, following a final decision, he has been entered in the patent register of such State instead of the previous proprietor, such person shall, at his request, replace the previous proprietor in respect of such State. By derogation from Article 118, the previous proprietor and the person making the request shall not be deemed to be joint proprietors unless both so request.

Article 100   Grounds for opposition

Opposition may only be filed on the grounds that—
    (a)   the subject-matter of the European patent is not patentable within the terms of Articles 52 to 57;
    (b)   the European patent does not disclose the invention in a manner sufficiently clear and complete for it to be carried out by a person skilled in the art;
    (c)   the subject-matter of the European patent extends beyond the content of the application as filed, or, if the patent was granted on a divisional application or on a new application filed in accordance with Article 61, beyond the content of the earlier application as filed.

Article 101   Examination of the opposition

(1)   If the opposition is admissible, the Opposition Division shall examine whether the grounds for opposition laid down in Article 100 prejudice the maintenance of the European patent.

(2)   In the examination of the opposition, which shall be conducted in accordance with the provisions of the Implementing Regulations, the Opposition Division shall invite the parties, as often as necessary, to file observations, within a period to be

fixed by the Opposition Division, on communications from another party or issued by itself.

Article 102   Revocation or maintenance of the European patent

(1)   If the Opposition Division is of the opinion that the grounds for opposition mentioned in Article 100 prejudice the maintenance of the European patent, it shall revoke the patent.

(2)   If the Opposition Division is of the opinion that the grounds for opposition mentioned in Article 100 do not prejudice the maintenance of the patent unamended, it shall reject the opposition.

(3)   If the Opposition Division is of the opinion that, taking into consideration the amendments made by the proprietor of the patent during the opposition proceedings, the patent and the invention to which it relates meet the requirements of this Convention, it shall decide to maintain the patent as amended, provided that—
  (a)   it is established, in accordance with the provisions of the Implementing Regulations, that the proprietor of the patent approves the text in which the Opposition Division intends to maintain the patent;
  (b)   the fee for the printing of a new specification of the European patent is paid within the time limit prescribed in the Implementing Regulations.

(4)   If the fee for the printing of a new specification is not paid in due time, the patent shall be revoked.

(5)   Provision may be made in the Implementing Regulations for the proprietor of the patent to file a translation of any amended claims in the two official languages of the European Patent Office other than the language of the proceedings. If the translation has not been filed in due time the patent shall be revoked.

Article 103   Publication of a new specification of the European patent

If a European patent is amended under Article 102 paragraph 3, the European Patent Office shall, at the same time as it publishes the mention of the opposition decision, publish a new specification of the European patent containing the description, the claims and any drawings, in the amended form.

Article 104   Costs

(1)   Each party to the proceedings shall meet the costs he has incurred unless a decision of an Opposition Division or Board of Appeal, for reasons of equity, orders, in accordance with the Implementing Regulations, a different apportionment of costs incurred during taking of evidence or in oral proceedings.

(2)   On request, the registry of the Opposition Division shall fix the amount of the costs to be paid under a decision apportioning them. The fixing of the costs by the registry may be reviewed by a decision of the Opposition Division on a request filed within the period laid down in the Implementing Regulations.

(3)   Any final decision of the European Patent Office fixing the amount of costs shall be dealt with, for the purpose of enforcement in the Contracting States, in the same way as a final decision given by a civil court of the State in the territory of which enforcement is to be carried out. Verification of such decisions shall be limited to its authenticity.

Article 105   Intervention of the assumed infringer

(1)   In the event of an opposition to a European patent being filed, any third party who proves that proceedings for infringement of the same patent have been instituted against him may, after the opposition period has expired, intervene in the opposition proceedings, if he gives notice of intervention within three months of the date on which the infringement proceedings were instituted. The same shall apply in respect of any third party who proves both that the proprietor of the patent has requested that he cease alleged infringement of the patent and that he has instituted proceedings for a court ruling that he is not infringing the patent.

(2)   Notice of intervention shall be filed in a written reasoned statement. It shall not be deemed to have been filed until the opposition fee has been paid. Thereafter the intervention shall, subject to any exceptions laid down in the Implementing Regulations, be treated as opposition.

[10]

PART VI
APPEALS PROCEDURE

Article 106   Decisions subject to appeal

(1)   An appeal shall lie from decisions of the Receiving Section, Examining Divisions, Opposition Divisions and the Legal Division. It shall have suspensive effect.

(2)   An appeal may be filed against the decision of the Opposition Division even if the European patent has been surrendered or has lapsed for all the designated States.

(3)   A decision which does not terminate proceedings as regards one of the parties can only be appealed together with the final decision, unless the decision allows separate appeal.

(4)   The apportionment of costs of opposition proceedings cannot be the sole subject of an appeal.

(5)   A decision fixing the amount of costs of opposition proceedings cannot be appealed unless the amount is in excess of that laid down in the Rules relating to Fees.

Article 107   Persons entitled to appeal and to be parties to appeal proceedings

Any party to proceedings adversely affected by a decision may appeal. Any other parties to the proceedings shall be parties to the appeal proceedings as of right.

[11]

PART VIII
IMPACT ON NATIONAL LAW

CHAPTER II. REVOCATION AND PRIOR RIGHTS

Article 138   Grounds for revocation

(1)   Subject to the provisions of Article 139, a European patent may only be revoked under the law of a Contracting State, with effect for its territory, on the following grounds—
    (a)   if the subject-matter of the European patent is not patentable within the terms of Articles 52 to 57;

(b) if the European patent does not disclose the invention in a manner sufficiently clear and complete for it to be carried out by a person skilled in the art;

(c) if the subject-matter of the European patent extends beyond the content of the application as filed or, if the patent was granted on a divisional application or on a new application filed in accordance with Article 61, beyond the content of the earlier application as filed;

(d) if the protection conferred by the European patent has been extended;

(e) if the proprietor of the European patent is not entitled under Article 60, paragraph 1.

(2) If the grounds for revocation only affect the European patent in part, revocation shall be pronounced in the form of a corresponding limitation of the said patent. If the national law so allows, the limitation may be effected in the form of an amendment to the claims, the description or the drawings.

[12]

PROTOCOL ON THE INTERPRETATION OF ARTICLE 69 OF THE CONVENTION

Article 69 should not be interpreted in the sense that the extent of the protection conferred by a European patent is to be understood as that defined by the strict, literal meaning of the wording used in the claims, the description and drawings being employed only for the purpose of resolving an ambiguity found in the claims. Neither should it be interpreted in the sense that the claims serve only as a guideline and that the actual protection conferred may extend to what, from a consideration of the description and drawings by a person skilled in the art, the patentee has contemplated. On the contrary, it is to be interpreted as defining a position between these extremes which combines a fair protection for the patentee with a reasonable degree of certainty for third parties.

[13]

(This Convention and Protocol are reproduced with the permission of the European Patent Office.)

AGREEMENT ON TRADE-RELATED ASPECTS OF INTELLECTUAL PROPERTY RIGHTS

PART I
GENERAL PROVISIONS AND BASIC PRINCIPLES

Article 1　Nature and Scope of Obligations

1. Members shall give effect to the provisions of this Agreement. Members may, but shall not be obliged to, implement in their law more extensive protection than is required by this Agreement, provided that such protection does not contravene the provisions of this Agreement. Members shall be free to determine the appropriate method of implementing the provisions of this Agreement within their own legal system and practice.

2. For the purposes of this Agreement, the term "intellectual property" refers to all categories of intellectual property that are the subject of Sections 1 through 7 of Part II.

3.   Members shall accord the treatment provided for in this Agreement to the nationals of other Members.[1] In respect of the relevant intellectual property right, the nationals of other Members shall be understood as those natural or legal persons that would meet the criteria for eligibility for protection provided for in the Paris Convention (1967), the Berne Convention (1971), the Rome Convention and the Treaty on Intellectual Property in Respect of Integrated Circuits, were all Members of the WTO members of those Conventions.[2] Any Member availing itself of the possibilities provided in paragraph 3 of Article 5 or paragraph 2 of Article 6 of the Rome Convention shall make a notification as foreseen in those provisions to the Council for Trade-Related Aspects of Intellectual Property Rights (the "Council for TRIPS").

NOTES

[1]   When "nationals" are referred to in this Agreement, they shall be deemed, in the case of a separate customs territory Member of the WTO, to mean persons, natural or legal, who are domiciled or who have a real and effective industrial or commercial establishment in that customs territory.

[2]   In this Agreement, "Paris Convention" refers to the Paris Convention for the Protection of Industrial Property: "Paris Convention (1967)" refers to the Stockholm Act of this Convention of 14 July 1967. "Berne Convention" refers to the Berne Convention for the Protection of Literary and Artistic Works: "Berne Convention (1971)" refers to the Paris Act of this Convention of 24 July 1971. "Rome Convention" refers to the International Convention for the Protection of Performers, Producers of Phonograms and Broadcasting Organisations, adopted at Rome on 26 October 1961. "Treaty on Intellectual Property in Respect of Integrated Circuits" (IPC Treaty) refers to the Treaty on Intellectual Property in Respect of Integrated Circuits, adopted at Washington on 26 May 1989. "WTO Agreement" refers to the Agreement Establishing the WTO.

Article 2   Intellectual Property Conventions

1.   In respect of Parts II, III and IV of this Agreement, Members shall comply with Articles 1 through 12, and Article 19, of the Paris Convention (1967).

2.   Nothing in Parts I to IV of this Agreement shall derogate from existing obligations that Members may have to each other under the Paris Convention, the Berne Convention, the Rome Convention and the Treaty on Intellectual Property in Respect of Integrated Circuits.

Article 3   National Treatment

1.   Each Member shall accord to the nationals of other Members treatment no less favourable than that it accords to its own nationals with regard to the protection[1] of intellectual property, subject to the exceptions already provided in, respectively, the Paris Convention (1967), the Berne Convention (1971), the Rome Convention or the Treaty on Intellectual Property in Respect of Integrated Circuits. In respect of performers, producers of phonograms and broadcasting organisations, this obligation only applies in respect of the rights provided under this Agreement. Any Member availing itself of the possibilities provided in Article 6 of the Berne Convention (1971) or paragraph 1(b) of Article 16 of the Rome Convention shall make a notification as foreseen in those provisions to the Council for TRIPS.

2.   Members may avail themselves of the exceptions permitted under paragraph 1 in relation to judicial and administrative procedures, including the designation of an address for service or the appointment of an agent within the jurisdiction of a Member, only where such exceptions are necessary to secure compliance with laws and regulations which are not inconsistent with the provisions of this Agreement and where such practices are not applied in a manner which would constitute a disguised restriction on trade.

NOTES
   ¹   For the purposes of Articles 3 and 4, "protection" shall include matters affecting the availability, acquisition, scope, maintenance and enforcement of intellectual property rights as well as those matters affecting the use of intellectual property rights specifically addressed in this Agreement.

Article 4   Most-Favoured-Nation Treatment

With regard to the protection of intellectual property, any advantage, favour, privilege or immunity granted by a Member to the nationals of any other country shall be accorded immediately and unconditionally to the nationals of all other Members. Exempted from this obligation are any advantage, favour, privilege or immunity accorded by a Member—

   (a)   deriving from international agreements on judicial assistance or law enforcement of a general nature and not particularly confined to the protection of intellectual property;

   (b)   granted in accordance with the provisions of the Berne Convention (1971) or the Rome Convention authorising that the treatment accorded be a function not of national treatment but of the treatment accorded in another country;

   (c)   in respect of the rights of performers, producers of phonograms and broadcasting organisations not provided under this Agreement;

   (d)   deriving from international agreements related to the protection of intellectual property which entered into force prior to the entry into force of the WTO Agreement, provided that such agreements are notified to the Council for TRIPS and do not constitute all arbitrary or unjustifiable discrimination against nationals of other Members.

Article 5   Multilateral Agreements on Acquisition or Maintenance of Protection

The obligations under Articles 3 and 4 do not apply to procedures provided in multilateral agreements concluded under the auspices of WIPO relating to the acquisition or maintenance of intellectual property rights.

Article 6   Exhaustion

For the purposes of dispute settlement under this Agreement, subject to the provisions of Articles 3 and 4 nothing in this Agreement shall be used to address the issue of the exhaustion of intellectual property rights.

Article 7   Objectives

The protection and enforcement of intellectual property rights should contribute to the promotion of technological innovation and to the transfer and dissemination of technology, to the mutual advantage of producers and users of technological knowledge and in a manner conducive to social and economic welfare, and to a balance of rights and obligations.

Article 8   Principles

1.   Members may, in formulating or amending their laws and regulations, adopt measures necessary to protect public health and nutrition, and to promote the public interest in sectors of vital importance to their socio-economic and technological development, provided that such measures are consistent with the provisions of this Agreement.

2.   Appropriate measures, provided that they are consistent with the provisions of this Agreement, may be needed to prevent the abuse of intellectual property rights by right holders or the resort to practices which unreasonably restrain trade or adversely affect the international transfer of technology.

[14]

PART II
STANDARDS CONCERNING THE AVAILABILITY, SCOPE AND USE OF INTELLECTUAL PROPERTY RIGHTS

SECTION 1: COPYRIGHT AND RELATED RIGHTS

Article 9   Relation to the Berne Convention

1.   Members shall comply with Articles 1 through 21 of the Berne Convention (1971) and the Appendix thereto. However, Members shall not have rights or obligations under this Agreement in respect of the rights conferred under Article 6[bis] of that Convention or of the rights derived therefrom.

2.   Copyright protection shall extend to expressions and not to ideas, procedures, methods of operation or mathematical concepts as such.

Article 10   Computer Programs and Compilations of Data

1.   Computer programs, whether in source or object code, shall be protected as literary works under the Berne Convention (1971).

2.   Compilations of data or other material, whether in machine readable or other form, which by reason of the selection or arrangement of their contents constitute intellectual creations shall be protected as such. Such protection, which shall not extend to the data or material itself, shall be without prejudice to any copyright subsisting in the data or material itself.

Article 11   Rental Rights

In respect of at least computer programs and cinematographic works, a Member shall provide authors and their successors in title the right to authorise or to prohibit the commercial rental to the public of originals or copies of their copyright works. A Member shall be excepted from this obligation in respect of cinematographic works unless such rental has led to widespread copying of such works which is materially impairing the exclusive right of reproduction conferred in that Member on authors and their successors in title. In respect of computer programs, this obligation does not apply to rentals where the program itself is not the essential object of the rental.

Article 12   Term of Protection

Whenever the term of protection of a work, other than a photographic work or a work of applied art, is calculated on a basis other than the life of a natural person, such term shall be no less than 50 years from the end of the calendar year of authorised publication, or, failing such authorised publication within 50 years from the making of the work, 50 years from the end of the calendar year of making.

Article 13   Limitations and Exceptions

Members shall confine limitations or exceptions to exclusive rights to certain special cases which do not conflict with a normal exploitation of the work and do not unreasonably prejudice the legitimate interests of the right holder.

Article 14   Protection of Performers, Producers of Phonograms (Sound Recordings) and Broadcasting Organisations

1.   In respect of a fixation of their performance on a phonogram, performers shall have the possibility of preventing the following acts when undertaken without their authorisation: the fixation of their unfixed performance and the reproduction of such fixation. Performers shall also have the possibility of preventing the following acts when undertaken without their authorisation: the broadcasting by wireless means and the communication to the public of their live performance.

2.   Producers of phonograms shall enjoy the right to authorise or prohibit the direct or indirect reproduction of their phonograms.

3.   Broadcasting organisations shall have the right to prohibit the following acts when undertaken without their authorisation: the fixation, the reproduction of fixations, and the rebroadcasting by wireless means of broadcasts, as well as the communication to the public of television broadcasts of the same. Where Members do not grant such rights to broadcasting organisations, they shall provide owners of copyright in the subject matter of broadcasts with the possibility of preventing the above acts, subject to the provisions of the Berne Convention (1971).

4.   The provisions of Article 11 in respect of computer programs shall apply *mutatis mutandis* to producers of phonograms and any other right holders in phonograms as determined in a Member's law. If on 15 April 1994 a Member has in force a system of equitable remuneration of right holders in respect of the rental of phonograms, it may maintain such system provided that the commercial rental of phonograms is not giving rise to the material impairment of the exclusive rights of reproduction of right holders.

5.   The term of the protection available under this Agreement to performers and producers of phonograms shall last at least until the end of a period of 50 years computed from the end of the calendar year in which the fixation was made or the performance took place. The term of protection granted pursuant to paragraph 3 shall last for at least 20 years from the end of the calendar year in which the broadcast took place.

6.   Any Member may, in relation to the rights conferred under paragraphs 1, 2 and 3, provide for conditions, limitations, exceptions and reservations to the extent permitted by the Rome Convention. However, the provisions of Article 18 of the Berne Convention (1971) shall also apply, *mutatis mutandis*, to the rights of performers and producers of phonograms in phonograms.

SECTION 2: TRADEMARKS

Article 15   Protectable Subject Matter

1.   Any sign, or any combination of signs, capable of distinguishing the goods or services of one undertaking from those of other undertakings, shall be capable of constituting a trademark. Such signs, in particular words including personal names, letters, numerals, figurative elements and combinations of colours as well as any combination of such signs, shall be eligible for registration as trademarks. Where signs are not inherently capable of distinguishing the relevant goods or services, Members may make registrability depend on distinctiveness acquired through use. Members may require, as a condition of registration, that signs be visually perceptible.

2.   Paragraph 1 shall not be understood to prevent a Member from denying registration of a trademark on other grounds, provided that they do not derogate from the provisions of the Paris Convention (1967).

3.   Members may make registrability depend on use. However, actual use of a trademark shall not be a condition for filing an application for registration. An application shall not be refused solely on the ground that intended use has not taken place before the expiry of a period of three years from the date of application.

4.   The nature of the goods or services to which a trademark is to be applied shall in no case form an obstacle to registration of the trademark.

5.   Members shall publish each trademark either before it is registered or promptly after it is registered and shall afford a reasonable opportunity for petitions to cancel the registration. In addition, Members may afford an opportunity for the registration of a trademark to be opposed.

Article 16   Rights Conferred

1.   The owner of a registered trademark shall have the exclusive right to prevent all third parties not having the owner's consent from using in the course of trade identical or similar signs for goods or services which are identical or similar to those in respect of which the trademark is registered where such use would result in a likelihood of confusion. In case of the use of an identical sign for identical goods or services, a likelihood of confusion shall be presumed. The rights described above shall not prejudice any existing prior rights, nor shall they affect the possibility of Members making rights available on the basis of use.

2.   Article 6bis of the Paris Convention (1967) shall apply, *mutatis mutandis*, to services. In determining whether a trademark is well known, Members shall take account of the knowledge of the trademark in the relevant sector of the public, including knowledge in the Member concerned which has been obtained as a result of the promotion of the trademark.

3.   Article 6bis of the Paris Convention (1967) shall apply, *mutatis mutandis*, to goods or services which are not similar to those in respect of which a trademark is registered, provided that use of that trademark in relation to those goods or services would indicate a connection between those goods or services and the owner of the registered trademark and provided that the interests of the owner of the registered trademark are likely to be damaged by such use.

Article 17   Exceptions

Members may provide limited exceptions to the rights conferred by a trademark, such as fair use of descriptive terms, provided that such exceptions take account of the legitimate interests of the owner of the trademark and of third parties.

Article 18   Term of Protection

Initial registration, and each renewal of registration, of a trademark shall be for a term of no less than seven years. The registration of a trademark shall be renewable indefinitely.

Article 19   Requirement of Use

1.   If use is required to maintain a registration, the registration may be cancelled only after an uninterrupted period of at least three years of non-use, unless valid reasons based on the existence of obstacles to such use are shown by the trademark owner. Circumstances arising independently of the will of the owner of the trademark which constitute an obstacle to the use of the trademark, such as import

restrictions on or other government requirements for goods or services protected by the trademark, shall be recognised as valid reasons for non-use.

2.   When subject to the control of its owner, use of a trademark by another person shall be recognised as use of the trademark for the purpose of maintaining the registration.

Article 20   Other Requirements

The use of a trademark in the course of trade shall not be unjustifiably encumbered by special requirements, such as use with another trademark, use in a special form or use in a manner detrimental to its capability to distinguish the goods or services of one undertaking from those of other undertakings. This will not preclude a requirement prescribing the use of the trademark identifying the undertaking producing the goods or services along with, but without linking it to, the trademark distinguishing the specific goods or services in question of that undertaking.

Article 21   Licensing and Assignment

Members may determine conditions on the licensing and assignment of trademarks, it being understood that the compulsory licensing of trademarks shall not be permitted and that the owner of a registered trademark shall have the right to assign the trademark with or without the transfer of the business to which the trademark belongs.

SECTION 3: GEOGRAPHICAL INDICATIONS

Article 22   Protection of Geographical Indications

1.   Geographical indications are, for the purposes of this Agreement, indications which identify a good as originating in the territory of a Member, or a region or locality in that territory, where a given quality, reputation or other characteristic of the good is essentially attributable to its geographical origin.

2.   In respect of geographical indications, Members shall provide the legal means for interested parties to prevent—
(a)   the use of any means in the designation or presentation of a good that indicates or suggests that the good in question originates in a geographical area other than the true place of origin in a manner which misleads the public as to the geographical origin of the good;
(b)   any use which constitutes an act of unfair competition within the meaning of Article 10bis of the Paris Convention (1967).

3.   A Member shall, *ex officio* if its legislation so permits or at the request of an interested party, refuse or invalidate the registration of a trademark which contains or consists of a geographical indication with respect to goods not originating in the territory indicated, if use of the indication in the trademark for such goods in that Member is of such a nature as to mislead the public as to the true place of origin.

4.   The protection under paragraphs 1, 2 and 3 shall be applicable against a geographical indication which, although literally true as to the territory, region or locality in which the goods originate, falsely represents to the public that the goods originate in another territory.

Article 23   Additional Protection for Geographical Indications for Wines and Spirits

1.   Each Member shall provide the legal means for interested parties to prevent use of a geographical indication identifying wines for wines not originating in the place

indicated by the geographical indication in question or identifying spirits for spirits not originating in the place indicated by the geographical indication in question, even where the true origin of the goods is indicated or the geographical indication is used in translation or accompanied by expressions such as "kind", "type", "style", "imitation" or the like[1].

2.   The registration of a trademark for wines which contains or consists of a geographical indication identifying wines or for spirits which contains or consists of a geographical indication identifying spirits shall be refused or invalidated, *ex officio* if a Member's legislation so permits or at the request of an interested party, with respect to such wines or spirits not having this origin.

3.   In the case of homonymous geographical indications for wines, protection shall be accorded to each indication, subject to the provisions of paragraph 4 of Article 22. Each Member shall determine the practical conditions under which the homonymous indications in question will be differentiated from each other, taking into account the need to ensure equitable treatment of the producers concerned and that consumers are not misled.

4.   In order to facilitate the protection of geographical indications for wines, negotiations shall be undertaken in the Council for TRIPS concerning the establishment of a multilateral system of notification and registration of geographical indications for wines eligible for protection in those Members participating in the system.

NOTES

[1]   Notwithstanding the first sentence of Article 42, Members may, with respect to these obligations, instead provide for enforcement by administrative action.

Article 24   International Negotiations: Exceptions

1.   Members agree to enter into negotiations aimed at increasing the protection of individual geographical indications under Article 23. The provisions of paragraphs 4 through 8 below shall not be used by a Member to refuse to conduct negotiations or to conclude bilateral or multilateral agreements. In the context of such negotiations, Members shall be willing to consider the continued applicability of these provisions to individual geographical indications whose use was the subject of such negotiations.

2.   The Council for TRIPS shall keep under review the application of the provisions of this Section: the first such review shall take place within two years of the entry into force of the WTO Agreement. Any matter affecting the compliance with the obligations under these provisions may be drawn to the attention of the Council, which, at the request of a Member, shall consult with any Member or Members in respect of such matter in respect of which it has not been possible to find a satisfactory solution through bilateral or plurilateral consultations between the Members concerned. The Council shall take such action as may be agreed to facilitate the operation and further the objectives of this Section.

3.   In implementing this Section, a Member shall not diminish the protection of geographical indications that existed in that Member immediately prior to the date of entry into force of the WTO Agreement.

4.   Nothing in this Section shall require a Member to prevent continued and similar use of a particular geographical indication of another Member identifying wines or spirits in connection with goods or services by any of its nationals or domiciliaries who have used that geographical indication in a continuous manner

with regard to the same or related goods or services in the territory of that Member either (a) for at least 10 years preceding 15 April 1994 or (b) in good faith preceding that date.

5.   Where a trademark has been applied for or registered in good faith, or where rights to a trademark have been acquired through use in good faith either—
  (a) before the date of application of these provisions in that Member as defined in Part VI; or
  (b) before the geographical indication is protected in its country of origin;

measures adopted to implement this Section shall not prejudice eligibility for or the validity of the registration of a trademark, or the right to use a trademark, on the basis that such a trademark is identical with, or similar to, a geographical indication.

6.   Nothing in this Section shall require a Member to apply its provisions in respect of a geographical indication of any other Member with respect to goods or services for which the relevant indication is identical with the term customary in common language as the common name for such goods or services in the territory of that Member. Nothing in this Section shall require a Member to apply its provisions in respect of a geographical indication of any other Member with respect to products of the vine for which the relevant indication is identical with the customary name of a grape variety existing in the territory of that Member as of the date of entry into force of the WTO Agreement.

7.   A Member may provide that any request made under this Section in connection with the use or registration of a trademark must be presented within five years after the adverse use of the protected indication has become generally known in that Member or after the date of registration of the trademark in that Member provided that the trademark has been published by that date, if such date is earlier than the date on which the adverse use became generally known in that Member, provided that the geographical indication is not used or registered in bad faith.

8.   The provisions of this Section shall in no way prejudice the right of any person to use, in the course of trade, that person's name or the name of that person's predecessor in business, except where such name is used in such a manner as to mislead the public.

9.   There shall be no obligation under this Agreement to protect geographical indications which are not or cease to be protected in their country of origin, or which have fallen in to disuse in that country.

SECTION 4: INDUSTRIAL DESIGNS

Article 25   Requirements for Protection

1.   Members shall provide for the protection of independently created industrial designs that are new or original. Members may provide that designs are not new or original if they do not significantly differ from known designs or combinations of known design features. Members may provide that such protection shall not extend to designs dictated essentially by technical or functional considerations.

2.   Each Member shall ensure that requirements for securing protection for textile designs, in particular in regard to any cost, examination or publication, do not unreasonably impair the opportunity to seek and obtain such protection. Members shall be free to meet this obligation through industrial design law or through copyright law.

Article 26   Protection

1.   The owner of a protected industrial design shall have the right to prevent third parties not having the owner's consent from making, selling or importing articles bearing or embodying a design which is a copy, or substantially a copy, of the protected design, when such acts are undertaken for commercial purposes.

2.   Members may provide limited exceptions to the protection of industrial designs, provided that such exceptions do not unreasonably conflict with the normal exploitation of protected industrial designs and do not unreasonably prejudice the legitimate interests of the owner of the protected design, taking account of the legitimate interests of third parties.

3.   The duration of protection available shall amount to at least 10 years.

SECTION 5: PATENTS

Article 27   Patentable Subject Matter

1.   Subject to the provisions of paragraphs 2 and 3, patents shall be available for any inventions, whether products or processes, in all fields of technology, provided that they are new, involve an inventive step and are capable of industrial application.[1] Subject to paragraph 4 of Article 65, paragraph 8 of Article 70 and paragraph 3 of this Article, patents shall be available and patent rights enjoyable without discrimination as to the place of invention, the field of technology and whether products are imported or locally produced.

2.   Members may exclude from patentability inventions, the prevention within their territory of the commercial exploitation of which is necessary to protect *ordre public* or morality, including to protect human, animal or plant life or health or to avoid serious prejudice to the environment, provided that such exclusion is not made merely because the exploitation is prohibited by their law.

3.   Members may also exclude from patentability—
   (a)   diagnostic, therapeutic and surgical methods for the treatment of humans or animals;
   (b)   plants and animals other than micro-organisms, and essentially biological processes for the production of plants or animals other than non-biological and microbiological processes. However, Members shall provide for the protection of plant varieties either by patents or by an effective *sui generis* system or by any combination thereof. The provisions of this subparagraph shall be reviewed four years after the date of entry into force of the WTO Agreement.

NOTES
   [1]   For the purposes of this Article, the terms "inventive step" and "capable of industrial application" may be deemed by a Member to be synonymous with the terms "non-obvious" and "useful" respectively.

Article 28   Rights Conferred

1.   A patent shall confer on its owner the following exclusive rights—
   (a)   where the subject matter of a patent is a product, to prevent third parties not having the owner's consent from the acts of: making, using, offering for sale, selling, or importing[1] for these purposes that product;
   (b)   where the subject matter of a patent is a process, to prevent third parties not having the owner's consent from the act of using the process, and from

the acts of: using, offering for sale, selling, or importing for these purposes at least the product obtained directly by that process.

2.   Patent owners shall also have the right to assign, or transfer by succession, the patent and to conclude licensing contracts.

NOTES

[1]   This right, like all other rights conferred under this Agreement in respect of the use, sale, importation or other distribution of goods, is subject to the provisions of Article 6.

Article 29   Conditions on Patent Applicants

1.   Members shall require that an applicant for a patent shall disclose the invention in a manner sufficiently clear and complete for the invention to be carried out by a person skilled in the art and may require the applicant to indicate the best mode for carrying out the invention known to the inventor at the filing date or, where priority is claimed, at the priority date of the application.

2.   Members may require an applicant for a patent to provide information concerning the applicant's corresponding foreign applications and grants.

Article 30   Exceptions to Rights Conferred

Members may provide limited exceptions to the exclusive rights conferred by a patent, provided that such exceptions do not unreasonably conflict with a normal exploitation of the patent and do not unreasonably prejudice the legitimate interests of the patent owner, taking account of the legitimate interests of third parties.

Article 31   Other Use Without Authorisation of the Right Holder

Where the law of a Member allows for other use[1] of the subject matter of a patent without the authorisation of the right holder, including use by the government or third parties authorised by the government, the following provisions shall be respected—

(a)   authorisation of such use shall be considered on its individual merits;

(b)   such use may only be permitted if, prior to such use, the proposed user has made efforts to obtain authorisation from the right holder on reasonable commercial terms and conditions and that such efforts have not been successful within a reasonable period of time. This requirement may be waived by a Member in the case of a national emergency or other circumstances of extreme urgency or in cases of public non-commercial use. In situations of national emergency or other circumstances of extreme urgency, the right holder shall, nevertheless, be notified as soon as reasonably practicable. In the case of public non-commercial use, where the government or contractor, without making a patent search, knows or has demonstrable grounds to know that a valid patent is or will be used by or for the government, the right holder shall be informed promptly;

(c)   the scope and duration of such use shall be limited to the purpose for which it was authorised, and in the case of semi-conductor technology shall only be for public non-commercial use or to remedy a practice determined after judicial or administrative process to be anti-competitive;

(d)   such use shall be non-exclusive;

(e)   such use shall be non-assignable, except with that part of the enterprise or goodwill which enjoys such use;

(f)   any such use shall be authorised predominantly for the supply of the domestic market of the Member authorising such use;

(g)   authorisation for such use shall be liable, subject to adequate protection of the legitimate interests of the persons so authorised, to be terminated if and when the circumstances which led to it cease to exist and are unlikely to recur. The competent authority shall have the authority to review, upon motivated request, the continued existence of these circumstances;

(h)   the right holder shall be paid adequate remuneration in the circumstances of each case, taking into account the economic value of the authorisation;

(i)   the legal validity of any decision relating to the authorisation of such use shall be subject to judicial review or other independent review by a distinct higher authority in that Member;

(j)   any decision relating to the remuneration provided in respect of such use shall be subject to judicial review or other independent review by a distinct higher authority in that Member;

(k)   Members are not obliged to apply the conditions set forth in subparagraphs (b) and (f) where such use is permitted to remedy a practice determined after judicial or administrative process to be anti-competitive. The need to correct anti-competitive practices may be taken into account in determining the amount of remuneration in such cases. Competent authorities shall have the authority to refuse termination of authorisation if and when the conditions which led to such authorisation are likely to recur;

(l)   where such use is authorised to permit the exploitation of a patent ("the second patent") which cannot be exploited without infringing another patent ("the first patent"), the following additional conditions shall apply—

    (i)   the invention claimed in the second patent shall involve an important technical advance of considerable economic significance in relation to the invention claimed in the first patent;

    (ii)   the owner of the first patent shall be entitled to a cross-licence on reasonable terms to use the invention claimed in the second patent; and

    (iii)   the use authorised in respect of the first patent shall be non-assignable except with the assignment of the second patent.

NOTES

[1]   "Other use" refers to use other than that allowed under Article 30.

Article 32   Revocation/Forfeiture

An opportunity for judicial review of any decision to revoke or forfeit a patent shall be available.

Article 33   Term of Protection

The term of protection available shall not end before the expiration of a period of twenty years counted from the filing date.[1]

NOTES

[1]   It is understood that those Members which do not have a system of original grant may provide that the term of protection shall be computed from the filing date in the system of original grant.

Article 34   Process Patents: Burden of Proof

1.   For the purposes of civil proceedings in respect of the infringement of the rights of the owner referred to in paragraph 1(b) of Article 28, if the subject matter of

a patent is a process for obtaining a product, the judicial authorities shall have the authority to order the defendant to prove that the process to obtain an identical product is different from the patented process. Therefore, Members shall provide, in at least one of the following circumstances, that any identical product when produced without the consent of the patent owner shall, in the absence of proof to the contrary, be deemed to have been obtained by the patented process—

    (a) if the product obtained by the patented process is new;

    (b) if there is a substantial likelihood that the identical product was made by the process and the owner of the patent has been unable through reasonable efforts to determine the process actually used.

2.   Any Member shall be free to provide that the burden of proof indicated in paragraph 1 shall be on the alleged infringer only if the condition referred to in subparagraph (a) is fulfilled or only if the condition referred to in subparagraph (b) is fulfilled.

3.   In the adduction of proof to the contrary, the legitimate interests of defendants in protecting their manufacturing and business secrets shall be taken into account.

SECTION 6: LAYOUT-DESIGNS (TOPOGRAPHIES) OF INTEGRATED CIRCUITS

Article 35   Relation to the IPIC Treaty

Members agree to provide protection to the layout-designs (topographies) of integrated circuits (referred to in this Agreement as "layout designs") in accordance with Articles 2 through 7 (other than paragraph 3 of Article 6), Article 12 and paragraph 3 of Article 16 of the Treaty on Intellectual Property in Respect of Integrated Circuits and, in addition, to comply with the following provisions.

Article 36   Scope of the Protection

Subject to the provisions of paragraph 1 of Article 37, Members shall consider unlawful the following acts if performed without the authorisation of the right holder:[1] importing, selling, or otherwise distributing for commercial purposes a protected layout-design, an integrated circuit in which a protected layout-design is incorporated, or an article incorporating such an integrated circuit only in so far as it continues to contain an unlawfully reproduced layout-design.

NOTES

  [1]   The term "right holder" in this Section shall be understood as having the same meaning as the term "holder of the right" in the IPIC Treaty.

Article 37   Acts Not Requiring the Authorisation of the Right Holder

1.   Notwithstanding Article 36, no Member shall consider unlawful the performance of any of the acts referred to in that Article in respect of an integrated circuit incorporating an unlawfully reproduced layout-design or any article incorporating such an integrated circuit where the person performing or ordering such acts did not know and had no reasonable ground to know, when acquiring the integrated circuit or article incorporating such an integrated circuit, that it incorporated an unlawfully reproduced layout-design. Members shall provide that, after the time that such person has received sufficient notice that the layout-design was unlawfully reproduced, that person may perform any of the acts with respect to

the stock on hand or ordered before such time, but shall be liable to pay to the right holder a sum equivalent to a reasonable royalty such as would be payable under a freely negotiated licence in respect of such a layout-design.

2.   The conditions set out in subparagraphs (a) through (k) of Article 31 shall apply *mutatis mutandis* in the event of any non-voluntary licensing of a layout-design or of its use by or for the government without the authorisation of the right holder.

Article 38   Term of Protection

1.   In Members requiring registration as a condition of protection, the term of protection of layout-designs shall not end before the expiration of a period of 10 years counted from the date of filing an application for registration or from the first commercial exploitation wherever in the world it occurs.

2.   In Members not requiring registration as a condition for protection, layout-designs shall be protected for a term of no less than 10 years from the date of the first commercial exploitation wherever in the world it occurs.

3.   Notwithstanding paragraphs 1 and 2, a Member may provide that protection shall lapse 15 years after the creation of the layout-design.

SECTION 7: PROTECTION OF UNDISCLOSED INFORMATION

Article 39

1.   In the course of ensuring effective protection against unfair competition as provided in Article 10bis of the Paris Convention (1967), Members shall protect undisclosed information in accordance with paragraph 2 and data submitted to governments or governmental agencies in accordance with paragraph 3.

2.   Natural and legal persons shall have the possibility of preventing information lawfully within their control from being disclosed to, acquired by, or used by others without their consent in a manner contrary to honest commercial practices[1] so long as such information—

    (a)   is secret in the sense that it is not, as a body or in the precise configuration and assembly of its components, generally known among or readily accessible to persons within the circles that normally deal with the kind of information in question;

    (b)   has commercial value because it is secret; and

    (c)   has been subject to reasonable steps under the circumstances, by the person lawfully in control of the information, to keep it secret.

3.   Members, when requiring, as a condition of approving the marketing of pharmaceutical or of agricultural chemical products which utilise new chemical entities, the submission of undisclosed test or other data, the origination of which involves a considerable effort, shall protect such data against unfair commercial use. In addition, Members shall protect such data against disclosure, except where necessary to protect the public, or unless steps are taken to ensure that the data are protected against unfair commercial use.

NOTES

[1]   For the purpose of this provision, "a manner contrary to honest commercial practices" shall mean at least practices such as breach of contract, breach of confidence and inducement to breach, and includes the acquisition of undisclosed information by third parties who knew, or were grossly negligent in failing to know, that such practices were involved in the acquisition.

SECTION 8: CONTROL OF ANTI-COMPETITIVE PRACTICES IN CONTRACTUAL LICENCES

Article 40

1.   Members agree that some licensing practices or conditions pertaining to intellectual property rights which restrain competition may have adverse effects on trade and may impede the transfer and dissemination of technology.

2.   Nothing in this Agreement shall prevent Members from specifying in their legislation licensing practices or conditions that may in particular cases constitute an abuse of intellectual property rights having an adverse effect on competition in the relevant market. As provided above, a Member may adopt, consistently with the other provisions of this Agreement, appropriate measures to prevent or control such practices, which may include for example exclusive grantback conditions, conditions preventing challenges to validity and coercive package licensing, in the light of the relevant laws and regulations of that Member.

3.   Each Member shall enter, upon request, into consultations with any other Member which has cause to believe that an intellectual property right owner that is a national or domiciliary of the Member to which the request for consultations has been addressed is undertaking practices in violation of the requesting Member's laws and regulations on the subject matter of this Section, and which wishes to secure compliance with such legislation, without prejudice to any action under the law and to the full freedom of an ultimate decision of either Member. The Member addressed shall accord full and sympathetic consideration to, and shall afford adequate opportunity for, consultations with the requesting Member, and shall cooperate through supply of publicly available non-confidential information of relevance to the matter in question and of other information available to the Member, subject to domestic law and to the conclusion of mutually satisfactory agreements concerning the safeguarding of its confidentiality by the requesting Member.

4.   A Member whose nationals or domiciliaries are subject to proceedings in another Member concerning alleged violation of that other Member's laws and regulations on the subject matter of this Section shall, upon request, be granted an opportunity for consultations by the other Member under the same conditions as those foreseen in paragraph 3.

[15]

PART III
ENFORCEMENT OF INTELLECTUAL PROPERTY RIGHTS

SECTION 1: GENERAL OBLIGATIONS

Article 41

1.   Members shall ensure that enforcement procedures as specified in this Part are available under their law so as to permit effective action against any act of infringement of intellectual property rights covered by this Agreement, including expeditious remedies to prevent infringements and remedies which constitute a deterrent to further infringements. These procedures shall be applied in such a manner as to avoid the creation of barriers to legitimate trade and to provide for safeguards against their abuse.

2.   Procedures concerning the enforcement of intellectual property rights shall be fair and equitable. They shall not be unnecessarily complicated or costly, or entail unreasonable time-limits or unwarranted delays.

3.   Decisions on the merits of a case shall preferably be in writing and reasoned. They shall be made available at least to the parties to the proceeding without undue delay. Decisions on the merits of a case shall be based only on evidence in respect of which parties were offered the opportunity to be heard.

4.   Parties to a proceeding shall have an opportunity for review by a judicial authority of final administrative decisions and, subject to jurisdictional provisions in a Member's law concerning the importance of a case, of at least the legal aspects of initial judicial decisions on the merits of a case. However, there shall be no obligation to provide an opportunity for review of acquittals in criminal cases.

5.   It is understood that this Part does not create any obligation to put in place a judicial system for the enforcement of intellectual property rights distinct from that for the enforcement of law in general, nor does it affect the capacity of Members to enforce their law in general. Nothing in this Part creates any obligation with respect to the distribution of resources as between enforcement of intellectual property rights and the enforcement of law in general.

Section 2: Civil and Administrative Procedures and Remedies

Article 42   Fair and Equitable Procedures

Members shall make available to right holders[1] civil judicial procedures concerning the enforcement of any intellectual property right covered by this Agreement. Defendants shall have the right to written notice which is timely and contains sufficient detail, including the basis of the claims. Parties shall be allowed to be represented by independent legal counsel, and procedures shall not impose overly burdensome requirements concerning mandatory personal appearances. All parties to such procedures shall be duly entitled to substantiate their claims and to present all relevant evidence. The procedure shall provide a means to identify and protect confidential information, unless this would be contrary to existing constitutional requirements.

NOTES
[1]   For the purpose of this Part, the term "right holder" includes federations and associations having legal standing to assert such rights.

Article 43   Evidence

1.   The judicial authorities shall have the authority, where a party has presented reasonably available evidence sufficient to support its claims and has specified evidence relevant to substantiation of its claims which lies in the control of the opposing party, to order that this evidence be produced by the opposing party, subject in appropriate cases to conditions which ensure the protection of confidential information.

2.   In cases in which a party to a proceeding voluntarily and without good reason refuses access to, or otherwise does not provide necessary information within a reasonable period, or significantly impedes a procedure relating to an enforcement action, a Member may accord judicial authorities the authority to make preliminary and final determinations, affirmative or negative, on the basis of the information

presented to them, including the complaint or the allegation presented by the party adversely affected by the denial of access to information, subject to providing the parties an opportunity to be heard on the allegations or evidence.

Article 44   Injunctions

1.   The judicial authorities shall have the authority to order a party to desist from an infringement, *inter alia* to prevent the entry into the channels of commerce in their jurisdiction of imported goods that involve the infringement of an intellectual property right, immediately after customs clearance of such goods. Members are not obliged to accord such authority in respect of protected subject matter acquired or ordered by a person prior to knowing or having reasonable grounds to know that dealing in such subject matter would entail the infringement of an intellectual property right.

2.   Notwithstanding the other provisions of this Part and provided that the provisions of Part II specifically addressing use by governments, or by third parties authorised by a government, without the authorisation of the right holder are complied with, Members may limit the remedies available against such use to payment of remuneration in accordance with subparagraph (h) of Article 31. In other cases, the remedies under this Part shall apply or, where these remedies are inconsistent with a Member's law, declaratory judgments and adequate compensation shall be available.

Article 45   Damages

1.   The judicial authorities shall have the authority to order the infringer to pay the right holder damages adequate to compensate for the injury the right holder has suffered because of an infringement of that person's intellectual property right by an infringer who knowingly, or with reasonable grounds to know, engaged in infringing activity.

2.   The judicial authorities shall also have the authority to order the infringer to pay the right holder expenses, which may include appropriate attorney's fees. In appropriate cases, Members may authorise the judicial authorities to order recovery of profits and/or payment of pre-established damages even where the infringer did not knowingly, or with reasonable grounds to know, engage in infringing activity.

Article 46   Other Remedies

In order to create an effective deterrent to infringement, the judicial authorities shall have the authority to order that goods that they have found to be infringing be, without compensation of any sort, disposed of outside the channels of commerce in such a manner as to avoid any harm caused to the right holder, or, unless this would be contrary to existing constitutional requirements, destroyed. The judicial authorities shall also have the authority to order that materials and implements the predominant use of which has been in the creation of infringing goods be, without compensation of any sort, disposed of outside the channels of commerce in such a manner as to minimise the risks of further infringements. In considering such requests, the need for proportionality between the seriousness of the infringement and the remedies ordered as well as the interests of third parties shall be taken into account. In regard to counterfeit trademark goods, the simple removal of the trademark unlawfully affixed shall not be sufficient, other than in exceptional cases, to permit release of the goods into the channels of commerce.

PART IV
ACQUISITION AND MAINTENANCE OF INTELLECTUAL PROPERTY RIGHTS AND RELATED *INTER PARTES* PROCEDURES

Article 62

1.   Members may require, as a condition of the acquisition or maintenance of the intellectual property rights provided for under Sections 2 through 6 of Part II, compliance with reasonable procedures and formalities. Such procedures and formalities shall be consistent with the provisions of this Agreement.

2.   Where the acquisition of an intellectual property right is subject to the right being granted or registered, Members shall ensure that the procedures for grant or registration, subject to compliance with the substantive conditions for acquisition of the right, permit the granting or registration of the right within a reasonable period of time so as to avoid unwarranted curtailment of the period of protection.

3.   Article 4 of the Paris Convention (1967) shall apply *mutatis mutandis* to service marks.

4.   Procedures concerning the acquisition or maintenance of intellectual property rights and, where a Member's law provides for such procedures, administrative revocation and *inter partes* procedures such as opposition, revocation and cancellation, shall be governed by the general principles set out in paragraphs 2 and 3 of Article 41.

5.   Final administrative decisions in any of the procedures referred to under paragraph 4 shall be subject to review by a judicial or quasi-judicial authority. However, there shall be no obligation to provide an opportunity for such review of decisions in cases of unsuccessful opposition or administrative revocation, provided that the grounds for such procedures can be the subject of invalidation procedures.

[17]

PART V
DISPUTE PREVENTION AND SETTLEMENT

Article 63   Transparency

1.   Laws and regulations, and final judicial decisions and administrative rulings of general application, made effective by a Member pertaining to the subject matter of this Agreement (the availability, scope, acquisition, enforcement and prevention of the abuse of intellectual property rights) shall be published, or where such publication is not practicable made publicly available, in a national language, in such a manner as to enable governments and right holders to become acquainted with them. Agreements concerning the subject matter of this Agreement which are in force between the government or a governmental agency of a Member and the government or a governmental agency of another Member shall also be published.

2.   Members shall notify the laws and regulations referred to in paragraph 1 to the Council for TRIPS in order to assist that Council in its review of the operation of this Agreement. The Council shall attempt to minimise the burden on Members in carrying out this obligation and may decide to waive the obligation to notify such laws and regulations directly to the Council if consultations with WIPO on the establishment of a common register containing these laws and regulations are successful. The Council shall also consider in this connection any action required regarding notifications pursuant to the obligations under this Agreement stemming from the provisions of Article 6ter of the Paris Convention (1967).

3.   Each Member shall be prepared to supply, in response to a written request from another Member, information of the sort referred to in paragraph 1. A Member, having reason to believe that a specific judicial decision or administrative ruling or bilateral agreement in the area of intellectual property rights affects its rights under this Agreement, may also request in writing to be given access to or be informed in sufficient detail of such specific judicial decisions or administrative rulings or bilateral agreements.

4.   Nothing in paragraphs 1, 2 and 3 shall require Members to disclose confidential information which would impede law enforcement or otherwise be contrary to the public interest or would prejudice the legitimate commercial interests of particular enterprises, public or private.

Article 64   Dispute Settlement

1.   The provisions of Articles XXII and XXIII of GATT 1994 as elaborated and applied by the Dispute Settlement Understanding shall apply to consultations and the settlement of disputes under this Agreement except as otherwise specifically provided herein.

2.   Subparagraphs 1(b) and 1(c) of Article XXIII of GATT 1994 shall not apply to the settlement of disputes under this Agreement for a period of five years from the date of entry into force of the WTO Agreement.

3.   During the time period referred to in paragraph 2, the Council for TRIPS shall examine the scope and modalities for complaints of the type provided for under subparagraphs 1(b) and 1(c) of Article XXIII of GATT 1994 made pursuant to this Agreement, and submit its recommendations to the Ministerial Conference for approval. Any decision of the Ministerial Conference to approve such recommendations or to extend the period in paragraph 2 shall be made only by consensus, and approved recommendations shall be effective for all Members without further formal acceptance process.

[18]

(This Agreement is reproduced with the permission of the World Trade Organisation.)

TREATY ESTABLISHING THE EUROPEAN COMMMUNITY (TREATY OF ROME)

[25 March 1957]

[PART THREE
COMMUNITY POLICIES]

TITLE I—FREE MOVEMENT OF GOODS

CHAPTER 2—ELIMINATION OF QUANTITATIVE
RESTRICTIONS BETWEEN MEMBER STATES

NOTES

Part Three heading grouped together with Part Two heading by the Treaty on European Union, art G(9).

Article 30

Quantitative restrictions on imports and all measures having equivalent effect shall, without prejudice to the following provisions, be prohibited between Member States.

Article 34

1.   Quantitative restrictions on exports, and all measures having equivalent effect, shall be prohibited between Member States.

2.   Member States shall, by the end of the first stage at the latest, abolish all quantitative restrictions on exports on exports and any measures having equivalent effect which are in existence when this Treaty enters into force.

Article 36

The provisions of Articles 30 to 34 shall not preclude prohibitions or restrictions on imports, exports or goods in transit justified on grounds of public morality, public policy or public security; the protection of health and life of humans, animals or plants; the protection of national treasures possessing artistic, historic or archaeological value; or the protection of industrial and commercial property. Such prohibitions or restrictions shall not, however, constitute a means of arbitrary discrimination or a disguised restriction on trade between Member States.

[19]

[TITLE V
COMMON RULES ON COMPETITION, TAXATION AND
APPROXIMATION OF LAWS]

CHAPTER 1—RULES ON COMPETITION

SECTION 1—RULES APPLYING TO UNDERTAKINGS

NOTES

Title V heading was substituted by the Treaty on European Union, art G(17).

Article 85

1.   The following shall be prohibited as incompatible with the common market: all agreements between undertakings, decisions by associations of undertakings and concerted practices which may affect trade between Member States and which have as their object or effect the prevention, restriction or distortion of competition within the common market, and in particular those which—
(a)   directly or indirectly fix purchase or selling prices or any other trading conditions;
(b)   limit or control production, markets, technical development, or investment;
(c)   share markets or sources of supply;
(d)   apply dissimilar conditions to equivalent transactions with other trading parties, thereby placing them at a competitive disadvantage;
(e)   make the conclusion of contracts subject to acceptance by the other parties of supplementary obligations which, by their nature or according to commercial usage, have no connection with the subject of such contracts.

2.   Any agreements or decisions prohibited pursuant to this Article shall be automatically void.

3.   The provisions of paragraph 1 may, however, be declared inapplicable in the case of—

— any agreement or category of agreements between undertakings;
— any decision or category of decisions by associations of undertakings;
— any concerted practice or category of concerted practices;

which contributes to improving the production or distribution of goods or to promoting technical or economic progress, while allowing consumers a fair share of the resulting benefit, and which does not—

(a) impose on the undertakings concerned restrictions which are not indispensable to the attainment of these objectives;

(b) afford such undertakings the possibility of eliminating competition in respect of a substantial part of the products in question.

Article 86

Any abuse by one or more undertakings of a dominant position within the common market or in a substantial part of it shall be prohibited as incompatible with the common market in so far as it may affect trade between Member States.

Such abuse may, in particular, consist in—

(a) directly or indirectly imposing unfair purchase or selling prices or other unfair trading conditions;

(b) limiting production, markets or technical development to the prejudice of consumers;

(c) applying dissimilar conditions to equivalent transactions with other trading parties, thereby placing them at a competitive disadvantage;

(d) making the conclusion of contracts subject to acceptance by the other parties of supplementary obligations which, by their nature or according to commercial usage, have no connection with the subject of such contracts.

[20]

PART SIX
GENERAL AND FINAL PROVISIONS

Article 222

This Treaty shall in no way prejudice the rules in Member States governing the system of property ownership

[21]–[50]

PART II
PATENTS

PATENTS ACT 1977

(c 37)

An Act to establish a new law of patents applicable to future patents and applications for patents; to amend the law of patents applicable to existing patents and applications for patents; to give effect to certain international conventions on patents; and for connected purposes

[29 July 1977]

NOTES

Trade marks and registered trade marks: note that references to trade marks and registered trade marks within the meaning of the Trade Marks Act 1938 shall, unless the context otherwise requires, be construed after the commencement of the Trade Marks Act 1994 as references to trade marks and registered trade marks within the meaning of that Act. See the Trade Marks Act 1994, s 106(1), Sch 4, para 1.

PART I
NEW DOMESTIC LAW

Patentability

1 Patentable inventions

(1) A patent may be granted only for an invention in respect of which the following conditions are satisfied, that is to say—

    (a) the invention is new;

    (b) it involves an inventive step;

    (c) it is capable of industrial application;

    (d) the grant of a patent for it is not excluded by subsections (2) and (3) below;

and references in this Act to a patentable invention shall be construed accordingly.

(2) It is hereby declared that the following (among other things) are not inventions for the purposes of this Act, that is to say, anything which consists of—

    (a) a discovery, scientific theory or mathematical method;

    (b) a literary, dramatic, musical or artistic work or any other aesthetic creation whatsoever;

    (c) a scheme, rule or method for performing a mental act, playing a game or doing business, or a program for a computer;

    (d) the presentation of information;

but the foregoing provision shall prevent anything from being treated as an invention for the purposes of this Act only to the extent that a patent or application for a patent relates to that thing as such.

(3) A patent shall not be granted—

    (a) for an invention the publication or exploitation of which would be generally expected to encourage offensive, immoral or anti-social behaviour;

    (b) for any variety of animal or plant or any essentially biological process for the production of animals or plants, not being a micro-biological process or the product of such a process.

(4) For the purposes of subsection (3) above behaviour shall not be regarded as offensive, immoral or anti-social only because it is prohibited by any law in force in the United Kingdom or any part of it.

(5)   The Secretary of State may by order vary the provisions of subsection (2) above for the purpose of maintaining them in conformity with developments in science and technology; and no such order shall be made unless a draft of the order has been laid before, and approved by resolution of, each House of Parliament.

[51]

2   Novelty

(1)   An invention shall be taken to be new if it does not form part of the state of the art.

(2)   The state of the art in the case of an invention shall be taken to comprise all matter (whether a product, a process, information about either, or anything else) which has at any time before the priority date of that invention been made available to the public (whether in the United Kingdom or elsewhere) by written or oral description, by use or in any other way.

(3)   The state of the art in the case of an invention to which an application for a patent or a patent relates shall be taken also to comprise matter contained in an application for another patent which was published on or after the priority date of that invention, if the following conditions are satisfied, that is to say—

    (a)   that matter was contained in the application for that other patent both as filed and as published; and

    (b)   the priority date of that matter is earlier than that of the invention.

(4)   For the purposes of this section the disclosure of matter constituting an invention shall be disregarded in the case of a patent or an application for a patent if occurring later than the beginning of the period of six months immediately preceding the date of filing the application for the patent and either—

    (a)   the disclosure was due to, or made in consequence of, the matter having been obtained unlawfully or in breach of confidence by any person—

        (i)   from the inventor or from any other person to whom the matter was made available in confidence by the inventor or who obtained it from the inventor because he or the inventor believed that he was entitled to obtain it; or

        (ii)   from any other person to whom the matter was made available in confidence by any person mentioned in sub-paragraph (i) above or in this sub-paragraph or who obtained it from any person so mentioned because he or the person from whom he obtained it believed that he was entitled to obtain it;

    (b)   the disclosure was made in breach of confidence by any person who obtained the matter in confidence from the inventor or from any other person to whom it was made available, or who obtained it, from the inventor; or

    (c)   the disclosure was due to, or made in consequence of the inventor displaying the invention at an international exhibition and the applicant states, on filing the application, that the invention has been so displayed and also, within the prescribed period, files written evidence in support of the statement complying with any prescribed conditions.

(5)   In this section references to the inventor include references to any proprietor of the invention for the time being.

(6)   In the case of an invention consisting of a substance or composition for use in a method of treatment of the human or animal body by surgery or therapy or of

diagnosis practised on the human or animal body, the fact that the substance or composition forms part of the state of the art shall not prevent the invention from being taken to be new if the use of the substance or composition in any such method does not form part of the state of the art.

[52]

3   Inventive step

An invention shall be taken to involve an inventive step if it is not obvious to a person skilled in the art, having regard to any matter which forms part of the state of the art by virtue only of section 2(2) above (and disregarding section 2(3) above).

[53]

4   Industrial application

(1)   Subject to subsection (2) below, an invention shall be taken to be capable of industrial application if it can be made or used in any kind of industry, including agriculture.

(2)   An invention of a method of treatment of the human or animal body by surgery or therapy or of diagnosis practised on the human or animal body shall not be taken to be capable of industrial application.

(3)   Subsection (2) above shall not prevent a product consisting of a substance or composition being treated as capable of industrial application merely because it is invented for use in any such method.

[54]

5   Priority date

(1)   For the purposes of this Act the priority date of an invention to which an application for a patent relates and also of any matter (whether or not the same as the invention) contained in any such application is, except as provided by the following provisions of this Act, the date of filing the application.

(2)   If in or in connection with an application for a patent (the application in suit) a declaration is made, whether by the applicant or any predecessor in title of his, complying with the relevant requirements of rules and specifying one or more earlier relevant applications for the purposes of this section made by the applicant or a predecessor in title of his and each having a date of filing during the period of twelve months immediately preceding the date of filing the application in suit, then—

   (a)   if an invention to which the application in suit relates is supported by matter disclosed in the earlier relevant application or applications, the priority date of that invention shall instead of being the date of filing the application in suit be the date of filing the relevant application in which that matter was disclosed or, if it was disclosed in more than one relevant application, the earliest of them;

   (b)   the priority date of any matter contained in the application in suit which was also disclosed in the earlier relevant application or applications shall be the date of filing the relevant application in which that matter was disclosed or, if it was disclosed in more than one relevant application, the earliest of them.

(3)   Where an invention or other matter contained in the application in suit was also disclosed in two earlier relevant applications filed by the same applicant as in the case

of the application in suit or a predecessor in title of his and the second of those relevant applications was specified in or in connection with the application in suit, the second of those relevant applications shall, so far as concerns that invention or matter, be disregarded unless—

    (a)   it was filed in or in respect of the same country as the first; and

    (b)   not later than the date of filing the second, the first (whether or not so specified) was unconditionally withdrawn, or was abandoned or refused, without—

        (i)   having been made available to the public (whether in the United Kingdom or elsewhere);

        (ii)   leaving any rights outstanding; and

        (iii)   having served to establish a priority date in relation to another application, wherever made.

(4)   The foregoing provisions of this section shall apply for determining the priority date of an invention for which a patent has been granted as they apply for determining the priority date of an invention to which an application for that patent relates.

(5)   In this section "relevant application" means any of the following applications which has a date of filing, namely—

    (a)   an application for a patent under this Act;

    (b)   an application in or for a convention country (specified under section 90 below) for protection in respect of an invention or an application which, in accordance with the law of a convention country or a treaty or international convention to which a convention country is a party, is equivalent to such an application.

                                                     [55]

6   Disclosure of matter, etc, between earlier and later applications

(1)   It is hereby declared for the avoidance of doubt that where an application (the application in suit) is made for a patent and a declaration is made in accordance with section 5(2) above in or in connection with that application specifying an earlier relevant application, the application in suit and any patent granted in pursuance of it shall not be invalidated by reason only of relevant intervening acts.

(2)   In this section—

    "relevant application" has the same meaning as in section 5 above; and

    "relevant intervening acts" means acts done in relation to matter disclosed in an earlier relevant application between the dates of the earlier relevant application and the application in suit, as for example, filing another application for the invention for which the earlier relevant application was made, making information available to the public about that invention or that matter or working that invention, but disregarding any application, or the disclosure to the public of matter contained in any application, which is itself to be disregarded for the purposes of section 5(3) above.

                                                     [56]

Right to apply for and obtain a patent and be mentioned as inventor

7   Right to apply for and obtain a patent

(1)   Any person may make an application for a patent either alone or jointly with another.

(2)   A patent for an invention may be granted—

    (a)   primarily to the inventor or joint inventors;

    (b)   in preference to the foregoing, to any person or persons who, by virtue of any enactment or rule of law, or any foreign law or treaty or international convention, or by virtue of an enforceable term of any agreement entered into with the inventor before the making of the invention, was or were at the time of the making of the invention entitled to the whole of the property in it (other than equitable interests) in the United Kingdom;

    (c)   in any event, to the successor or successors in title of any person or persons mentioned in paragraph (a) or (b) above or any person so mentioned and the successor or successors in title of another person so mentioned;

and to no other person.

(3)   In this Act "inventor" in relation to an invention means the actual deviser of the invention and "joint inventor" shall be construed accordingly.

(4)   Except so far as the contrary is established, a person who makes an application for a patent shall be taken to be the person who is entitled under subsection (2) above to be granted a patent and two or more persons who make such an application jointly shall be taken to be the persons so entitled.

[57]

8   Determination before grant of questions about entitlement to patents, etc

(1)   At any time before a patent has been granted for an invention (whether or not an application has been made for it)—

    (a)   any person may refer to the comptroller the question whether he is entitled to be granted (alone or with any other persons) a patent for that invention or has or would have any right in or under any patent so granted or any application for such a patent; or

    (b)   any of two or more co-proprietors of an application for a patent for that invention may so refer the question whether any right in or under the application should be transferred or granted to any other person;

and the comptroller shall determine the question and may make such order as he thinks fit to give effect to the determination.

(2)   Where a person refers a question relating to an invention under subsection (1)(a) above to the comptroller after an application for a patent for the invention has been filed and before a patent is granted in pursuance of the application, then, unless the application is refused or withdrawn before the reference is disposed of by the comptroller, the comptroller may, without prejudice to the generality of subsection (1) above and subject to subsection (6) below,—

    (a)   order that the application shall proceed in the name of that person, either solely or jointly with that of any other applicant, instead of in the name of the applicant or any specified applicant;

    (b)   where the reference was made by two or more persons, order that the application shall proceed in all their names jointly;

    (c)   refuse to grant a patent in pursuance of the application or order the application to be amended so as to exclude any of the matter in respect of which the question was referred;

    (d)   make an order transferring or granting any licence or other right in or under the application and give directions to any person for carrying out the provisions of any such order.

(3)   Where a question is referred to the comptroller under subsection (1)(a) above and—

(a)   the comptroller orders an application for a patent for the invention to which the question relates to be so amended;

(b)   any such application is refused under subsection 2(c) above before the comptroller has disposed of the reference (whether the reference was made before or after the publication of the application); or

(c)   any such application is refused under any other provision of this Act or is withdrawn before the comptroller has disposed of the reference, but after the publication of the application;

the comptroller may order that any person by whom the reference was made may within the prescribed period make a new application for a patent for the whole or part of any matter comprised in the earlier application or, as the case may be, for all or any of the matter excluded from the earlier application, subject in either case to section 76 below, and in either case that, if such a new application is made, it shall be treated as having been filed on the date of filing the earlier application.

(4)   Where a person refers a question under subsection (1)(b) above relating to an application, any order under subsection (1) above may contain directions to any person for transferring or granting any right in or under the application.

(5)   If any person to whom directions have been given under subsection (2)(d) or (4) above fails to do anything necessary for carrying out any such directions within 14 days after the date of the directions, the comptroller may, on application made to him by any person in whose favour or on whose reference the directions were given, authorise him to do that thing on behalf of the person to whom the directions were given.

(6)   Where on a reference under this section it is alleged that, by virtue of any transaction, instrument or event relating to an invention or an application for a patent, any person other than the inventor or the applicant for the patent has become entitled to be granted (whether alone or with any other persons) a patent for the invention or has or would have any right in or under any patent so granted or any application for any such patent, an order shall not be made under subsection (2)(a), (b) or (d) above on the reference unless notice of the reference is given to the applicant and any such person, except any of them who is a party to the reference.

(7)   If it appears to the comptroller on a reference of a question under this section that the question involves matters which would more properly be determined by the court, he may decline to deal with it and, without prejudice to the court's jurisdiction to determine any such question and make a declaration, or any declaratory jurisdiction of the court in Scotland, the court shall have jurisdiction to do so.

(8)   No directions shall be given under this section so as to affect the mutual rights or obligations of trustees or of the personal representatives of deceased persons, or their rights or obligations as such.

[58]

9   Determination after grant of questions referred before grant

If a question with respect to a patent or application is referred by any person to the comptroller under section 8 above, whether before or after the making of an application for the patent, and is not determined before the time when the application is first in order for a grant of a patent in pursuance of the application, that fact shall not prevent the grant of a patent, but on its grant that person shall be treated as having referred to the comptroller under section 37 below any question mentioned in that section which the comptroller thinks appropriate.

[59]

10   Handling of application by joint applicants

If any dispute arises between joint applicants for a patent whether or in what manner the application should be proceeded with, the comptroller may, on a request made by any of the parties, give such directions as he thinks fit for enabling the application to proceed in the name of one or more of the parties alone or for regulating the manner in which it shall be proceeded with, or for both those purposes, according as the case may require.

[60]

11   Effect of transfer of application under s 8 or 10

(1)   Where an order is made or directions are given under section 8 or 10 above that an application for a patent shall proceed in the name of one or some of the original applicants (whether or not it is also to proceed in the name of some other person), any licences or other rights in or under the application shall, subject to the provisions of the order and any directions under either of those sections, continue in force and be treated as granted by the persons in whose name the application is to proceed.

(2)   Where an order is made or directions are given under section 8 above that an application for a patent shall proceed in the name of one or more persons none of whom was an original applicant (on the ground that the original applicant or applicants was or were not entitled to be granted the patent), any licences or other rights in or under the application shall, subject to the provisions of the order and any directions under that section and subject to subsection (3) below, lapse on the registration of that person or those persons as the applicant or applicants or, where the application has not been published, on the making of the order.

(3)   If before registration of a reference under section 8 above resulting in the making of any order mentioned in subsection (2) above—

    (a)   the original applicant or any of the applicants, acting in good faith, worked the invention in question in the United Kingdom or made effective and serious preparations to do so; or

    (b)   a licensee of the applicant, acting in good faith, worked the invention in the United Kingdom or made effective and serious preparations to do so;

that or those original applicant or applicants or the licensee shall, on making a request within the prescribed period to the person in whose name the application is to proceed, be entitled to be granted a licence (but not an exclusive licence) to continue working or, as the case may be, to work the invention.

(4)   Any such licence shall be granted for a reasonable period and on reasonable terms.

(5)   Where an order is made as mentioned in subsection (2) above, the person in whose name the application is to proceed or any person claiming that he is entitled to be granted any such licence may refer to the comptroller the question whether the latter is so entitled and whether any such period is or terms are reasonable, and

the comptroller shall determine the question and may, if he considers it appropriate, order the grant of such a licence.

12 Determination of questions about entitlement to foreign and convention patents, etc

(1) At any time before a patent is granted for an invention in pursuance of an application made under the law of any country other than the United Kingdom or under any treaty or international convention (whether or not that application has been made)—

    (a) any person may refer to the comptroller the question whether he is entitled to be granted (alone or with any other persons) any such patent for that invention or has or would have any right in or under any such patent or an application for such a patent; or

    (b) any of two or more co-proprietors of an application for such a patent for that invention may so refer the question whether any right in or under the application should be transferred or granted to any other person;

and the comptroller shall determine the question so far as he is able to and may make such order as he thinks fit to give effect to the determination.

(2) If it appears to the comptroller on a reference of a question under this section that the question involves matters which would more properly be determined by the court, he may decline to deal with it and, without prejudice to the court's jurisdiction to determine any such question and make a declaration, or any declaratory jurisdiction of the court in Scotland, the court shall have jurisdiction to do so.

(3) Subsection (1) above, in its application to a European patent and an application for any such patent, shall have effect subject to section 82 below.

(4) Section 10 above, except so much of it as enables the comptroller to regulate the manner in which an application is to proceed, shall apply to disputes between joint applicants for any such patent as is mentioned in subsection (1) above as it applies to joint applicants for a patent under this Act.

(5) Section 11 above shall apply in relation to—

    (a) any orders made under subsection (1) above and any directions given under section 10 above by virtue of subsection (4) above; and

    (b) any orders made and directions given by the relevant convention court with respect to a question corresponding to any question which may be determined under subsection (1) above;

as it applies to orders made and directions given apart from this section under section 8 or 10 above.

(6) In the following cases, that is to say—

    (a) where an application for a European patent (UK) is refused or withdrawn, or the designation of the United Kingdom in the application is withdrawn, after publication of the application but before a question relating to the right to the patent has been referred to the comptroller under subsection (1) above or before proceedings relating to that right have begun before the relevant convention court;

    (b) where an application has been made for a European patent (UK) and on a reference under subsection (1) above or any such proceedings as are mentioned in paragraph (a) above the comptroller, the court or the relevant convention court determines by a final decision (whether before or after publication of the application) that a person other than the applicant has the right to the patent, but that person requests the European Patent Office that the application for the patent should be refused; or

(c) where an international application for a patent (UK) is withdrawn, or the designation of the United Kingdom in the application is withdrawn, whether before or after the making of any reference under subsection (1) above but after publication of the application;

the comptroller may order that any person (other than the applicant) appearing to him to be entitled to be granted a patent under this Act may within the prescribed period make an application for such a patent for the whole or part of any matter comprised in the earlier application (subject, however, to section 76 below) and that if the application for a patent under this Act is filed, it shall be treated as having been filed on the date of filing the earlier application.

(7) In this section—

(a) references to a patent and an application for a patent include respectively references to protection in respect of an invention and an application which, in accordance with the law of any country other than the United Kingdom or any treaty or international convention, is equivalent to an application for a patent or for such protection; and

(b) a decision shall be taken to be final for the purposes of this section when the time for appealing from it has expired without an appeal being brought or, where an appeal is brought, when it is finally disposed of.

[62]

13 Mention of inventor

(1) The inventor or joint inventors of an invention shall have a right to be mentioned as such in any patent granted for the invention and shall also have a right to be so mentioned if possible in any published application for a patent for the invention and, if not so mentioned, a right to be so mentioned in accordance with rules in a prescribed document.

(2) Unless he has already given the Patent Office the information hereinafter mentioned, an applicant for a patent shall within the prescribed period file with the Patent Office a statement—

(a) identifying the person or persons whom he believes to be the inventor or inventors; and

(b) where the applicant is not the sole inventor or the applicants are not the joint inventors, indicating the derivation of his or their right to be granted the patent;

and, if he fails to do so, the application shall be taken to be withdrawn.

(3) Where a person has been mentioned as sole or joint inventor in pursuance of this section, any other person who alleges that the former ought not to have been so mentioned may at any time apply to the comptroller for a certificate to that effect, and the comptroller may issue such a certificate; and if he does so, he shall accordingly rectify any undistributed copies of the patent and of any documents prescribed for the purposes of subsection (1) above.

[63]

Applications

14 Making of application

(1) Every application for a patent—
   (a) shall be made in the prescribed form and shall be filed at the Patent Office in the prescribed manner; and
   (b) shall be accompanied by the fee prescribed for the purposes of this subsection (hereafter in this Act referred to as the filing fee).

(2) Every application for a patent shall contain—
   (a) a request for the grant of a patent;
   (b) a specification containing a description of the invention, a claim or claims and any drawing referred to in the description or any claim; and
   (c) an abstract;

but the foregoing provision shall not prevent an application being initiated by documents complying with section 15(1) below.

(3) The specification of an application shall disclose the invention in a manner which is clear enough and complete enough for the invention to be performed by a person skilled in the art.

(4) *(Repealed by the Copyright, Designs and Patents Act 1988, s 303(2), Sch 8.)*

(5) The claim or claims shall—
   (a) define the matter for which the applicant seeks protection;
   (b) be clear and concise;
   (c) be supported by the description; and
   (d) relate to one invention or to a group of inventions which are so linked as to form a single inventive concept.

(6) Without prejudice to the generality of subsection (5)(d) above, rules may provide for treating two or more inventions as being so linked as to form a single inventive concept for the purposes of this Act.

(7) The purpose of the abstract is to give technical information and on publication it shall not form part of the state of the art by virtue of section 2(3) above, and the comptroller may determine whether the abstract adequately fulfils its purpose and, if it does not, may reframe it so that it does.

(8) *(Repealed by the Copyright, Designs and Patents Act 1988, s 303(2), Sch 8.)*

(9) An application for a patent may be withdrawn at any time before the patent is granted and any withdrawal of such an application may not be revoked.

[64]

15 Date of filing application

(1) The date of filing an application for a patent shall, subject to the following provisions of this Act, be taken to be the earliest date on which the following conditions are satisfied in relation to the application, that is to say—
   (a) the documents filed at the Patent Office contain an indication that a patent is sought in pursuance of the application;
   (b) those documents identify the applicant or applicants for the patent;
   (c) those documents contain a description of the invention for which a patent is sought (whether or not the description complies with the other provisions of this Act and with any relevant rules); and

(d) the applicant pays the filing fee.

(2)   If any drawing referred to in any such application is filed later than the date which by virtue of subsection (1) above is to be treated as the date of filing the application, but before the beginning of the preliminary examination of the application under section 17 below, the comptroller shall give the applicant an opportunity of requesting within the prescribed period that the date on which the drawing is filed shall be treated for the purposes of this Act as the date of filing the application, and—

(a) if the applicant makes any such request, the date of filing the drawing shall be so treated; but

(b) otherwise any reference to the drawing in the application shall be treated as omitted.

(3)   If on the preliminary examination of an application under section 17 below it is found that any drawing referred to in the application has not been filed, then—

(a) if the drawing is subsequently filed within the prescribed period, the date on which it is filed shall be treated for the purposes of this Act as the date of filing the application; but

(b) otherwise any reference to the drawing in the application shall be treated as omitted.

[(3A) Nothing in subsection (2) or (3) above shall be construed as affecting the power of the comptroller under section 117(1) below to correct errors or mistakes with respect to the filing of drawings.]

(4)   Where, after an application for a patent has been filed and before the patent is granted, a new application is filed by the original applicant or his successor in title in accordance with rules in respect of any part of the matter contained in the earlier application and the conditions mentioned in subsection (1) above are satisfied in relation to the new application (without the new application contravening section 76 below) the new application shall be treated as having, as its date of filing, the date of filing the earlier application.

(5)   An application which has a date of filing by virtue of the foregoing provisions of this section shall be taken to be withdrawn at the end of the relevant prescribed period, unless before that end the applicant—

(a) files at the Patent Office one or more claims for the purposes of the application and also the abstract; and

(b) makes a request for a preliminary examination and search under the following provisions of this Act and pays the search fee.

[65]

NOTES
    Sub-s (3A): inserted in relation to applications filed after 7 January 1991 by the Copyright, Designs and Patents Act 1988, s 295, Sch 5, para 2.

16   Publication of application

(1)   Subject to section 22 below, where an application has a date of filing, then, as soon as possible after the end of the prescribed period, the comptroller shall, unless the application is withdrawn or refused before preparations for its publication have been completed by the Patent Office, publish it as filed (including not only the original claims but also any amendments of those claims and new claims subsisting

immediately before the completion of those preparations) and he may, if so requested by the applicant, publish it as aforesaid during that period, and in either event shall advertise the fact and date of its publication in the journal.

(2) The comptroller may omit from the specification of a published application for a patent any matter—

    (a) which in his opinion disparages any person in a way likely to damage him, or

    (b) the publication or exploitation of which would in his opinion be generally expected to encourage offensive, immoral or anti-social behaviour.

[66]

Examination and search

17 Preliminary examination and search

(1) Where an application for a patent has a date of filing and is not withdrawn, and before the end of the prescribed period—

    (a) a request is made by the applicant to the Patent Office in the prescribed form for a preliminary examination and a search; and

    (b) the prescribed fee is paid for the examination and search (the search fee);

the comptroller shall refer the application to an examiner for a preliminary examination and search, except that he shall not refer the application for a search until it includes one or more claims.

(2) On a preliminary examination of an application the examiner shall determine whether the application complies with those requirements of this Act and the rules which are designated by the rules as formal requirements for the purposes of this Act and shall report his determination to the comptroller.

(3) If it is reported to the comptroller under subsection (2) above that not all the formal requirements are complied with, he shall give the applicant an opportunity to make observations on the report and to amend the application within a specified period (subject to section 15(5) above) so as to comply with those requirements (subject, however, to section 76 below), and if the applicant fails to do so the comptroller may refuse the application.

(4) Subject to subsections (5) and (6) below, on a search requested under this section, the examiner shall make such investigation as in his opinion is reasonably practicable and necessary for him to identify the documents which he thinks will be needed to decide, on a substantive examination under section 18 below, whether the invention for which a patent is sought is new and involves an inventive step.

(5) On any such search the examiner shall determine whether or not the search would serve any useful purpose on the application as for the time being constituted and—

    (a) if he determines that it would serve such a purpose in relation to the whole or part of the application, he shall proceed to conduct the search so far as it would serve such a purpose and shall report on the results of the search to the comptroller; and

    (b) if he determines that the search would not serve such a purpose in relation to the whole or part of the application, he shall report accordingly to the comptroller;

and in either event the applicant shall be informed of the examiner's report.

(6)   If it appears to the examiner, either before or on conducting a search under this section, that an application relates to two or more inventions, but that they are not so linked as to form a single inventive concept, he shall initially only conduct a search in relation to the first invention specified in the claims of the application, but may proceed to conduct a search in relation to another invention so specified if the applicant pays the search fee in respect of the application so far as it relates to that other invention.

(7)   After a search has been requested under this section for an application the comptroller may at any time refer the application to an examiner for a supplementary search, and [subsections (4) and (5) above] shall apply in relation to a supplementary search as [they apply] in relation to any other search under this section.

[(8)   A reference for a supplementary search in consequence of—
   (a)   an amendment of the application made by the applicant under section 18(3) or 19(1) below, or
   (b)   a correction of the application, or of a document filed in connection with the application, under section 117 below,

shall be made only on payment of the prescribed fee, unless the comptroller directs otherwise.]

[67]

NOTES

Sub-s (7): words in square brackets substituted by the Copyright, Designs and Patents Act 1988, s 295, Sch 5, para 3(2).

Sub-s (8): added by the Copyright, Designs and Patents Act 1988, s 295, Sch 5, para 3(3).

18   Substantive examination and grant or refusal of patent

(1)   Where the conditions imposed by section 17(1) above for the comptroller to refer an application to an examiner for a preliminary examination and search are satisfied and at the time of the request under that subsection or within the prescribed period—
   (a)   a request is made by the applicant to the Patent Office in the prescribed form for a substantive examination; and
   (b)   the prescribed fee is paid for the examination;

the comptroller shall refer the application to an examiner for a substantive examination; and if no such request is made or the prescribed fee is not paid within that period, the application shall be treated as having been withdrawn at the end of that period.

[(1A)   If the examiner forms the view that a supplementary search under section 17 above is required for which a fee is payable, he shall inform the comptroller, who may decide that the substantive examination should not proceed until the fee is paid; and if he so decides, then unless within such period as he may allow—
   (a)   the fee is paid, or
   (b)   the application is amended so as to render the supplementary search unnecessary,

he may refuse the application.]

(2)   On a substantive examination of an application the examiner shall investigate, to such extent as he considers necessary in view of any examination and search carried out under section 17 above, whether the application complies with the requirements of this Act and the rules and shall determine that question and report his determination to the comptroller.

(3) If the examiner reports that any of those requirements are not complied with, the comptroller shall give the applicant an opportunity within a specified period to make observations on the report and to amend the application so as to comply with those requirements (subject, however, to section 76 below), and if the applicant fails to satisfy the comptroller that those requirements are complied with, or to amend the application so as to comply with them, the comptroller may refuse the application.

(4) If the examiner reports that the application, whether as originally filed or as amended in pursuance of section 17 above, this section or section 19 below, complies with those requirements at any time before the end of the prescribed period, the comptroller shall notify the applicant of that fact and, subject to subsection (5) and sections 19 and 22 below and on payment within the prescribed period of any fee prescribed for the grant, grant him a patent.

(5) Where two or more applications for a patent for the same invention having the same priority date are filed by the same applicant or his successor in title, the comptroller may on that ground refuse to grant a patent in pursuance of more than one of the applications.

[68]

NOTES
  Sub-s (1A): inserted by the Copyright, Designs and Patents Act 1988, s 295, Sch 5, para 4.

19   General power to amend application before grant

(1) At any time before a patent is granted in pursuance of an application the applicant may, in accordance with the prescribed conditions and subject to section 76 below, amend the application of his own volition.

(2) The comptroller may, without an application being made to him for the purpose, amend the specification and abstract contained in an application for a patent so as to acknowledge a registered trade mark.

[69]

NOTES
  Reference to a registered trade mark in sub-s (2) includes reference to a registered service mark, by virtue of the Patents, Designs and Marks Act 1986, s 2(3), Sch 2, Part I.

20   Failure of application

(1) If it is not determined that an application for a patent complies before the end of the prescribed period with all the requirements of this Act and the rules, the application shall be treated as having been refused by the comptroller at the end of that period, and section 97 below shall apply accordingly.

(2) If at the end of that period an appeal to the court is pending in respect of the application or the time within which such an appeal could be brought has not expired, that period—

(a) where such an appeal is pending, or is brought within the said time or before the expiration of any extension of that time granted (in the case of a first extension) on an application made within that time or (in the case of a subsequent extension) on an application made before the expiration of the last previous extension, shall be extended until such date as the court may determine;

(b)   where no such appeal is pending or is so brought, shall continue until the end of the said time or, if any extension of that time is so granted, until the expiration of the extension or last extension so granted.

[70]

21   Observations by third party on patentability

(1)   Where an application for a patent has been published but a patent has not been granted to the applicant, any other person may make observations in writing to the comptroller on the question whether the invention is a patentable invention, stating reasons for the observations, and the comptroller shall consider the observations in accordance with rules.

(2)   It is hereby declared that a person does not become a party to any proceedings under this Act before the comptroller by reason only that he makes observations under this section.

[71]

Security and safety

22   Information prejudicial to defence of realm or safety of public

(1)   Where an application for a patent is filed in the Patent Office (whether under this Act or any treaty or international convention to which the United Kingdom is a party and whether before or after the appointed day) and it appears to the comptroller that the application contains information of a description notified to him by the Secretary of State as being information the publication of which might be prejudicial to the defence of the realm, the comptroller may give directions prohibiting or restricting the publication of that information or its communication to any specified person or description of persons.

(2)   If it appears to the comptroller that any application so filed contains information the publication of which might be prejudicial to the safety of the public, he may give directions prohibiting or restricting the publication of that information or its communication to any specified person or description of persons until the end of a period not exceeding three months from the end of the period prescribed for the purposes of section 16 above.

(3)   While directions are in force under this section with respect to an application—
    (a)   if the application is made under this Act, it may proceed to the stage where it is in order for the grant of a patent, but it shall not be published and that information shall not be so communicated and no patent shall be granted in pursuance of the application;
    (b)   if it is an application for a European patent, it shall not be sent to the European Patent Office; and
    (c)   if it is an international application for a patent, a copy of it shall not be sent to the International Bureau or any international searching authority appointed under the Patent Co-operation Treaty.

(4)   Subsection (3)(b) above shall not prevent the comptroller from sending the European Patent Office any information which it is his duty to send that office under the European Patent Convention.

(5)   Where the comptroller gives directions under this section with respect to any application, he shall give notice of the application and of the directions to the Secretary of State, and the following provisions shall then have effect:—

(a) the Secretary of State shall, on receipt of the notice, consider whether the publication of the application or the publication or communication of the information in question would be prejudicial to the defence of the realm or the safety of the public;

(b) if the Secretary of State determines under paragraph (a) above that the publication of the application or the publication or communication of that information would be prejudicial to the safety of the public, he shall notify the comptroller who shall continue his directions under subsection (2) above until they are revoked under paragraph (e) below;

(c) if the Secretary of State determines under paragraph (a) above that the publication of the application or the publication or communication of that information would be prejudicial to the defence of the realm or the safety of the public, he shall (unless a notice under paragraph (d) below has previously been given by the Secretary of State to the comptroller) reconsider that question during the period of nine months from the date of filing the application and at least once in every subsequent period of twelve months;

(d) if on consideration of an application at any time it appears to the Secretary of State that the publication of the application or the publication or communication of the information contained in it would not, or would no longer, be prejudicial to the defence of the realm or the safety of the public, he shall give notice to the comptroller to that effect; and

(e) on receipt of such a notice the comptroller shall revoke the directions and may, subject to such conditions (if any) as he thinks fit, extend the time for doing anything required or authorised to be done by or under this Act in connection with the application, whether or not that time has previously expired.

(6) The Secretary of State may do the following for the purpose of enabling him to decide the question referred to in subsection (5)(c) above—

(a) where the application contains information relating to the production or use of atomic energy or research into matters connected with such production or use, he may at any time do one or both of the following, that is to say, inspect and authorise the United Kingdom Atomic Energy Authority to inspect the application and any documents sent to the comptroller in connection with it; and

(b) in any other case, he may at any time after (or, with the applicant's consent, before) the end of the period prescribed for the purposes of section 16 above inspect the application and any such documents;

and where that Authority are authorised under paragraph (a) above they shall as soon as practicable report on their inspection to the Secretary of State.

(7) Where directions have been given under this section in respect of an application for a patent for an invention and, before the directions are revoked, that prescribed period expires and the application is brought in order for the grant of a patent, then—

(a) if while the directions are in force the invention is worked by (or with the written authorisation of or to the order of) a government department, the provisions of sections 55 to 59 below shall apply as if—

(i) the working were use made by virtue of section 55;

(ii) the application had been published at the end of that period; and

      (iii) a patent had been granted for the invention at the time the application is brought in order for the grant of a patent (taking the terms of the patent to be those of the application as it stood at the time it was so brought in order); and

    (b) if it appears to the Secretary of State that the applicant for the patent has suffered hardship by reason of the continuance in force of the directions, the Secretary of State may, with the consent of the Treasury, make such payment (if any) by way of compensation to the applicant as appears to the Secretary of State and the Treasury to be reasonable having regard to the inventive merit and utility of the invention, the purpose for which it is designed and any other relevant circumstances.

(8)   Where a patent is granted in pursuance of an application in respect of which directions have been given under this section, no renewal fees shall be payable in respect of any period during which those directions were in force.

(9)   A person who fails to comply with any direction under this section shall be liable—

    (a) on summary conviction, to a fine not exceeding [the prescribed sum]; or

    (b) on conviction on indictment, to imprisonment for a term not exceeding two years or a fine, or both.

[72]

NOTES

Sub-s (9): words in square brackets substituted by virtue of the Magistrates' Courts Act 1980, s 32(2).

23   Restrictions on applications abroad by United Kingdom residents

(1)   Subject to the following provisions of this section, no person resident in the United Kingdom shall, without written authority granted by the comptroller, file or cause to be filed outside the United Kingdom an application for a patent for invention unless—

    (a) an application for a patent for the same invention has been filed in the Patent Office (whether before, on or after the appointed day) not less than six weeks before the application outside the United Kingdom; and

    (b) either no directions have been given under section 22 above in relation to the application in the United Kingdom or all such directions have been revoked.

(2)   Subsection (1) above does not apply to an application for a patent for an invention for which an application for a patent has first been filed (whether before or after the appointed day) in a country outside the United Kingdom by a person resident outside the United Kingdom.

(3)   A person who files or causes to be filed an application for the grant of a patent in contravention of this section shall be liable—

    (a) on summary conviction, to a fine not exceeding [the prescribed sum]; or

    (b) on conviction on indictment, to imprisonment for a term not exceeding two years or a fine, or both.

(4)   In this section—

    (a) any reference to an application for a patent includes a reference to an application for other protection for an invention;

(b) any reference to either kind of application is a reference to an application under this Act, under the law of any country other than the United Kingdom or under any treaty or international convention to which the United Kingdom is a party.

[73]

NOTES

Sub-s (3): words in square brackets substituted by virtue of the Magistrates' Courts Act 1980, s 32(2).

Provisions as to patents after grant

24 Publication and certificate of grant

(1) As soon as practicable after a patent has been granted under this Act the comptroller shall publish in the journal a notice that it has been granted.

(2) The comptroller shall, as soon as practicable after he publishes a notice under subsection (1) above, send the proprietor of the patent a certificate in the prescribed form that the patent has been granted to the proprietor.

(3) The comptroller shall, at the same time as he publishes a notice under subsection (1) above in relation to a patent publish the specification of the patent, the names of the proprietor and (if different) the inventor and any other matters constituting or relating to the patent which in the comptroller's opinion it is desirable to publish.

[74]

25 Term of patent

(1) A patent granted under this Act shall be treated for the purposes of the following provisions of this Act as having been granted, and shall take effect, on the date on which notice of its grant is published in the journal and, subject to subsection (3) below, shall continue in force until the end of the period of 20 years beginning with the date of filing the application for the patent or with such other date as may be prescribed.

(2) A rule prescribing any such other date under this section shall not be made unless a draft of the rule has been laid before, and approved by resolution of, each House of Parliament.

(3) A patent shall cease to have effect at the end of the period prescribed for the payment of any renewal fee if it is not paid within that period.

(4) If during the period of six months immediately following the end of the prescribed period the renewal fee and any prescribed additional fee are paid, the patent shall be treated for the purposes of this Act as if it had never expired, and accordingly—
  (a) anything done under or in relation to it during that further period shall be valid;
  (b) an act which would constitute an infringement of it if it had not expired shall constitute such an infringement; and
  (c) an act which would constitute the use of the patented invention for the services of the Crown if the patent had not expired shall constitute that use.

(5) Rules shall include provision requiring the comptroller to notify the registered proprietor of a patent that a renewal fee has not been received from him in the Patent Office before the end of the prescribed period and before the framing of the notification.

[75]

26   Patent not to be impugned for lack of unity

No person may in any proceeding object to a patent or to an amendment of a specification of a patent on the ground that the claims contained in the specification of the patent, as they stand or, as the case may be, as proposed to be amended, relate—

   (a)   to more than one invention, or
   (b)   to a group of inventions which are not so linked as to form a single inventive concept.

[76]

27   General power to amend specification after grant

(1)   Subject to the following provisions of this section and to section 76 below, the comptroller may, on an application made by the proprietor of a patent, allow the specification of the patent to be amended subject to such conditions, if any, as he thinks fit.

(2)   No such amendment shall be allowed under this section where there are pending before the court or the comptroller proceedings in which the validity of the patent may be put in issue.

(3)   An amendment of a specification of a patent under this section shall have effect and be deemed always to have had effect from the grant of the patent.

(4)   The comptroller may, without an application being made to him for the purpose, amend the specification of a patent so as to acknowledge a registered trademark.

(5)   A person may give notice to the comptroller of his opposition to an application under this section by the proprietor of a patent, and if he does so the comptroller shall notify the proprietor and consider the opposition in deciding whether to grant the application.

[77]

NOTES

   Reference to a registered trade mark in sub-s (4) includes reference to a registered service mark, by virtue of the Patents, Designs and Marks Act 1986, s 2(3), Sch 2, Part I.

---

28   Restoration of lapsed patents

[(1)   Where a patent has ceased to have effect by reason of a failure to pay any renewal fee, an application for the restoration of the patent may be made to the comptroller within the prescribed period.

(1A)   Rules prescribing that period may contain such transitional provisions and savings as appear to the Secretary of State to be necessary or expedient.]

(2)   An application under this section may be made by the person who was the proprietor of the patent or by any other person who would have been entitled to the patent if it had not ceased to have effect; and where the patent was held by two or more persons jointly, the application may, with the leave of the comptroller, be made by one or more of them without joining the others.

[(2A) Notice of the application shall be published by the comptroller in the prescribed manner.]

(3)   If the comptroller is satisfied that—

(a)   the proprietor of the patent took reasonable care to see that any renewal fee was paid within the prescribed period or that that fee and any prescribed additional fee were paid within the six months immediately following the end of that period, . . .

(b)   . . .

the comptroller shall by order restore the patent on payment of any unpaid renewal fee and any prescribed additional fee.

(4)   An order under this section may be made subject to such conditions as the comptroller thinks fit (including a condition requiring compliance with any provisions of the rules relating to registration which have not been complied with), and if the proprietor of the patent does not comply with any condition of such an order the comptroller may revoke the order and give such directions consequential on the revocation as he thinks fit.

(5)–(9) . . .

[78]

NOTES

Sub-ss (1), (1A): substituted for sub-s (1), as originally enacted, by the Copyright, Designs and Patents Act 1988, s 295, Sch 5, para 6(2).

Sub-s (2A): inserted by the Copyright, Designs and Patents Act 1988, s 295, Sch 5, para 6(3).

Sub-s (3): words omitted repealed by the Copyright, Designs and Patents Act 1988, ss 295, 303(2), Sch 5, para 6(4), Sch 8.

[28A   Effect of order for restoration of patent

(1)   The effect of an order for the restoration of a patent is as follows.

(2)   Anything done under or in relation to the patent during the period between expiry and restoration shall be treated as valid.

(3)   Anything done during that period which would have constituted an infringement if the patent had not expired shall be treated as an infringement—

(a)   if done at a time when it was possible for the patent to be renewed under section 25(4), or

(b)   if it was a continuation or repetition of an earlier infringing act.

(4)   If after it was no longer possible for the patent to be so renewed, and before publication of notice of the application for restoration, a person—

(a)   began in good faith to do an act which would have constituted an infringement of the patent if it had not expired, or

(b)   made in good faith effective and serious preparations to do such an act,

he has the right to continue to do the act or, as the case may be, to do the act, notwithstanding the restoration of the patent; but this right does not extend to granting a licence to another person to do the act.

(5)   If the act was done, or the preparations were made, in the course of a business, the person entitled to the right conferred by subsection (4) may—

(a)   authorise the doing of that act by any partners of his for the time being in that business, and

(b)   assign that right, or transmit it on death (or in the case of a body corporate on its dissolution), to any person who acquires that part of the business in the course of which the act was done or the preparations were made.

(6)   Where a product is disposed of to another in exercise of the rights conferred by subsection (4) or (5), that other and any person claiming through him may deal with the product in the same way as if it had been disposed of by the registered proprietor of the patent.

(7)   The above provisions apply in relation to the use of a patent for the services of the Crown as they apply in relation to infringement of the patent.]

                                                                            [79]

NOTES
   Inserted by the Copyright, Designs and Patents Act 1988, s 295, Sch 5, para 7.

29   Surrender of patents

(1)   The proprietor of a patent may at any time by notice given to the comptroller offer to surrender his patent.

(2)   A person may give notice to the comptroller of his opposition to the surrender of a patent under this section, and if he does so the comptroller shall notify the proprietor of the patent and determine the question.

(3)   If the comptroller is satisfied that the patent may properly be surrendered, he may accept the offer and, as from the date when notice of his acceptance is published in the journal, the patent shall cease to have effect, but no action for infringement shall lie in respect of any act done before that date and no right to compensation shall accrue for any use of the patented invention before that date for the services of the Crown.

                                                                            [80]

Property in patents and applications, and registration

30   Nature of, and transactions in, patents and applications for patents

(1)   Any patent or application for a patent is personal property (without being a thing in action), and any patent or any such application and rights in or under it may be transferred, created or granted in accordance with subsections (2) to (7) below.

(2)   Subject to section 36(3) below, any patent or any such application, or any right in it, may be assigned or mortgaged.

(3)   Any patent or any such application or right shall vest by operation of law in the same way as any other personal property and may be vested by an assent of personal representatives.

(4)   Subject to section 36(3) below, a licence may be granted under any patent or any such application for working the invention which is the subject of the patent or the application; and—
   (a)   to the extent that the licence so provides, a sub-licence may be granted under any such licence and any such licence or sub-licence may be assigned or mortgaged; and
   (b)   any such licence or sub-licence shall vest by operation of law in the same way as any other personal property and may be vested by an assent of personal representatives.

(5)   Subsections (2) to (4) above shall have effect subject to the following provisions of this Act.

(6) Any of the following transactions, that is to say—

    (a) any assignment or mortgage of a patent or any such application, or any right in a patent or any such application;

    (b) any assent relating to any patent or any such application or right;

shall be void unless it is in writing and is signed by or on behalf of the parties to the transaction (or, in the case of an assent or other transaction by a personal representative, by or on behalf of the personal representative) or in the case of a body corporate is so signed or is under the seal of that body.

(7) An assignment of a patent or any such application or a share in it, and an exclusive licence granted under any patent or any such application, may confer on the assignee or licensee the right of the assignor or licensor to bring proceedings by virtue of section 61 or 69 below for a previous infringement or to bring proceedings under section 58 below for a previous act.

[81]

31 Nature of, and transactions in, patents and applications for patents in Scotland

(1) Section 30 above shall not extend to Scotland, but instead the following provisions of this section shall apply there.

(2) Any patent or application for a patent, and any right in or under any patent or any such application, is incorporeal moveable property, and the provisions of the following subsections and of section 36(3) below shall apply to any grant of licences, assignations and securities in relation to such property.

(3) Any patent or any such application, or any right in it, may be assigned and security may be granted over a patent or any such application or right.

(4) A licence may be granted, under any patent or any application for a patent, for working the invention which is the subject of the patent or application.

(5) To the extent that any licence granted under subsection (4) above so provides, a sub-licence may be granted under any such licence and any such licence or sub-licence may be assigned and security granted over it.

(6) Any assignation or grant of security under this section may be carried out only by writing probative or holograph of the parties to the transaction.

(7) Any assignation of a patent or application for a patent or a share in it, and an exclusive licence granted under any patent or any such application, may confer on the assignee or licensee the right of the assignor or licensor to bring proceedings by virtue of section 61 or 69 below for a previous infringement or to bring proceedings under section 58 below for a previous act.

[82]

[32 Register of patents etc

(1) The comptroller shall maintain the register of patents, which shall comply with rules made by virtue of this section and shall be kept in accordance with such rules.

(2) Without prejudice to any other provision of this Act or rules, rules may make provision with respect to the following matters, including provision imposing requirements as to any of those matters—

    (a) the registration of patents and of published applications for patents;

(b) the registration of transactions, instruments or events affecting rights in or under patents and applications;

(c) the furnishing to the comptroller of any prescribed documents or description of documents in connection with any matter which is required to be registered;

(d) the correction of errors in the register and in any documents filed at the Patent Office in connection with registration; and

(e) the publication and advertisement of anything done under this Act or rules in relation to the register.

(3) Notwithstanding anything in subsection (2)(b) above, no notice of any trust, whether express, implied or constructive, shall be entered in the register and the comptroller shall not be affected by any such notice.

(4) The register need not be kept in documentary form.

(5) Subject to rules, the public shall have a right to inspect the register at the Patent Office at all convenient times.

(6) Any person who applies for a certified copy of an entry in the register or a certified extract from the register shall be entitled to obtain such a copy or extract on payment of a fee prescribed in relation to certified copies and extracts; and rules may provide that any person who applies for an uncertified copy or extract shall be entitled to such a copy or extract on payment of a fee prescribed in relation to uncertified copies and extracts.

(7) Applications under subsection (6) above or rules made by virtue of that subsection shall be made in such manner as may be prescribed.

(8) In relation to any portion of the register kept otherwise than in documentary form—

(a) the right of inspection conferred by subsection (5) above is a right to inspect the material on the register; and

(b) the right to a copy or extract conferred by subsection (6) above or rules is a right to a copy or extract in a form in which it can be taken away and in which it is visible and legible.

(9) Subject to subsection (12) below, the register shall be prima facie evidence of anything required or authorised by this Act or rules to be registered and in Scotland shall be sufficient evidence of any such thing.

(10) A certificate purporting to be signed by the comptroller and certifying that any entry which he is authorised by this Act or rules to make has or has not been made, or that any other thing which he is so authorised to do has or has not been done, shall be prima facie evidence, and in Scotland shall be evidence, of the matters so certified.

(11) Each of the following, that is to say—

(a) a copy of an entry in the register or an extract from the register which is supplied under subsection (6) above;

(b) a copy of any document kept in the Patent Office or an extract from any such document, any specification of a patent or any application for a patent which has been published,

which purports to be a certified copy or a certified extract shall, subject to subsection (12) below, be admitted in evidence without further proof and without production of any original; and in Scotland such evidence shall be sufficient evidence.

(12) In the application of this section to England and Wales nothing in it shall be taken as detracting from section 69 or 70 of the Police and Criminal Evidence Act 1984 or any provision made by virtue of either of them.

(13) In this section "certified copy" and "certified extract" mean a copy and extract certified by the comptroller and sealed with the seal of the Patent Office.

(14) In this Act, except so far as the context otherwise requires—
"register", as a noun, means the register of patents;
"register", as a verb, means, in relation to any thing, to register or register particulars, or enter notice, of that thing in the register and, in relation to a person, means to enter his name in the register;

and cognate expressions shall be construed accordingly.]

[83]

NOTES
Substituted by the Patents, Designs and Marks Act 1986, s 1, Sch 1, para 4.

33   Effect of registration, etc, on rights in patents

(1) Any person who claims to have acquired the property in a patent or application for a patent by virtue of any transaction, instrument or event to which this section applies shall be entitled as against any other person who claims to have acquired that property by virtue of an earlier transaction, instrument or event to which this section applies if, at the time of the later transaction, instrument or event—
(a) the earlier transaction, instrument or event was not registered, or
(b) in the case of any application which has not been published, notice of the earlier transaction, instrument or event had not been given to the comptroller, and
(c) in any case, the person claiming under the later transaction, instrument or event, did not know of the earlier transaction, instrument or event.

(2) Subsection (1) above shall apply equally to the case where any person claims to have acquired any right in or under a patent or application for a patent, by virtue of a transaction, instrument or event to which this section applies, and that right is incompatible with any such right acquired by virtue of an earlier transaction, instrument or event to which this section applies.

(3) This section applies to the following transactions, instruments and events:—
(a) the assignment or assignation of a patent or application for a patent, or a right in it;
(b) the mortgage of a patent or application or the granting of security over it;
(c) the grant, assignment or assignation of a licence or sub-licence, or mortgage of a licence or sub-licence, under a patent or application;
(d) the death of the proprietor or one of the proprietors of any such patent or application or any person having a right in or under a patent or application and the vesting by an assent of personal representatives of a patent, application or any such right; and
(e) any order or directions of a court or other competent authority—
(i) transferring a patent or application or any right in or under it to any person; or
(ii) that an application should proceed in the name of any person;
and in either case the event by virtue of which the court or authority had power to make any such order or give any such directions.

(4)   Where an application for the registration of a transaction, instrument or event has been made, but the transaction, instrument or event has not been registered, then, for the purposes of subsection (1)(a) above, registration of the application shall be treated as registration of the transaction, instrument or event.

[84]

34   Rectification of register

(1)   The court may, on the application of any person aggrieved, order the register to be rectified by the making, or the variation or deletion, of any entry in it.

(2)   In proceedings under this section the court may determine any question which it may be necessary or expedient to decide in connection with the rectification of the register.

(3)   Rules of court may provide for the notification of any application under this section to the comptroller and for his appearance on the application and for giving effect to any order of the court on the application.

[85]

(S 35 repealed by the Patents, Designs and Marks Act 1986, s 3, Sch 3, Pt I.)

36   Co-ownership of patents and applications for patents

(1)   Where a patent is granted to two or more persons, each of them shall, subject to any agreement to the contrary, be entitled to an equal undivided share in the patent.

(2)   Where two or more persons are proprietors of a patent, then, subject to the provisions of this section and subject to any agreement to the contrary—
  (a)   each of them shall be entitled, by himself or his agents, to do in respect of the invention concerned, for his own benefit and without the consent of or the need to account to the other or others, any act which would apart from this subsection and section 55 below, amount to an infringement of the patent concerned; and
  (b)   any such act shall not amount to an infringement of the patent concerned.

(3)   Subject to the provisions of sections 8 and 12 above and section 37 below and to any agreement for the time being in force, where two or more persons are proprietors of a patent one of them shall not without the consent of the other or others grant a licence under the patent or assign or mortgage a share in the patent or in Scotland cause or permit security to be granted over it.

(4)   Subject to the provisions of those sections, where two or more persons are proprietors of a patent, anyone else may supply one of those persons with the means, relating to an essential element of the invention, for putting the invention into effect, and the supply of those means by virtue of this subsection shall not amount to an infringement of the patent.

(5)   Where a patented product is disposed of by any of two or more proprietors to any person, that person and any other person claiming through him shall be entitled to deal with the product in the same way as if it had been disposed of by a sole registered proprietor.

(6)   Nothing in subsection (1) or (2) above shall affect the mutual rights or obligations of trustees or of the personal representatives of a deceased person, or their rights or obligations as such.

(7) The foregoing provisions of this section shall have effect in relation to an application for a patent which is filed as they have effect in relation to a patent and—

(a) references to a patent and a patent being granted shall accordingly include references respectively to any such application and to the application being filed; and

(b) the reference in subsection (5) above to a patented product shall be construed accordingly.

[86]

37 Determination of right to patent after grant

[(1) After a patent has been granted for an invention any person having or claiming a proprietary interest in or under the patent may refer to the comptroller the question—

(a) who is or are the true proprietor or proprietors of the patent,

(b) whether the patent should have been granted to the person or persons to whom it was granted, or

(c) whether any right in or under the patent should be transferred or granted to any other person or persons;

and the comptroller shall determine the question and make such order as he thinks fit to give effect to the determination.]

(2) Without prejudice to the generality of subsection (1) above, an order under that subsection may contain provision—

(a) directing that the person by whom the reference is made under that subsection shall be included (whether or not to the exclusion of any other person) among the persons registered as proprietors of the patent;

(b) directing the registration of a transaction, instrument or event by virtue of which that person has acquired any right in or under the patent;

(c) granting any licence or other right in or under the patent;

(d) directing the proprietor of the patent or any person having any right in or under the patent to do anything specified in the order as necessary to carry out the other provisions of the order.

(3) If any person to whom directions have been given under subsection (2)(d) above fails to do anything necessary for carrying out any such directions within 14 days after the date of the order containing the directions, the comptroller may, on application made to him by any person in whose favour or on whose reference the order containing the directions was made, authorise him to do that thing on behalf of the person to whom the directions were given.

(4) Where the comptroller finds on a reference under [this section] that the patent was granted to a person not entitled to be granted that patent (whether alone or with other persons) and on an application made under section 72 below makes an order on the ground for the conditional or unconditional revocation of the patent, the comptroller may order that the person by whom the application was made or his successor in title may, subject to section 76 below, make a new application for a patent—

(a) in the case of unconditional revocation, for the whole of the matter comprised in the specification of that patent; and

(b) in the case of conditional revocation, for the matter which in the opinion of the comptroller should be excluded from that specification by amendment under section 75 below;

and where such a new application is made, it shall be treated as having been filed on the date of filing the application for the patent to which the reference relates.

(5)   On any such reference no order shall be made under this section transferring the patent to which the reference relates on the ground that the patent was granted to a person not so entitled, and no order shall be made under subsection (4) above on that ground, if the reference was made after the end of the period of two years beginning with the date of the grant, unless it is shown that any person registered as a proprietor of the patent knew at the time of the grant or, as the case may be, of the transfer of the patent to him that he was not entitled to the patent.

(6)   An order under this section shall not be so made as to affect the mutual rights or obligations of trustees or of the personal representatives of a deceased person, or their rights or obligations as such.

(7)   Where a question is referred to the comptroller under [this section] an order shall not be made by virtue of subsection (2) or under subsection (4) above on the reference unless notice of the reference is given to all persons registered as proprietor of the patent or as having a right in or under the patent, except those who are parties to the reference.

(8)   If it appears to the comptroller on a reference under [this section] that the question referred to him would more properly be determined by the court, he may decline to deal with it and, without prejudice to the court's jurisdiction to determine any such question and make a declaration, or any declaratory jurisdiction of the court in Scotland, the court shall have jurisdiction to do so.

(9)   The court shall not in the exercise of any such declaratory jurisdiction determine a question whether a patent was granted to a person not entitled to be granted the patent if the proceedings in which the jurisdiction is invoked were commenced after the end of the period of two years beginning with the date of the grant of the patent, unless it is shown that any person registered as a proprietor of the patent knew at the time of the grant or, as the case may be, of the transfer of the patent to him that he was not entitled to the patent.

                                                              [87]

NOTES

Sub-s (1): substituted by the Copyright, Designs and Patents Act 1988, s 295, Sch 5, para 9(2).

Sub-ss (4), (7), (8): words in square brackets substituted by the Copyright, Designs and Patents Act 1988, s 295, Sch 5, para 9(3).

38   Effect of transfer of patent under s 37

(1)   Where an order is made under section 37 above that a patent shall be transferred from any person or persons (the old proprietor or proprietors) to one or more persons (whether or not including an old proprietor), then, except in a case falling within subsection (2) below, any licences or other rights granted or created by the old proprietor or proprietors shall, subject to section 33 above and to the provisions of the order, continue in force and be treated as granted by the person or persons to whom the patent is ordered to be transferred (the new proprietor or proprietors).

(2)   Where an order is so made that a patent shall be transferred from the old proprietor or proprietors to one or more persons none of whom was an old proprietor (on the ground that the patent was granted to a person not entitled to be granted the patent), any licences or other rights in or under the patent shall, subject

to the provisions of the order and subsection (3) below, lapse on the registration of that person or those persons as the new proprietor or proprietors of the patent.

(3)   Where an order is so made that a patent shall be transferred as mentioned in subsection (2) above or that a person other than an old proprietor may make a new application for a patent and before the reference of the question under that section resulting in the making of any such order is registered, the old proprietor or proprietors or a licensee of the patent, acting in good faith, worked the invention in question in the United Kingdom or made effective and serious preparations to do so, the old proprietor or proprietors or the licensee shall, on making a request to the new proprietor or proprietors within the prescribed period, be entitled to be granted a licence (but not an exclusive licence) to continue working or, as the case may be, to work the invention, so far as it is the subject of the new application.

(4)   Any such licence shall be granted for a reasonable period and on reasonable terms.

(5)   The new proprietor or proprietors of the patent or any person claiming that he is entitled to be granted any such licence may refer to the comptroller the question whether that person is so entitled and whether any such period is or terms are reasonable, and the comptroller shall determine the question and may, if he considers it appropriate, order the grant of such a licence.

[88]

Employees' inventions

39   Right to employees' inventions

(1)   Notwithstanding anything in any rule of law, an invention made by an employee shall, as between him and his employer, be taken to belong to his employer for the purposes of this Act and all other purposes if—

(a)   it was made in the course of the normal duties of the employee or in the course of duties falling outside his normal duties, but specifically assigned to him, and the circumstances in either case were such that an invention might reasonably be expected to result from the carrying out of his duties; or

(b)   the invention was made in the course of the duties of the employee and, at the time of making the invention, because of the nature of his duties and the particular responsibilities arising from the nature of his duties he had a special obligation to further the interests of the employer's undertaking.

(2)   Any other invention made by an employee shall, as between him and his employer, be taken for those purposes to belong to the employee.

[(3)   Where by virtue of this section an invention belongs, as between him and his employer, to an employee, nothing done—

(a)   by or on behalf of the employee or any person claiming under him for the purposes of pursuing an application for a patent, or

(b)   by any person for the purpose of performing or working the invention,

shall be taken to infringe any copyright or design right to which, as between him and his employer, his employer is entitled in any model or document relating to the invention.]

[89]

NOTES
Sub-s (3): added by the Copyright, Designs and Patents Act 1988, s 295, Sch 5, para 11(1).

40   Compensation of employees for certain inventions

(1)   Where it appears to the court or the comptroller on an application made by an employee within the prescribed period that the employee has made an invention belonging to the employer for which a patent has been granted, that the patent is (having regard among other things to the size and nature of the employer's undertaking) of outstanding benefit to the employer and that by reason of those facts it is just that the employee should be awarded compensation to be paid by the employer, the court or the comptroller may award him such compensation of an amount determined under section 41 below.

(2)   Where it appears to the court or the comptroller on an application made by an employee within the prescribed period that—

(a)   a patent has been granted for an invention made by and belonging to the employee;

(b)   his rights in the invention, or in any patent or application for a patent for the invention, have since the appointed day been assigned to the employer or an exclusive licence under the patent or application has since the appointed day been granted to the employer;

(c)   the benefit derived by the employee from the contract of assignment, assignation or grant or any ancillary contract ("the relevant contract") is inadequate in relation to the benefit derived by the employer from the patent; and

(d)   by reason of those facts it is just that the employee should be awarded compensation to be paid by the employer in addition to the benefit derived from the relevant contract;

the court or the comptroller may award him such compensation of an amount determined under section 41 below.

(3)   Subsections (1) and (2) above shall not apply to the invention of an employee where a relevant collective agreement provides for the payment of compensation in respect of inventions of the same description as that invention to employees of the same description as that employee.

(4)   Subsection (2) above shall have effect notwithstanding anything in the relevant contract or any agreement applicable to the invention (other than any such collective agreement).

(5)   If it appears to the comptroller on an application under this section that application involves matters which would more properly be determined by the court, he may decline to deal with it.

(6)   In this section—

"the prescribed period", in relation to proceedings before the court, means the period prescribed by rules of court, and

"relevant collective agreement" means a collective agreement within the meaning of [the Trade Union and Labour Relations (Consolidation) Act 1992], made by or on behalf of a trade union to which the employee belongs, and by the employer or an employers' association to which the employer belongs which is in force at the time of the making of the invention.

(7)   References in this section to an invention belonging to an employer or employee are references to it so belonging as between the employer and the employee.

NOTES
  Sub-s (6): words in square brackets substituted by the Trade Union and Labour Relations (Consolidation) Act 1992, s 300(2), Sch 2, para 9.

41   Amount of compensation

(1)   An award of compensation to an employee under section 41(1) or (2) above in relation to a patent for an invention shall be such as will secure for the employee a fair share (having regard to all the circumstances) of the benefit which the employer has derived, or may reasonably be expected to derive, from the patent or from the assignment, assignation or grant to a person connected with the employer of the property or any right in the invention or the property in, or any right in or under, an application for that patent.

(2)   For the purposes of subsection (1) above the amount of any benefit derived or expected to be derived by an employer from the assignment, assignation or grant of—

  (a)   the property in, or any right in or under, a patent for the invention or an application for such a patent; or

  (b)   the property or any right in the invention;

to a person connected with him shall be taken to be the amount which could reasonably be expected to be so derived by the employer if that person had not been connected with him.

(3)   Where the Crown or a Research Council in its capacity as employer assigns or grants the property in, or any right in or under, an invention, patent or application for a patent to a body having among its functions that of developing or exploiting inventions resulting from public research and does so for no consideration or only a nominal consideration, any benefit derived from the invention, patent or application by that body shall be treated for the purposes of the foregoing provisions of this section as so derived by the Crown or, as the case may be, Research Council.

  In this subsection "Research Council" means a body which is a Research Council for the purposes of the Science and Technology Act 1965.

(4)   In determining the fair share of the benefit to be secured for an employee in respect of a patent for an invention which has always belonged to an employer, the court or the comptroller shall, among other things, take the following matters into account, that is to say—

  (a)   the nature of the employee's duties, his remuneration and the other advantages he derives or has derived from his employment or has derived in relation to the invention under this Act;

  (b)   the effort and skill which the employee has devoted to making the invention;

  (c)   the effort and skill which any other person has devoted to making the invention jointly with the employee concerned, and the advice and other assistance contributed by any other employee who is not a joint inventor of the invention; and

  (d)   the contribution made by the employer to the making, developing and working of the invention by the provision of advice, facilities and other assistance, by the provision of opportunities and by his managerial and commercial skill and activities.

(5)   In determining the fair share of the benefit to be secured for an employee in respect of a patent for an invention which originally belonged to him, the court or the comptroller shall, among other things, take the following matters into account, that is to say—

    (a)   any conditions in a licence or licences granted under this Act or otherwise in respect of the invention or the patent;

    (b)   the extent to which the invention was made jointly by the employee with any other person; and

    (c)   the contribution made by the employer to the making, developing and working of the invention as mentioned in subsection (4)(d) above.

(6)   Any order for the payment of compensation under section 40 above may be an order for the payment of a lump sum or for periodical payment, or both.

(7)   Without prejudice to section 32 of the Interpretation Act 1889 (which provides that a statutory power may in general be exercised from time to time), the refusal of the court or the comptroller to make any such order on an application made by an employee under section 40 above shall not prevent a further application being made under that section by him or any successor in title of his.

(8)   Where the court or the comptroller has made any such order, the court or he may on the application of either the employer or the employee vary or discharge it or suspend any provision of the order and revive any provision so suspended, and section 40(5) above shall apply to the application as it applies to an application under that section.

(9)   In England and Wales any sums awarded by the comptroller under section 40 above shall, if a county court so orders, be recoverable by execution issued from the county court or otherwise as if they were payable under an order of that court.

(10)   In Scotland an order made under section 40 above by the comptroller for the payment of any sums may be enforced in like manner as a recorded decree arbitral.

(11)   In Northern Ireland an order made under section 40 above by the comptroller for the payment of any sums may be enforced as if it were a money judgment.

[91]

42   Enforceability of contracts relating to employees' inventions

(1)   This section applies to any contract (whenever made) relating to inventions made by an employee, being a contract entered into by him—

    (a)   with the employer (alone or with another); or

    (b)   with some other person at the request of the employer or in pursuance of the employee's contract of employment.

(2)   Any term in a contract to which this section applies which diminishes the employee's rights in inventions of any description made by him after the appointed day and the date of the contract, or in or under patents for those inventions or applications for such patents, shall be unenforceable against him to the extent that it diminishes his rights in an invention of that description so made, or in or under a patent for such an invention or an application for any such patent.

(3)   Subsection (2) above shall not be construed as derogating from any duty of confidentiality owed to his employer by an employee by virtue of any rule of law of otherwise.

(4)   This section applies to any arrangement made with a Crown employee by or on behalf of the Crown as his employer as it applies to any contract made between an employee and an employer other than the Crown, and for the purposes of this section "Crown employee" means a person employed under or for the purposes of a government department or any officer or body exercising on behalf of the Crown functions conferred by any enactment [or a person serving in the naval, military or air forces of the Crown].

[92]

NOTES

Sub-s (4): words in square brackets added with retrospective effect by the Armed Forces Act 1981, s 22(1), (2).

43   Supplementary

(1)   Sections 39 to 42 above shall not apply to an invention made before the appointed day.

(2)   Sections 39 to 42 above shall not apply to an invention made by an employee unless at the time he made the invention one of the following conditions was satisfied in his case, that is to say—

(a)   he was mainly employed in the United Kingdom; or

(b)   he was not mainly employed anywhere or his place of employment could not be determined, but his employer had a place of business in the United Kingdom to which the employee was attached, whether or not he was also attached elsewhere.

(3)   In sections 39 to 42 above and this section, except so far as the context otherwise requires, references to the making of an invention by an employee are references to his making it alone or jointly with any other person, but do not include references to his merely contributing advice or other assistance in the making of an invention by another employee.

(4)   Any references [in sections 39 to 42] above to a patent and to a patent being granted are respectively references to a patent or other protection and to its being granted whether under the law of the United Kingdom or the law in force in any other country or under any treaty or international convention.

(5)   For the purposes of sections 40 and 41 above the benefit derived or expected to be derived by an employer from a patent shall, where he dies before any award is made under section 40 above in respect of the patent, include any benefit derived or expected to be derived from the patent by his personal representatives or by any person in whom it was vested by their assent.

(6)   Where an employee dies before an award is made under section 40 above in respect of a patented invention made by him, his personal representatives or their successors in title may exercise his right to make or proceed with an application for compensation under subsection (1) or (2) of that section.

(7)   In sections 40 and 41 above and this section "benefit" means benefit in money or money's worth.

(8)   Section 533 of the Income and Corporation Taxes Act 1970 (definition of connected persons) shall apply for determining for the purposes of section 41(2) above whether one person is connected with another as it applies for determining that question for the purposes of the Tax Acts.

[93]

NOTES

Sub-s (4): words in square brackets substituted by the Copyright, Designs and Patents Act 1988, s 295, Sch 5, para 11(2).

Contracts as to patented products, etc

44   Avoidance of certain restrictive conditions

(1)   Subject to the provisions of this section, any condition or term of a contract for the supply of a patented product or of a licence to work a patented invention, or of a contract relating to any such supply or licence, shall be void in so far as it purports—

   (a)   in the case of a contract for supply, to require the person supplied to acquire from the supplier, or his nominee, or prohibit him from acquiring from any specified person, or from acquiring except from the supplier or his nominee, anything other than the patented product;

   (b)   in the case of a licence to work a patented invention, to require the licensee to acquire from the licensor or his nominee, or prohibit him from acquiring from any specified person, or from acquiring except from the licensor or his nominee, anything other than the product which is the patented invention or (if it is a process) other than any product obtained directly by means of the process or to which the process has been applied;

   (c)   in either case, to prohibit the person supplied or licensee from using articles (whether patented products or not) which are not supplied by, or any patented process which does not belong to, the supplier or licensor, or his nominee, or to restrict the right of the person supplied or licensee to use any such articles or process.

(2)   Subsection (1) above applies to contracts and licences whether made or granted before or after the appointed day, but not to those made or granted before 1st January 1950.

(3)   In proceedings against any person for infringement of a patent it shall be a defence to prove that at the time of the infringement there was in force a contract relating to the patent made by or with the consent of the plaintiff or pursuer or a licence under the patent granted by him or with his consent and containing in either case a condition or term void by virtue of this section.

(4)   A condition or term of a contract or licence shall not be void by virtue of this section if—

   (a)   at the time of the making of the contract or granting of the licence the supplier or licensor was willing to supply the product, or grant a licence to work the invention, as the case may be, to the person supplied or licensee, on reasonable terms specified in the contract or licence and without any such condition or term as is mentioned in subsection (1) above; and

   (b)   the person supplied or licensee is entitled under the contract or licence to relieve himself of his liability to observe the condition or term on giving to the other party three months' notice in writing and subject to payment to that other party of such compensation (being, in the case of a contract to supply, a lump sum or rent for the residue of the term of the contract and, in the case of a licence, a royalty for the residue of the term of the licence) as may be determined by an arbitrator or arbiter appointed by the Secretary of State.

(5)   If in any proceeding it is alleged that any condition or term of a contract or licence is void by virtue of this section it shall lie on the supplier or licensor to prove the matters set out in paragraph (a) of subsection (4) above.

(6)   A condition or term of a contract or licence shall not be void by virtue of this section by reason only that it prohibits any person from selling goods other than those supplied by a specific person or, in the case of a contract for the hiring of or licence to use a patented product, that it reserves to the bailor (or in Scotland, hirer) or licensor, or his nominee, the right to supply such new parts of the patented product as may be required to put or keep it in repair.

[94]

45   Determination of parts of certain contracts

(1)   Any contract for the supply of a patented product or licence to work a patented invention, or contract relating to any such supply or licence, may at any time after the patent or all the patents by which the product or invention was protected at the time of the making of the contract or granting of the licence has or have ceased to be in force, and notwithstanding anything to the contrary in the contract or licence or in any other contract, be determined, to the extent (and only to the extent) that the contract or licence relates to the product or invention, by either party on giving three months' notice in writing to the other party.

(2)   In subsection (1) above "patented product" and "patented invention" include respectively a product and an invention which is the subject of an application for a patent, and that subsection shall apply in relation to a patent by which any such product or invention was protected and which was granted after the time of the making of the contract or granting of the licence in question, on an application which had been filed before that time, as it applies to a patent in force at that time.

(3)   If, on an application under this subsection made by either party to a contract or licence falling within subsection (1) above, the court is satisfied that, in consequence of the patent or patents concerned ceasing to be in force, it would be unjust to require the applicant to continue to comply with all the terms and conditions of the contract or licence, it may make such order varying those terms or conditions as, having regard to all the circumstances of the case, it thinks just as between the parties.

(4)   Without prejudice to any other right of recovery, nothing is subsection (1) above shall be taken to entitle any person to recover property bailed under a hire-purchase agreement (within the meaning of the Consumer Credit Act 1974).

(5)   The foregoing provisions of this section apply to contracts and licences whether made before or after the appointed day.

(6)   The provisions of this section shall be without prejudice to any rule of law relating to the frustration of contracts and any right of determining a contract or licence exercisable apart from this section.

[95]

Licences of right and compulsory licences

46   Patentee's application for entry in register that licences are available as of right

(1)   At any time after the grant of a patent its proprietor may apply to the comptroller for an entry to be made in the register to the effect that licences under the patent are to be available as of right.

(2)   Where such an application is made, the comptroller shall give notice of the application to any person registered as having a right in or under the patent and, if satisfied that the proprietor of the patent is not precluded by contract from granting licences under the patent, shall make that entry.

(3)   Where such an entry is made in respect of a patent—

    (a)   any person shall, at any time after the entry is made, be entitled as of right to a licence under the patent on such terms as may be settled by agreement or, in default of agreement, by the comptroller on the application of the proprietor of the patent or the person requiring the licence;

    (b)   the comptroller may, on the application of the holder of any licence granted under the patent before the entry was made, order the licence to be exchanged for a licence of right on terms so settled;

    (c)   if in proceedings for infringement of the patent (otherwise than by the importation of any article [from a country which is not a member State of the European Economic Community]) the defendant or defender undertakes to take a licence on such terms, no injunction or interdict shall be granted against him and the amount (if any) recoverable against him by way of damages shall not exceed double the amount which would have been payable by him as licensee if such a licence on those terms had been granted before the earliest infringement;

    (d)   the renewal fee payable in respect of the patent after the date of the entry shall be half the fee which would be payable if the entry had not been made.

[(3A)   An undertaking under subsection (3)(c) above may be given at any time before final order in the proceedings, without any admission of liability.]

(4)   The licensee under a licence of right may (unless, in the case of a licence the terms of which are settled by agreement, the licence otherwise expressly provides) request the proprietor of the patent to take proceedings to prevent any infringement of the patent; and if the proprietor refuses or neglects to do so within two months after being so requested, the licensee may institute proceedings for the infringement in his own name as if he were proprietor, making the proprietor a defendant or defender.

(5)   A proprietor so added as defendant or defender shall not be liable for any costs or expenses unless he enters an appearance and takes part in the proceedings.

[96]

NOTES

    Sub-s (3): words in square brackets inserted by the Copyright, Designs and Patents Act 1988, s 295, Sch 5, para 12(2).

    Sub-s (3A): inserted by the Copyright, Designs and Patents Act 1988, s 295, Sch 5, para 12(3).

---

47   Cancellation of entry made under s 46

(1)   At any time after an entry has been made under section 46 above in respect of a patent, the proprietor of the patent may apply to the comptroller for cancellation of the entry.

(2)   Where such an application is made and the balance paid of all renewal fees which would have been payable if the entry had not been made, the comptroller may cancel the entry, if satisfied that there is no existing licence under the patent or that all licensees under the patent consent to the application.

(3)   Within the prescribed period after an entry has been made under section 46 above in respect of a patent, any person who claims that the proprietor of the patent is, and was at the time of the entry, precluded by a contract in which the claimant is interested from granting licences under the patent may apply to the comptroller for cancellation of the entry.

(4)   Where the comptroller is satisfied, on an application under subsection (3) above, that the proprietor of the patent is and was so precluded, he shall cancel the entry; and the proprietor shall then be liable to pay, within a period specified by the comptroller, a sum equal to the balance of all renewal fees which would have been payable if the entry had not been made, and the patent shall cease to have effect at the expiration of that period if that sum is not so paid.

(5)   Where an entry is cancelled under this section, the rights and liabilities of the proprietor of the patent shall afterwards be the same as if the entry had not been made.

(6)   Where an application has been made under this section then—
   (a)   in the case of an application under subsection (1) above, any person, and
   (b)   in the case of an application under subsection (3) above, the proprietor of the patent,

may within the prescribed period give notice to the comptroller of opposition to the cancellation; and the comptroller shall, in considering the application, determine whether the opposition is justified.

[97]

48   Compulsory licences

(1)   At any time after the expiration of three years, or of such other period as may be prescribed, from the date of the grant of a patent, any person may apply to the comptroller on one or more of the grounds specified in subsection (3) below—
   (a)   for a licence under the patent,
   (b)   for an entry to be made in the register to the effect that licences under the patent are to be available as of right, or
   (c)   where the applicant is a government department, for the grant to any person specified in the application of a licence under the patent.

(2)   A rule prescribing any such other period under subsection (1) above shall not be made unless a draft of the rule has been laid before, and approved by resolution of, each House of Parliament.

(3)   The grounds are:—
   (a)   where the patented invention is capable of being commercially worked in the United Kingdom, that it is not being so worked or is not being so worked to the fullest extent that is reasonably practicable;
   (b)   where the patented invention is a product, that a demand for the product in the United Kingdom—
      (i)   is not being met on reasonable terms, or
      (ii) is being met to a substantial extent by importation;
   (c)   where the patented invention is capable of being commercially worked in the United Kingdom, that it is being prevented or hindered from being so worked—
      (i)   where the invention is a product, by the importation of the product,

    (ii) where the invention is a process, by the importation of a product obtained directly by means of the process or to which the process has been applied;

(d) that by reason of the refusal of the proprietor of the patent to grant a licence or licences on reasonable terms—

    (i) a market for the export of any patented product made in the United Kingdom is not being supplied, or

    (ii) the working or efficient working in the United Kingdom of any other patented invention which makes a substantial contribution to the art is prevented or hindered, or

    (iii) the establishment or development of commercial or industrial activities in the United Kingdom is unfairly prejudiced;

(e) that by reason of conditions imposed by the proprietor of the patent on the grant of licences under the patent, or on the disposal or use of the patented product or on the use of the patented process, the manufacture, use or disposal of materials not protected by the patent, or the establishment or development of commercial or industrial activities in the United Kingdom, is unfairly prejudiced.

(4)   Subject to the provisions of subsections (5) to (7) below, if he is satisfied that any of those grounds are established, the comptroller may—

(a) where the application is under subsection (1)(a) above, order the grant of a licence to the applicant on such terms as the comptroller thinks fit;

(b) where the application is under subsection (1)(b) above, make such an entry as is there mentioned;

(c) where the application is under subsection (1)(c) above, order the grant of a licence to the person specified in the application on such terms as comptroller thinks fit.

(5)   Where the application is made on the ground that the patented invention is not being commercially worked in the United Kingdom or is not being so worked to the fullest extent that is reasonably practicable, and it appears to the comptroller that the time which has elapsed since the publication in the journal of a notice of the grant of the patent has for any reason been insufficient to enable the invention to be so worked, he may by order adjourn the application for such period as will in his opinion give sufficient time for the invention to be so worked.

(6)   No entry shall be made in the register under this section on the ground mentioned in subsection (3)(d)(i) above, and any licence granted under this section on that ground shall contain such provisions as appear to the comptroller to be expedient for restricting the countries in which any product concerned may be disposed of or used by the licensee.

(7)   No order or entry shall be made under this section in respect of a patent (the patent concerned) on the ground mentioned in subsection (3)(d)(ii) above unless the comptroller is satisfied that the proprietor of the patent for the other invention is able and willing to grant to the proprietor of the patent concerned and his licensees a licence under the patent for the other invention on reasonable terms.

(8)   An application may be made under this section in respect of a patent notwithstanding that the applicant is already the holder of a licence under the patent; and no person shall be estopped or barred from alleging any of the matters specified in subsection (3) above by reason of any admission made by him, whether in such a licence or otherwise, or by reason of his having accepted a licence.

49 Provisions about licences under s 48

(1) Where the comptroller is satisfied, on an application made under section 48 above in respect of a patent, that the manufacture, use or disposal of materials not protected by the patent is unfairly prejudiced by reason of conditions imposed by the proprietor of the patent on the grant of licences under the patent, or on the disposal or use of the patented product or the use of the patented process, he may (subject to the provisions of that section) order the grant of licences under the patent to such customers of the applicant as he thinks fit as well as to the applicant.

(2) Where an application under section 48 above is made in respect of a patent by a person who holds a licence under the patent, the comptroller—
  (a) may, if he orders the grant of a licence to the applicant, order the existing licence to be cancelled, or
  (b) may, instead of ordering the grant of a licence to the applicant, order the existing licence to be amended.

(3) *(Repealed by the Copyright, Designs and Patents Act 1988, ss 295, 303(2), Sch 5, para 13, Sch 8.)*

(4) Section 46(4) and (5) above shall apply to a licence granted in pursuance of an order under section 48 above and to a licence granted by virtue of an entry under that section as it applies to a licence granted by virtue of an entry under section 46 above.

[99]

50 Exercise of powers on applications under s 48

(1) The powers of the comptroller on an application under section 48 above in respect of a patent shall be exercised with a view to securing the following general purposes:—
  (a) that inventions which can be worked on a commercial scale in the United Kingdom and which should in the public interest be so worked shall be worked there without undue delay and to the fullest extent that is reasonably practicable;
  (b) that the inventor or other person beneficially entitled to a patent shall receive reasonable remuneration having regard to the nature of the invention;
  (c) that the interests of any person for the time being working or developing an invention in the United Kingdom under the protection of a patent shall not be unfairly prejudiced.

(2) Subject to subsection (1) above, the comptroller shall, in determining whether to make an order or entry in pursuance of such an application, take account of the following matters, that is to say—
  (a) the nature of the invention, the time which has elapsed since the publication in the journal of a notice of the grant of the patent and the measures already taken by the proprietor of the patent or any licensee to make full use of the invention;
  (b) the ability of any person to whom a licence would be granted under the order concerned to work the invention to the public advantage; and
  (c) the risks to be undertaken by that person in providing capital and working the invention if the application for an order is granted,

but shall not be required to take account of matters subsequent to the making of the application.

[100]

[51 Powers exercisable in consequence of report of Monopolies and Mergers Commission

(1)   Where a report of the Monopolies and Mergers Commission has been laid before Parliament containing conclusions to the effect—

  (a) on a monopoly reference, that a monopoly situation exists and facts found by the Commission operate or may be expected to operate against the public interest,

  (b) on a merger reference, that a merger situation qualifying for investigation has been created and the creation of the situation, or particular elements in or consequences of it specified in the report, operate or may be expected to operate against the public interest,

  (c) on a competition reference, that a person was engaged in an anti-competitive practice which operated or may be expected to operate against the public interest, or

  (d) on a reference under section 11 of the Competition Act 1980 (reference of public bodies and certain other persons), that a person is pursuing a course of conduct which operates against the public interest,

the appropriate Minister or Ministers may apply to the comptroller to take action under this section.

(2)   Before making an application the appropriate Minister or Ministers shall publish, in such manner as he or they think appropriate, a notice describing the nature of the proposed application and shall consider any representations which may be made within 30 days of such publication by persons whose interests appear to him or them to be affected.

(3)   If on an application under this section it appears to the comptroller that the matters specified in the Commission's report as being those which in the Commission's opinion operate, or operated or may be expected to operate, against the public interest include—

  (a) conditions in licences granted under a patent by its proprietor restricting the use of the invention by the licensee or the right of the proprietor to grant other licences, or

  (b) a refusal by the proprietor of a patent to grant licences on reasonable terms

he may by order cancel or modify any such condition or may, instead or in addition, make an entry in the register to the effect that licences under the patent are to be available as of right.

(4)   In this section "the appropriate Minister or Ministers" means the Minister or Ministers to whom the report of the Commission was made.]

[101]

NOTES
Substituted by the Copyright, Designs and Patents Act 1988, s 295, Sch 5, para 14.

52   Opposition, appeal and arbitration

(1)   The proprietor of the patent concerned or any other person wishing to oppose an application under sections 48 to 51 above may, in accordance with rules, give to the comptroller notice of opposition; and the comptroller shall consider the opposition in deciding whether to grant the application.

(2)   Where an appeal is brought from an order made by the comptroller in pursuance of an application under sections 48 to 51 above or from a decision of his to

make an entry in the register in pursuance of such an application or from a refusal of his to make such an order or entry, the Attorney General, Lord Advocate or Attorney General for Northern Ireland, or such other counsel as any of them may appoint, shall be entitled to appear and be heard.

(3) Where an application under sections 48 to 51 above is opposed under subsection (1) above, and either—

(a) the parties consent, or

(b) the proceedings require a prolonged examination of documents or any scientific or local investigation which cannot in the opinion of the comptroller conveniently be made before him,

the comptroller may at any time order the whole proceedings, or any question or issue of fact arising in them, to be referred to an arbitrator or arbiter agreed on by the parties or, in default of agreement, appointed by the comptroller.

(4) Where the whole proceedings are so referred, section 21 of the Arbitration Act 1950 or, as the case may be, section 22 of the Arbitration Act (Northern Ireland) 1937 (statement of cases by arbitrators) shall not apply to the arbitration; but unless the parties otherwise agree before the award of the arbitrator or arbiter is made an appeal shall lie from the award to the court.

(5) Where a question or issue of fact is so referred, the arbitrator or arbiter shall report his findings to the comptroller.

[102]

53 Compulsory licences; supplementary provisions

(1) Without prejudice to section 86 below (by virtue of which the Community Patent Convention has effect in the United Kingdom), sections 48 to 51 above shall have effect subject to any provision of that convention relating to the grant of compulsory licences for lack or insufficiency of exploitation as that provision applies by virtue of that section.

(2) In any proceedings on an [application made under section 48 above in respect of a patent], any statement with respect to any activity in relation to the patented invention, or with respect to the grant or refusal of licences under the patent, contained in a report of the Monopolies and Mergers Commission laid before Parliament under Part VII of the Fair Trading Act 1973 [or section 17 of the Competition Act 1980] shall be prima facie evidence of the matters stated, and in Scotland shall be sufficient evidence of those matters.

(3) The comptroller may make an entry in the register under sections 48 to 51 above notwithstanding any contract which would have precluded the entry on the application of the proprietor of the patent under section 46 above.

(4) An entry made in the register under sections 48 to 51 above shall for all purposes have the same effect as an entry made under section 46 above.

(5) No order or entry shall be made in pursuance of an application under sections 48 to 51 above which would be at variance with any treaty or international convention to which the United Kingdom is a party.

[103]

NOTES

Commencement: 1 June 1978 (sub-ss (2)–(5)); to be appointed (sub-s (1)); (SI 1978/586).

Sub-s (2): first words in square brackets substituted and second words in square brackets inserted by the Copyright, Designs and Patents Act 1988, s 295, Sch 5, para 15.

54   Special provisions where patented invention is being worked abroad

(1)   Her Majesty may by Order in Council provide that the comptroller may not (otherwise than for purposes of the public interest) make an order or entry in respect of a patent in pursuance of an application under sections 48 to 51 above if the invention concerned is being commercially worked in any relevant country specified in the Order and demand in the United Kingdom for any patented product resulting from that working is being met by importation from that country.

(2)   In subsection (1) above "relevant country" means a country other than a member state whose law in the opinion of Her Majesty in Council incorporates or will incorporate provisions treating the working of an invention in, and importation from, the United Kingdom in a similar way to that in which the Order in Council would (if made) treat the working of an invention in, and importation from, that country.

[104]

Use of patented inventions for services of the Crown

55   Use of patented inventions for services of the Crown

(1)   Notwithstanding anything in this Act, any government department and any person authorised in writing by a government department may, for the services of the Crown and in accordance with this section, do any of the following acts in the United Kingdom in relation to a patented invention without the consent of the proprietor of the patent, that is to say—
  (a)   where the invention is a product, may—
      (i)   make, use, import or keep the product, or sell or offer to sell it where to do so would be incidental or ancillary to making, using, importing or keeping it; or
      (ii) in any event, sell or offer to sell it for foreign defence purposes or for the production or supply of specified drugs and medicines, or dispose or offer to dispose of it (otherwise than by selling it) for any purpose whatever;
  (b)   where the invention is a process, may use it or do in relation to any product obtained directly by means of the process anything mentioned in paragraph (a) above;
  (c)   without prejudice to the foregoing, where the invention or any product obtained directly by means of the invention is a specified drug or medicine, may sell or offer to sell the drug or medicine;
  (d)   may supply or offer to supply to any person any of the means, relating to an essential element of the invention, for putting the invention into effect;
  (e)   may dispose or offer to dispose of anything which was made, used, imported or kept in the exercise of the powers conferred by this section and which is no longer required for the purpose for which it was made, used, imported or kept (as the case may be),

and anything done by virtue of this subsection shall not amount to an infringement of the patent concerned.

(2)   Any act done in relation to an invention by virtue of this section is in the following provisions of this section referred to as use of the invention; and "use", in relation to an invention, in sections 56 to 58 below shall be construed accordingly.

(3) So far as the invention has before its priority date been duly recorded by or tried by or on behalf of a government department or the United Kingdom Atomic Energy Authority otherwise than in consequence of a relevant communication made in confidence, any use of the invention by virtue of this section may be made free of any royalty or other payment to the proprietor.

(4) So far as the invention has not been so recorded or tried, any use of it made by virtue of this section at any time either—

(a) after the publication of the application for the patent for the invention; or

(b) without prejudice to paragraph (a) above, in consequence of a relevant communication made after the priority date of the invention otherwise than in confidence;

shall be made on such terms as may be agreed either before or after the use by the government department and the proprietor of the patent with the approval of the Treasury or as may in default of agreement be determined by the court on a reference under section 58 below.

(5) Where an invention is used by virtue of this section at any time after publication of an application for a patent for the invention but before such a patent is granted, and the terms for its use agreed or determined as mentioned in subsection (4) above include terms as to payment for the use, then (notwithstanding anything in those terms) any such payment shall be recoverable only—

(a) after such a patent is granted; and

(b) if (apart from this section) the use would, if the patent had been granted on the date of the publication of the application, have infringed not only the patent but also the claims (as interpreted by the description and any drawings referred to in the description or claims) in the form in which they were contained in the application immediately before the preparations for its publication were completed by the Patent Office.

(6) The authority of a government department in respect of an invention may be given under this section either before or after the patent is granted and either before or after the use in respect of which the authority is given is made, and may be given to any person whether or not he is authorised directly or indirectly by the proprietor of the patent to do anything in relation to the invention.

(7) Where any use of an invention is made by or with the authority of a government department under this section, then, unless it appears to the department that it would be contrary to the public interest to do so, the department shall notify the proprietor of the patent as soon as practicable after the second of the following events, that is to say, the use is begun and the patent is granted, and furnish him with such information as to the extent of the use as he may from time to time require.

(8) A person acquiring anything disposed of in the exercise of powers conferred by this section, and any person claiming through him, may deal with it in the same manner as if the patent were held on behalf of the Crown.

(9) In this section "relevant communication", in relation to an invention, means a communication of the invention directly or indirectly by the proprietor of the patent or any person from whom he derives title.

(10) Subsection (4) above is without prejudice to any rule of law relating to the confidentiality of information.

(11) In the application of this section to Northern Ireland, the reference in subsection (4) above to the Treasury shall, where the government department referred to in that subsection is a department of the Government of Northern Ireland, be construed as a reference to the Department of Finance for Northern Ireland.

[105]

56   Interpretation, etc, of provisions about Crown use

(1)   Any reference in section 55 above to a patented invention, in relation to any time, is a reference to an invention for which a patent has before that time been, or is subsequently, granted.

(2)   In this Act, except so far as the context otherwise requires, "the services of the Crown" includes—
- (a)   the supply of anything for foreign defence purposes;
- (b)   the production or supply of specified drugs and medicines; and
- (c)   such purposes relating to the production or use of atomic energy or research into matters connected therewith as the Secretary of State thinks necessary or expedient;

and "use for the services of the Crown" shall be construed accordingly.

(3)   In section 55(1)(a) above and subsection (2)(a) above, references to a sale or supply of anything for foreign defence purposes are references to a sale or supply of the thing—
- (a)   to the government of any country outside the United Kingdom, in pursuance of an agreement or arrangement between Her Majesty's Government in the United Kingdom and the government of that country, where the thing is required for the defence of that country or of any other country whose government is party to any agreement or arrangement with Her Majesty's Government in respect of defence matters; or
- (b)   to the United Nations, or to the government of any country belonging to that organisation, in pursuance of an agreement or arrangement between Her Majesty's Government and that organisation or government, where the thing is required for any armed forces operating in pursuance of a resolution of that organisation or any organ of that organisation.

(4)   For the purposes of section 55(1)(a) and (c) above and subsection (2)(b) above, specified drugs and medicines are drugs and medicines which are both—
- (a)   required for the provision of pharmaceutical services, general medical services or general dental services, that is to say, services of those respective kinds under Part II of the National Health Service Act 1977, [Part II of the National Health Service (Scotland) Act 1978] or the corresponding provisions of the law in force in Northern Ireland or the Isle of Man, and
- (b)   specified for the purposes of this subsection in regulations made by the Secretary of State.

[106]

NOTES

    Sub-s (4): words in square brackets substituted by the National Health Service (Scotland) Act 1978, Sch 16, para 45.

57   Rights of third parties in respect of Crown use

(1)   In relation to—

(a)   any use made for the services of the Crown of an invention by a government department, or a person authorised by a government department, by virtue of section 55 above, or

(b)   anything done for the services of the Crown to the order of a government department by the proprietor of a patent in respect of a patented invention or by the proprietor of an application in respect of an invention for which an application for a patent has been filed and is still pending,

the provisions of any licence, assignment, assignation or agreement to which this subsection applies shall be of no effect so far as those provisions restrict or regulate the working of the invention, or the use of any model, document or information relating to it, or provide for the making of payments in respect of, or calculated by reference to, such working or use; and the reproduction or publication of any model or document in connection with the said working or use shall not be deemed to be an infringement of any copyright [or design right] subsisting in the model or document.

(2)   Subsection (1) above applies to a licence, assignment, assignation or agreement which is made, whether before or after the appointed day, between (on the one hand) any person who is a proprietor of or an applicant for the patent, or anyone who derives title from any such person or from whom such person derives title, and (on the other hand) any person whatever other than a government department.

(3)   Where an exclusive licence granted otherwise than for royalties or other benefits determined by reference to the working of the invention is in force under the patent or application concerned, then—

(a)   in relation to anything done in respect of the invention which, but for the provisions of this section and section 55 above, would constitute an infringement of the rights of the licensee, subsection (4) of that section shall have effect as if for the reference to the proprietor of the patent there were substituted a reference to the licensee; and

(b)   in relation to anything done in respect of the invention by the licensee by virtue of an authority given under that section, that section shall have effect as if the said subsection (4) were omitted.

(4)   Subject to the provisions of subsection (3) above, where the patent, or the right to the grant of the patent, has been assigned to the proprietor of the patent or application in consideration of royalties or other benefits determined by reference to the working of the invention, then—

(a)   in relation to any use of the invention by virtue of section 55 above, subsection (4) of that section shall have effect as if the reference to the proprietor of the patent included a reference to the assignor, and any sum payable by virtue of that subsection shall be divided between the proprietor of the patent or application and the assignor in such proportion as may be agreed on by them or as may in default of agreement be determined by the court on a reference under section 58 below; and

(b)   in relation to any act done in respect of the invention for the services of the Crown by the proprietor of the patent or application to the order of a government department, section 55(4) above shall have effect as if that act were use made by virtue of an authority given under that section.

(5)   Where section 55(4) above applies to any use of an invention and a person holds an exclusive licence under the patent or application concerned (other than such a

licence as is mentioned in subsection (3) above) authorising him to work the invention, then subsections (7) and (8) below shall apply.

(6)   In those subsections "the section 55(4)" payment means such payment (if any) as the proprietor of the patent or application and the department agree under section 55 above, or the court determines under section 58 below, should be made by the department to the proprietor in respect of the use of the invention.

(7)   The licensee shall be entitled to recover from the proprietor of the patent or application such part (if any) of the section 55(4) payment as may be agreed on by them or as may in default of agreement be determined by the court under section 58 below to be just having regard to any expenditure incurred by the licensee—
(a)   in developing the invention, or
(b)   in making payments to the proprietor in consideration of the licence, other than royalties or other payments determined by reference to the use of the invention.

(8)   Any agreement by the proprietor of the patent or application and the department under section 55(4) above as to the amount of the section 55(4) payment shall be of no effect unless the licensee consents to the agreement; and any determination by the court under section 55(4) above as to the amount of that payment shall be of no effect unless the licensee has been informed of the reference to the court and is given an opportunity to be heard.

(9)   Where any models, documents or information relating to an invention are used in connection with any use of the invention which falls within subsection (1)(a) above, or with anything done in respect of the invention which falls within subsection (1)(b) above, subsection (4) of section 55 above shall (whether or not it applies to any such use of the invention) apply to the use of the models, documents or information as if for the reference in it to the proprietor of the patent there were substituted a reference to the person entitled to the benefit of any provision of an agreement which is rendered inoperative by this section in relation to that use; and in section 58 below the references to terms for the use of an invention shall be construed accordingly.

(10)   Nothing in this section shall be construed as authorising the disclosure to a government department or any other person of any model, document or information to the use of which this section applies in contravention of any such licence, assignment, assignation or agreement as is mentioned in this section.

[107]

NOTES
      Sub-s (1): words in square brackets added by the Copyright, Designs and Patents Act 1988, s 303(1), Sch 7, para 20.

[57A   Compensation for loss of profit

(1)   Where use is made of an invention for the services of the Crown, the government department concerned shall pay—
(a)   to the proprietor of the patent, or
(b)   if there is an exclusive licence in force in respect of the patent, to the exclusive licensee,

compensation for any loss resulting from his not being awarded a contract to supply the patented product or, as the case may be, to perform the patented process or supply a thing made by means of the patented process.

(2) Compensation is payable only to the extent that such a contract could have been fulfilled from his existing manufacturing or other capacity; but is payable notwithstanding the existence of circumstances rendering him ineligible for the award of such a contract.

(3) In determining the loss, regard shall be had to the profit which would have been made on such a contract and to the extent to which any manufacturing or other capacity was under-used.

(4) No compensation is payable in respect of any failure to secure contracts to supply the patented product or, as the case may be, to perform the patented process or supply a thing made by means of the patented process, otherwise than for the services of the Crown.

(5) The amount payable shall, if not agreed between the proprietor or licensee and the government department concerned with the approval of the Treasury, be determined by the court on a reference under section 58, and is in addition to any amount payable under section 55 or 57.

(6) In this section "the government department concerned", in relation to any use of an invention for the services of the Crown, means the government department by whom or on whose authority the use was made.

(7) In the application of this section to Northern Ireland, the reference in subsection (5) above to the Treasury shall, where the government department concerned is a department of the Government of Northern Ireland, be construed as a reference to the Department of Finance and Personnel.]

                                                                            [108]

_____

NOTES
Inserted with savings by the Copyright, Designs and Patents Act 1988, s 295, Sch 5, para 16(1), (4).

_____

58   References of disputes as to Crown use

[(1) Any dispute as to—
  (a) the exercise by a government department, or a person authorised by a government department, of the powers conferred by section 55 above,
  (b) terms for the use of an invention for the services of the Crown under that section,
  (c) the right of any person to receive any part of a payment made in pursuance of subsection (4) of that section, or
  (d) the right of any person to receive a payment under section 57A,

may be referred to the court by either party to the dispute after a patent has been granted for the invention.]

(2) If in such proceedings any question arises whether an invention has been recorded or tried as mentioned in section 55 above, and the disclosure of any document recording the invention, or of any evidence of the trial thereof, would in the opinion of the department be prejudicial to the public interest, the disclosure may be made confidentially to counsel for the other party or to an independent expert mutually agreed upon.

(3) In determining under this section any dispute between a government department and any person as to the terms for the use of an invention for the services of the Crown, the court shall have regard—
  (a) to any benefit or compensation which that person or any person from whom he derives title may have received or may be entitled to receive

directly or indirectly from any government department in respect of the invention in question;

(b) to whether that person or any person from whom he derives title has in the court's opinion without reasonable cause failed to comply with a request of the department to use the invention for the services of the Crown on reasonable terms.

(4) In determining whether or not to grant any relief [under subsection (1)(a), (b) or (c) above] and the nature and extent of the relief granted the court shall, subject to the following provisions of this section, apply the principles applied by the court immediately before the appointed day to the granting of relief under section 48 of the 1949 Act.

(5) On a reference under this section the court may refuse to grant relief by way of compensation in respect of the use of an invention for the services of the Crown during any further period specified under section 25(4) above, but before the payment of the renewal fee and any additional fee prescribed for the purposes of that section.

(6) Where an amendment of the specification of a patent has been allowed under any of the provisions of this Act, the court shall not grant relief by way of compensation under this section in respect of any such use before the decision to allow the amendment unless the court is satisfied that the specification of the patent as published was framed in good faith and with reasonable skill and knowledge.

(7) If the validity of a patent is put in issue in proceedings under this section and it is found that the patent is only partially valid, the court may, subject to subsection (8) below, grant relief to the proprietor of the patent in respect of that part of the patent which is found to be valid and to have been used for the services of the Crown.

(8) Where in any such proceedings it is found that a patent is only partially valid, the court shall not grant relief by way of compensation, costs or expenses except where the proprietor of the patent proves that the specification of the patent was framed in good faith and with reasonable skill and knowledge, and in that event the court may grant relief in respect of that part of the patent which is valid and has been so used, subject to the discretion of the court as to costs and expenses and as to the date from which compensation should be awarded.

(9) As a condition of any such relief the court may direct that the specification of the patent shall be amended to its satisfaction upon an application made for that purpose under section 75 below, and an application may be so made accordingly, whether or not all other issues in the proceedings have been determined.

(10) In considering the amount of any compensation for the use of an invention for the services of the Crown after publication of an application for a patent for the invention and before such a patent is granted, the court shall consider whether or not it would have been reasonable to expect, from a consideration of the application as published under section 16 above, that a patent would be granted conferring on the proprietor of the patent protection for an act of the same description as that found to constitute that use, and if the court finds that it would not have been reasonable, it shall reduce the compensation to such amount as it thinks just.

(11) Where by virtue of a transaction, instrument or event to which section 33 above applies a person becomes the proprietor or one of the proprietors or an exclusive licensee of a patent (the new proprietor or licensee) and a government

department or a person authorised by a government department subsequently makes use under section 55 above of the patented invention, the new proprietor or licensee shall not be entitled to any compensation under section 55(4) above (as it stands or as modified by section 57(3) above)[, or to any compensation under section 57A above,] in respect of a subsequent use of the invention before the transaction, instrument or event is registered unless—

    (a)   the transaction, instrument or event is registered within the period of six months beginning with its date; or

    (b)   the court is satisfied that it was not practicable to register the transaction, instrument or event before the end of that period and that it was registered as soon as practicable thereafter.

(12) In any proceedings under this section the court may at any time order the whole proceedings or any question or issue of fact arising in them to be referred, on such terms as the court may direct, to a Circuit judge discharging the functions of an official referee or an arbitrator in England and Wales or Northern Ireland, or to an arbiter in Scotland; and references to the court in the foregoing provisions of this section shall be construed accordingly.

(13) One of two or more joint proprietors of a patent or application for a patent may without the concurrence of the others refer a dispute to the court under this section, but shall not do so unless the others are made parties to the proceedings; but any of the others made a defendant or defender shall not be liable for any costs or expenses unless he enters an appearance and takes part in the proceedings.

[109]

NOTES

Sub-s (1): substituted with savings by the Copyright, Designs and Patents Act 1988, s 295, Sch 5, para 16(2), (4).

Sub-s (4): words in square brackets substituted with savings by the Copyright, Designs and Patents Act 1988, s 295, Sch 5, para 16(2), (4).

Sub-s (11): words in square brackets inserted with savings by the Copyright, Designs and Patents Act 1988, s 295, Sch 5, para 16(3), (4).

59   Special provisions as to Crown use during emergency

(1)   During any period of emergency within the meaning of this section the powers exercisable in relation to an invention by a government department or a person authorised by a government department under section 55 above shall include power to use the invention for any purpose which appears to the department necessary or expedient—

    (a)   for the efficient prosecution of any war in which Her Majesty may be engaged;

    (b)   for the maintenance of supplies and services essential to the life of the community;

    (c)   for securing a sufficiency of supplies and services essential to the well-being of the community;

    (d)   for promoting the productivity of industry, commerce and agriculture;

    (e)   for fostering and directing exports and reducing imports, or imports of any classes, from all or any countries and for redressing the balance of trade;

    (f)   generally for ensuring that the whole resources of the community are available for use, and are used, in a manner best calculated to serve the interests of the community; or

(g) for assisting the relief of suffering and the restoration and distribution of essential supplies and services in any country or territory outside the United Kingdom which is in grave distress as the result of war;

and any reference in this Act to the services of the Crown shall, as respects any period of emergency, include a reference to those purposes.

(2) In this section the use of an invention includes, in addition to any act constituting such use by virtue of section 55 above, any act which would, apart from that section and this section, amount to an infringement of the patent concerned or, as the case may be, give rise to a right under section 69 below to bring proceedings in respect of the application concerned, and any reference in this Act to "use for the services of the Crown" shall, as respects any period of emergency, be construed accordingly.

(3) In this section "period of emergency" means any period beginning with such date as may be declared by Order in Council to be the commencement, and ending with such date as may be so declared to be the termination, of a period of emergency for the purposes of this section.

(4) A draft of an Order under this section shall not be submitted to Her Majesty unless it has been laid before, and approved by resolution of, each House of Parliament.

[110]

Infringement

60 Meaning of infringement

(1) Subject to the provisions of this section, a person infringes a patent for an invention if, but only if, while the patent is in force, he does any of the following things in the United Kingdom in relation to the invention without the consent of the proprietor of the patent, that is to say—
  (a) where the invention is a product, he makes, disposes of, offers to dispose of, uses or imports the product or keeps it whether for disposal of otherwise;
  (b) where the invention is a process, he uses the process or he offers it for use in the United Kingdom when he knows, or it is obvious to a reasonable person in the circumstances, that its use there without the consent of the proprietor would be an infringement of the patent;
  (c) where the invention is a process, he disposes of, offers to dispose of, uses or imports any product obtained directly by means of that process or keeps any such product whether for disposal or otherwise.

(2) Subject to the following provisions of this section, a person (other than the proprietor of the patent) also infringes a patent for an invention if, while the patent is in force and without the consent of the proprietor, he supplies or offers to supply in the United Kingdom a person other than a licensee or other person entitled to work the invention with any of the means, relating to an essential element of the invention, for putting the invention into effect when he knows, or it is obvious to a reasonable person in the circumstances, that those means are suitable for putting, and are intended to put, the invention into effect in the United Kingdom.

(3) Subsection (2) above shall not apply to the supply or offer of a staple commercial product unless the supply or the offer is made for the purpose of

inducing the person supplied or, as the case may be, the person to whom the offer is made to do an act which constitutes an infringement of the patent by virtue of subsection (1) above.

(4)   Without prejudice to section 86 below, subsections (1) and (2) above shall not apply to any act which, under any provision of the Community Patent Convention relating to the exhaustion of the rights of the proprietor of a patent, as that provision applies by virtue of that section, cannot be prevented by the proprietor of the patent.

(5)   An act which, apart from this subsection, would constitute an infringement of a patent for an invention shall not do so if—

    (a)   it is done privately and for purposes which are not commercial;

    (b)   it is done for experimental purposes relating to the subject-matter of the invention;

    (c)   it consists of the extemporaneous preparation in a pharmacy of a medicine for an individual in accordance with a prescription given by a registered medical or dental practitioner or consists of dealing with a medicine so prepared;

    (d)   it consists of the use, exclusively for the needs of a relevant ship, of a product or process in the body of such a ship or in its machinery, tackle, apparatus or other accessories, in a case where the ship has temporarily or accidentally entered the internal or territorial waters of the United Kingdom;

    (e)   it consists of the use of a product or process in the body or operation of a relevant aircraft, hovercraft or vehicle which has temporarily or accidentally entered or is crossing the United Kingdom (including the air space above it and its territorial waters) or the use of accessories for such a relevant aircraft, hovercraft or vehicle;

    (f)   it consists of the use of an exempted aircraft which has lawfully entered or is lawfully crossing the United Kingdom as aforesaid or of the importation into the United Kingdom, or the use or storage there, of any part or accessory for such an aircraft.

(6)   For the purposes of subsection (2) above a person who does an act in relation to an invention which is prevented only by virtue of paragraph (a), (b) or (c) of subsection (5) above from constituting an infringement of a patent for the invention shall not be treated as a person entitled to work the invention, but—

    (a)   the reference in that subsection to a person entitled to work an invention includes a reference to a person so entitled by virtue of section 55 above, and

    (b)   a person who by virtue of [section 28A(4) or (5)] above or section 64 below is entitled to do an act in relation to the invention without it constituting such an infringement shall, so far as concerns that act, be treated as a person entitled to work the invention.

(7)   In this section—

    "relevant ship" and "relevant aircraft, hovercraft or vehicle" mean respectively a ship and an aircraft, hovercraft or vehicle registered in, or belonging to, any country, other than the United Kingdom, which is a party to the Convention for the Protection of Industrial Property signed at Paris on 20th March 1883; and

    "exempted aircraft" means an aircraft to which [section 89 of the Civil Aviation Act 1982] (aircraft exempted from seizure in respect of patent claims) applies.

[111]

NOTES

Commencement: 1 June 1978 (sub-ss (1)–(3), (5)–(7)); to be appointed (remainder).

Sub-s (6): in para (b) words in square brackets substituted by the Copyright, Designs and Patents Act 1988, s 295, Sch 5, para 8(a).

Sub-s (7): words in square brackets substituted by the Civil Aviation Act 1982, s 109, Sch 15.

61   Proceedings for infringement of patent

(1) Subject to the following provisions of this Part of this Act, civil proceedings may be brought in the court by the proprietor of a patent in respect of any act alleged to infringe the patent and (without prejudice to any other jurisdiction of the court) in those proceedings a claim may be made—

    (a) for an injunction or interdict restraining the defendant or defender from any apprehended act of infringement;

    (b) for an order for him to deliver up or destroy any patented product in relation to which the patent is infringed or any article in which that product is inextricably comprised;

    (c) for damages in respect of the infringement;

    (d) for an account of the profits derived by him from the infringement;

    (e) for a declaration or declarator that the patent is valid and has been infringed by him.

(2) The court shall not, in respect of the same infringement, both award the proprietor of a patent damages and order that he shall be given an account of the profits.

(3) The proprietor of a patent and any other person may by agreement with each other refer to the comptroller the question whether that other person has infringed the patent and on the reference the proprietor of the patent may make any claim mentioned in subsection (1)(c) or (e) above.

(4) Except so far as the context requires, in the following provisions of this Act—

    (a) any reference to proceedings for infringement and the bringing of such proceedings includes a reference to a reference under subsection (3) above and the making of such a reference;

    (b) any reference to a plaintiff or pursuer includes a reference to the proprietor of the patent; and

    (c) any reference to a defendant or defender includes a reference to any other party to the reference.

(5) If it appears to the comptroller on a reference under subsection (3) above that the question referred to him would more properly be determined by the court, he may decline to deal with it and the court shall have jurisdiction to determine the question as if the reference were proceedings brought in the court.

(6) Subject to the following provisions of this Part of this Act, in determining whether or not to grant any kind of relief claimed under this section and the extent of the relief granted the court or the comptroller shall apply the principles applied by the court in relation to that kind of relief immediately before the appointed day.

[112]

62   Restrictions on recovery of damages for infringement

(1) In proceedings for infringement of a patent damages shall not be awarded, and no order shall be made for an account of profits, against a defendant or defender who

proves that at the date of the infringement he was not aware, and had no reasonable grounds for supposing, that the patent existed; and a person shall not be taken to have been so aware or to have had reasonable grounds for so supposing by reason only of the application to a product of the word "patent" or "patented", or any word or words expressing or implying that a patent has been obtained for the product, unless the number of the patent accompanied the word or words in question.

(2)   In proceedings for infringement of a patent the court or the comptroller may, if it or he thinks fit, refuse to award any damages or make any such order in respect of an infringement committed during any further period specified under section 25(4) above, but before the payment of the renewal fee and any additional fee prescribed for the purposes of that subsection.

(3)   Where an amendment of the specification of a patent has been allowed under any of the provisions of this Act, no damages shall be awarded in proceedings for an infringement of the patent committed before the decision to allow the amendment unless the court or the comptroller is satisfied that the specification of the patent as published was framed in good faith and with reasonable skill and knowledge.

[113]

63   Relief for infringement of partially valid patent

(1)   If the validity of a patent is put in issue in proceedings for infringement of the patent and it is found that the patent is only partially valid, the court or the comptroller may, subject to subsection (2) below, grant relief in respect of that part of the patent which is found to be valid and infringed.

(2)   Where in any such proceedings it is found that a patent is only partially valid, the court or the comptroller shall not grant relief by way of damages, costs or expenses, except where the plaintiff or pursuer proves that the specification for the patent was framed in good faith and with reasonable skill and knowledge, and in that event the court or the comptroller may grant relief in respect of that part of the patent which is valid and infringed, subject to the discretion of the court or the comptroller as to costs or expenses and as to the date from which damages should be reckoned.

(3)   As a condition of relief under this section the court or the comptroller may direct that the specification of the patent shall be amended to its or his satisfaction upon an application made for that purpose under section 75 below, and an application may be so made accordingly, whether or not all other issues in the proceedings have been determined.

[114]

[64   Right to continue use begun before priority date

(1)   Where a patent is granted for an invention, a person who in the United Kingdom before the priority date of the invention—

   (a)   does in good faith an act which would constitute an infringement of the patent if it were in force, or

   (b)   makes in good faith effective and serious preparations to do such an act,

has the right to continue to do the act or, as the case may be, to do the act, notwithstanding the grant of the patent; but this right does not extend to granting a licence to another person to do the act.

(2)   If the act was done, or the preparations were made, in the course of a business, the person entitled to the right conferred by subsection (1) may—

(a) authorise the doing of that act by any partners of his for the time being in that business, and

(b) assign that right, or transmit it on death (or in the case of a body corporate on its dissolution), to any person who acquires that part of the business in the course of which the act was done or the preparations were made.

(3) Where a product is disposed of to another in exercise of the rights conferred by subsection (1) or (2), that other and any person claiming through him may deal with the product in the same way as if it had been disposed of by the registered proprietor of the patent.]

[115]

NOTES
Substituted by the Copyright, Designs and Patents Act 1988, s 295, Sch 5, para 17.

65 Certificate of contested validity of patent

(1) If in any proceedings before the court or the comptroller the validity of a patent to any extent is contested and that patent is found by the court or the comptroller to be wholly or partially valid, the court or the comptroller may certify the finding and the fact that the validity of the patent was so contested.

(2) Where a certificate is granted under this section, then, if in any subsequent proceedings before the court or the comptroller for infringement of the patent concerned or for revocation of the patent a final order or judgment or interlocutor is made or given in favour of the party relying on the validity of the patent as found in the earlier proceedings, that party shall, unless the court or the comptroller otherwise directs, be entitled to his costs or expenses as between solicitor and own client (other than the costs or expenses of any appeal in the subsequent proceedings).

[116]

66 Proceedings for infringement by a co-owner

(1) In the application of section 60 above to a patent of which there are two or more joint proprietors the reference to the proprietor shall be construed—

(a) in relation to any act, as a reference to that proprietor or those proprietors who, by virtue of section 36 above or any agreement referred to in that section, is or are entitled to do that act without its amounting to an infringement; and

(b) in relation to any consent, as a reference to that proprietor or those proprietors who, by virtue of section 36 above or any such agreement, is or are the proper person or persons to give the requisite consent.

(2) One of two or more joint proprietors of a patent may without the concurrence of the others bring proceedings in respect of an act alleged to infringe the patent, but shall not do so unless the others are made parties to the proceedings; but any of the others made a defendant or defender shall not be liable for any costs or expenses unless he enters an appearance and takes part in the proceedings.

[117]

67 Proceedings for infringement by exclusive licensee

(1) Subject to the provisions of this section, the holder of an exclusive licence under a patent shall have the same right as the proprietor of the patent to bring proceedings in respect of any infringement of the patent committed after the date of

the licence; and references to the proprietor of the patent in the provisions of this Act relating to infringement shall be construed accordingly.

(2) In awarding damages or granting any other relief in any such proceedings the court or the comptroller shall take into consideration any loss suffered or likely to be suffered by the exclusive licensee as such as a result of the infringement, or, as the case may be, the profits derived from the infringement, so far as it constitutes an infringement of the rights of the exclusive licensee as such.

(3) In any proceedings taken by an exclusive licensee by virtue of this section the proprietor of the patent shall be made a party to the proceedings, but if made a defendant or defender shall not be liable for any costs or expenses unless he enters an appearance and takes part in the proceedings.

[118]

68 Effect of non-registration on infringement proceedings

Where by virtue of a transaction, instrument or event to which section 33 above applies a person becomes the proprietor or one of the proprietors or an exclusive licensee of a patent and the patent is subsequently infringed, the court or the comptroller shall not award him damages or order that he be given an account of the profits in respect of such a subsequent infringement occurring before the transaction, instrument or event is registered unless—

(a) the transaction, instrument or event is registered within the period of six months beginning with its date; or

(b) the court or the comptroller is satisfied that it was not practicable to register the transaction, instrument or event before the end of that period and that it was registered as soon as practicable thereafter.

[119]

69 Infringement of rights conferred by publication of application

(1) Where an application for a patent for an invention is published, then, subject to subsections (2) and (3) below, the applicant shall have, as from the publication and until the grant of the patent, the same right as he would have had, if the patent had been granted on the date of the publication of the application, to bring proceedings in the court or before the comptroller for damages in respect of any act which would have infringed the patent; and (subject to subsections (2) and (3) below) references in sections 60 to 62 and 66 to 68 above to a patent and the proprietor of a patent shall be respectively construed as including references to any such application and the applicant, and references to a patent being in force, being granted, being valid or existing shall be construed accordingly.

(2) The applicant shall be entitled to bring proceedings by virtue of this section in respect of any act only—

(a) after the patent has been granted; and

(b) if the act would, if the patent had been granted on the date of the publication of the application, have infringed not only the patent, but also the claims (as interpreted by the description and any drawings referred to in the description or claims) in the form in which they were contained in the application immediately before the preparations for its publication were completed by the Patent Office.

(3) Section 62(2) and (3) above shall not apply to an infringement of the rights conferred by this section, but in considering the amount of any damages for such

an infringement, the court or the comptroller shall consider whether or not it would have been reasonable to expect, from a consideration of the application as published under section 16 above, that a patent would be granted conferring on the proprietor of the patent protection from an act of the same description as that found to infringe those rights, and if the court or the comptroller finds that it would not have been reasonable, it or he shall reduce the damages to such an amount as it or he thinks just.

[120]

70   Remedy for groundless threats of infringement proceedings

(1)   Where a person (whether or not the proprietor of, or entitled to any right in, a patent) by circulars, advertisements or otherwise threatens another person with proceedings for any infringement of a patent, a person aggrieved by the threats (whether or not he is the person to whom the threats are made) may, subject to subsection (4) below, bring proceedings in the court against the person making the threats, claiming any relief mentioned in subsection (3) below.

(2)   In any such proceedings the plaintiff or pursuer shall, if he proves that the threats were so made and satisfies the court that he is a person aggrieved by them, be entitled to the relief claimed unless—

    (a)   the defendant or defender proves that the acts in respect of which proceedings were threatened constitute or, if done, would constitute an infringement of a patent; and

    (b)   the patent alleged to be infringed is not shown by the plaintiff or pursuer to be invalid in a relevant respect.

(3)   The said relief is—

    (a)   a declaration or declarator to the effect that the threats are unjustifiable;

    (b)   an injunction or interdict against the continuance of the threats; and

    (c)   damages in respect of any loss which the plaintiff or pursuer has sustained by the threats.

(4)   Proceedings may not be brought under this section for a threat to bring proceedings for an infringement alleged to consist of making or importing a product for disposal or of using a process.

(5)   It is hereby declared that a mere notification of the existence of a patent does not constitute a threat of proceedings within the meaning of this section.

[121]

71   Declaration or declarator as to non-infringement

(1)   Without prejudice to the court's jurisdiction to make a declaration or declarator apart from this section, a declaration or declarator that an act does not, or a proposed act would not, constitute an infringement of a patent may be made by the court or the comptroller in proceedings between the person doing or proposing to do the act and the proprietor of the patent, notwithstanding that no assertion to the contrary has been made by the proprietor, if it is shown—

    (a)   that that person has applied in writing to the proprietor for a written acknowledgment to the effect of the declaration or declarator claimed, and has furnished him with full particulars in writing of the act in question; and

    (b)   that the proprietor has refused or failed to give any such acknowledgment.

(2)   Subject to section 72(5) below, a declaration made by the comptroller under this section shall have the same effect as a declaration or declarator by the court.

Revocation of patents

72   Power to revoke patents on application

(1)   Subject to the following provisions of this Act, the court or the comptroller may on the application of any person by order revoke a patent for an invention on (but only on) any of the following grounds, that is to say—

(a)   the invention is not a patentable invention;

[(b)   that the patent was granted to a person who was not entitled to be granted that patent;]

(c)   the specification of the patent does not disclose the invention clearly enough and completely enough for it to be performed by a person skilled in the art;

(d)   the matter disclosed in the specification of the patent extends beyond that disclosed in the application for the patent, as filed, or, if the patent was granted on a new application filed under section 8(3), 12 or 37(4) above or as mentioned in section 15(4) above, in the earlier application, as filed;

(e)   the protection conferred by the patent has been extended by an amendment which should not have been allowed.

(2)   An application for the revocation of a patent on the ground mentioned in subsection (1)(b) above—

(a)   may only be made by a person found by the court in an action for a declaration or declarator, or found by the court or the comptroller on a reference under section 37 above, to be entitled to be granted that patent or to be granted a patent for part of the matter comprised in the specification of the patent sought to be revoked; and

(b)   may not be made if that action was commenced or that reference was made after the end of the period of two years beginning with the date of the grant of the patent sought to be revoked, unless it is shown that any person registered as a proprietor of the patent knew at the time of the grant or of the transfer of the patent to him that he was not entitled to the patent.

(3)   *(Repealed by the Copyright, Designs and Patents Act 1988, s 303(2), Sch 8.)*

(4)   An order under this section may be an order for the unconditional revocation of the patent or, where the court or the comptroller determines that one of the grounds mentioned in subsection (1) above has been established, but only so as to invalidate the patent to a limited extent, an order that the patent should be revoked unless within a specified time the specification is amended under section 75 below to the satisfaction of the court or the comptroller, as the case may be.

(5)   A decision of the comptroller or on appeal from the comptroller shall not estop any party to civil proceedings in which infringement of a patent is in issue from alleging invalidity of the patent on any of the grounds referred to in subsection (1) above, whether or not any of the issues involved were decided in the said decision.

(6)   Where the comptroller refuses to grant an application made to him by any person under this section, no application (otherwise than by way of appeal or by way of putting validity in issue in proceedings for infringement) may be made to

the court by that person under this section in relation to the patent concerned, without the leave of the court.

(7)   Where the comptroller has not disposed of an application made to him under this section, the applicant may not apply to the court under this section in respect of the patent concerned unless either—

(a)   the proprietor of the patent agrees that the applicant may so apply, or
(b)   the comptroller certifies in writing that it appears to him that the question whether the patent should be revoked is one which would more properly be determined by the court.

[123]

NOTES

Sub-s (1): para (b) substituted by the Copyright, Designs and Patents Act 1988, s 295, Sch 5, para 18.

73   Comptroller's power to revoke patents on his own initiative

(1)   If it appears to the comptroller that an invention for which a patent has been granted formed part of the state of the art by virtue only of section 2(3) above, he may on his own initiative by order revoke the patent, but shall not do so without giving the proprietor of the patent an opportunity of making any observations and of amending the specification of the patent so as to exclude any matter which formed part of the state of the art as aforesaid without contravening section 76 below.

[(2)   If it appears to the comptroller that a patent under this Act and a European patent (UK) have been granted for the same invention having the same priority date, and that the applications for the patents were filed by the same applicant or his successor in title, he shall give the proprietor of the patent under this Act an opportunity of making observations and of amending the specification of the patent, and if the proprietor fails to satisfy the comptroller that there are not two patents in respect of the same invention, or to amend the specification so as to prevent there being two patents in respect of the same invention, the comptroller shall revoke the patent.

(3)   The comptroller shall not take action under subsection (2) above before—

(a)   the end of the period for filing an opposition to the European patent (UK) under the European Patent Convention, or
(b)   if later, the date on which opposition proceedings are finally disposed of;

and he shall not then take any action if the decision is not to maintain the European patent or if it is amended so that there are not two patents in respect of the same invention.

(4)   The comptroller shall not take action under subsection (2) above if the European patent (UK) has been surrendered under section 29(1) above before the date on which by virtue of section 25(1) above the patent under this Act is to be treated as having been granted or, if proceedings for the surrender of the European patent (UK) have been begun before that date, until those proceedings are finally disposed of; and he shall not then take any action if the decision is to accept the surrender of the European patent.]

[124]

NOTES

Sub-ss (2)–(4): substituted for sub-ss (2), (3), as originally enacted, by the Copyright, Designs and Patents Act 1988, s 295, Sch 5, para 19.

Putting validity in issue

74   Proceedings in which validity of patent may be put in issue

(1)   Subject to the following provisions of this section, the validity of a patent may be put in issue—

  (a) by way of defence, in proceedings for infringement of the patent under section 61 above or proceedings under section 69 above for infringement of rights conferred by the publication of an application;

  (b) in proceedings under section 70 above;

  (c) in proceedings in which a declaration in relation to the patent is sought under section 71 above;

  (d) in proceedings before the court or the comptroller under section 72 above for the revocation of the patent;

  (e) in proceedings under section 58 above.

(2)   The validity of a patent may not be put in issue in any other proceedings and, in particular, no proceedings may be instituted (whether under this Act or otherwise) seeking only a declaration as to the validity or invalidity of a patent.

(3)   The only grounds on which the validity of a patent may be put in issue (whether in proceedings for revocation under section 72 above or otherwise) are the grounds on which the patent may be revoked under that section.

(4)   No determination shall be made in any proceedings mentioned in subsection (1) above on the validity of a patent which any person puts in issue on the ground mentioned in section 72(1)(b) above unless—

  (a) it has been determined in entitlement proceedings commenced by that person or in the proceedings in which the validity of the patent is in issue that the patent should have been granted to him and not some other person; and

  (b) except where it has been so determined in entitlement proceedings, the proceedings in which the validity of the patent is in issue are commenced before the end of the period of two years beginning with the date of the grant of the patent or it is shown that any person registered as a proprietor of the patent knew at the time of the grant or of the transfer of the patent to him that he was not entitled to the patent.

(5)   Where the validity of a patent is put in issue by way of defence or counterclaim the court or the comptroller shall, if it or he thinks it just to do so, give the defendant an opportunity to comply with the condition in subsection (4)(a) above.

(6)   In subsection (4) above "entitlement proceedings", in relation to a patent, means a reference under [section 37(1) above] on the ground that the patent was granted to a person not entitled to it or proceedings for a declaration or declarator that it was so granted.

(7)   Where proceedings with respect to a patent are pending in the court under any provision of this Act mentioned in subsection (1) above, no proceedings may be instituted without the leave of the court before the comptroller with respect to that patent under section 61(3), 69, 71 or 72 above.

(8)   It is hereby declared that for the purposes of this Act the validity of a patent is not put in issue merely because the comptroller is considering its validity in order to decide whether to revoke it under section 73 above.

NOTES

Sub-s (6): words in square brackets substituted by the Copyright, Designs and Patents Act 1988, s 295, Sch 5, para 10.

General provisions as to amendment of patents and applications

75   Amendment of patent in infringement or revocation proceedings

(1)   In any proceedings before the court or the comptroller in which the validity of a patent is put in issue the court or, as the case may be, the comptroller may, subject to section 76 below, allow the proprietor of the patent to amend the specification of the patent in such manner, and subject to such terms as to advertising the proposed amendment and as to costs, expenses or otherwise, as the court or comptroller thinks fit.

(2)   A person may give notice to the court or the comptroller of his opposition to an amendment proposed by the proprietor of the patent under this section, and if he does so the court or the comptroller shall notify the proprietor and consider the opposition in deciding whether the amendment or any amendment should be allowed.

(3)   An amendment of a specification of a patent under this section shall have effect and be deemed always to have had effect from the grant of the patent.

(4)   Where an application for an order under this section is made to the court, the applicant shall notify the comptroller, who shall be entitled to appear and be heard and shall appear if so directed by the court.

[126]

[76   Amendments of applications and patents not to include added matter

(1)   An application for a patent which—
     (a)   is made in respect of matter disclosed in an earlier application, or in the specification of a patent which has been granted, and
     (b)   discloses additional matter, that is, matter extending beyond that disclosed in the earlier application, as filed, or the application for the patent, as filed,

may be filed under section 8(3), 12 or 37(4) above, or as mentioned in section 15(4) above, but shall not be allowed to proceed unless it is amended so as to exclude the additional matter.

(2)   No amendment of an application for a patent shall be allowed under section 17(3), 18(3) or 19(1) if it results in the application disclosing matter extending beyond that disclosed in the application as filed.

(3)   No amendment of the specification of a patent shall be allowed under section 27(1), 73 or 75 if it—
     (a)   results in the specification disclosing additional matter, or
     (b)   extends the protection conferred by the patent.]

[127]

NOTES

Substituted by the Copyright, Designs and Patents Act 1988, s 295, Sch 5, para 20.

PART II
PROVISIONS ABOUT INTERNATIONAL CONVENTIONS

European patents and patent applications

77   Effect of European patent (UK)

(1)   Subject to the provisions of this Act, a European patent (UK) shall, as from the publication of the mention of its grant in the European Patent Bulletin, be treated for the purposes of Parts I and III of this Act as if it were a patent under this Act granted in pursuance of an application made under this Act and as if notice of the grant of the patent had, on the date of that publication, been published under section 24 above in the journal; and—

    (a)   the proprietor of a European patent (UK) shall accordingly as respects the United Kingdom have the same rights and remedies, subject to the same conditions, as the proprietor of a patent under this Act;

    (b)   references in Parts I and III of this Act to a patent shall be construed accordingly; and

    (c)   any statement made and any certificate filed for the purposes of the provision of the convention corresponding to section 2(4)(c) above shall be respectively treated as a statement made and written evidence filed for the purposes of the said paragraph (c).

(2)   Subsection (1) above shall not affect the operation in relation to a European patent (UK) of any provisions of the European Patent Convention relating to the amendment or revocation of such a patent in proceedings before the European Patent Office.

[(3)   Where in the case of a European patent (UK)—

    (a)   proceedings for infringement, or proceedings under section 58 above, have been commenced before the court or the comptroller and have not been finally disposed of, and

    (b)   it is established in proceedings before the European Patent Office that the patent is only partially valid,

the provisions of section 63 or, as the case may be, of subsections (7) to (9) of section 58 apply as they apply to proceedings in which the validity of a patent is put in issue and in which it is found that the patent is only partially valid.]

[(4)   Where a European patent (UK) is amended in accordance with the European Patent Convention, the amendment shall have effect for the purposes of Parts I and III of this Act as if the specification of the patent had been amended under this Act; but subject to subsection (6)(b) below.

(4A)   Where a European patent (UK) is revoked in accordance with the European Patent Convention, the patent shall be treated for the purposes of Parts I and III of this Act as having been revoked under this Act.]

(5)   Where—

    (a)   under the European Patent Convention a European patent (UK) is revoked for failure to observe a time limit and is subsequently restored; and

    (b)   between the revocation and publication of the fact that it has been restored a person begins in good faith to do an act which would, apart from section 55 above, constitute an infringement of the patent or makes in good faith effective and serious preparations to do such an act;

he shall have the rights conferred by [section 28A(4) and (5) above, and subsections (6) and (7) of that section shall apply accordingly.]

(6) While this subsection is in force—
    (a) subsection (1) above shall not apply to a European patent (UK) the specification of which was published in French or German, unless a translation of the specification into English is filed at the Patent Office and the prescribed fee is paid before the end of the prescribed period;
    (b) subsection (4) above shall not apply to an amendment made in French or German unless [a translation into English of the specification as amended] is filed at the Patent Office and the prescribed fee is paid before the end of the prescribed period.

(7) Where [such a translation is not filed], the patent shall be treated as always having been void.

(8) The comptroller shall publish any translation filed at the Patent Office under subsection (6) above.

(9) Subsection (6) above shall come into force on a day appointed for the purpose by rules and shall cease to have effect on a day so appointed, without prejudice, however, to the power to bring it into force again.

[128]

NOTES
    Sub-s (3): substituted by the Copyright, Designs and Patents Act 1988, s 295, Sch 5, para 21.
    Sub-ss (4), (4A): substituted for sub-s (4), as originally enacted, by the Copyright, Designs and Patent Act 1988, s 295, Sch 5, para 21.
    Sub-ss (5), (6), (7): words in square brackets substituted by the Copyright, Designs and Patents Act 1988, s 295, Sch 5, paras 8, 21.

Miscellaneous

91 Evidence of conventions and instruments under conventions

(1) Judicial notice shall be taken of the following, that is to say—
    (a) the European Patent Convention, the Community Patent Convention and the Patent Co-operation Treaty (each of which is hereafter in this section referred to as the relevant convention);
    (b) any bulletin, journal or gazette published under the relevant convention and the register of European or Community patents kept under it; and
    (c) any decision of, or expression of opinion by, the relevant convention court on any question arising under or in connection with the relevant convention.

(2) Any document mentioned in subsection (1)(b) above shall be admissible as evidence of any instrument or other act thereby communicated of any convention institution.

(3) Evidence of any instrument issued under the relevant convention by any such institution, including any judgment or order of the relevant convention court, or of any document in the custody of any such institution or reproducing in legible form any information in such custody otherwise than in legible form, or any entry in or extract from such a document, may be given in any legal proceedings by production of a copy certified as a true copy by an official of that institution; and

any document purporting to be such a copy shall be received in evidence without proof of the official position or handwriting of the person signing the certificate.

(4)   Evidence of any such instrument may also be given in any legal proceedings—

(a) by production of a copy purporting to be printed by the Queen's Printer;

(b) where the instrument is in the custody of a government department, by production of a copy certified on behalf of the department to be a true copy by an officer of the department generally or specially authorised to do so;

and any document purporting to be such a copy as is mentioned in paragraph (b) above of an instrument in the custody of a department shall be received in evidence without proof of the official position or handwriting of the person signing the certificate, or of his authority to do so, or of the document being in the custody of the department.

(5)   In any legal proceedings in Scotland evidence of any matter given in a manner authorised by this section shall be sufficient evidence of it.

(6)   In this section—

"convention institution" means an institution established by or having functions under the relevant convention;

"relevant convention court" does not include a court of the United Kingdom or of any other country which is a party to the relevant convention; and

"legal proceedings", in relation to the United Kingdom, includes proceedings before the comptroller.

[129]

PART III
MISCELLANEOUS AND GENERAL

Supplemental

125   Extent of invention

(1)   For the purposes of this Act an invention for a patent for which an application has been made or for which a patent has been granted shall, unless the context otherwise requires, be taken to be that specified in a claim of the specification of the application or patent, as the case may be, as interpreted by the description and any drawings contained in that specification, and the extent of the protection conferred by a patent or application for a patent shall be determined accordingly.

(2)   It is hereby declared for the avoidance of doubt that where more than one invention is specified in any such claim, each invention may have a different priority date under section 5 above.

(3)   The Protocol on the Interpretation of Article 69 of the European Patent Convention (which Article contains a provision corresponding to subsection (1) above) shall, as for the time being in force, apply for the purposes of subsection (1) above as it applies for the purposes of that Article.

[130]

130   Interpretation

(1)   In this Act, except so far as the context otherwise requires—

"application for a European patent (UK)" and "international application for a patent (UK)" each mean an application of the relevant description which, on its date of filing, designates the United Kingdom;

"appointed day", in any provision of this Act, means the day appointed under section 132 below for the coming into operation of that provision;

"Community Patent Convention" means the Convention for the European Patent for the Common Market and "Community patent" means a patent granted under that convention;

"comptroller" means the Comptroller-General of Patents, Designs and Trade Marks;

"Convention on International Exhibitions" means the Convention relating to International Exhibitions signed in Paris on 22nd November 1928, as amended or supplemented by any protocol to that convention which is for the time being in force;

"court" means

[(a)   as respects England and Wales, the High Court or any patents county court having jurisdiction by virtue of an order under section 287 of the Copyright, Designs and Patents Act 1988;]

(b)   as respects Scotland, the Court of Session;

(c)   as respects Northern Ireland, the High Court in Northern Ireland;

"date of filing" means—

(a)   in relation to an application for a patent made under this Act, the date which is the date of filing that application by virtue of section 15 above; and

(b)   in relation to any other application, the date which, under the law of the country where the application was made or in accordance with the terms of a treaty or convention to which that country is a party, is to be treated as the date of filing that application or is equivalent to the date of filing an application in that country (whatever the outcome of the application);

"designate" in relation to an application or a patent, means designate the country or countries (in pursuance of the European Patent Convention or the Patent Co-operation Treaty) in which protection is sought for the invention which is the subject of the application or patent;

"employee" means a person who works or (where the employment has ceased) worked under a contract of employment or in employment under or for the purposes of a government department [or a person who serves (or served) in the naval, military or air forces of the Crown];

"employer", in relation to an employee, means the person by whom the employee is or was employed;

"European Patent Convention" means the Convention on the Grant of European Patents, "European patent" means a patent granted under that convention, "European patent (UK)" means a European patent designating the United Kingdom, "European Patent Bulletin" means the bulletin of that name published under that convention, and "European Patent Office" means the office of that name established by that convention;

"exclusive licence" means a licence from the proprietor of or applicant for a patent conferring on the licensee, or on him and persons authorised by him, to the exclusion of all other persons (including the proprietor or applicant), any right in respect of the invention to which the patent or application relates, and "exclusive licensee" and "non-exclusive licence" shall be construed accordingly;

"filing fee" means the fee prescribed for the purposes of section 14 above;

"formal requirements" means those requirements designated as such by rules made for the purposes of section 17 above;

"international application for a patent" means an application made under the Patent Co-operation Treaty;

"International Bureau" means the secretariat of the World Intellectual Property Organisation established by a convention signed at Stockholm on 14th July 1967;

"international exhibition" means an official or officially recognised international exhibition falling within the terms of the Convention on International Exhibitions or falling within the terms of any subsequent treaty or convention replacing that convention;

"inventor" has the meaning assigned to it by section 7 above;

"journal" has the meaning assigned to it by section 123(6) above;

"mortgage", when used as a noun, includes a charge for securing money or money's worth and, when used as a verb, shall be construed accordingly;

"1949 Act" means the Patents Act 1949;

"patent" means a patent under this Act;

. . . . .

"Patent Co-operation Treaty" means the treaty of that name signed at Washington on 19th June 1970;

"patented invention" means an invention for which a patent is granted and "patented process" shall be construed accordingly;

"patented product" means a product which is a patented invention or, in relation to a patented process, a product obtained directly by means of the process or to which the process has been applied;

"prescribed" and "rules" have the meanings assigned to them by section 123 above;

"priority date" means the date determined as such under section 5 above;

"published" means made available to the public (whether in the United Kingdom or elsewhere) and a document shall be taken to be published under any provision of this Act if it can be inspected as of right at any place in the United Kingdom by members of the public, whether on payment of a fee or not; and "republished" shall be construed accordingly;

"register" and cognate expressions have the meanings assigned to them by section 32 above;

"relevant convention court", in relation to any proceedings under the European Patent Convention, the Community Patent Convention or the Patent Co-operation Treaty, means that court or other body which under that convention or treaty has jurisdiction over those proceedings, including (where it has such jurisdiction) any department of the European Patent Office;

"right", in relation to any patent or application, includes an interest in the patent or application and, without prejudice to the foregoing, any reference to a right in a patent includes a reference to a share in the patent;

"search fee" means the fee prescribed for the purposes of [section 17(1) above];

"services of the Crown" and "use for the services of the Crown" have the meanings assigned to them by section 56(2) above, including, as respects any period of emergency within the meaning of section 59 above, the meanings assigned to them by the said section 59.

(2) Rules may provide for stating in the journal that an exhibition falls within the definition of international exhibition in subsection (1) above and any such statement shall be conclusive evidence that the exhibition falls within that definition.

(3) For the purposes of this Act matter shall be taken to have been disclosed in any relevant application within the meaning of section 5 above or in the specification of a patent if it was either claimed or disclosed (otherwise than by way of disclaimer or acknowledgment of prior art) in that application or specification.

(4) References in this Act to an application for a patent, as filed, are references to such an application in the state it was on the date of filing.

(5) References in this Act to an application for a patent being published are references to its being published under section 16 above.

(6) References in this Act to any of the following conventions, that is to say—
(a) The European Patent Convention;
(b) The Community Patent Convention;
(c) The Patent Co-operation Treaty;

are references to that convention or any other international convention or agreement replacing it, as amended or supplemented by any convention or international agreement (including in either case any protocol or annex), or in accordance with the terms of any such convention or agreement, and include references to any instrument made under any such convention or agreement.

(7) Whereas by a resolution made on the signature of the Community Patent Convention the governments of the member states of the European Economic Community resolved to adjust their laws relating to patents so as (among other things) to bring those laws into conformity with the corresponding provisions of the European Patent Convention, the Community Patent Convention and the Patent Co-operation Treaty, it is hereby declared that the following provisions of this Act, this is to say, sections 1(1) to (4), 2 to 6, 14(3), (5) and (6), 37(5), 54, 60, 69, 72(1) and (2), 74(4), 82, 83, . . . 100 and 125, are so framed as to have, as nearly as practicable, the same effects in the United Kingdom as the corresponding provisions of the European Patent Convention, the Community Patent Convention and the Patent Co-operation Treaty have in the territories to which those Conventions apply.

(8) The Arbitration Act 1950 shall not apply to any proceedings before the comptroller under this Act.

(9) Except so far as the context otherwise requires, any reference in this Act to any enactment shall be construed as a reference to that enactment as amended or extended by or under any other enactment, including this Act.

[131]

NOTES

Sub-s (1): in the definition of "court", para (a) substituted by the Copyright, Designs and Patents Act 1988, s 303(1); in definition "employee", words in square brackets added with retrospective effect by the Armed Forces Act 1981, s 22(1), (3); definition "patent agent" repealed by the Copyright, Designs and Patents Act 1988, s 303(2), Sch 8; in definition "search fee", words in square brackets substituted by the Copyright, Designs and Patents Act 1988, s 295, Sch 5, para 5.

Sub-s (7): words omitted repealed by the Copyright, Designs and Patents Act 1988, s 303(2), Sch 8.

132   Short title, extent, commencement, consequential amendments and repeals

(1)   This Act may be cited as the Patents Act 1977.

(2)–(7) . . .

NOTES
>   Sub-ss (2)–(7): not relevant to this work.

COMMISSION REGULATION (EEC) 240/96

of 31 January 1996

on the application of Article 85(3) of the Treaty to certain categories of technology transfer agreements

NOTES
>   Date of publication in OJ: OJ L31, 9.2.96, p 2.

Article 1

1.   Pursuant to Article 85(3) of the Treaty and subject to the conditions set out below, it is hereby declared that Article 85(1) of the Treaty shall not apply to pure patent licensing or know-how licensing agreements and to mixed patent and know-how licensing agreements, including those agreements containing ancillary provisions relating to intellectual property rights other than patents, to which only two undertakings are party and which include one or more of the following obligations—

>   (1)   an obligation on the licensor not to license other undertakings to exploit the licensed technology in the licensed territory;

>   (2)   an obligation on the licensor not to exploit the licensed technology in the licensed territory himself;

>   (3)   an obligation on the licensee not to exploit the licensed technology in the territory of the licensor within the common market;

>   (4)   an obligation on the licensee not to manufacture or use the licensed product, or use the licensed process, in territories within the common market which are licensed to other licensees;

>   (5)   an obligation on the licensee not to pursue an active policy of putting the licensed product on the market in the territories within the common market which are licensed to other licensees, and in particular not to engage in advertising specifically aimed at those territories or to establish any branch or maintain a distribution depot there;

>   (6)   an obligation on the licensee not to put the licensed product on the market in the territories licensed to other licensees within the common market in response to unsolicited orders;

>   (7)   an obligation on the licensee to use only the licensor's trademark or get up to distinguish the licensed product during the term of the agreement, provided that the licensee is not prevented from identifying himself as the manufacturer of the licensed products;

>   (8)   an obligation on the licensee to limit his production of the licensed product to the quantities he requires in manufacturing his own products and to sell

the licensed product only as an integral part of or a replacement part for his own products or otherwise in connection with the sale of his own products, provided that such quantities are freely determined by the licensee.

2.   Where the agreement is a pure patent licensing agreement, the exemption of the obligations referred to in paragraph 1 is granted only to the extent that and for as long as the licensed product is protected by parallel patents, in the territories respectively of the licensee (points (1), (2), (7) and (8)), the licensor (point (3)) and other licensees (points (4) and (5)). The exemption of the obligation referred to in point (6) of paragraph 1 is granted for a period not exceeding five years from the date when the licensed product is first put on the market within the common market by one of the licensees, to the extent that and for as long as, in these territories, this product is protected by parallel patents.

3.   Where the agreement is a pure know-how licensing agreement, the period for which the exemption of the obligations referred to in points (1) to (5) of paragraph 1 is granted may not exceed ten years from the date when the licensed product is first put on the market within the common market by one of the licensees.

The exemption of the obligation referred to in point (6) of paragraph 1 is granted for a period not exceeding five years from the date when the licensed product is first put on the market within the common market by one of the licensees.

The obligations referred to in points (7) and (8) of paragraph 1 are exempted during the lifetime of the agreement for as long as the know-how remains secret and substantial.

However, the exemption in paragraph 1 shall apply only where the parties have identified in any appropriate form the initial know-how and any subsequent improvements to it which become available to one party and are communicated to the other party pursuant to the terms of the agreement and to the purpose thereof, and only for as long as the know-how remains secret and substantial.

4.   Where the agreement is a mixed patent and know-how licensing agreement, the exemption of the obligations referred to in points (1) to (5) of paragraph 1 shall apply in Member States in which the licensed technology is protected by necessary patents for as long as the licensed product is protected in those Member States by such patents if the duration of such protection exceeds the periods specified in paragraph 3.

The duration of the exemption provided in point (6) of paragraph 1 may not exceed the five-year period provided for in paragraphs 2 and 3.

However, such agreements qualify for the exemption referred to in paragraph 1 only for as long as the patents remain in force or to the extent that the know-how is identified and for as long as it remains secret and substantial whichever period is the longer.

5.   The exemption provided for in paragraph 1 shall also apply where in a particular agreement the parties undertake obligations of the types referred to in that paragraph but with a more limited scope than is permitted by that paragraph.

[133]

Article 2

1.   Article 1 shall apply notwithstanding the presence in particular of any of the following clauses, which are generally not restrictive of competition—

(1) an obligation on the licensee not to divulge the know-how communicated by the licensor; the licensee may be held to this obligation after the agreement has expired;

(2) an obligation on the licensee not to grant sublicences or assign the licence;

(3) an obligation on the licensee not to exploit the licensed know-how or patents after termination of the agreement in so far and as long as the know-how is still secret or the patents are still in force;

(4) an obligation on the licensee to grant to the licensor a licence in respect of his own improvements to or his new applications of the licensed technology, provided—

     — that, in the case of severable improvements, such a licence is not exclusive, so that the licensee is free to use his own improvements or to license them to third parties, in so far as that does not involve disclosure of the know-how communicated by the licensor that is still secret,

     — and that the licensor undertakes to grant an exclusive or non-exclusive licence of his own improvements to the licensee;

(5) an obligation on the licensee to observe minimum quality specifications, including technical specifications, for the licensed product or to procure goods or services from the licensor or from an undertaking designated by the licensor, in so far as these quality specifications, products or services are necessary for—

     (a) a technically proper exploitation of the licensed technology; or

     (b) ensuring that the product of the licensee conforms to the minimum quality specifications that are applicable to the licensor and other licensees;

and to allow the licensor to carry out related checks;

(6) obligations—

     (a) to inform the licensor of misappropriation of the know-how or of infringements of the licensed patents; or

     (b) to take or to assist the licensor in taking legal action against such misappropriation or infringements;

(7) an obligation on the licensee to continue paying the royalties—

     (a) until the end of the agreement in the amounts, for the periods and according to the methods freely determined by the parties, in the event of the know-how becoming publicly known other than by action of the licensor, without prejudice to the payment of any additional damages in the event of the know-how becoming publicly known by the action of the licensee in breach of the agreement;

     (b) over a period going beyond the duration of the licensed patents, in order to facilitate payment;

(8) an obligation on the licensee to restrict his exploitation of the licensed technology to one or more technical fields of application covered by the licensed technology or to one or more product markets;

(9) an obligation on the licensee to pay a minimum royalty or to produce a minimum quantity of the licensed product or to carry out a minimum number of operations exploiting the licensed technology;

(10) an obligation on the licensor to grant the licensee any more favourable terms that the licensor may grant to another undertaking after the agreement is entered into;

(11) an obligation on the licensee to mark the licensed product with an indication of the licensor's name or of the licensed patent;

(12) an obligation on the licensee not to use the licensor's technology to construct facilities for third parties; this is without prejudice to the right of the licensee to increase the capacity of his facilities or to set up additional facilities for his own use on normal commercial terms, including the payment of additional royalties;

(13) an obligation on the licensee to supply only a limited quantity of the licensed product to a particular customer, where the licence was granted so that the customer might have a second source of supply inside the licensed territory; this provision shall also apply where the customer is the licensee, and the licence which was granted in order to provide a second source of supply provides that the customer is himself to manufacture the licensed products or to have them manufactured by a subcontractor;

(14) a reservation by the licensor of the right to exercise the rights conferred by a patent to oppose the exploitation of the technology by the licensee outside the licensed territory;

(15) a reservation by the licensor of the right to terminate the agreement if the licensee contests the secret or substantial nature of the licensed know-how or challenges the validity of licensed patents within the common market belonging to the licensor or undertakings connected with him;

(16) a reservation by the licensor of the right to terminate the licence agreement of a patent if the licensee raises the claim that such a patent is not necessary;

(17) an obligation on the licensee to use his best endeavours to manufacture and market the licensed product;

(18) a reservation by the licensor of the right to terminate the exclusivity granted to the licensee and to stop licensing improvements to him when the licensee enters into competition within the common market with the licensor, with undertakings connected with the licensor or with other undertakings in respect of research and development, production, use or distribution of competing products, and to require the licensee to prove that the licensed know-how is not being used for the production of products and the provision of services other than those licensed.

2.   In the event that, because of particular circumstances, the clauses referred to in paragraph 1 fall within the scope of Article 85(1), they shall also be exempted even if they are not accompanied by any of the obligations exempted by Article 1.

3.   The exemption in paragraph 2 shall also apply where an agreement contains clauses of the types referred to in paragraph 1 but with a more limited scope than is permitted by that paragraph.

[134]

Article 3

Article 1 and Article 2(2) shall not apply where—

(1) one party is restricted in the determination of prices, components of prices or discounts for the licensed products;

(2) one party is restricted from competing within the common market with the other party, with undertakings connected with the other party or with other undertakings in respect of research and development, production, use or distribution of competing products without prejudice to the provisions of Article 2(1)(17) and (18);

(3) one or both of the parties are required without any objectively justified reason—

    (a) to refuse to meet orders from users or resellers in their respective territories who would market products in other territories within the common market;

    (b) to make it difficult for users or resellers to obtain the products from other resellers within the common market, and in particular to exercise intellectual property rights or take measures so as to prevent users or resellers from obtaining outside, or from putting on the market in the licensed territory products which have been lawfully put on the market within the common market by the licensor or with his consent;

    or do so as a result of a concerted practice between them;

(4) the parties were already competing manufacturers before the grant of the licence and one of them is restricted, within the same technical field of use or within the same product market, as to the customers he may serve, in particular by being prohibited from supplying certain classes of user, employing certain forms of distribution or, with the aim of sharing customers, using certain types of packaging for the products, save as provided in Article 1(1)(7) and Article 2(1)(13);

(5) the quantity of the licensed products one party may manufacture or sell or the number of operations exploiting the licensed technology he may carry out are subject to limitations, save as provided in Article (1)(8) and Article 2(1)(13);

(6) the licensee is obliged to assign in whole or in part to the licensor rights to improvements to or new applications of the licensed technology;

(7) the licensor is required, albeit in separate agreements or through automatic prolongation of the initial duration of the agreement by the inclusion of any new improvements, for a period exceeding that referred to in Article 1(2) and (3) not to license other undertakings to exploit the licensed technology in the licensed territory, or a party is required for a period exceeding that referred to in Article 1(2) and (3) or Article 1(4) not to exploit the licensed technology in the territory of the other party or of other licensees.

[135]

Article 4

1.   The exemption provided for in Articles 1 and 2 shall also apply to agreements containing obligations restrictive of competition which are not covered by those Articles and do not fall within the scope of Article 3, on condition that the agreements in question are notified to the Commission in accordance with the provisions of Articles 1, 2 and 3 of Regulation (EC) No 3385/94 and that the Commission does not oppose such exemption within a period of four months.

2.   Paragraph 1 shall apply, in particular, where—

    (a) the licencee is obliged at the time the agreement is entered into to accept quality specifications or further licences or to procure goods or services which are not necessary for a technically satisfactory exploitation of the licensed technology or for ensuring that the production of the licensee conforms to the quality standards that are respected by the licensor and other licencees;

    (b) the licensee is prohibited from contesting the secrecy or the substantiality of the licensed know-how or from challenging the validity of patents licensed within the common market belonging to the licensor or undertakings connected with him.

3.   The period of four months referred to in paragraph 1 shall run from the date on which the notification takes effect in accordance with Article 4 of Regulation (EC) No 3385/94.

4.   The benefit of paragraphs 1 and 2 may be claimed for agreements notified before the entry into force of this Regulation by submitting a communication to the Commission referring expressly to this Article and to the notification. Paragraph 3 shall apply *mutatis mutandis.*

5.   The Commission may oppose the exemption within a period of four months. It shall oppose exemption if it receives a request to do so from a Member State within two months of the transmission to the Member State of the notification referred to in paragraph 1 or of the communication referred to in paragraph 4. This request must be justified on the basis of considerations relating to the competition rules of the Treaty.

6.   The Commission may withdraw the opposition to the exemption at any time. However, where the opposition was raised at the request of a Member State and this request is maintained, it may be withdrawn only after consultation of the Advisory Committee on Restrictive Practices and Dominant Positions.

7.   If the opposition is withdrawn because the undertakings concerned have shown that the conditions of Article 85(3) are satisfied, the exemption shall apply from the date of notification.

8.   If the opposition is withdrawn because the undertakings concerned have amended the agreement so that the conditions of Article 85(3) are satisfied, the exemption shall apply from the date on which the amendments take effect.

9.   If the Commission opposes exemption and the opposition is not withdrawn, the effects of the notification shall be governed by the provisions of Regulation No 17.

[136]

Article 5

1.   This Regulation shall not apply to—
    (1)   agreements between members of a patent or know-how pool which relate to the pooled technologies;
    (2)   licensing agreements between competing undertakings which hold interests in a joint venture, or between one of them and the joint venture, if the licensing agreements relate to the activities of the joint venture;
    (3)   agreements under which one party grants the other a patent and/or know-how licence and in exchange the other party, albeit in separate agreements or through connected undertakings, grants the first party a patent, trademark or know-how licence or exclusive sales rights, where the parties are competitors in relation to the products covered by those agreements;
    (4)   licensing agreements containing provisions relating to intellectual property rights other than patents which are not ancillary;
    (5)   agreements entered into solely for the purpose of sale.

2.   This Regulation shall nevertheless apply—
    (1)   to agreements to which paragraph 1(2) applies, under which a parent undertaking grants the joint venture a patent or know-how licence, provided that the licensed products and the other goods and services of the participating undertakings which are considered by users to be interchangeable or substitutable in view of their characteristics, price and intended use represent—

— in case of a licence limited to production, not more than 20%, and

— in case of a licence covering production and distribution, not more than 10%;

of the market for the licensed products and all interchangeable or substitutable goods and services;

(2) to agreements to which paragraph 1(1) applies and to reciprocal licences within the meaning of paragraph 1(3), provided the parties are not subject to any territorial restriction within the common market with regard to the manufacture, use or putting on the market of the licensed products or to the use of the licensed or pooled technologies.

3. This Regulation shall continue to apply where, for two consecutive financial years, the market shares in paragraph 2(1) are not exceeded by more than one-tenth; where that limit is exceeded, this Regulation shall continue to apply for a period of six months from the end of the year in which the limit was exceeded.

[137]

Article 6

This Regulation shall also apply to—

(1) agreements where the licensor is not the holder of the know-how or the patentee, but is authorised by the holder or the patentee to grant a licence;

(2) assignments of know-how, patents or both where the risk associated with exploitation remains with the assignor, in particular where the sum payable in consideration of the assignment is dependent on the turnover obtained by the assignee in respect of products made using the know-how or the patents, the quantity of such products manufactured or the number of operations carried out employing the know-how or the patents;

(3) licensing agreements in which the rights or obligations of the licensor or the licensee are assumed by undertakings connected with them.

[138]

Article 7

The Commission may withdraw the benefit of this Regulation, pursuant to Article 7 of Regulation No 19/65/EEC, where it finds in a particular case that an agreement exempted by this Regulation nevertheless has certain effects which are incompatible with the conditions laid down in Article 85(3) of the Treaty, and in particular where—

(1) the effect of the agreement is to prevent the licensed products from being exposed to effective competition in the licensed territory from identical goods or services or from goods or services considered by users as interchangeable or substitutable in view of their characteristics, price and intended use, which may in particular occur where the licensee's market share exceeds 40%;

(2) without prejudice to Article 1(1)(6), the licensee refuses, without any objectively justified reason, to meet unsolicited orders from users or resellers in the territory of other licensees;

(3) the parties—

(a) without any objectively justified reason, refuse to meet orders from users or resellers in their respective territories who would market the products in other territories within the common market; or

    (b) make it difficult for users or resellers to obtain the products from other resellers within the common market, and in particular where they exercise intellectual property rights or take measures so as to prevent resellers or users from obtaining outside, or from putting on the market in the licensed territory products which have been lawfully put on the market within the common market by the licensor or with his consent;

    (4) the parties were competing manufacturers at the date of the grant of the licence and obligations on the licensee to produce a minimum quantity or to use his best endeavours as referred to in Article 2(1), (9) and (17) respectively have the effect of preventing the licensee from using competing technologies.

[139]

Article 8

1.   For purposes of this Regulation—

    (a) patent applications;
    (b) utility models;
    (c) applications for registration of utility models;
    (d) topographies of semiconductor products;
    (e) *certificats d'utilité* and *certificats d'addition* under French law;
    (f) applications for *certificats d'utilité* and *certificats d'addition* under French law;
    (g) supplementary protection certificates for medicinal products or other products for which such supplementary protection certificates may be obtained;
    (h) plant breeder's certificates,

shall be deemed to be patents.

2.   This Regulation shall also apply to agreements relating to the exploitation of an invention if an application within the meaning of paragraph 1 is made in respect of the invention for a licensed territory after the date when the agreements were entered into but within the time-limits set by the national law or the international convention to be applied.

3.   This Regulation shall furthermore apply to pure patent or know-how licensing agreements or to mixed agreements whose initial duration is automatically prolonged by the inclusion of any new improvements, whether patented or not, communicated by the licensor, provided that the licensee has the right to refuse such improvements or each party has the right to terminate the agreement at the expiry of the initial term of an agreement and at least every three years thereafter.

[140]

Article 9

1.   Information acquired pursuant to Article 4 shall be used only for the purposes of this Regulation.

2.   The Commission and the authorities of the Member States, their officials and other servants shall not disclose information acquired by them pursuant to this Regulation of the kind covered by the obligation of professional secrecy.

3.   The provisions of paragraphs 1 and 2 shall not prevent publication of general information or surveys which do not contain information relating to particular undertakings or associations of undertakings.

[141]

Article 10

For purposes of this Regulation—
  (1) "know-how" means a body of technical information that is secret, substantial and identified in any appropriate form;
  (2) "secret" means that the know-how package as a body or in the precise configuration and assembly of its components is not generally known or easily accessible, so that part of its value consists in the lead which the licensee gains when it is communicated to him; it is not limited to the narrow sense that each individual component of the know-how should be totally unknown or unobtainable outside the licensor's business;
  (3) "substantial" means that the know-how includes information which must be useful, ie can reasonably be expected at the date of conclusion of the agreement to be capable of improving the competitive position of the licensee, for example by helping him to enter a new market or giving him an advantage in competition with other manufacturers or providers of services who do not have access to the licensed secret know-how or other comparable secret know-how;
  (4) "identified" means that the know-how is described or recorded in such a manner as to make it possible to verify that it satisfies the criteria of secrecy and substantiality and to ensure that the licensee is not unduly restricted in his exploitation of his own technology, to be identified the know-how can either be set out in the licence agreement or in a separate document or recorded in any other appropriate form at the latest when the know-how is transferred or shortly thereafter, provided that the separate document or other record can be made available if the need arises;
  (5) "necessary patents" are patents where a licence under the patent is necessary for the putting into effect of the licensed technology in so far as, in the absence of such a licence, the realisation of the licensed technology would not be possible or would be possible only to a lesser extent or in more difficult or costly conditions. Such patents must therefore be of technical, legal or economic interest to the licensee;
  (6) "licensing agreement" means pure patent licensing agreements and pure know-how licensing agreements as well as mixed patent and know-how licensing agreements;
  (7) "licensed technology" means the initial manufacturing know-how or the necessary product and process patents, or both, existing at the time the first licensing agreement is concluded, and improvements subsequently made to the know-how or patents, irrespective of whether and to what extent they are exploited by the parties or by other licensees;
  (8) "the licensed products" are goods or services the production or provision of which requires the use of the licensed technology;
  (9) "the licensee's market share" means the proportion which the licensed products and other goods or services provided by the licensee, which are considered by users to be interchangeable or substitutable for the licensed products in view of their characteristics, price and intended use, represent the entire market for the licensed products and all other interchangeable or substitutable goods and services in the common market or a substantial part of it;
  (10) "exploitation" refers to any use of the licensed technology in particular in the production, active or passive sales in a territory even if not coupled with manufacture in that territory, or leasing of the licensed products;

(11) "the licensed territory" is the territory covering all or at least part of the common market where the licensee is entitled to exploit the licensed technology;

(12) "territory of the licensor" means territories in which the licensor has not granted any licences for patents and/or know-how covered by the licensing agreement;

(13) "parallel patents" means patents which, in spite of the divergences which remain in the absence of any unification of national rules concerning industrial property, protect the same invention in various Member States;

(14) "connected undertakings" means—

(a) undertakings in which a party to the agreement, directly or indirectly—
— owns more than half the capital or business assets, or
— has the power to exercise more than half the voting rights, or
— has the power to appoint more than half the members of the supervisory board, board of directors or bodies legally representing the undertaking, or
— has the right to manage the affairs of the undertaking;

(b) undertakings which, directly or indirectly, have in or over a party to the agreement the rights or powers listed in (a);

(c) undertakings in which an undertaking referred to in (b), directly or indirectly, has the rights or powers listed in (a);

(d) undertakings in which the parties to the agreement or undertakings connected with them jointly have the rights or powers listed in (a): such jointly controlled undertakings are considered to be connected with each of the parties to the agreement;

(15) "ancillary provisions" are provisions relating to the exploitation of intellectual property rights other than patents, which contain no obligations restrictive of competition other than those also attached to the licensed know-how or patents and exempted under this Regulation;

(16) "obligation" means both contractual obligation and a concerted practice;

(17) "competing manufacturers" or manufacturers of "competing products" means manufacturers who sell products which, in view of their characteristics, price and intended use, are considered by users to be interchangeable or substitutable for the licensed products.

[142]

Article 11

1.   Regulation (EEC) No 556/89 is hereby repealed with effect from 1 April 1996.

2.   Regulation (EEC) No 2349/84 shall continue to apply until 31 March 1996.

3.   The prohibition in Article 85(1) of the Treaty shall not apply to agreements in force on 31 March 1996 which fulfil the exemption requirements laid down by Regulation (EEC) No 2349/84 or (EEC) No 556/89.

[143]

Article 12

1.   The Commission shall undertake regular assessments of the application of this Regulation, and in particular of the opposition procedure provided for in Article 4.

2.   The Commission shall draw up a report on the operation of this Regulation before the end of the fourth year following its entry into force and shall, on that basis, assess whether any adaptation of the Regulation is desirable.

[144]

Article 13

This Regulation shall enter into force on 1 April 1996.

It shall apply until 31 March 2006.

Article 11(2) of this Regulation shall, however, enter into force on 1 January 1996.

[145]–[200]

PART III
COPYRIGHT

COPYRIGHT, DESIGNS AND PATENTS ACT 1988

(c 48)

An Act to restate the law of copyright, with amendments; to make fresh provision as to the rights of performers and others in performances; to confer a design right in original designs; to amend the Registered Designs Act 1949; to make provision with respect to patent agents and trade mark agents; to confer patents and designs jurisdiction on certain county courts; to amend the law of patents; to make provision with respect to devices designed to circumvent copy-protection of works in electronic form; to make fresh provision penalising the fraudulent reception of transmissions; to make the fraudulent application or use of a trade mark an offence; to make provision for the benefit of the Hospital for Sick Children, Great Ormond Street, London; to enable financial assistance to be given to certain international bodies; and for connected purposes

[15 November 1988]

NOTES

Trade marks and registered trade marks: note that references to trade marks and registered trade marks within the meaning of the Trade Marks Act 1938 shall, unless the context otherwise requires, be construed after the commencement of the Trade Marks Act 1994 as references to trade marks and registered trade marks within the meaning of that Act. See the Trade Marks Act 1994, s 106(1), Sch 4, para 1.

PART I
COPYRIGHT

CHAPTER I
SUBSISTENCE, OWNERSHIP AND DURATION OF COPYRIGHT

Introductory

1 Copyright and copyright works

(1) Copyright is a property right which subsists in accordance with this Part in the following descriptions of work—

(a) original literary, dramatic, musical or artistic works,

(b) sound recordings, films, broadcasts or cable programmes, and

(c) the typographical arrangement of published editions.

(2) In this Part "copyright work" means a work of any of those descriptions in which copyright subsists.

(3) Copyright does not subsist in a work unless the requirements of this Part with respect to qualification for copyright protection are met (see section 153 and the provisions referred to there).

[201]

2 Rights subsisting in copyright works

(1) The owner of the copyright in a work of any description has the exclusive right to do the acts specified in Chapter II as the acts restricted by the copyright in a work of that description.

(2)   In relation to certain descriptions of copyright work the following rights conferred by Chapter IV (moral rights) subsist in favour of the author, director or commissioner of the work, whether or not he is the owner of the copyright—

    (a)   section 77 (right to be identified as author or director),

    (b)   section 80 (right to object to derogatory treatment of work), and

    (c)   section 85 (right to privacy of certain photographs and films).

[202]

Descriptions of work and related provisions

3   Literary, dramatic and musical works

(1)   In this Part—

"literary work" means any work, other than a dramatic or musical work, which is written, spoken or sung, and accordingly includes—

    (a)   a table or compilation, *and*

    (b)   a computer program[, and

    (c)   preparatory design material for a computer program];

"dramatic work" includes a work of dance or mime; and

"musical work" means a work consisting of music, exclusive of any words or action intended to be sung, spoken or performed with the music.

(2)   Copyright does not subsist in a literary, dramatic or musical work unless and until it is recorded, in writing or otherwise; and references in this Part to the time at which such a work is made are to the time at which it is so recorded.

(3)   It is immaterial for the purposes of subsection (2) whether the work is recorded by or with the permission of the author; and where it is not recorded by the author, nothing in that subsection affects the question whether copyright subsists in the record as distinct from the work recorded.

[203]

NOTES

    Sub-s (1): in definition "literary work" word in italics repealed and words in square brackets added by the Copyright (Computer Programs) Regulations 1992, SI 1992/3233, regs 2, 3, subject to reg 12(2) thereof (agreements entered into before 1 January 1993 to remain unaffected).

4   Artistic works

(1)   In this Part "artistic work" means—

    (a)   a graphic work, photograph, sculpture or collage, irrespective of artistic quality,

    (b)   a work of architecture being a building or a model for a building, or

    (c)   a work of artistic craftsmanship.

(2)   In this Part—

"building" includes any fixed structure, and a part of a building or fixed structure;

"graphic work" includes—

    (a)   any painting, drawing, diagram, map, chart or plan, and

    (b)   any engraving, etching, lithograph, woodcut or similar work;

"photograph" means a recording of light or other radiation on any medium on which an image is produced or from which an image may by any means be produced, and which is not part of a film;

"sculpture" includes a cast or model made for purposes of sculpture.

[204]

[5A   Sound recordings

(1)   In this Part "sound recording" means—

(a)   a recording of sounds, from which the sounds may be reproduced, or

(b)   a recording of the whole or any part of a literary, dramatic or musical work, from which sounds reproducing the work or part may be produced,

regardless of the medium on which the recording is made or the method by which the sounds are reproduced or produced.

(2)   Copyright does not subsist in a sound recording which is, or to the extent that it is, a copy taken from a previous sound recording.]

[205]

NOTES

Commencement: 1 January 1996.

This section and s 5B substituted for original s 5 by the Duration of Copyright and Rights in Performances Regulations 1995, SI 1995/3297, reg 9(1), subject to transitional provisions and savings specified in regs 12–35 thereof.

[5B   Films

(1)   In this Part "film" means a recording on any medium from which a moving image may by any means be produced.

(2)   The sound track accompanying a film shall be treated as part of the film for the purposes of this Part.

(3)   Without prejudice to the generality of subsection (2), where that subsection applies—

(a)   references in this Part to showing a film include playing the film sound track to accompany the film, and

(b)   references to playing a sound recording do not include playing the film sound track to accompany the film.

(4)   Copyright does not subsist in a film which is, or to the extent that it is, a copy taken from a previous film.

(5)   Nothing in this section affects any copyright subsisting in a film sound track as a sound recording.]

[206]

NOTES

Commencement: 1 January 1996.

This section and s 5A substituted for original s 5 by the Duration of Copyright and Rights in Performances Regulations 1995, SI 1995/3297, reg 9(1), subject to transitional provisions and savings specified in regs 12–35 thereof.

6   Broadcasts

(1)   In this Part a "broadcast" means a transmission by wireless telegraphy of visual images, sounds or other information which—

(a)   is capable of being lawfully received by members of the public, or

(b)   is transmitted for presentation to members of the public;

and references to broadcasting shall be construed accordingly.

(2)   An encrypted transmission shall be regarded as capable of being lawfully received by members of the public only if decoding equipment has been made available to members of the public by or with the authority of the person making the transmission or the person providing the contents of the transmission.

(3)   References in this Part to the person making a broadcast, broadcasting a work, or including a work in a broadcast are—

(a)   to the person transmitting the programme, if he has responsibility to any extent for its contents, and

(b)   to any person providing the programme who makes with the person transmitting it the arrangements necessary for its transmission;

and references in this Part to a programme, in the context of broadcasting, are to any item included in a broadcast.

(4)   For the purposes of this Part the place from which a broadcast is made is, in the case of a satellite transmission, the place from which the signals carrying the broadcast are transmitted to the satellite.

(5)   References in this Part to the reception of a broadcast include reception of a broadcast relayed by means of a telecommunications system.

(6)   Copyright does not subsist in a broadcast which infringes, or to the extent that it infringes, the copyright in another broadcast or in a cable programme.

[207]

7   Cable programmes

(1)   In this Part—

"cable programme" means any item included in a cable programme service; and

"cable programme service" means a service which consists wholly or mainly in sending visual images, sounds or other information by means of a telecommunications system, otherwise than by wireless telegraphy, for reception—

(a)   at two or more places (whether for simultaneous reception or at different times in response to requests by different users), or

(b)   for presentation to members of the public,

and which is not, or so far as it is not, excepted by or under the following provisions of this section.

(2)   The following are excepted from the definition of "cable programme service"—

(a)   a service or part of a service of which it is an essential feature that while visual images, sounds or other information are being conveyed by the person providing the service there will or may be sent from each place of reception, by means of the same system or (as the case may be) the same part of it, information (other than signals sent for the operation or control of the service) for reception by the person providing the service or other persons receiving it;

(b)   a service run for the purposes of a business where—

(i)   no person except the person carrying on the business is concerned in the control of the apparatus comprised in the system,

(ii)   the visual images, sounds or other information are conveyed by the system solely for purposes internal to the running of the business and not by way of rendering a service or providing amenities for others, and

    (iii) the system is not connected to any other telecommunications system;

  (c) a service run by a single individual where—

    (i) all the apparatus comprised in the system is under his control,

    (ii) the visual images, sounds or other information conveyed by the system are conveyed solely for domestic purposes of his, and

    (iii) the system is not connected to any other telecommunications system;

  (d) services where—

    (i) all the apparatus comprised in the system is situated in, or connects, premises which are in single occupation, and

    (ii) the system is not connected to any other telecommunications system, other than services operated as part of the amenities provided for residents or inmates of premises run as a business;

  (e) services which are, or to the extent that they are, run for persons providing broadcasting or cable programme services or providing programmes for such services.

(3)   The Secretary of State may by order amend subsection (2) so as to add or remove exceptions, subject to such transitional provision as appears to him to be appropriate.

(4)   An order shall be made by statutory instrument; and no order shall be made unless a draft of it has been laid before and approved by resolution of each House of Parliament.

(5)   References in this Part to the inclusion of a cable programme or work in a cable programme service are to its transmission as part of the service; and references to the person including it are to the person providing the service.

(6)   Copyright does not subsist in a cable programme—

  (a) if it is included in a cable programme service by reception and immediate re-transmission of a broadcast, or

  (b) if it infringes, or to the extent that it infringes, the copyright in another cable programme or in a broadcast.

[208]

8 Published editions

(1)   In this Part "published edition", in the context of copyright in the typographical arrangement of a published edition, means a published edition of the whole or any part of one or more literary, dramatic or musical works.

(2)   Copyright does not subsist in the typographical arrangement of a published edition if, or to the extent that, it reproduces the typographical arrangement of a previous edition.

[209]

Authorship and ownership of copyright

9 Authorship of work

(1)   In this Part "author", in relation to a work, means the person who creates it.

(2)   That person shall be taken to be—

    (a) in the case of a sound recording or film, the person by whom the arrangements necessary for the making of the recording or film are undertaken;

    (b) in the case of a broadcast, the person making the broadcast (see section 6(3)) or, in the case of a broadcast which relays another broadcast by reception and immediate re-transmission, the person making that other broadcast;

    (c) in the case of a cable programme, the person providing the cable programme service in which the programme is included;

    (d) in the case of the typographical arrangement of a published edition, the publisher.

(3)   In the case of a literary, dramatic, musical or artistic work which is computer-generated, the author shall be taken to be the person by whom the arrangements necessary for the creation of the work are undertaken.

(4)   For the purposes of this Part a work is of "unknown authorship" if the identity of the author is unknown or, in the case of a work of joint authorship, if the identity of none of the authors is known.

(5)   For the purposes of this Part the identity of an author shall be regarded as unknown if it is not possible for a person to ascertain his identity by reasonable inquiry; but if his identity is once known it shall not subsequently be regarded as unknown.

[210]

10   Works of joint authorship

(1)   In this Part a "work of joint authorship" means a work produced by the collaboration of two or more authors in which the contribution of each author is not distinct from that of the other author or authors.

(2)   A broadcast shall be treated as a work of joint authorship in any case where more than one person is to be taken as making the broadcast (see section 6(3)).

(3)   References in this Part to the author of a work shall, except as otherwise provided, be construed in relation to a work of joint authorship as references to all the authors of the work.

[211]

11   First ownership of copyright

(1)   The author of a work is the first owner of any copyright in it, subject to the following provisions.

(2)   Where a literary, dramatic, musical or artistic work is made by an employee in the course of his employment, his employer is the first owner of any copyright in the work subject to any agreement to the contrary.

(3)   This section does not apply to Crown copyright or Parliamentary copyright (see sections 163 and 165) or to copyright which subsists by virtue of section 168 (copyright of certain international organisations).

[212]

Duration of copyright

[12   Duration of copyright in literary, dramatic, musical or artistic works

(1)   The following provisions have effect with respect to the duration of copyright in a literary, dramatic, musical or artistic work.

(2)   Copyright expires at the end of the period of 70 years from the end of the calendar year in which the author dies, subject as follows.

(3)   If the work is of unknown authorship, copyright expires—

(a)   at the end of the period of 70 years from the end of the calendar year in which the work was made, or

(b)   if during that period the work is made available to the public, at the end of the period of 70 years from the end of the calendar year in which it is first so made available,

subject as follows.

(4)   Subsection (2) applies if the identity of the author becomes known before the end of the period specified in paragraph (a) or (b) of subsection (3).

(5)   For the purposes of subsection (3) making available to the public includes—

(a)   in the case of a literary, dramatic or musical work—

(i)   performance in public, or

(ii)   being broadcast or included in a cable programme service;

(b)   in the case of an artistic work—

(i)   exhibition in public,

(ii)   a film including the work being shown in public, or

(iii)   being included in a broadcast or cable programme service;

but in determining generally for the purposes of that subsection whether a work has been made available to the public no account shall be taken of any unauthorised act.

(6)   Where the country of origin of the work is not an EEA state and the author of the work is not a national of an EEA state, the duration of copyright is that to which the work is entitled in the country of origin, provided that does not exceed the period which would apply under subsections (2) to (5).

(7)   If the work is computer-generated the above provisions do not apply and copyright expires at the end of the period of 50 years from the end of the calendar year in which the work was made.

(8)   The provisions of this section are adapted as follows in relation to a work of joint authorship—

(a)   the reference in subsection (2) to the death of the author shall be construed—

(i)   if the identity of all the authors is known, as a reference to the death of the last of them to die, and

(ii)   if the identity of one or more of the authors is known and the identity of one or more others is not, as a reference to the death of the last whose identity is known;

(b)   the reference in subsection (4) to the identity of the author becoming known shall be construed as a reference to the identity of any of the authors becoming known;

(c)   the reference in subsection (6) to the author not being a national of an EEA state shall be construed as a reference to none of the authors being a national of an EEA state.

(9)   This section does not apply to Crown copyright or Parliamentary copyright (see sections 163 to 166) or to copyright which subsists by virtue of section 168 (copyright of certain international organisations).]

[213]

NOTES

Commencement: 1 January 1996.

Substituted by the Duration of Copyright and Rights in Performances Regulations 1995, SI 1995/3297, reg 5(1), subject to transitional provisions and savings specified in regs 12–35 thereof.

[13A   Duration of copyright in sound recordings

(1)   The following provisions have effect with respect to the duration of copyright in a sound recording.

(2)   Copyright expires—
    (a)   at the end of the period of 50 years from the end of the calendar year in which it is made, or
    (b)   if during that period it is released, 50 years from the end of the calendar year in which it is released;

subject as follows.

(3)   For the purposes of subsection (2) a sound recording is "released" when it is first published, played in public, broadcast or included in a cable programme service; but in determining whether a sound recording has been released no account shall be taken of any unauthorised act.

(4)   Where the author of a sound recording is not a national of an EEA state, the duration of copyright is that to which the sound recording is entitled in the country of which the author is a national, provided that does not exceed the period which would apply under subsections (2) and (3).

(5)   If or to the extent that the application of subsection (4) would be at variance with an international obligation to which the United Kingdom became subject prior to 29th October 1993, the duration of copyright shall be as specified in subsections (2) and (3).]

[214]

NOTES

Commencement: 1 January 1996.

This section and s 13B substituted for original s 13 by the Duration of Copyright and Rights in Performances Regulations 1995, SI 1995/3297, reg 6(1), subject to transitional provisions and savings specified in regs 12–35 thereof.

[13B   Duration of copyright in films

(1)   The following provisions have effect with respect to the duration of copyright in a film.

(2)   Copyright expires at the end of the period of 70 years from the end of the calendar year in which the death occurs of the last to die of the following persons—
    (a)   the principal director,
    (b)   the author of the screenplay,
    (c)   the author of the dialogue, or

(d) the composer of music specially created for and used in the film;

subject as follows.

(3) If the identity of one or more of the persons referred to in subsection (2)(a) to (d) is known and the identity of one or more others is not, the reference in that subsection to the death of the last of them to die shall be construed as a reference to the death of the last whose identity is known.

(4) If the identity of the persons referred to in subsection (2)(a) to (d) is unknown, copyright expires at—

    (a) the end of the period of 70 years from the end of the calendar year in which the film was made, or

    (b) if during that period the film is made available to the public, at the end of the period of 70 years from the end of the calendar year in which it is first so made available.

(5) Subsections (2) and (3) apply if the identity of any of those persons becomes known before the end of the period specified in paragraph (a) or (b) of subsection (4).

(6) For the purposes of subsection (4) making available to the public includes—

    (a) showing in public, or

    (b) being broadcast or included in a cable programme service;

but in determining generally for the purposes of that subsection whether a film has been made available to the public no account shall be taken of any unauthorised act.

(7) Where the country of origin is not an EEA state and the author of the film is not a national of an EEA state, the duration of copyright is that to which the work is entitled in the country of origin, provided that does not exceed the period which would apply under subsections (2) to (6).

(8) In relation to a film of which there are joint authors, the reference in subsection (7) to the author not being a national of an EEA state shall be construed as a reference to none of the authors being a national of an EEA state.

(9) If in any case there is no person falling within paragraphs (a) to (d) of subsection (2), the above provisions do not apply and copyright expires at the end of the period of 50 years from the end of the calendar year in which the film was made.

(10) For the purposes of this section the identity of any of the persons referred to in subsection (2)(a) to (d) shall be regarded as unknown if it is not possible for a person to ascertain his identity by reasonable inquiry; but if the identity of any such person is once known it shall not subsequently be regarded as unknown.]

[215]

NOTES

Commencement: 1 January 1996.

This section and s 13A substituted for original s 13 by the Duration of Copyright and Rights in Performances Regulations 1995, SI 1995/3297, reg 6(1), subject to transitional provisions and savings specified in regs 12–35 thereof.

[14 Duration of copyright in broadcasts and cable programmes

(1) The following provisions have effect with respect to the duration of copyright in a broadcast or cable programme.

(2) Copyright in a broadcast or cable programme expires at the end of the period of 50 years from the end of the calendar year in which the broadcast was made or the programme was included in a cable programme service, subject as follows.

(3) Where the author of the broadcast or cable programme is not a national of an EEA state, the duration of copyright in the broadcast or cable programme is that to which it is entitled in the country of which the author is a national, provided that does not exceed the period which would apply under subsection (2).

(4) If or to the extent that the application of subsection (3) would be at variance with an international obligation to which the United Kingdom became subject prior to 29th October 1993, the duration of copyright shall be as specified in subsection (2).

(5) Copyright in a repeat broadcast or cable programme expires at the same time as the copyright in the original broadcast or cable programme; and accordingly no copyright arises in respect of a repeat broadcast or cable programme which is broadcast or included in a cable programme service after the expiry of the copyright in the original broadcast or cable programme.

(6) A repeat broadcast or cable programme means one which is a repeat either of a broadcast previously made or of a cable programme previously included in a cable programme service.]

[216]

NOTES
Commencement: 1 January 1996.
Substituted by the Duration of Copyright and Rights in Performances Regulations 1995, SI 1995/3297, reg 7(1), subject to transitional provisions and savings as specified in regs 12–35 thereof.

15   Duration of copyright in typographical arrangement of published editions

Copyright in the typographical arrangement of a published edition expires at the end of the period of 25 years from the end of the calendar year in which the edition was first published.

[217]

[15A   Meaning of country of origin

(1) For the purposes of the provisions of this Part relating to the duration of copyright the country of origin of a work shall be determined as follows.

(2) If the work is first published in a Berne Convention country and is not simultaneously published elsewhere, the country of origin is that country.

(3) If the work is first published simultaneously in two or more countries only one of which is a Berne Convention country, the country of origin is that country.

(4) If the work is first published simultaneously in two or more countries of which two or more are Berne Convention countries, then—

   (a) if any of those countries is an EEA state, the country of origin is that country; and

   (b) if none of those countries is an EEA state, the country of origin is the Berne Convention country which grants the shorter or shortest period of copyright protection.

(5)   If the work is unpublished or is first published in a country which is not a Berne Convention country (and is not simultaneously published in a Berne Convention country), the country of origin is—

(a)   if the work is a film and the maker of the film has his headquarters in, or is domiciled or resident in a Beme Convention country, that country;

(b)   if the work is—

(i)   a work of architecture constructed in a Beme Convention country, or

(ii)   an artistic work incorporated in a building or other structure situated in a Berne Convention country,

that country;

(c)   in any other case, the country of which the author of the work is a national.

(6)   In this section—

(a)   a "Berne Convention country" means a country which is a party to any Act of the International Convention for the Protection of Literary and Artistic Works signed at Berne on 9th September 1886; and

(b)   references to simultaneous publication are to publication within 30 days of first publication.]

[218]

NOTES

Commencement: 1 January 1996.

Inserted by the Duration of Copyright and Rights in Performances Regulations 1995, SI 1995/3297, reg 8(1), subject to transitional provisions and savings specified in regs 12–35 thereof.

CHAPTER II
RIGHTS OF COPYRIGHT OWNER

The acts restricted by copyright

16   The acts restricted by copyright in a work

(1)   The owner of the copyright in a work has, in accordance with the following provisions of this Chapter, the exclusive right to do the following acts in the United Kingdom—

(a)   to copy the work (see section 17);

(b)   to issue copies of the work to the public (see section 18);

(c)   to perform, show or play the work in public (see section 19);

(d)   to broadcast the work or include it in a cable programme service (see section 20);

(e)   to make an adaptation of the work or do any of the above in relation to an adaptation (see section 21);

and those acts are referred to in this Part as the "acts restricted by the copyright".

(2)   Copyright in a work is infringed by a person who without the licence of the copyright owner does, or authorises another to do, any of the acts restricted by the copyright.

(3)   References in this Part to the doing of an act restricted by the copyright in a work are to the doing of it—

(a)   in relation to the work as a whole or any substantial part of it, and

(b)   either directly or indirectly;

and it is immaterial whether any intervening acts themselves infringe copyright.

(4)   This Chapter has effect subject to—

     (a)   the provisions of Chapter III (acts permitted in relation to copyright works), and

     (b)   the provisions of Chapter VII (provisions with respect to copyright licensing).

[219]

17   Infringement of copyright by copying

(1)   The copying of the work is an act restricted by the copyright in every description of copyright work; and references in this Part to copying and copies shall be construed as follows.

(2)   Copying in relation to a literary, dramatic, musical or artistic work means reproducing the work in any material form.

    This includes storing the work in any medium by electronic means.

(3)   In relation to an artistic work copying includes the making of a copy in three dimensions of a two-dimensional work and the making of a copy in two dimensions of a three-dimensional work.

(4)   Copying in relation to a film, television broadcast or cable programme includes making a photograph of the whole or any substantial part of any image forming part of the film, broadcast or cable programme.

(5)   Copying in relation to the typographical arrangement of a published edition means making a facsimile copy of the arrangement.

(6)   Copying in relation to any description of work includes the making of copies which are transient or are incidental to some other use of the work.

[220]

18   Infringement by issue of copies to the public

(1)   The issue to the public of copies of the work is an act restricted by the copyright in every description of copyright work.

(2)   References in this Part to the issue to the public of copies of a work are [except where the work is a computer program] to the act of putting into circulation copies not previously put into circulation, in the United Kingdom or elsewhere, and not to—

     (a)   any subsequent distribution, sale, hiring or loan of those copies, or

     (b)   any subsequent importation of those copies into the United Kingdom;

except that in relation to sound recordings [and films] the restricted act of issuing copies to the public includes any rental of copies to the public.

[(3)   References in this Part to the issue to the public of copies of a work where the work is a computer program are to the act of putting into circulation copies of that program not previously put into circulation in the United Kingdom or any other member State, by or with the consent of the copyright owner, and not to—

     (a)   any subsequent distribution, sale, hiring or loan of those copies, or

     (b)   any subsequent importation of those copies into the United Kingdom,

except that the restricted act of issuing copies to the public includes any rental of copies to the public.]

[221]

19 Infringement by performance, showing or playing of work in public

(1) The performance of the work in public is an act restricted by the copyright in a literary, dramatic or musical work.

(2) In this Part "performance", in relation to a work—
(a) includes delivery in the case of lectures, addresses, speeches and sermons, and
(b) in general, includes any mode of visual or acoustic presentation, including presentation by means of a sound recording, film, broadcast or cable programme of the work.

(3) The playing or showing of the work in public is an act restricted by the copyright in a sound recording, film, broadcast or cable programme.

(4) Where copyright in a work is infringed by its being performed, played or shown in public by means of apparatus for receiving visual images or sounds conveyed by electronic means, the person by whom the visual images or sounds are sent, and in the case of a performance the performers, shall not be regarded as responsible for the infringement.

[222]

20 Infringement by broadcasting or inclusion in a cable programme service

The broadcasting of the work or its inclusion in a cable programme service is an act restricted by the copyright in—
(a) a literary, dramatic, musical or artistic work,
(b) a sound recording or film, or
(c) a broadcast or cable programme.

[223]

21 Infringement by making adaptation or act done in relation to adaptation

(1) The making of an adaptation of the work is an act restricted by the copyright in a literary, dramatic or musical work.

For this purpose an adaptation is made when it is recorded, in writing or otherwise.

(2) The doing of any of the acts specified in sections 17 to 20, or subsection (1) above, in relation to an adaptation of the work is also an act restricted by the copyright in a literary, dramatic or musical work.

For this purpose it is immaterial whether the adaptation has been recorded, in writing or otherwise, at the time the act is done.

(3) In this Part "adaptation"—
(a) in relation to a literary [work, other than a computer program,] or dramatic work, means—
(i) a translation of the work;

    (ii) a version of a dramatic work in which it is converted into a non-dramatic work or, as the case may be, of a non-dramatic work in which it is converted into a dramatic work;

    (iii) a version of the work in which the story or action is conveyed wholly or mainly by means of pictures in a form suitable for reproduction in a book, or in a newspaper, magazine or similar periodical;

  [(ab) in relation to a computer program, means an arrangement or altered version of the program or a translation of it;]

  (b) in relation to a musical work, means an arrangement or transcription of the work.

(4)   In relation to a computer program a "translation" includes a version of the program in which it is converted into or out of a computer language or code or into a different computer language or code *otherwise than incidentally in the course of running the program.*

(5)   No inference shall be drawn from this section as to what does or does not amount to copying a work.

[224]

NOTES

Sub-s (3): words in square brackets inserted by the Copyright (Computer Programs) Regulations 1992, SI 1992/3233, regs 2, 5(1), (2), subject to reg 12(2) thereof (agreements entered into before 1 January 1993 to remain unaffected).

Sub-s (4): words in italics repealed by the Copyright (Computer Programs) Regulations 1992, SI 1992/3233, regs 2, 5(3), subject to reg 12(2) thereof (agreements entered into before 1 January 1993 to remain unaffected).

Secondary infringement of copyright

22   Secondary infringement: importing infringing copy

The copyright in a work is infringed by a person who, without the licence of the copyright owner, imports into the United Kingdom, otherwise than for his private and domestic use, an article which is, and which he knows or has reason to believe is, an infringing copy of the work.

[225]

23   Secondary infringement: possessing or dealing with infringing copy

The copyright in a work is infringed by a person who, without the licence of the copyright owner—

  (a) possesses in the course of a business,

  (b) sells or lets for hire, or offers or exposes for sale or hire,

  (c) in the course of a business exhibits in public or distributes, or

  (d) distributes otherwise than in the course of a business to such an extent as to affect prejudicially the owner of the copyright,

an article which is, and which he knows or has reason to believe is, an infringing copy of the work.

[226]

24   Secondary infringement: providing means for making infringing copies

(1)   Copyright in a work is infringed by a person who, without the licence of the copyright owner—

  (a) makes,

    (b)   imports into the United Kingdom,

    (c)   possesses in the course of a business, or

    (d)   sells or lets for hire, or offers or exposes for sale or hire,

an article specifically designed or adapted for making copies of that work, knowing or having reason to believe that it is to be used to make infringing copies.

(2)   Copyright in a work is infringed by a person who without the licence of the copyright owner transmits the work by means of a telecommunications system (otherwise than by broadcasting or inclusion in a cable programme service), knowing or having reason to believe that infringing copies of the work will be made by means of the reception of the transmission in the United Kingdom or elsewhere.

[227]

25   Secondary infringement: permitting use of premises for infringing performance

(1)   Where the copyright in a literary, dramatic or musical work is infringed by a performance at a place of public entertainment, any person who gave permission for that place to be used for the performance is also liable for the infringement unless when he gave permission he believed on reasonable grounds that the performance would not infringe copyright.

(2)   In this section "place of public entertainment" includes premises which are occupied mainly for other purposes but are from time to time made available for hire for the purposes of public entertainment.

[228]

26   Secondary infringement: provision of apparatus for infringing performance, etc

(1)   Where copyright in a work is infringed by a public performance of the work, or by the playing or showing of the work in public, by means of apparatus for—

    (a)   playing sound recordings,

    (b)   showing films, or

    (c)   receiving visual images or sounds conveyed by electronic means,

the following persons are also liable for the infringement.

(2)   A person who supplied the apparatus, or any substantial part of it, is liable for the infringement if when he supplied the apparatus or part—

    (a)   he knew or had reason to believe that the apparatus was likely to be so used as to infringe copyright, or

    (b)   in the case of apparatus whose normal use involves a public performance, playing or showing, he did not believe on reasonable grounds that it would not be so used as to infringe copyright.

(3)   An occupier of premises who gave permission for the apparatus to be brought onto the premises is liable for the infringement if when he gave permission he knew or had reason to believe that the apparatus was likely to be so used as to infringe copyright.

(4)   A person who supplied a copy of a sound recording or film used to infringe copyright is liable for the infringement if when he supplied it he knew or had reason to believe that what he supplied, or a copy made directly or indirectly from it, was likely to be so used as to infringe copyright.

[229]

Infringing copies

27   Meaning of "infringing copy"

(1)   In this Part "infringing copy", in relation to a copyright work, shall be construed in accordance with this section.

(2)   An article is an infringing copy if its making constituted an infringement of the copyright in the work in question.

(3)   [Subject to subsection (3A)] an article is also an infringing copy if—

    (a)   it has been or is proposed to be imported into the United Kingdom, and

    (b)   its making in the United Kingdom would have constituted an infringement of the copyright in the work in question, or a breach of an exclusive licence agreement relating to that work.

[(3A)   A copy of a computer program which has previously been sold in any other member State, by or with the consent of the copyright owner, is not an infringing copy for the purposes of subsection (3).]

(4)   Where in any proceedings the question arises whether an article is an infringing copy and it is shown—

    (a)   that the article is a copy of the work, and

    (b)   that copyright subsists in the work or has subsisted at any time,

it shall be presumed until the contrary is proved that the article was made at a time when copyright subsisted in the work.

(5)   Nothing in subsection (3) shall be construed as applying to an article which may lawfully be imported into the United Kingdom by virtue of any enforceable Community right within the meaning of section 2(1) of the European Communities Act 1972.

(6)   In this Part "infringing copy" includes a copy falling to be treated as an infringing copy by virtue of any of the following provisions—

    section 32(5) (copies made for purposes of instruction or examination),

    section 35(3) (recordings made by educational establishments for educational purposes),

    section 36(5) (reprographic copying by educational establishments for purposes of instruction),

    section 37(3)(b) (copies made by librarian or archivist in reliance on false declaration),

    section 56(2) (further copies, adaptations, etc. of work in electronic form retained on transfer of principal copy),

    section 63(2) (copies made for purpose of advertising artistic work for sale),

    section 68(4) (copies made for purpose of broadcast or cable programme), or

    any provision of an order under section 141 (statutory licence for certain reprographic copying by educational establishments).

[230]

NOTES

    Commencement: 1 January 1993 (sub-s (3A)); 1 August 1989 (remainder) (SI 1989/816).

    Sub-s (3): words in square brackets inserted by the Copyright (Computer Programs) Regulations 1992, SI 1992/3233, regs 2, 6, subject to reg 12(2) thereof (agreements entered into before 1 January 1993 to remain unaffected).

    Sub-s (3A): inserted by the Copyright (Computer Programs) Regulations 1992, SI 1992/3233, regs 2, 6, subject to reg 12(2) thereof (agreements entered into before 1 January 1993 to remain unaffected).

CHAPTER III
ACTS PERMITTED IN RELATION TO COPYRIGHT WORKS

Introductory

28   Introductory provisions

(1)   The provisions of this Chapter specify acts which may be done in relation to copyright works notwithstanding the subsistence of copyright; they relate only to the question of infringement of copyright and do not affect any other right or obligation restricting the doing of any of the specified acts.

(2)   Where it is provided by this Chapter that an act does not infringe copyright, or may be done without infringing copyright, and no particular description of copyright work is mentioned, the act in question does not infringe the copyright in a work of any description.

(3)   No inference shall be drawn from the description of any act which may by virtue of this Chapter be done without infringing copyright as to the scope of the acts restricted by the copyright in any description of work.

(4)   The provisions of this Chapter are to be construed independently of each other, so that the fact that an act does not fall within one provision does not mean that it is not covered by another provision.

[231]

General

29   Research and private study

(1)   Fair dealing with a literary, dramatic, musical or artistic work for the purposes of research or private study does not infringe any copyright in the work or, in the case of a published edition, in the typographical arrangement.

(2)   Fair dealing with the typographical arrangement of a published edition for the purposes mentioned in subsection (1) does not infringe any copyright in the arrangement.

(3)   Copying by a person other than the researcher or student himself is not fair dealing if—

(a)   in the case of a librarian, or a person acting on behalf of a librarian, he does anything which regulations under section 40 would not permit to be done under section 38 or 39 (articles or parts of published works: restriction on multiple copies of same material), or

(b)   in any other case, the person doing the copying knows or has reason to believe that it will result in copies of substantially the same material being provided to more than one person at substantially the same time and for substantially the same purpose.

[(4)   It is not fair dealing—

(a)   to convert a computer program expressed in a low level language into a version expressed in a higher level language, or

(b)   incidentally in the course of so converting the program, to copy it,

(these acts being permitted if done in accordance with section 50B (decompilation)).]

[232]

NOTES

Commencement: 1 January 1993 (sub-s (4)); 1 August 1989 (remainder) (SI 1989/816).

Sub-s (4): added by the Copyright (Computer Programs) Regulations 1992, SI 1992/3233, regs 2, 7, subject to reg 12(2) thereof (agreements entered into before 1 January 1993 to remain unaffected).

30   Criticism, review and news reporting

(1)   Fair dealing with a work for the purpose of criticism or review, of that or another work or of a performance of a work, does not infringe any copyright in the work provided that it is accompanied by a sufficient acknowledgement.

(2)   Fair dealing with a work (other than a photograph) for the purpose of reporting current events does not infringe any copyright in the work provided that (subject to subsection (3)) it is accompanied by a sufficient acknowledgement.

(3)   No acknowledgement is required in connection with the reporting of current events by means of a sound recording, film, broadcast or cable programme.

[233]

31   Incidental inclusion of copyright material

(1)   Copyright in a work is not infringed by its incidental inclusion in an artistic work, sound recording, film, broadcast or cable programme.

(2)   Nor is the copyright infringed by the issue to the public of copies, or the playing, showing, broadcasting or inclusion in a cable programme service, of anything whose making was, by virtue of subsection (1), not an infringement of the copyright.

(3)   A musical work, words spoken or sung with music, or so much of a sound recording, broadcast or cable programme as includes a musical work or such words, shall not be regarded as incidentally included in another work if it is deliberately included.

[234]

Education

32   Things done for purposes of instruction or examination

(1)   Copyright in a literary, dramatic, musical or artistic work is not infringed by its being copied in the course of instruction or of preparation for instruction, provided the copying—

(a)   is done by a person giving or receiving instruction, and

(b)   is not by means of a reprographic process.

(2)   Copyright in a sound recording, film, broadcast or cable programme is not infringed by its being copied by making a film or film sound-track in the course of instruction, or of preparation for instruction, in the making of films or film sound-tracks, provided the copying is done by a person giving or receiving instruction.

(3)   Copyright is not infringed by anything done for the purposes of an examination by way of setting the questions, communicating the questions to the candidates or answering the questions.

(4)   Subsection (3) does not extend to the making of a reprographic copy of a musical work for use by an examination candidate in performing the work.

(5)   Where a copy which would otherwise be an infringing copy is made in accordance with this section but is subsequently dealt with, it shall be treated as an infringing copy for the purpose of that dealing, and if that dealing infringes copyright for all subsequent purposes.

For this purpose "dealt with" means sold or let for hire or offered or exposed for sale or hire.

[235]

33   Anthologies for educational use

(1)   The inclusion of a short passage from a published literary or dramatic work in a collection which—
   (a)   is intended for use in educational establishments and is so described in its title, and in any advertisements issued by or on behalf of the publisher, and
   (b)   consists mainly of material in which no copyright subsists,

does not infringe the copyright in the work if the work itself is not intended for use in such establishments and the inclusion is accompanied by a sufficient acknowledgement.

(2)   Subsection (1) does not authorise the inclusion of more than two excerpts from copyright works by the same author in collections published by the same publisher over any period of five years.

(3)   In relation to any given passage the reference in subsection (2) to excerpts from works by the same author—
   (a)   shall be taken to include excerpts from works by him in collaboration with another, and
   (b)   if the passage in question is from such a work, shall be taken to include excerpts from works by any of the authors, whether alone or in collaboration with another.

(4)   References in this section to the use of a work in an educational establishment are to any use for the educational purposes of such an establishment.

[236]

34   Performing, playing or showing work in course of activities of educational establishment

(1)   The performance of a literary, dramatic or musical work before an audience consisting of teachers and pupils at an educational establishment and other persons directly connected with the activities of the establishment—
   (a)   by a teacher or pupil in the course of the activities of the establishment, or
   (b)   at the establishment by any person for the purposes of instruction,

is not a public performance for the purposes of infringement of copyright.

(2)   The playing or showing of a sound recording, film, broadcast or cable programme before such an audience at an educational establishment for the purposes of instruction is not a playing or showing of the work in public for the purposes of infringement of copyright.

(3)   A person is not for this purpose directly connected with the activities of the educational establishment simply because he is the parent of a pupil at the establishment.

[237]

35   Recording by educational establishments of broadcasts and cable programmes

(1)   A recording of a broadcast or cable programme, or a copy of such a recording, may be made by or on behalf of an educational establishment for the educational purposes of that establishment without thereby infringing the copyright in the broadcast or cable programme, or in any work included in it.

(2)   This section does not apply if or to the extent that there is a licensing scheme certified for the purposes of this section under section 143 providing for the grant of licences.

(3)   Where a copy which would otherwise be an infringing copy is made in accordance with this section but is subsequently dealt with, it shall be treated as an infringing copy for the purposes of that dealing, and if that dealing infringes copyright for all subsequent purposes.

For this purpose "dealt with" means sold or let for hire or offered or exposed for sale or hire.

[238]

36   Reprographic copying by educational establishments of passages from published works

(1)   Reprographic copies of passages from published literary, dramatic or musical works may, to the extent permitted by this section, be made by or on behalf of an educational establishment for the purposes of instruction without infringing any copyright in the work, or in the typographical arrangement.

(2)   Not more than one per cent. of any work may be copied by or on behalf of an establishment by virtue of this section in any quarter, that is, in any period 1st January to 31st March, 1st April to 30th June, 1st July to 30th September or 1st October to 31st December.

(3)   Copying is not authorised by this section if, or to the extent that, licences are available authorising the copying in question and the person making the copies knew or ought to have been aware of that fact.

(4)   The terms of a licence granted to an educational establishment authorising the reprographic copying for the purposes of instruction of passages from published literary, dramatic or musical works are of no effect so far as they purport to restrict the proportion of a work which may be copied (whether on payment or free of charge) to less than that which would be permitted under this section.

(5)   Where a copy which would otherwise be an infringing copy is made in accordance with this section but is subsequently dealt with, it shall be treated as an infringing copy for the purposes of that dealing, and if that dealing infringes copyright for all subsequent purposes.

For this purpose "dealt with" means sold or let for hire or offered or exposed for sale or hire.

[239]

Libraries and archives

37   Libraries and archives: introductory

(1)   In sections 38 to 43 (copying by librarians and archivists)—

   (a)   references in any provision to a prescribed library or archive are to a library or archive of a description prescribed for the purposes of that provision by regulations made by the Secretary of State; and

   (b)   references in any provision to the prescribed conditions are to the conditions so prescribed.

(2)   The regulations may provide that, where a librarian or archivist is required to be satisfied as to any matter before making or supplying a copy of a work—

   (a)   he may rely on a signed declaration as to that matter by the person requesting the copy, unless he is aware that it is false in a material particular, and

   (b)   in such cases as may be prescribed, he shall not make or supply a copy in the absence of a signed declaration in such form as may be prescribed.

(3)   Where a person requesting a copy makes a declaration which is false in a material particular and is supplied with a copy which would have been an infringing copy if made by him—

   (a)   he is liable for infringement of copyright as if he had made the copy himself, and

   (b)   the copy shall be treated as an infringing copy.

(4)   The regulations may make different provision for different descriptions of libraries or archives and for different purposes.

(5)   Regulations shall be made by statutory instrument which shall be subject to annulment in pursuance of a resolution of either House of Parliament.

(6)   References in this section, and in sections 38 to 43, to the librarian or archivist include a person acting on his behalf.

[240]

38   Copying by librarians: articles in periodicals

(1)   The librarian of a prescribed library may, if the prescribed conditions are complied with, make and supply a copy of an article in a periodical without infringing any copyright in the text, in any illustrations accompanying the text or in the typographical arrangement.

(2)   The prescribed conditions shall include the following—

   (a)   that copies are supplied only to persons satisfying the librarian that they require them for purposes of research or private study, and will not use them for any other purpose;

   (b)   that no person is furnished with more than one copy of the same article or with copies of more than one article contained in the same issue of a periodical; and

   (c)   that persons to whom copies are supplied are required to pay for them a sum not less than the cost (including a contribution to the general expenses of the library) attributable to their production.

[241]–[242]

39   Copying by librarians: parts of published works

(1)   The librarian of a prescribed library may, if the prescribed conditions are complied with, make and supply from a published edition a copy of part of a literary, dramatic or musical work (other than an article in a periodical) without infringing any copyright in the work, in any illustrations accompanying the work or in the typographical arrangement.

(2)   The prescribed conditions shall include the following—

   (a)   that copies are supplied only to persons satisfying the librarian that they require them for purposes of research or private study, and will not use them for any other purpose;

   (b)   that no person is furnished with more than one copy of the same material or with a copy of more than a reasonable proportion of any work; and

   (c)   that person to whom copies are supplied are required to pay for them a sum not less than the cost (including a contribution to the general expenses of the library) attributable to their production.

[243]

40   Restriction on production of multiple copies of the same material

(1)   Regulations for the purposes of sections 38 and 39 (copying by librarian of article or part of published work) shall contain provision to the effect that a copy shall be supplied only to a person satisfying the librarian that his requirement is not related to any similar requirement of another person.

(2)   The regulations may provide—

   (a)   that requirements shall be regarded as similar if the requirements are for copies of substantially the same material at substantially the same time and for substantially the same purpose; and

   (b)   that requirements of persons shall be regarded as related if those persons receive instruction to which the material is relevant at the same time and place.

[244]

41   Copying by librarians: supply of copies to other libraries

(1)   The librarian of a prescribed library may, if the prescribed conditions are complied with, make and supply to another prescribed library a copy of—

   (a)   an article in a periodical, or

   (b)   the whole or part of a published edition of a literary, dramatic or musical work,

without infringing any copyright in the text of the article or, as the case may be, in the work, in any illustrations accompanying it or in the typographical arrangement.

(2)   Subsection (1)(b) does not apply if at the time the copy is made the librarian making it knows, or could by reasonable inquiry ascertain, the name and address of a person entitled to authorise the making of the copy.

[245]

42   Copying by librarians or archivists: replacement copies of works

(1)   The librarian or archivist of a prescribed library or archive may, if the prescribed conditions are complied with, make a copy from any item in the permanent collection of the library or archive—

    (a)   in order to preserve or replace that item by placing the copy in its permanent collection in addition to or in place of it, or

    (b)   in order to replace in the permanent collection of another prescribed library or archive an item which has been lost, destroyed or damaged,

without infringing the copyright in any literary, dramatic or musical work, in any illustrations accompanying such a work or, in the case of a published edition, in the typographical arrangement.

(2)   The prescribed conditions shall include provision for restricting the making of copies to cases where it is not reasonably practicable to purchase a copy of the item in question to fulfil that purpose.

                        [246]

43   Copying by librarians or archivists: certain unpublished works

(1)   The librarian or archivist of a prescribed library or archive may, if the prescribed conditions are complied with, make and supply a copy of the whole or part of a literary, dramatic or musical work from a document in the library or archive without infringing any copyright in the work or any illustrations accompanying it.

(2)   This section does not apply if—

    (a)   the work had been published before the document was deposited in the library or archive, or

    (b)   the copyright owner has prohibited copying of the work,

and at the time the copy is made the librarian or archivist making it is, or ought to be, aware of that fact.

(3)   The prescribed conditions shall include the following—

    (a)   that copies are supplied only to persons satisfying the librarian or archivist that they require them for purposes of research or private study and will not use them for any other purpose;

    (b)   that no person is furnished with more than one copy of the same material; and

    (c)   that persons to whom copies are supplied are required to pay for them a sum not less than the cost (including a contribution to the general expenses of the library or archive) attributable to their production.

                        [247]

44   Copy of work required to be made as condition of export

If an article of cultural or historical importance or interest cannot lawfully be exported from the United Kingdom unless a copy of it is made and deposited in an appropriate library or archive, it is not an infringement of copyright to make that copy.

                        [248]

Public administration

45   Parliamentary and judicial proceedings

(1)   Copyright is not infringed by anything done for the purposes of parliamentary or judicial proceedings.

(2)   Copyright is not infringed by anything done for the purposes of reporting such proceedings; but this shall not be construed as authorising the copying of a work which is itself a published report of the proceedings.

[249]

46   Royal Commissions and statutory inquiries

(1)   Copyright is not infringed by anything done for the purposes of the proceedings of a Royal Commission or statutory inquiry.

(2)   Copyright is not infringed by anything done for the purpose of reporting any such proceedings held in public; but this shall not be construed as authorising the copying of a work which is itself a published report of the proceedings.

(3)   Copyright in a work is not infringed by the issue to the public of copies of the report of a Royal Commission or statutory inquiry containing the work or material from it.

(4)   In this section—

"Royal Commission" includes a Commission appointed for Northern Ireland by the Secretary of State in pursuance of the prerogative powers of Her Majesty delegated to him under section 7(2) of the Northern Ireland Constitution Act 1973; and

"statutory inquiry" means an inquiry held or investigation conducted in pursuance of a duty imposed or power conferred by or under an enactment.

[250]

47   Material open to public inspection or on official register

(1)   Where material is open to public inspection pursuant to a statutory requirement, or is on a statutory register, any copyright in the material as a literary work is not infringed by the copying of so much of the material as contains factual information of any description, by or with the authority of the appropriate person, for a purpose which does not involve the issuing of copies to the public.

(2)   Where material is open to public inspection pursuant to a statutory requirement, copyright is not infringed by the copying or issuing to the public of copies of the material, by or with the authority of the appropriate person, for the purpose of enabling the material to be inspected at a more convenient time or place or otherwise facilitating the exercise of any right for the purpose of which the requirement is imposed.

(3)   Where material which is open to public inspection pursuant to a statutory requirement, or which is on a statutory register, contains information about matters of general scientific, technical, commercial or economic interest, copyright is not infringed by the copying or issuing to the public of copies of the material, by or with the authority of the appropriate person, for the purpose of disseminating that information.

(4)   The Secretary of State may by order provide that subsection (1), (2) or (3) shall, in such cases as may be specified in the order, apply only to copies marked in such manner as may be so specified.

(5)   The Secretary of State may by order provide that subsections (1) to (3) apply, to such extent and with such modifications as may be specified in the order—

(a)   to material made open to public inspection by—
    (i)   an international organisation specified in the order, or
    (ii) a person so specified who has functions in the United Kingdom under an international agreement to which the United Kingdom is party, or
(b)   to a register maintained by an international organisation specified in the order,

as they apply in relation to material open to public inspection pursuant to a statutory requirement or to a statutory register.

(6)   In this section—
    "appropriate person" means the person required to make the material open to public inspection or, as the case may be, the person maintaining the register;
    "statutory register" means a register maintained in pursuance of a statutory requirement; and
    "statutory requirement" means a requirement imposed by provision made by or under an enactment.

(7)   An order under this section shall be made by statutory instrument which shall be subject to annulment in pursuance of a resolution of either House of Parliament.

[251]

NOTES
    Modified by the Copyright (Material Open to Public Inspection) (International Organisations) Order 1989, SI 1989/1098, arts 2, 3, the Copyright (Material Open to Public Inspection) (Marking of Copies of Maps) Order 1989, SI 1989/1099, art 2, and the Copyright (Material Open to Public Inspection) (Marking of Copies of Plans and Drawings) Order 1990, SI 1990/1427, art 2.

48   Material communicated to the Crown in the course of public business

(1)   This section applies where a literary, dramatic, musical or artistic work has in the course of public business been communicated to the Crown for any purpose, by or with the licence of the copyright owner and a document or other material thing recording or embodying the work is owned by or in the custody or control of the Crown.

(2)   The Crown may, for the purpose for which the work was communicated to it, or any related purpose which could reasonably have been anticipated by the copyright owner, copy the work and issue copies of the work to the public without infringing any copyright in the work.

(3)   The Crown may not copy a work, or issue copies of a work to the public, by virtue of this section if the work has previously been published otherwise than by virtue of this section.

(4)   In subsection (1) "public business" includes any activity carried on by the Crown.

(5)   This section has effect subject to any agreement to the contrary between the Crown and the copyright owner.

[(6)   In this section "the Crown" includes a health service body, as defined in section 60(7) of the National Health Service and Community Care Act 1990, and a National Health Service trust established under Part I of that Act or the National Health Service (Scotland) Act 1978 [and also includes a health and social services body, as defined in Article 7(6) of the Health and Personal Social Services (Northern Ireland) Order 1991, and a Health and Social Services trust established under that Order]; and the reference in subsection (1) above to public business shall be construed accordingly.]

[252]

NOTES

Commencement: 1 April 1991 (sub-s (6)); 1 August 1989 (remainder) (SI 1989/816).

Sub-s (6): added by the National Health Service and Community Care Act 1990, s 60, Sch 8, Pt I, para 3; words in square brackets inserted by the Health and Personal Social Services (Northern Ireland) Order 1991, SI 1991/194, art 7(2), Sch 2, Pt I.

49   Public records

Material which is comprised in public records within the meaning of the Public Records Act 1958, the Public Records (Scotland) Act 1937 or the Public Records Act (Northern Ireland) 1923 which are open to public inspection in pursuance of that Act, may be copied, and a copy may be supplied to any person, by or with the authority of any officer appointed under that Act, without infringement of copyright.

[253]

50   Acts done under statutory authority

(1)   Where the doing of a particular act is specifically authorised by an Act of Parliament, whenever passed, then, unless the Act provides otherwise, the doing of that act does not infringe copyright.

(2)   Subsection (1) applies in relation to an enactment contained in Northern Ireland legislation as it applies in relation to an Act of Parliament.

(3)   Nothing in this section shall be construed as excluding any defence of statutory authority otherwise available under or by virtue of any enactment.

[254]

[Computer programs: lawful users

50A   Back up copies

(1)   It is not an infringement of copyright for a lawful user of a copy of a computer program to make any back up copy of it which it is necessary for him to have for the purposes of his lawful use.

(2)   For the purposes of this section and sections 50B and 50C a person is a lawful user of a computer program if (whether under a licence to do any acts restricted by the copyright in the program or otherwise), he has a right to use the program.

(3)   Where an act is permitted under this section, it is irrelevant whether or not there exists any term or condition in an agreement which purports to prohibit or restrict the act (such terms being, by virtue of section 296A, void).]

[255]

NOTES

Commencement: 1 January 1993.

Inserted, together with the preceding cross heading and ss 50B, 50C below, by the Copyright (Computer Programs) Regulations 1992, SI 1992/3233, regs 2, 8, subject to reg 12(2) thereof (agreements entered into before 1 January 1993 to remain unaffected).

[50B   Decompilation

(1)   It is not an infringement of copyright for a lawful user of a copy of a computer program expressed in a low level language—
    (a)   to convert it into a version expressed in a higher level language, or
    (b)   incidentally in the course of so converting the program, to copy it,

(that is, to "decompile" it), provided that the conditions in subsection (2) are met.

(2)   The conditions are that—
    (a)   it is necessary to decompile the program to obtain the information necessary to create an independent program which can be operated with the program decompiled or with another program ("the permitted objective"); and
    (b)   the information so obtained is not used for any purpose other than the permitted objective.

(3)   In particular, the conditions in subsection (2) are not met if the lawful user—
    (a)   has readily available to him the information necessary to achieve the permitted objective;
    (b)   does not confine the decompiling to such acts as are necessary to achieve the permitted objective;
    (c)   supplies the information obtained by the decompiling to any person to whom it is not necessary to supply it in order to achieve the permitted objective; or
    (d)   uses the information to create a program which is substantially similar in its expression to the program decompiled or to do any act restricted by copyright.

(4)   Where an act is permitted under this section, it is irrelevant whether or not there exists any term or condition in an agreement which purports to prohibit or restrict the act (such terms being, by virtue of section 296A, void).]

[256]

NOTES
Commencement: 1 January 1993.
Inserted, as noted to s 50A above, by the Copyright (Computer Programs) Regulations 1992, SI 1992/3233, regs 2, 8, 12(2).

[50C   Other acts permitted to lawful users

(1)   It is not an infringement of copyright for a lawful user of a copy of a computer program to copy or adapt it, provided that the copying or adapting—
    (a)   is necessary for his lawful use; and
    (b)   is not prohibited under any term or condition of an agreement regulating the circumstances in which his use is lawful.

(2)   It may, in particular, be necessary for the lawful use of a computer program to copy it or adapt it for the purpose of correcting errors in it.

(3)   This section does not apply to any copying or adapting permitted under section 50A or 50B.]

[257]

NOTES
Commencement: 1 January 1993.
Inserted, as noted to s 50A above, by the Copyright (Computer Programs) Regulations 1992, SI 1992/3233, regs 2, 8, 12(2).

Designs

51 Design documents and models

(1) It is not an infringement of any copyright in a design document or model recording or embodying a design for anything other than an artistic work or a typeface to make an article to the design or to copy an article made to the design.

(2) Nor is it an infringement of the copyright to issue to the public, or include in a film, broadcast or cable programme service, anything the making of which was, by virtue of subsection (1), not an infringement of that copyright.

(3) In this section—
  "design" means the design of any aspect of the shape or configuration (whether internal or external) of the whole or part of an article, other than surface decoration; and
  "design document" means any record of a design, whether in the form of a drawing, a written description, a photograph, data stored in a computer or otherwise.

[258]

52 Effect of exploitation of design derived from artistic work

(1) This section applies where an artistic work has been exploited, by or with the licence of the copyright owner, by—
  (a) making by an industrial process articles falling to be treated for the purposes of this Part as copies of the work, and
  (b) marketing such articles, in the United Kingdom or elsewhere.

(2) After the end of the period of 25 years from the end of the calendar year in which such articles are first marketed, the work may be copied by making articles of any description, or doing anything for the purpose of making articles of any description, and anything may be done in relation to articles so made, without infringing copyright in the work.

(3) Where only part of an artistic work is exploited as mentioned in subsection (1), subsection (2) applies only in relation to that part.

(4) The Secretary of State may by order make provision—
  (a) as to the circumstances in which an article, or any description of article, is to be regarded for the purposes of this section as made by an industrial process;
  (b) excluding from the operation of this section such articles of a primarily literary or artistic character as he thinks fit.

(5) An order shall be made by statutory instrument which shall be subject to annulment in pursuance of a resolution of either House of Parliament.

(6) In this section—
  (a) references to articles do not include films; and
  (b) references to the marketing of an article are to its being sold or let for hire or offered or exposed for sale or hire.

[259]

53 Things done in reliance on registration of design

(1) The copyright in an artistic work is not infringed by anything done—

    (a) in pursuance of an assignment or licence made or granted by a person registered under the Registered Designs Act 1949 as the proprietor of a corresponding design, and

    (b) in good faith in reliance on the registration and without notice of any proceedings for the cancellation of the registration or for rectifying the relevant entry in the register of designs;

and this is so notwithstanding that the person registered as the proprietor was not the proprietor of the design for the purposes of the 1949 Act.

(2)   In subsection (1) a "corresponding design", in relation to an artistic work, means a design within the meaning of the 1949 Act which if applied to an article would produce something which would be treated for the purposes of this Part as a copy of the artistic work.

[260]

Typefaces

54   Use of typeface in ordinary course of printing

(1)   It is not an infringement of copyright in an artistic work consisting of the design of a typeface—

    (a) to use the typeface in the ordinary course of typing, composing text, typesetting or printing,

    (b) to possess an article for the purpose of such use, or

    (c) to do anything in relation to material produced by such use;

and this is so notwithstanding that an article is used which is an infringing copy of the work.

(2)   However, the following provisions of this Part apply in relation to persons making, importing or dealing with articles specifically designed or adapted for producing material in a particular typeface, or possessing such articles for the purpose of dealing with them, as if the production of material as mentioned in subsection (1) did infringe copyright in the artistic work consisting of the design of the typeface—

    section 24 (secondary infringement: making, importing, possessing or dealing with article for making infringing copy),

    sections 99 and 100 (order for delivery up and right of seizure),

    section 107(2) (offence of making or possessing such an article), and

    section 108 (order for delivery up in criminal proceedings).

(3)   The references in subsection (2) to "dealing with" an article are to selling, letting for hire, or offering or exposing for sale or hire, exhibiting in public, or distributing.

[261]

55   Articles for producing material in particular typeface

(1)   This section applies to the copyright in an artistic work consisting of the design of a typeface where articles specifically designed or adapted for producing material in that typeface have been marketed by or with the licence of the copyright owner.

(2)   After the period of 25 years from the end of the calendar year in which the first such articles are marketed, the work may be copied by making further such articles, or doing anything for the purpose of making such articles, and anything may be done in relation to articles so made, without infringing copyright in the work.

(3)   In subsection (1) "marketed" means sold, let for hire or offered or exposed for sale or hire, in the United Kingdom or elsewhere.

[262]

Works in electronic form

56   Transfers of copies of works in electronic form

(1)   This section applies where a copy of a work in electronic form has been purchased on terms which, expressly or impliedly or by virtue of any rule of law, allow the purchaser to copy the work, or to adapt it or make copies of an adaptation, in connection with his use of it.

(2)   If there are no express terms—
  (a) prohibiting the transfer of the copy by the purchaser, imposing obligations which continue after a transfer, prohibiting the assignment of any licence or terminating any licence on a transfer, or
  (b) providing for the terms on which a transferee may do the things which the purchaser was permitted to do,

anything which the purchaser was allowed to do may also be done without infringement of copyright by a transferee; but any copy, adaptation or copy of an adaptation made by the purchaser which is not also transferred shall be treated as an infringing copy for all purposes after the transfer.

(3)   The same applies where the original purchased copy is no longer usable and what is transferred is a further copy used in its place.

(4)   The above provisions also apply on a subsequent transfer, with the substitution for references in subsection (2) to the purchaser of references to the subsequent transferor.

[263]

Miscellaneous: literary, dramatic, musical and artistic works

57   Anonymous or pseudonymous works: acts permitted on assumptions as to expiry of copyright or death of author

(1)   Copyright in a literary, dramatic, musical or artistic work is not infringed by an act done at a time when, or in pursuance of arrangements made at a time when—
  (a) it is not possible by reasonable inquiry to ascertain the identity of the author, and
  (b) it is reasonable to assume—
    (i) that copyright has expired, or
    (ii) that the author died [70 years] or more before the beginning of the calendar year in which the act is done or the arrangements are made.

(2)   Subsection (1)(b)(ii) does not apply in relation to—
  (a) a work in which Crown copyright subsists, or
  (b) a work in which copyright originally vested in an international organisation by virtue of section 168 and in respect of which an Order under that section specifies a copyright period longer than [70 years].

(3)   In relation to a work of joint authorship—

(a) the reference in subsection (1) to its being possible to ascertain the identity of the author shall be construed as a reference to its being possible to ascertain the identity of any of the authors, and

(b) the reference in subsection (1)(b)(ii) to the author having died shall be construed as a reference to all the authors having died.

[264]

NOTES

Sub-ss (1), (2): words in square brackets substituted by the Duration of Copyright and Rights in Performances Regulations 1995, SI 1995/3297, reg 5(2), subject to transitional provisions and savings specified in regs 12–35 thereof (see, in particular, reg 15 of the 1995 Regulations).

58 Use of notes or recordings of spoken words in certain cases

(1) Where a record of spoken words is made, in writing or otherwise, for the purpose—

(a) of reporting current events, or

(b) of broadcasting or including in a cable programme service the whole or part of the work,

it is not an infringement of any copyright in the words as a literary work to use the record or material taken from it (or to copy the record, or any such material, and use the copy) for that purpose, provided the following conditions are met.

(2) The conditions are that—

(a) the record is a direct record of the spoken words and is not taken from a previous record or from a broadcast or cable programme;

(b) the making of the record was not prohibited by the speaker and, where copyright already subsisted in the work, did not infringe copyright;

(c) the use made of the record or material taken from it is not of a kind prohibited by or on behalf of the speaker or copyright owner before the record was made; and

(d) the use is by or with the authority of a person who is lawfully in possession of the record.

[265]

59 Public reading or recitation

(1) The reading or recitation in public by one person of a reasonable extract from a published literary or dramatic work does not infringe any copyright in the work if it is accompanied by a sufficient acknowledgement.

(2) Copyright in a work is not infringed by the making of a sound recording, or the broadcasting or inclusion in a cable programme service, of a reading or recitation which by virtue of subsection (1) does not infringe copyright in the work, provided that the recording, broadcast or cable programme consists mainly of material in relation to which it is not necessary to rely on that subsection.

[266]

60 Abstracts of scientific or technical articles

(1) Where an article on a scientific or technical subject is published in a periodical accompanied by an abstract indicating the contents of the article, it is not an infringement of copyright in the abstract, or in the article, to copy the abstract or issue copies of it to the public.

(2) This section does not apply if or to the extent that there is a licensing scheme certified for the purposes of this section under section 143 providing for the grant of licences.

[267]

61 Recordings of folksongs

(1) A sound recording of a performance of a song may be made for the purpose of including it in an archive maintained by a designated body without infringing any copyright in the words as a literary work or in the accompanying musical work, provided the conditions in subsection (2) below are met.

(2) The conditions are that—
    (a) the words are unpublished and of unknown authorship at the time the recording is made,
    (b) the making of the recording does not infringe any other copyright, and
    (c) its making is not prohibited by any performer.

(3) Copies of a sound recording made in reliance on subsection (1) and included in an archive maintained by a designated body may, if the prescribed conditions are met, be made and supplied by the archivist without infringing copyright in the recording or the works included in it.

(4) The prescribed conditions shall include the following—
    (a) that copies are only supplied to persons satisfying the archivist that they require them for purposes of research or private study and will not use them for any other purpose, and
    (b) that no person is furnished with more than one copy of the same recording.

(5) In this section—
    (a) "designated" means designated for the purposes of this section by order of the Secretary of State, who shall not designate a body unless satisfied that it is not established or conducted for profit,
    (b) "prescribed" means prescribed for the purposes of this section by order of the Secretary of State, and
    (c) references to the archivist include a person acting on his behalf.

(6) An order under this section shall be made by statutory instrument which shall be subject to annulment in pursuance of a resolution of either House of Parliament.

[268]

62 Representation of certain artistic works on public display

(1) This section applies to—
    (a) buildings, and
    (b) sculptures, models for buildings and works of artistic craftsmanship, if permanently situated in a public place or in premises open to the public.

(2) The copyright in such a work is not infringed by—
    (a) making a graphic work representing it,
    (b) making a photograph or film of it, or
    (c) broadcasting or including in a cable programme service a visual image of it.

(3)　Nor is the copyright infringed by the issue to the public of copies, or the broadcasting or inclusion in a cable programme service, of anything whose making was, by virtue of this section, not an infringement of the copyright.

[269]

63　Advertisement of sale of artistic work

(1)　It is not an infringement of copyright in an artistic work to copy it, or to issue copies to the public, for the purpose of advertising the sale of the work.

(2)　Where a copy which would otherwise be an infringing copy is made in accordance with this section but is subsequently dealt with for any other purpose, it shall be treated as an infringing copy for the purposes of that dealing, and if that dealing infringes copyright for all subsequent purposes.

For this purpose "dealt with" means sold or let for hire, offered or exposed for sale or hire, exhibited in public or distributed.

[270]

64　Making of subsequent works by same artist

Where the author of an artistic work is not the copyright owner, he does not infringe the copyright by copying the work in making another artistic work, provided he does not repeat or imitate the main design of the earlier work.

[271]

65　Reconstruction of buildings

Anything done for the purposes of reconstructing a building does not infringe any copyright—
  (a)　in the building, or
  (b)　in any drawings or plans in accordance with which the building was, by or with the licence of the copyright owner, constructed.

[272]

Miscellaneous: sound recordings, films and computer programs

66　Rental of sound recordings, films and computer programs

(1)　The Secretary of State may by order provide that in such cases as may be specified in the order the rental to the public of copies of sound recordings, films or computer programs shall be treated as licensed by the copyright owner subject only to the payment of such reasonable royalty or other payment as may be agreed or determined in default of agreement by the Copyright Tribunal.

(2)　No such order shall apply if, or to the extent that, there is a licensing scheme certified for the purposes of this section under section 143 providing for the grant of licences.

(3)　An order may make different provision for different cases and may specify cases by reference to any factor relating to the work, the copies rented, the renter or the circumstances of the rental.

(4)　An order shall be made by statutory instrument; and no order shall be made unless a draft of it has been laid before and approved by a resolution of each House of Parliament.

(5)   Copyright in a computer program is not infringed by the rental of copies to the public after the end of the period of 50 years from the end of the calendar year in which copies of it were first issued to the public in electronic form.

(6)   Nothing in this section affects any liability under section 23 (secondary infringement) in respect of the rental of infringing copies.

[273]

[Miscellaneous: films and sound recordings

66A   Films: acts permitted on assumptions as to expiry of copyright, &c

(1)   Copyright in a film is not infringed by an act done at a time when, or in pursuance of arrangements made at a time when—
  (a)   it is not possible by reasonable inquiry to ascertain the identity of any of the persons referred to in section 13B(2)(a) to (d) (persons by reference to whose life the copyright period is ascertained), and
  (b)   it is reasonable to assume—
     (i)   that copyright has expired, or
     (ii) that the last to die of those persons died 70 years or more before the beginning of the calendar year in which the act is done or the arrangements are made.

(2)   Subsection (1)(b)(ii) does not apply in relation to—
  (a)   a film in which Crown copyright subsists, or
  (b)   a film in which copyright originally vested in an international organisation by virtue of section 168 and in respect of which an Order under that section specifies a copyright period longer than 70 years.]

[274]

NOTES
Commencement: 1 January 1996.
Inserted, together with the cross-heading immediately preceding it, by the Duration of Copyright and Rights in Performances Regulations 1995, SI 1995/3297, reg 6(2), subject to transitional provisions and savings specified in regs 12–35 thereof.

67   Playing of sound recordings for purposes of club, society, etc

(1)   It is not an infringement of the copyright in a sound recording to play it as part of the activities of, or for the benefit of, a club, society or other organisation if the following conditions are met.

(2)   The conditions are—
  (a)   that the organisation is not established or conducted for profit and its main objects are charitable or are otherwise concerned with the advancement of religion, education or social welfare, and
  (b)   that the proceeds of any charge for admission to the place where the recording is to be heard are applied solely for the purposes of the organisation.

[275]

Miscellaneous: broadcasts and cable programmes

68   Incidental recording for purposes of broadcast or cable programme

(1)   This section applies where by virtue of a licence or assignment of copyright a person is authorised to broadcast or include in a cable programme service—

(a)   a literary, dramatic or musical work, or an adaptation of such a work,

(b)   an artistic work, or

(c)   a sound recording or film.

(2)   He shall by virtue of this section be treated as licensed by the owner of the copyright in the work to do or authorise any of the following for the purposes of the broadcast or cable programme—

(a)   in the case of a literary, dramatic or musical work, or an adaptation of such a work, to make a sound recording or film of the work or adaptation;

(b)   in the case of an artistic work, to take a photograph or make a film of the work;

(c)   in the case of a sound recording or film, to make a copy of it.

(3)   That licence is subject to the condition that the recording, film, photograph or copy in question—

(a)   shall not be used for any other purpose, and

(b)   shall be destroyed within 28 days of being first used for broadcasting the work or, as the case may be, including it in a cable programme service.

(4)   A recording, film, photograph or copy made in accordance with this section shall be treated as an infringing copy—

(a)   for the purposes of any use in breach of the condition mentioned in subsection (3)(a), and

(b)   for all purposes after that condition or the condition mentioned in subsection (3)(b) is broken.

[276]

69   Recording for purposes of supervision and control of broadcasts and cable programmes

(1)   Copyright is not infringed by the making or use by the British Broadcasting Corporation, for the purpose of maintaining supervision and control over programmes broadcast by them, of recordings of those programmes.

[(2)   Copyright is not infringed by anything done in pursuance of—

(a)   section 11(1), 95(1), 145(4), (5) or (7), 155(3) or 167(1) of the Broadcasting Act 1990;

(b)   a condition which, by virtue of section 11(2) or 95(2) of that Act, is included in a licence granted under Part I or III of that Act; or

(c)   a direction given under section 109(2) of that Act (power of Radio Authority to require production of recordings etc).

(3)   Copyright is not infringed by—

(a)   the use by the Independent Television Commission or the Radio Authority, in connection with the performance of any of their functions under the Broadcasting Act 1990, of any recording, script or transcript which is provided to them under or by virtue of any provision of that Act; or

(b)   the use by the Broadcasting Complaints Commission or the Broadcasting Standards Council, in connection with any complaint made to them under that Act, of any recording or transcript requested or required to be provided to them, and so provided, under section 145(4) or (7) or section 155(3) of that Act.]

[277]

NOTES

Commencement: 1 January 1991 (sub-ss (2), (3)); 1 August 1989 (remainder). (SI 1989/816).
Sub-ss (2), (3): substituted by the Broadcasting Act 1990, s 203(1), Sch 20, para 50.

70   Recording for purposes of time-shifting

The making for private and domestic use of a recording of a broadcast or cable programme solely for the purpose of enabling it to be viewed or listened to at a more convenient time does not infringe any copyright in the broadcast or cable programme or in any work included in it.

[278]

71   Photographs of television broadcasts or cable programmes

The making for private and domestic use of a photograph of the whole or any part of an image forming part of a television broadcast or cable programme, or a copy of such a photograph, does not infringe any copyright in the broadcast or cable programme or in any film included in it.

[279]

72   Free public showing or playing of broadcast or cable programme

(1)   The showing or playing in public of a broadcast or cable programme to an audience who have not paid for admission to the place where the broadcast or programme is to be seen or heard does not infringe any copyright in—
    (a)   the broadcast or cable programme, or
    (b)   any sound recording or film included in it.

(2)   The audience shall be treated as having paid for admission to a place—
    (a)   if they have paid for admission to a place of which that place forms part; or
    (b)   if goods or services are supplied at that place (or a place of which it forms part)—
        (i)   at prices which are substantially attributable to the facilities afforded for seeing or hearing the broadcast or programme, or
        (ii)   at prices exceeding those usually charged there and which are partly attributable to those facilities.

(3)   The following shall not be regarded as having paid for admission to a place—
    (a)   persons admitted as residents or inmates of the place;
    (b)   persons admitted as members of a club or society where the payment is only for membership of the club or society and the provision of facilities for seeing or hearing broadcasts or programmes is only incidental to the main purposes of the club or society.

(4)   Where the making of the broadcast or inclusion of the programme in a cable programme service was an infringement of the copyright in a sound recording or film, the fact that it was heard or seen in public by the reception of the broadcast or programme shall be taken into account in assessing the damages for that infringement.

[280]

73   Reception and re-transmission of broadcast in cable programme service

(1)   This section applies where a broadcast made from a place in the United Kingdom is, by reception and immediate re-transmission, included in a cable programme service.

(2)   The copyright in the broadcast is not infringed—
   (a)   . . .
   (b)   if and to the extent that the broadcast is made for reception in the area in which the cable programme service is provided and is not a satellite transmission or an encrypted transmission.

(3)   The copyright in any work included in the broadcast is not infringed—
   (a)   . . .
   (b)   if and to the extent that the broadcast is made for reception in the area in which the cable programme service is provided;

but where the making of the broadcast was an infringement of the copyright in the work, the fact that the broadcast was re-transmitted as a programme in a cable programme service shall be taken into account in assessing the damages for that infringement.

[281]

NOTES
Sub-ss (2), (3): para (a) repealed by the Broadcasting Act 1990, s 203(3), Sch 21.

---

74   Provision of sub-titled copies of broadcast or cable programme

(1)   A designated body may, for the purpose of providing people who are deaf or hard of hearing, or physically or mentally handicapped in other ways, with copies which are sub-titled or otherwise modified for their special needs, make copies of television broadcasts or cable programmes and issue copies to the public, without infringing any copyright in the broadcasts or cable programmes or works included in them.

(2)   A "designated body" means a body designated for the purposes of this section by order of the Secretary of State, who shall not designate a body unless he is satisfied that it is not established or conducted for profit.

(3)   An order under this section shall be made by statutory instrument which shall be subject to annulment in pursuance of a resolution of either House of Parliament.

(4)   This section does not apply if, or to the extent that, there is a licensing scheme certified for the purposes of this section under section 143 providing for the grant of licences.

[282]

75   Recording for archival purposes

(1)   A recording of a broadcast or cable programme of a designated class, or a copy of such a recording, may be made for the purpose of being placed in an archive maintained by a designated body without thereby infringing any copyright in the broadcast or cable programme or in any work included in it.

(2)   In subsection (1) "designated" means designated for the purposes of this section by order of the Secretary of State, who shall not designate a body unless he is satisfied that it is not established or conducted for profit.

(3)   An order under this section shall be made by statutory instrument which shall be subject to annulment in pursuance of a resolution of either House of Parliament.

[283]

Adaptations

76   Adaptations

An act which by virtue of this Chapter may be done without infringing copyright in a literary, dramatic or musical work does not, where that work is an adaptation, infringe any copyright in the work from which the adaptation was made.

[284]

CHAPTER IV
MORAL RIGHTS

Right to be identified as author or director

77   Right to be identified as author or director

(1)   The author of a copyright literary, dramatic, musical or artistic work, and the director of a copyright film, has the right to be identified as the author or director of the work in the circumstances mentioned in this section; but the right is not infringed unless it has been asserted in accordance with section 78.

(2)   The author of a literary work (other than words intended to be sung or spoken with music) or a dramatic work has the right to be identified whenever—
    (a)   the work is published commercially, performed in public, broadcast or included in a cable programme service; or
    (b)   copies of a film or sound recording including the work are issued to the public;

and that right includes the right to be identified whenever any of those events occur in relation to an adaptation of the work as the author of the work from which the adaptation was made.

(3)   The author of a musical work, or a literary work consisting of words intended to be sung or spoken with music, has the right to be identified whenever—
    (a)   the work is published commercially;
    (b)   copies of a sound recording of the work are issued to the public; or
    (c)   a film of which the sound-track includes the work is shown in public or copies of such a film are issued to the public;

and that right includes the right to be identified whenever any of those events occur in relation to an adaptation of the work as the author of the work from which the adaptation was made.

(4)   The author of an artistic work has the right to be identified whenever—
    (a)   the work is published commercially or exhibited in public, or a visual image of it is broadcast or included in a cable programme service;
    (b)   a film including a visual image of the work is shown in public or copies of such a film are issued to the public; or
    (c)   in the case of a work of architecture in the form of a building or a model for a building, a sculpture or a work of artistic craftsmanship, copies of a graphic work representing it, or of a photograph of it, are issued to the public.

(5)   The author of a work of architecture in the form of a building also has the right to be identified on the building as constructed or, where more than one building is constructed to the design, on the first to be constructed.

(6) The director of a film has the right to be identified whenever the film is shown in public, broadcast or included in a cable programme service or copies of the film are issued to the public.

(7) The right of the author or director under this section is—

(a) in the case of commercial publication or the issue to the public of copies of a film or sound recording, to be identified in or on each copy or, if that is not appropriate, in some other manner likely to bring his identity to the notice of a person acquiring a copy,

(b) in the case of identification on a building, to be identified by appropriate means visible to persons entering or approaching the building, and

(c) in any other case, to be identified in a manner likely to bring his identity to the attention of a person seeing or hearing the performance, exhibition, showing, broadcast or cable programme in question;

and the identification must in each case be clear and reasonably prominent.

(8) If the author or director in asserting his right to be identified specifies a pseudonym, initials or some other particular form of identification, that form shall be used; otherwise any reasonable form of identification may be used.

(9) This section has effect subject to section 79 (exceptions to right).

[285]

78 Requirement that right be asserted

(1) A person does not infringe the right conferred by section 77 (right to be identified as author or director) by doing any of the acts mentioned in that section unless the right has been asserted in accordance with the following provisions so as to bind him in relation to that act.

(2) The right may be asserted generally, or in relation to any specified act or description of acts—

(a) on an assignment of copyright in the work, by including in the instrument effecting the assignment a statement that the author or director asserts in relation to that work his right to be identified, or

(b) by instrument in writing signed by the author or director.

(3) The right may also be asserted in relation to the public exhibition of an artistic work—

(a) by securing that when the author or other first owner of copyright parts with possession of the original, or of a copy made by him or under his direction or control, the author is identified on the original or copy, or on a frame, mount or other thing to which it is attached, or

(b) by including in a licence by which the author or other first owner of copyright authorises the making of copies of the work a statement signed by or on behalf of the person granting the licence that the author asserts his right to be identified in the event of the public exhibition of a copy made in pursuance of the licence.

(4) The persons bound by an assertion of the right under subsection (2) or (3) are—

(a) in the case of an assertion under subsection (2)(a), the assignee and anyone claiming through him, whether or not he has notice of the assertion;

(b) in the case of an assertion under subsection (2)(b), anyone to whose notice the assertion is brought;

(c) in the case of an assertion under subsection (3)(a), anyone into whose hands that original or copy comes, whether or not the identification is still present or visible;

(d) in the case of an assertion under subsection (3)(b), the licensee and anyone into whose hands a copy made in pursuance of the licence comes, whether or not he has notice of the assertion.

(5) In an action for infringement of the right the court shall, in considering remedies, take into account any delay in asserting the right.

[286]

79 Exceptions to right

(1) The right conferred by section 77 (right to be identified as author or director) is subject to the following exceptions.

(2) The right does not apply in relation to the following descriptions of work—
(a) a computer program;
(b) the design of a typeface;
(c) any computer-generated work.

(3) The right does not apply to anything done by or with the authority of the copyright owner where copyright in the work originally vested—
(a) in the author's employer by virtue of section 11(2) (works produced in course of employment), or
(b) in the director's employer by virtue of section 9(2)(a) (person to be treated as author of film).

(4) The right is not infringed by an act which by virtue of any of the following provisions would not infringe copyright in the work—
(a) section 30 (fair dealing for certain purposes), so far as it relates to the reporting of current events by means of a sound recording, film, broadcast or cable programme;
(b) section 31 (incidental inclusion of work in an artistic work, sound recording, film, broadcast or cable programme);
(c) section 32(3) (examination questions);
(d) section 45 (parliamentary and judicial proceedings);
(e) section 46(1) or (2) (Royal Commissions and statutory inquiries);
(f) section 51 (use of design documents and models);
(g) section 52 (effect of exploitation of design derived from artistic work);
(h) [section 57 or 66A (acts permitted on assumptions as to expiry of copyright, etc)].

(5) The right does not apply in relation to any work made for the purpose of reporting current events.

(6) The right does not apply in relation to the publication in—
(a) a newspaper, magazine or similar periodical, or
(b) an encyclopaedia, dictionary, yearbook or other collective work of reference,

of a literary, dramatic, musical or artistic work made for the purposes of such publication or made available with the consent of the author for the purposes of such publication.

(7)   The right does not apply in relation to—

(a)   a work in which Crown copyright or Parliamentary copyright subsists, or

(b)   a work in which copyright originally vested in an international organisation by virtue of section 168,

unless the author or director has previously been identified as such in or on published copies of the work.

[287]

_____

NOTES

Sub-s (4): words in square brackets substituted by the Duration of Copyright and Rights in Performances Regulations 1995, SI 1995/3297, reg 6(3), subject to transitional provisions and savings specified in regs 12–35 thereof.

_____

Right to object to derogatory treatment of work

80   Right to object to derogatory treatment of work

(1)   The author of a copyright literary, dramatic, musical or artistic work, and the director of a copyright film, has the right is the circumstances mentioned in this section not to have his work subjected to derogatory treatment.

(2)   For the purposes of this section—

(a)   "treatment" of a work means any addition to, deletion from or alteration to or adaptation of the work, other than—

(i)   a translation of a literary or dramatic work, or

(ii)   an arrangement or transcription of a musical work involving no more than a change of key or register; and

(b)   the treatment of a work is derogatory if it amounts to distortion or mutilation of the work or is otherwise prejudicial to the honour or reputation of the author or director;

and in the following provisions of this section references to a derogatory treatment of a work shall be construed accordingly.

(3)   In the case of a literary, dramatic or musical work the right is infringed by a person who—

(a)   publishes commercially, performs in public, broadcasts or includes in a cable programme service a derogatory treatment of the work; or

(b)   issues to the public copies of a film or sound recording of, or including, a derogatory treatment of the work.

(4)   In the case of an artistic work the right is infringed by a person who—

(a)   publishes commercially or exhibits in public a derogatory treatment of the work, or broadcasts or includes in a cable programme service a visual image of a derogatory treatment of the work,

(b)   shows in public a film including a visual image of a derogatory treatment of the work or issues to the public copies of such a film, or

(c)   in the case of—

(i)   a work of architecture in the form of a model for a building,

(ii)   a sculpture, or

(iii) a work of artistic craftsmanship,

issues to the public copies of a graphic work representing, or of a photograph of, a derogatory treatment of the work.

(5)   Subsection (4) does not apply to a work of architecture in the form of a building; but where the author of such a work is identified on the building and it is the subject of derogatory treatment he has the right to require the identification to be removed.

(6)   In the case of a film, the right is infringed by a person who—

  (a)   shows in public, broadcasts or includes in a cable programme service a derogatory treatment of the film; or

  (b)   issues to the public copies of a derogatory treatment of the film,

  . . .

(7)   The right conferred by this section extends to the treatment of parts of a work resulting from a previous treatment by a person other than the author or director, if those parts are attributed to, or are likely to be regarded as the work of, the author or director.

(8)   This section has effect subject to sections 81 and 82 (exceptions to and qualifications of right).

[288]

NOTES

   Sub-s (6): words omitted repealed by the Duration of Copyright and Rights in Performances Regulations 1995, SI 1995/3297, reg 9(2), subject to transitional provisions and savings specified in regs 12–35 thereof.

---

81   Exceptions to right

(1)   The right conferred by section 80 (right to object to derogatory treatment of work) is subject to the following exceptions.

(2)   The right does not apply to a computer program or to any computer-generated work.

(3)   The right does not apply in relation to any work made for the purpose of reporting current events.

(4)   The right does not apply in relation to the publication in—

  (a)   a newspaper, magazine or similar periodical, or

  (b)   an encyclopaedia, dictionary, yearbook or other collective work of reference,

of a literary, dramatic, musical or artistic work made for the purposes of such publication or made available with the consent of the author for the purposes of such publication.

   Nor does the right apply in relation to any subsequent exploitation elsewhere of such a work without any modification of the published version.

(5)   The right is not infringed by an act which by virtue of [section 57 or 66A (acts permitted on assumptions as to expiry of copyright, etc)] would not infringe copyright.

(6)   The right is not infringed by anything done for the purpose of—

  (a)   avoiding the commission of an offence,

  (b)   complying with a duty imposed by or under an enactment, or

  (c)   in the case of the British Broadcasting Corporation, avoiding the inclusion in a programme broadcast by them of anything which offends against good taste or decency or which is likely to encourage or incite to crime or to lead to disorder or to be offensive to public feeling, provided, where the author or director is identified at the time of the relevant act or has previously been identified in or on published copies of the work, that there is a sufficient disclaimer.

[289]

_____

NOTES

Sub-s (5): words in square brackets substituted by the Duration of Copyright and Rights in Performances Regulations 1995, SI 1995/3297, reg 6(3), subject to transitional provisions and savings specified in regs 12–35 thereof.

_____

82   Qualification of right in certain cases

(1)   This section applies to—
   (a) works in which copyright originally vested in the author's employer by virtue of section 11(2) (works produced in course of employment) or in the director's employer by virtue of section 9(2)(a) (person to be treated as author of film),
   (b) works in which Crown copyright or Parliamentary copyright subsists, and
   (c) works in which copyright originally vested in an international organisation by virtue of section 168.

(2)   The right conferred by section 80 (right to object to derogatory treatment of work) does not apply to anything done in relation to such a work by or with the authority of the copyright owner unless the author or director—
   (a) is identified at the time of the relevant act, or
   (b) has previously been identified in or on published copies of the work;

and where in such a case the right does apply, it is not infringed if there is a sufficient disclaimer.

[290]

83   Infringement of right by possessing or dealing with infringing article

(1)   The right conferred by section 80 (right to object to derogatory treatment of work) is also infringed by a person who—
   (a) possesses in the course of a business, or
   (b) sells or lets for hire, or offers or exposes for sale or hire, or
   (c) in the course of a business exhibits in public or distributes, or
   (d) distributes otherwise than in the course of a business so as to affect prejudicially the honour or reputation of the author or director,

an article which is, and which he knows or has reason to believe is, an infringing article.

(2)   An "infringing article" means a work or a copy of a work which—
   (a) has been subjected to derogatory treatment within the meaning of section 80, and
   (b) has been or is likely to be the subject of any of the acts mentioned in that section in circumstances infringing that right.

[291]

False attribution of work

84   False attribution of work

(1)   A person has the right in the circumstances mentioned in this section—

    (a) not to have a literary, dramatic, musical or artistic work falsely attributed to him as author, and

    (b) not to have a film falsely attributed to him as director;

and in this section an "attribution", in relation to such a work, means a statement (express or implied) as to who is the author or director.

(2)   The right is infringed by a person who—

    (a) issues to the public copies of a work of any of those descriptions in or on which there is a false attribution, or

    (b) exhibits in public an artistic work, or a copy of an artistic work, in or on which there is a false attribution.

(3)   The right is also infringed by a person who—

    (a) in the case of a literary, dramatic or musical work, performs the work in public, broadcasts it or includes it in a cable programme service as being the work of a person, or

    (b) in the case of a film, shows it in public, broadcasts it or includes it in a cable programme service as being directed by a person,

knowing or having reason to believe that the attribution is false.

(4)   The right is also infringed by the issue to the public or public display of material containing a false attribution in connection with any of the acts mentioned in subsection (2) or (3).

(5)   The right is also infringed by a person who in the course of a business—

    (a) possesses or deals with a copy of a work of any of the descriptions mentioned in subsection (1) in or on which there is a false attribution, or

    (b) in the case of an artistic work, possesses or deals with the work itself when there is a false attribution in or on it,

knowing or having reason to believe that there is such an attribution and that it is false.

(6)   In the case of an artistic work the right is also infringed by a person who in the course of a business—

    (a) deals with a work which has been altered after the author parted with possession of it as being the unaltered work of the author, or

    (b) deals with a copy of such a work as being a copy of the unaltered work of the author,

knowing or having reason to believe that that is not the case.

(7)   References in this section to dealing are to selling or letting for hire, offering or exposing for sale or hire, exhibiting in public, or distributing.

(8)   This section applies where, contrary to the fact—

    (a) a literary, dramatic or musical work is falsely represented as being an adaptation of the work of a person, or

    (b) a copy of an artistic work is falsely represented as being a copy made by the author of the artistic work,

as it applies where the work is falsely attributed to a person as author.

Right to privacy of certain photographs and films

85   Right to privacy of certain photographs and films

(1)   A person who for private and domestic purposes commissions the taking of a photograph or the making of a film has, where copyright subsists in the resulting work, the right not to have—

    (a)   copies of the work issued to the public,

    (b)   the work exhibited or shown in public, or

    (c)   the work broadcast or included in a cable programme service;

and, except as mentioned in subsection (2), a person who does or authorises the doing of any of those acts infringes that right.

(2)   The right is not infringed by an act which by virtue of any of the following provisions would not infringe copyright in the work—

    (a)   section 31 (incidental inclusion of work in an artistic work, film, broadcast or cable programme);

    (b)   section 45 (parliamentary and judicial proceedings);

    (c)   section 46 (Royal Commissions and statutory inquiries);

    (d)   section 50 (acts done under statutory authority);

    (e)   [section 57 or 66A (acts permitted on assumptions as to expiry of copyright, etc)].

[293]

NOTES

Sub-s (2): words in square brackets substituted by the Duration of Copyright and Rights in Performances Regulations 1995, SI 1995/3297, reg 6(3), subject to transitional provisions and savings specified in regs 12–35 thereof.

Supplementary

86   Duration of rights

(1)   The rights conferred by section 77 (right to be identified as author or director), section 80 (right to object to derogatory treatment of work) and section 85 (right to privacy of certain photographs and films) continue to subsist so long as copyright subsists in the work.

(2)   The right conferred by section 84 (false attribution) continues to subsist until 20 years after a person's death.

[294]

87   Consent and waiver of rights

(1)   It is not an infringement of any of the rights conferred by this Chapter to do any act to which the person entitled to the right has consented.

(2)   Any of those rights may be waived by instrument in writing signed by the person giving up the right.

(3)   A waiver—

    (a)   may relate to a specific work, to works of a specified description or to works generally, and may relate to existing or future works, and

(b)   may be conditional or unconditional and may be expressed to be subject to revocation;

and if made in favour of the owner or prospective owner of the copyright in the work or works to which it relates, it shall be presumed to extend to his licensees and successors in title unless a contrary intention is expressed.

(4)   Nothing in this Chapter shall be construed as excluding the operation of the general law of contract or estoppel in relation to an informal waiver or other transaction in relation to any of the rights mentioned in subsection (1).

[295]

88   Application of provisions to joint works

(1)   The right conferred by section 77 (right to be identified as author or director) is, in the case of a work of joint authorship, a right of each joint author to be identified as a joint author and must be asserted in accordance with section 78 by each joint author in relation to himself.

(2)   The right conferred by section 80 (right to object to derogatory treatment of work) is, in the case of a work of joint authorship, a right of each joint author and his right is satisfied if he consents to the treatment in question.

(3)   A waiver under section 87 of those rights by one joint author does not affect the rights of the other joint authors.

(4)   The right conferred by section 84 (false attribution) is infringed, in the circumstances mentioned in that section—

(a)   by any false statement as to the authorship of a work of joint authorship, and

(b)   by the false attribution of joint authorship in relation to a work of sole authorship;

and such a false attribution infringes the right of every person to whom authorship of any description is, whether rightly or wrongly, attributed.

(5)   The above provisions also apply (with any necessary adaptations) in relation to a film which was, or is alleged to have been, jointly directed, as they apply to a work which is, or is alleged to be, a work of joint authorship.

A film is "jointly directed" if it is made by the collaboration of two or more directors and the contribution of each director is not distinct from that of the other director or directors.

(6)   The right conferred by section 85 (right to privacy of certain photographs and films) is, in the case of a work made in pursuance of a joint commission, a right of each person who commissioned the making of the work, so that—

(a)   the right of each is satisfied if he consents to the act in question, and

(b)   a waiver under section 87 by one of them does not affect the rights of the others.

[296]

89   Application of provisions to parts of works

(1)   The rights conferred by section 77 (right to be identified as author or director) and section 85 (right to privacy of certain photographs and films) apply in relation to the whole or any substantial part of a work.

(2)   The rights conferred by section 80 (right to object to derogatory treatment of work) and section 84 (false attribution) apply in relation to the whole or any part of a work.

[297]

CHAPTER V
DEALINGS WITH RIGHTS IN COPYRIGHT WORKS

Copyright

90   Assignment and licences

(1)   Copyright is transmissible by assignment, by testamentary disposition or by operation of law, as personal or moveable property.

(2)   An assignment or other transmission of copyright may be partial, that is, limited so as to apply—
    (a)   to one or more, but not all, of the things the copyright owner has the exclusive right to do;
    (b)   to part, but not the whole, of the period for which the copyright is to subsist.

(3)   An assignment of copyright is not effective unless it is in writing signed by or on behalf of the assignor.

(4)   A licence granted by a copyright owner is binding on every successor in title to his interest in the copyright, except a purchaser in good faith for valuable consideration and without notice (actual or constructive) of the licence or a person deriving title from such a purchaser; and references in this Part to doing anything with, or without, the licence of the copyright owner shall be construed accordingly.

[298]

91   Prospective ownership of copyright

(1)   Where by an agreement made in relation to future copyright, and signed by or on behalf of the prospective owner of the copyright, the prospective owner purports to assign the future copyright (wholly or partially) to another person, then if, on the copyright coming into existence, the assignee or another person claiming under him would be entitled as against all other persons to require the copyright to be vested in him, the copyright shall vest in the assignee or his successor in title by virtue of this subsection.

(2)   In this Part—
    "future copyright" means copyright which will or may come into existence in respect of a future work or class of works or on the occurrence of a future event; and
    "prospective owner" shall be construed accordingly, and includes a person who is prospectively entitled to copyright by virtue of such an agreement as is mentioned in subsection (1).

(3)   A licence granted by a prospective owner of copyright is binding on every successor in title to his interest (or prospective interest) in the right, except a purchaser in good faith for valuable consideration and without notice (actual or constructive) of the licence or a person deriving title from such a purchaser; and

references in this Part to doing anything with, or without, the licence of the copyright owner shall be construed accordingly.

[299]

92   Exclusive licences

(1)   In this Part an "exclusive licence" means a licence in writing signed by or on behalf of the copyright owner authorising the licensee to the exclusion of all other persons, including the person granting the licence, to exercise a right which would otherwise be exercisable exclusively by the copyright owner.

(2)   The licensee under an exclusive licence has the same rights against a successor in title who is bound by the licence as he has against the person granting the licence.

[300]

93   Copyright to pass under will with unpublished work

Where under a bequest (whether specific or general) a person is entitled, beneficially or otherwise, to—

    (a)   an original document or other material thing recording or embodying a literary, dramatic, musical or artistic work which was not published before the death of the testator, or

    (b)   an original material thing containing a sound recording or film which was not published before the death of the testator,

the bequest shall, unless a contrary intention is indicated in the testator's will or a codicil to it, be construed as including the copyright in the work in so far as the testator was the owner of the copyright immediately before his death.

[301]

Moral rights

94   Moral rights not assignable

The rights conferred by Chapter IV (moral rights) are not assignable.

[302]

95   Transmission of moral rights on death

(1)   On the death of a person entitled to the right conferred by section 77 (right to identification of author or director), section 80 (right to object to derogatory treatment of work) or section 85 (right to privacy of certain photographs and films)—

    (a)   the right passes to such person as he may by testamentary disposition specifically direct,

    (b)   if there is no such direction but the copyright in the work in question forms part of his estate, the right passes to the person to whom the copyright passes, and

    (c)   if or to the extent that the right does not pass under paragraph (a) or (b) it is exercisable by his personal representatives.

(2)   Where copyright forming part of a person's estate passes in part to one person and in part to another, as for example where a bequest is limited so as to apply—

    (a)   to one or more, but not all, of the things the copyright owner has the exclusive right to do or authorise, or

(b)   to part, but not the whole, of the period for which the copyright is to subsist,

any right which passes with the copyright by virtue of subsection (1) is correspondingly divided.

(3)   Where by virtue of subsection (1)(a) or (b) a right becomes exercisable by more than one person—

(a)   it may, in the case of the right conferred by section 77 (right to identification of author or director), be asserted by any of them;

(b)   it is, in the case of the right conferred by section 80 (right to object to derogatory treatment of work) or section 85 (right to privacy of certain photographs and films), a right exercisable by each of them and is satisfied in relation to any of them if he consents to the treatment or act in question; and

(c)   any waiver of the right in accordance with section 87 by one of them does not affect the rights of the others.

(4)   A consent or waiver previously given or made binds any person to whom a right passes by virtue of subsection (1).

(5)   Any infringement after a person's death of the right conferred by section 84 (false attribution) is actionable by his personal representatives.

(6)   Any damages recovered by personal representatives by virtue of this section in respect of an infringement after a person's death shall devolve as part of his estate as if the right of action had subsisted and been vested in him immediately before his death.

[303]

CHAPTER VI
REMEDIES FOR INFRINGEMENT

Rights and remedies of copyright owner

96   Infringement actionable by copyright owner

(1)   An infringement of copyright is actionable by the copyright owner.

(2)   In an action for infringement of copyright all such relief by way of damages, injunctions, accounts or otherwise is available to the plaintiff as is available in respect of the infringement of any other property right.

(3)   This section has effect subject to the following provisions of this Chapter.

[304]

97   Provisions as to damages in infringement action

(1)   Where in an action for infringement of copyright it is shown that at the time of the infringement the defendant did not know, and had no reason to believe, that copyright subsisted in the work to which the action relates, the plaintiff is not entitled to damages against him, but without prejudice to any other remedy.

(2)   The court may in an action for infringement of copyright having regard to all the circumstances, and in particular to—

(a)   the flagrancy of the infringement, and

(b)   any benefit accruing to the defendant by reason of the infringement,

award such additional damages as the justice of the case may require.

[305]

98   Undertaking to take licence of right in infringement proceedings

(1)   If in proceedings for infringement of copyright in respect of which a licence is available as of right under section 144 (powers exercisable in consequence of report of Monopolies and Mergers Commission) the defendant undertakes to take a licence on such terms as may be agreed or, in default of agreement, settled by the Copyright Tribunal under that section—

    (a)   no injunction shall be granted against him,

    (b)   no order for delivery up shall be made under section 99, and

    (c)   the amount recoverable against him by way of damages or on an account of profits shall not exceed double the amount which would have been payable by him as licensee if such a licence on those terms had been granted before the earliest infringement.

(2)   An undertaking may be given at any time before final order in the proceedings, without any admission of liability.

(3)   Nothing in this section affects the remedies available in respect of an infringement committed before licences of right were available.

[306]

99   Order for delivery up

(1)   Where a person—

    (a)   has an infringing copy of a work in his possession, custody or control in the course of a business, or

    (b)   has in his possession, custody or control an article specifically designed or adapted for making copies of a particular copyright work, knowing or having reason to believe that it has been or is to be used to make infringing copies,

the owner of the copyright in the work may apply to the court for an order that the infringing copy or article be delivered up to him or to such other person as the court may direct.

(2)   An application shall not be made after the end of the period specified in section 113 (period after which remedy of delivery up not available); and no order shall be made unless the court also makes, or it appears to the court that there are grounds for making, an order under section 114 (order as to disposal of infringing copy or other article).

(3)   A person to whom an infringing copy or other article is delivered up in pursuance of an order under this section shall, if an order under section 114 is not made, retain it pending the making of an order, or the decision not to make an order, under that section.

(4)   Nothing in this section affects any other power of the court.

[307]

100   Right to seize infringing copies and other articles

(1)   An infringing copy of a work which is found exposed or otherwise immediately available for sale or hire, and in respect of which the copyright owner would be entitled to apply for an order under section 99, may be seized and detained by him or a person authorised by him.

The right to seize and detain is exercisable subject to the following conditions and is subject to any decision of the court under section 114.

(2)   Before anything is seized under this section notice of the time and place of the proposed seizure must be given to a local police station.

(3)   A person may for the purpose of exercising the right conferred by this section enter premises to which the public have access but may not seize anything in the possession, custody or control of a person at a permanent or regular place of business of his, and may not use any force.

(4)   At the time when anything is seized under this section there shall be left at the place where it was seized a notice in the prescribed form containing the prescribed particulars as to the person by whom or on whose authority the seizure is made and the grounds on which it is made.

(5)   In this section—

"premises" includes land, buildings, moveable structures, vehicles, vessels, aircraft and hovercraft; and

"prescribed" means prescribed by order of the Secretary of State.

(6)   An order of the Secretary of State under this section shall be made by statutory instrument which shall be subject to annulment in pursuance of a resolution of either House of Parliament.

[308]

Rights and remedies of exclusive licensee

101   Rights and remedies of exclusive licensee

(1)   An exclusive licensee has, except against the copyright owner, the same rights and remedies in respect of matters occurring after the grant of the licence as if the licence had been an assignment.

(2)   His rights and remedies are concurrent with those of the copyright owner; and references in the relevant provisions of this Part to the copyright owner shall be construed accordingly.

(3)   In an action brought by an exclusive licensee by virtue of this section a defendant may avail himself of any defence which would have been available to him if the action had been brought by the copyright owner.

[309]

102   Exercise of concurrent rights

(1)   Where an action for infringement of copyright brought by the copyright owner or an exclusive licensee relates (wholly or partly) to an infringement in respect of which they have concurrent rights of action, the copyright owner or, as the case may be, the exclusive licensee may not, without the leave of the court, proceed with the action unless the other is either joined as a plaintiff or added as a defendant.

(2)   A copyright owner or exclusive licensee who is added as a defendant in pursuance of subsection (1) is not liable for any costs in the action unless he takes part in the proceedings.

(3)   The above provisions do not affect the granting of interlocutory relief on an application by a copyright owner or exclusive licensee alone.

(4)   Where an action for infringement of copyright is brought which relates (wholly or partly) to an infringement in respect of which the copyright owner and

an exclusive licensee have or had concurrent rights of action—

    (a)   the court shall in assessing damages take into account—

        (i)   the terms of the licence, and

        (ii) any pecuniary remedy already awarded or available to either of them in respect of the infringement;

    (b)   no account of profits shall be directed if an award of damages has been made, or an account of profits has been directed, in favour of the other of them in respect of the infringement; and

    (c)   the court shall if an account of profits is directed apportion the profits between them as the court considers just, subject to any agreement between them;

and these provisions apply whether or not the copyright owner and the exclusive licensee are both parties to the action.

(5)   The copyright owner shall notify any exclusive licensee having concurrent rights before applying for an order under section 99 (order for delivery up) or exercising the right conferred by section 100 (right of seizure); and the court may on the application of the licensee make such order under section 99 or, as the case may be, prohibiting or permitting the exercise by the copyright owner of the right conferred by section 100, as it thinks fit having regard to the terms of the licence.

[310]

Remedies for infringement of moral rights

103   Remedies for infringement of moral rights

(1)   An infringement of a right conferred by Chapter IV (moral rights) is actionable as a breach of statutory duty owed to the person entitled to the right.

(2)   In proceedings for infringement of the right conferred by section 80 (right to object to derogatory treatment of work) the court may, if it thinks it is an adequate remedy in the circumstances, grant an injunction on terms prohibiting the doing of any act unless a disclaimer is made, in such terms and in such manner as may be approved by the court, dissociating the author or director from the treatment of the work.

[311]

Presumptions

104   Presumptions relevant to literary, dramatic, musical and artistic works

(1)   The following presumptions apply in proceedings brought by virtue of this Chapter with respect to a literary, dramatic, musical or artistic work.

(2)   Where a name purporting to be that of the author appeared on copies of the work as published or on the work when it was made, the person whose name appeared shall be presumed, until the contrary is proved—

    (a)   to be the author of the work;

    (b)   to have made it in circumstances not falling within section 11(2), 163, 165 or 168 (works produced in course of employment, Crown copyright, Parliamentary copyright or copyright of certain international organisations).

(3)   In the case of a work alleged to be a work of joint authorship, subsection (2) applies in relation to each person alleged to be one of the authors.

(4)   Where no name purporting to be that of the author appeared as mentioned in subsection (2) but—

   (a)   the work qualifies for copyright protection by virtue of section 155 (qualification by reference to country of first publication), and

   (b)   a name purporting to be that of the publisher appeared on copies of the work as first published,

the person whose name appeared shall be presumed, until the contrary is proved, to have been the owner of the copyright at the time of publication.

(5)   If the author of the work is dead or the identity of the author cannot be ascertained by reasonable inquiry, it shall be presumed, in the absence of evidence to the contrary—

   (a)   that the work is an original work, and

   (b)   that the plaintiff's allegations as to what was the first publication of the work and as to the country of first publication are correct.

[312]

105   Presumptions relevant to sound recordings and films

(1)   In proceedings brought by virtue of this Chapter with respect to a sound recording, where copies of the recording as issued to the public bear a label or other mark stating—

   (a)   that a named person was the owner of copyright in the recording at the date of issue of the copies, or

   (b)   that the recording was first published in a specified year or in a specified country,

the label or mark shall be admissible as evidence of the facts stated and shall be presumed to be correct until the contrary is proved.

(2)   In proceedings brought by virtue of this Chapter with respect to a film, where copies of the film as issued to the public bear a statement—

   (a)   that a named person was the author or director of the film,

   [(aa)   that a named person was the principal director, the author of the screenplay, the author of the dialogue or the composer of music specifically created for and used in the film,]

   (b)   that a named person was the owner of copyright in the film at the date of issue of the copies, or

   (c)   that the film was first published in a specified year or in a specified country,

the statement shall be admissible as evidence of the facts stated and shall be presumed to be correct until the contrary is proved.

(3)   In proceedings brought by virtue of this Chapter with respect to a computer program, where copies of the program are issued to the public in electronic form bearing a statement—

   (a)   that a named person was the owner of copyright in the program at the date of issue of the copies, or

   (b)   that the program was first published in a specified country or that copies of it were first issued to the public in electronic form in a specified year,

the statement shall be admissible as evidence of the facts stated and shall be presumed to be correct until the contrary is proved.

(4) The above presumptions apply equally in proceedings relating to an infringement alleged to have occurred before the date on which the copies were issued to the public.

(5) In proceedings brought by virtue of this Chapter with respect to a film, where the film as shown in public, broadcast or included in a cable programme service bears a statement—

(a) that a named person was the author or director of the film, or

(b) that a named person was the owner of copyright in the film immediately after it was made,

the statement shall be admissible as evidence of the facts stated and shall be presumed to be correct until the contrary is proved.

This presumption applies equally in proceedings relating to an infringement alleged to have occurred before the date on which the film was shown in public, broadcast or included in a cable programme service.

[313]

NOTES

Sub-s (2): para (aa) inserted by the Duration of Copyright and Rights in Performances Regulations 1995, SI 1995/3297, reg 6(4), subject to transitional provisions and savings specified in regs 12–35 thereof.

106 Presumptions relevant to works subject to Crown copyright

In proceedings brought by virtue of this Chapter with respect to a literary, dramatic or musical work in which Crown copyright subsists, where there appears on printed copies of the work a statement of the year in which the work was first published commercially, that statement shall be admissible as evidence of the fact stated and shall be presumed to be correct in the absence of evidence to the contrary.

[314]

Offences

107 Criminal liability for making or dealing with infringing articles, etc

(1) A person commits an offence who, without the licence of the copyright owner—

(a) makes for sale or hire, or

(b) imports into the United Kingdom otherwise than for his private and domestic use, or

(c) possesses in the course of a business with a view to committing any act infringing the copyright, or

(d) in the course of a business—

(i) sells or lets for hire, or

(ii) offers or exposes for sale or hire, or

(iii) exhibits in public, or

(iv) distributes, or

(e) distributes otherwise than in the course of a business to such an extent as to affect prejudicially the owner of the copyright,

an article which is, and which he knows or has reason to believe is, an infringing copy of a copyright work.

(2) A person commits an offence who—

(a) makes an article specifically designed or adapted for making copies of a particular copyright work, or

(b) has such an article in his possession,

knowing or having reason to believe that it is to be used to make infringing copies for sale or hire or for use in the course of a business.

(3) Where copyright is infringed (otherwise than by reception of a broadcast or cable programme)—
(a) by the public performance of a literary, dramatic or musical work, or
(b) by the playing or showing in public of a sound recording or film,

any person who caused the work to be so performed, played or shown is guilty of an offence if he knew or had reason to believe that copyright would be infringed.

(4) A person guilty of an offence under subsection (1)(a), (b), (d)(iv) or (e) is liable—
(a) on summary conviction to imprisonment for a term not exceeding six months or a fine not exceeding the statutory maximum, or both;
(b) on conviction on indictment to a fine or imprisonment for a term not exceeding two years, or both.

(5) A person guilty of any other offence under this section is liable on summary conviction to imprisonment for a term not exceeding six months or a fine not exceeding level 5 on the standard scale, or both.

(6) Sections 104 to 106 (presumptions as to various matters connected with copyright) do not apply to proceedings for an offence under this section; but without prejudice to their application in proceedings for an order under section 108 below.

[315]

[107A   Enforcement by local weights and measures authority

(1) It is the duty of every local weights and measures authority to enforce within their area the provisions of section 107.

(2) The following provisions of the Trade Descriptions Act 1968 apply in relation to the enforcement of that section by such an authority as in relation to the enforcement of that Act—
    section 27 (power to make test purchases),
    section 28 (power to enter premises and inspect and seize goods and documents),
    section 29 (obstruction of authorised officers), and
    section 33 (compensation for loss, &c of goods seized).

(3) Subsection (1) above does not apply in relation to the enforcement of section 107 in Northern Ireland, but it is the duty of the Department of Economic Development to enforce that section in Northern Ireland.

For that purpose the provisions of the Trade Descriptions Act 1968 specified in subsection (2) apply as if for the references to a local weights and measures authority and any officer of such an authority there were substituted references to that Department and any of its officers.

(4) Any enactment which authorises the disclosure of information for the purpose of facilitating the enforcement of the Trade Descriptions Act 1968 shall apply as if section 107 were contained in that Act and as if the functions of any person in relation to the enforcement of that section were functions under that Act.

(5)   Nothing in this section shall be construed as authorising a local weights and measures authority to bring proceedings in Scotland for an offence.]

NOTES

Commencement: to be appointed.

Inserted by the Criminal Justice and Public Order 1994, s 165(1), (2).

108   Order for delivery up in criminal proceedings

(1)   The court before which proceedings are brought against a person for an offence under section 107 may, if satisfied that at the time of his arrest or charge—

(a)   he had in his possession, custody or control in the course of a business an infringing copy of a copyright work, or

(b)   he had in his possession, custody or control an article specifically designed or adapted for making copies of a particular copyright work, knowing or having reason to believe that it had been or was to be used to make infringing copies,

order that the infringing copy or article be delivered up to the copyright owner or to such other person as the court may direct.

(2)   For this purpose a person shall be treated as charged with an offence—

(a)   in England, Wales and Northern Ireland, when he is orally charged or is served with a summons or indictment;

(b)   in Scotland, when he is cautioned, charged or served with a complaint or indictment.

(3)   An order may be made by the court of its own motion or on the application of the prosecutor (or, in Scotland, the Lord Advocate or procurator-fiscal), and may be made whether or not the person is convicted of the offence, but shall not be made—

(a)   after the end of the period specified in section 113 (period after which remedy of delivery up not available), or

(b)   if it appears to the court unlikely that any order will be made under section 114 (order as to disposal of infringing copy or other article).

(4)   An appeal lies from an order made under this section by a magistrates' court—

(a)   in England and Wales, to the Crown Court, and

(b)   in Northern Ireland, to the county court;

and in Scotland, where an order has been made under this section, the person from whose possession, custody or control the infringing copy or article has been removed may, without prejudice to any other form of appeal under any rule of law, appeal against that order in the same manner as against sentence.

(5)   A person to whom an infringing copy or other article is delivered up in pursuance of an order under this section shall retain it pending the making of an order, or the decision not to make an order, under section 114.

(6)   Nothing in this section affects the powers, of the court under section 43 of the Powers of Criminal Courts Act 1973, [Part II of the Proceeds of Crime (Scotland) Act 1995] or Article 7 of the Criminal Justice (Northern Ireland) Order 1980 (general provisions as to forfeiture in criminal proceedings).

NOTES

Sub-s (6): words in square brackets substituted by the Criminal Procedure (Consequential Provisions) (Scotland) Act 1995, ss 4, 5, Sch 3 (see in particular para 16 thereof), Sch 4, para 70(1), (2); words "Article 7 of the Criminal Justice (Northern Ireland) Order 1980" substituted for the words "Article 11 of the Criminal Justice (Northern Ireland) Order 1994" by the Criminal Justice (Northern Ireland) Order 1994, SI 1994/2795 (NI 15), art 26(1), Sch 2, para 13, as from a day to be appointed.

109   Search warrants

(1)   Where a justice of the peace (in Scotland, a sheriff or justice of the peace) is satisfied by information on oath given by a constable (in Scotland, by evidence on oath) that there are reasonable grounds for believing—

   (a)   that an offence under section 107(1)(a), (b), (d)(iv) or (e) has been or is about to be committed in any premises, and

   (b)   that evidence that such an offence has been or is about to be committed is in those premises,

he may issue a warrant authorising a constable to enter and search the premises, using such reasonable force as is necessary.

(2)   The power conferred by subsection (1) does not, in England and Wales, extend to authorising a search for material of the kinds mentioned in section 9(2) of the Police and Criminal Evidence Act 1984 (certain classes of personal or confidential material).

(3)   A warrant under this section—

   (a)   may authorise persons to accompany any constable executing the warrant, and

   (b)   remains in force for 28 days from the date of its issue.

(4)   In executing a warrant issued under this section a constable may seize an article if he reasonably believes that it is evidence that any offence under section 107(1) has been or is about to be committed.

(5)   In this section "premises" includes land, buildings, moveable structures, vehicles, vessels, aircraft and hovercraft.

[318]

110   Offence by body corporate: liability of officers

(1)   Where an offence under section 107 committed by a body corporate is proved to have been committed with the consent or connivance of a director, manager, secretary or other similar officer of the body, or a person purporting to act in any such capacity, he as well as the body corporate is guilty of the offence and liable to be proceeded against and punished accordingly.

(2)   In relation to a body corporate whose affairs are managed by its members "director" means a member of the body corporate.

[319]

Provision for preventing importation of infringing copies

111   Infringing copies may be treated as prohibited goods

(1)   The owner of the copyright in a published literary, dramatic or musical work may give notice in writing to the Commissioners of Customs and Excise—

   (a)   that he is the owner of the copyright in the work, and

(b) that he requests the Commissioners, for a period specified in the notice, to treat as prohibited goods printed copies of the work which are infringing copies.

(2) The period specified in a notice under subsection (1) shall not exceed five years and shall not extend beyond the period for which copyright is to subsist.

(3) The owner of the copyright in a sound recording or film may give notice in writing to the Commissioners of Customs and Excise—

(a) that he is the owner of the copyright in the work,

(b) that infringing copies of the work are expected to arrive in the United Kingdom at a time and a place specified in the notice, and

(c) that he requests the Commissioners to treat the copies as prohibited goods.

[(3A) The Commissioners may treat as prohibited goods only infringing copies of works which arrive in the United Kingdom—

(a) from outside the European Economic Area, or

(b) from within that Area but not having been entered for free circulation.

(3B) This section does not apply to goods entered, or expected to be entered, for free circulation, export, re-export or for a suspensive procedure in respect of which an application may be made under Article 3(1) of Council Regulation (EC) No 3295/94 laying down measures to prohibit the release for free circulation, export, re-export or entry for a suspensive procedure of counterfeit and pirated goods.]

(4) When a notice is in force under this section the importation of goods to which the notice relates, otherwise than by a person for his private and domestic use, [subject to subsections (3A) and (3B), is prohibited]; but a person is not by reason of the prohibition liable to any penalty other than forfeiture of the goods.

[320]

NOTES

Sub-ss (3A), (3B): inserted by the Copyright (EC Measures Relating to Pirated Goods and Abolition of Restrictions on the Import of Goods) Regulations 1995, SI 1995/1445, reg 2(1), (2).

Sub-s (4): words in square brackets substituted by the Copyright (EC Measures Relating to Pirated Goods and Abolition of Restrictions on the Import of Goods) Regulations 1995, SI 1995/1445, reg 2(1), (3).

112   Power of Commissioners of Customs and Excise to make regulations

(1) The Commissioners of Customs and Excise may make regulations prescribing the form in which notice is to be given under section 111 and requiring a person giving notice—

(a) to furnish the Commissioners with such evidence as may be specified in the regulations, either on giving notice or when the goods are imported, or at both those times, and

(b) to comply with such other conditions as may be specified in the regulations.

(2) The regulations may, in particular, require a person giving such a notice—

(a) to pay such fees in respect of the notice as may be specified by the regulations;

(b) to give such security as may be so specified in respect of any liability or expense which the Commissioners may incur in consequence of the notice by reason of the detention of any article or anything done to an article detained;

(c) to indemnify the Commissioners against any such liability or expense, whether security has been given or not.

(3)   The regulations may make different provision as respects different classes of case to which they apply and may include such incidental and supplementary provisions as the Commissioners consider expedient.

(4)   Regulations under this section shall be made by statutory instrument which shall be subject to annulment in pursuance of a resolution of either House of Parliament.

(5)   Section 17 of the Customs and Excise Management Act 1979 (general provisions as to Commissioners' receipts) applies to fees paid in pursuance of regulations under this section as to receipts under the enactments relating to customs and excise.

[321]

Supplementary

113   Period after which remedy of delivery up not available

(1)   An application for an order under section 99 (order for delivery up in civil proceedings) may not be made after the end of the period of six years from the date on which the infringing copy or article in question was made, subject to the following provisions.

(2)   If during the whole or any part of that period the copyright owner—
     (a)   is under a disability, or
     (b)   is prevented by fraud or concealment from discovering the facts entitling him to apply for an order,

an application may be made at any time before the end of the period of six years from the date on which he ceased to be under a disability or, as the case may be, could with reasonable diligence have discovered those facts.

(3)   In subsection (2) "disability"—
     (a)   in England and Wales, has the same meaning as in the Limitation Act 1980;
     (b)   in Scotland, means legal disability within the meaning of the Prescription and Limitation (Scotland) Act 1973;
     (c)   in Northern Ireland, has the same meaning as in the Statute of Limitations (Northern Ireland) 1958.

(4)   An order under section 108 (order for delivery up in criminal proceedings) shall not, in any case, be made after the end of the period of six years from the date on which the infringing copy or article in question was made.

[322]

114   Order as to disposal of infringing copy or other article

(1)   An application may be made to the court for an order that an infringing copy or other article delivered up in pursuance of an order under section 99 or 108, or seized and detained in pursuance of the right conferred by section 100, shall be—
     (a)   forfeited to the copyright owner, or
     (b)   destroyed or otherwise dealt with as the court may think fit,

or for a decision that no such order should be made.

(2)   In considering what order (if any) should be made, the court shall consider whether other remedies available in an action for infringement of copyright would be adequate to compensate the copyright owner and to protect his interests.

(3) Provision shall be made by rules of court as to the service of notice on persons having an interest in the copy or other articles, and any such person is entitled—

    (a) to appear in proceedings for an order under this section, whether or not he was served with notice, and

    (b) to appeal against any order made, whether or not he appeared;

and an order shall not take effect until the end of the period within which notice of an appeal may be given or, if before the end of that period notice of appeal is duly given, until the final determination or abandonment of the proceedings on the appeal.

(4) Where there is more than one person interested in a copy or other article, the court shall make such order as it thinks just and may (in particular) direct that the article be sold, or otherwise dealt with, and the proceeds divided.

(5) If the court decides that no order should be made under this section, the person in whose possession, custody or control the copy or other article was before being delivered up or seized is entitled to its return.

(6) References in this section to a person having an interest in a copy or other article include any person in whose favour an order could be made in respect of it under this section or under section 204 or 231 of this Act or [section 19 of the Trade Marks Act 1994] (which make similar provision in relation to infringement of rights in performances, design right and trade marks).

[323]

NOTES

    Sub-s (6): words in square brackets substituted by the Trade Marks Act 1994, s 106(1), Sch 4, paras 8(1), (2).

---

115 Jurisdiction of county court and sheriff court

(1) In England, Wales and Northern Ireland a county court may entertain proceedings under—

    section 99 (order for delivery up of infringing copy or other article),

    section 101(5) (order as to exercise of rights by copyright owner where
         ⁃ exclusive licensee has concurrent rights), or

    section 114 (order as to disposal of infringing copy or other article),

[save that, in Northern Ireland, a county court may entertain such proceedings only] where the value of the infringing copies and other articles in question does not exceed the county court limit for actions in tort.

(2) In Scotland proceedings for an order under any of those provisions may be brought in the sheriff court.

(3) Nothing in this section shall be construed as affecting the jurisdiction of the High Court or, in Scotland, the Court of Session.

[324]

NOTES

    Sub-s (1): words in square brackets inserted by the High Court and County Courts Jurisdiction Order 1991, SI 1991/724, art 2(8), Schedule, Pt I.

    It is believed that the reference in sub-s (1) to "section 101(5)" should be to "section 102(5)".

CHAPTER IX
QUALIFICATION FOR AND EXTENT OF COPYRIGHT PROTECTION

Qualification for copyright protection

153   Qualification for copyright protection

(1)   Copyright does not subsist in a work unless the qualification requirements of this Chapter are satisfied as regards—
- (a)   the author (see section 154), or
- (b)   the country in which the work was first published (see section 155), or
- (c)   in the case of a broadcast or cable programme, the country from which the broadcast was made or the cable programme was sent (see section 156).

(2)   Subsection (1) does not apply in relation to Crown copyright or Parliamentary copyright (see sections 163 to 166) or to copyright subsisting by virtue of section 168 (copyright of certain international organisations).

(3)   If the qualification requirements of this Chapter, or section 163, 165 or 168, are once satisfied in respect of a work, copyright does not cease to subsist by reason of any subsequent event.

[325]

154   Qualification by reference to author

(1)   A work qualifies for copyright protection if the author was at the material time a qualifying person, that is—
- (a)   a British citizen, a British Dependent Territories citizen, a British National (Overseas), a British Overseas citizen, a British subject or a British protected person within the meaning of the British Nationality Act 1981, or
- (b)   an individual domiciled or resident in the United Kingdom or another country to which the relevant provisions of this Part extend, or
- (c)   a body incorporated under the law of a part of the United Kingdom or of another country to which the relevant provisions of this Part extend.

(2)   Where, or so far as, provision is made by Order under section 159 (application of this Part to countries to which it does not extend), a work also qualifies for copyright protection if at the material time the author was a citizen or subject of, an individual domiciled or resident in, or a body incorporated under the law of, a country to which the Order relates.

(3)   A work of joint authorship qualifies for copyright protection if at the material time any of the authors satisfies the requirements of subsection (1) or (2); but where a work qualifies for copyright protection only under this section, only those authors who satisfy those requirements shall be taken into account for the purposes of—
> section 11(1) and (2) (first ownership of copyright; entitlement of author or author's employer),
> [section 12 (duration of copyright), and section 9(4) (meaning of "unknown authorship") so far as it applies for the purposes of section 12, and]
> section 57 (anonymous or pseudonymous works: acts permitted on assumptions as to expiry of copyright or death of author).

(4)   The material time in relation to a literary, dramatic, musical or artistic work is—
- (a)   in the case of an unpublished work, when the work was made or, if the

making of the work extended over a period, a substantial part of that period;

(b) in the case of a published work, when the work was first published or, if the author had died before that time, immediately before his death.

(5) The material time in relation to other descriptions of work is as follows—

(a) in the case of a sound recording or film, when it was made;

(b) in the case of a broadcast, when the broadcast was made;

(c) in the case of a cable programme, when the programme was included in a cable programme service;

(d) in the case of the typographical arrangement of a published edition, when the edition was first published.

[326]

NOTES

Sub-s (3): words in square brackets substituted by the Duration of Copyright and Rights in Performances Regulations 1995, SI 1995/3297, reg 5(3), subject to transitional provisions and savings specified in regs 12–35 thereof.

155 Qualification by reference to country of first publication

(1) A literary, dramatic, musical or artistic work, a sound recording or film, or the typographical arrangement of a published edition, qualifies for copyright protection if it is first published—

(a) in the United Kingdom, or

(b) in another country to which the relevant provisions of this Part extend.

(2) Where, or so far as, provision is made by Order under section 159 (application of this Part to countries to which it does not extend), such a work also qualifies for copyright protection if it is first published in a country to which the Order relates.

(3) For the purposes of this section, publication in one country shall not be regarded as other than the first publication by reason of simultaneous publication elsewhere; and for this purpose publication elsewhere within the previous 30 days shall be treated as simultaneous.

[327]

156 Qualification by reference to place of transmission

(1) A broadcast qualifies for copyright protection if it is made from, and a cable programme qualifies for copyright protection if it is sent from, a place in—

(a) the United Kingdom, or

(b) another country to which the relevant provisions of this Part extend.

(2) Where, or so far as, provision is made by Order under section 159 (application of this Part to countries to which it does not extend), a broadcast or cable programme also qualifies for copyright protection if it is made from or, as the case may be, sent from a place in a country to which the Order relates.

[328]

Extent and application of this Part

157 Countries to which this Part extends

(1) This Part extends to England and Wales, Scotland and Northern Ireland.

(2) Her Majesty may by Order in Council direct that this Part shall extend, subject to such exceptions and modifications as may be specified in the Order, to—

(a)   any of the Channel Islands,
(b)   the Isle of Man, or
(c)   any colony.

(3)   That power includes power to extend, subject to such exceptions and modifications as may be specified in the Order, any Order in Council made under the following provisions of this Chapter.

(4)   The legislature of a country to which this Part has been extended may modify or add to the provisions of this Part, in their operation as part of the law of that country, as the legislature may consider necessary to adapt the provisions to the circumstances of that country—
(a)   as regards procedure and remedies, or
(b)   as regards works qualifying for copyright protection by virtue of a connection with that country.

(5)   Nothing in this section shall be construed as restricting the extent of paragraph 36 of Schedule 1 (transitional provisions: dependent territories where the Copyright Act 1956 or the Copyright Act 1911 remains in force) in relation to the law of a dependent territory to which this Part does not extend.

[329]

158   Countries ceasing to be colonies

(1)   The following provisions apply where a country to which this Part has been extended ceases to be a colony of the United Kingdom.

(2)   As from the date on which it ceases to be a colony it shall cease to be regarded as a country to which this Part extends for the purposes of—
(a)   section 160(2)(a) (denial of copyright protection to citizens of countries not giving adequate protection to British works), and
(b)   sections 163 and 165 (Crown and Parliamentary copyright).

(3)   But it shall continue to be treated as a country to which this Part extends for the purposes of sections 154 to 156 (qualification for copyright protection) until—
(a)   an Order in Council is made in respect of that country under section 159 (application of this Part to countries to which it does not extend), or
(b)   an Order in Council is made declaring that it shall cease to be so treated by reason of the fact that the provisions of this Part as part of the law of that country have been repealed or amended.

(4)   A statutory instrument containing an Order in Council under subsection (3)(b) shall be subject to annulment in pursuance of a resolution of either House of Parliament.

[330]

159   Application of this Part to countries to which it does not extend

(1)   Her Majesty may by Order in Council make provision for applying in relation to a country to which this Part does not extend any of the provisions of this Part specified in the Order, so as to secure that those provisions—
(a)   apply in relation to persons who are citizens or subjects of that country or are domiciled or resident there, as they apply to persons who are British citizens or are domiciled or resident in the United Kingdom, or
(b)   apply in relation to bodies incorporated under the law of that country as they apply in relation to bodies incorporated under the law of a part of the United Kingdom, or

    (c)   apply in relation to works first published in that country as they apply in relation to works first published in the United Kingdom, or

    (d)   apply in relation to broadcasts made from or cable programmes sent from that country as they apply in relation to broadcasts made from or cable programmes sent from the United Kingdom.

(2)   An Order may make provision for all or any of the matters mentioned in subsection (1) and may—

    (a)   apply any provisions of this Part subject to such exceptions and modifications as are specified in the Order; and

    (b)   direct that any provisions of this Part apply either generally or in relation to such classes of works, or other classes of case, as are specified in the Order.

(3)   Except in the case of a Convention country or another member State of the European Economic Community, Her Majesty shall not make an Order in Council under this section in relation to a country unless satisfied that provision has been or will be made under the law of that country, in respect of the class of works to which the Order relates, giving adequate protection to the owners of copyright under this Part.

(4)   In subsection (3) "Convention country" means a country which is a party to a Convention relating to copyright to which the United Kingdom is also a party.

(5)   A statutory instrument containing an Order in Council under this section shall be subject to annulment in pursuance of a resolution of either House of Parliament.

[331]

160   Denial of copyright protection to citizens of countries not giving adequate protection to British works

(1)   If it appears to Her Majesty that the law of a country fails to give adequate protection to British works to which this section applies, or to one or more classes of such works, Her Majesty may make provision by Order in Council in accordance with this section restricting the rights conferred by this Part in relation to works of authors connected with that country.

(2)   An Order in Council under this section shall designate the country concerned and provide that, for the purposes specified in the Order, works first published after a date specified in the Order shall not be treated as qualifying for copyright protection by virtue of such publication if at that time the authors are—

    (a)   citizens or subjects of that country (not domiciled or resident in the United Kingdom or another country to which the relevant provisions of this Part extend), or

    (b)   bodies incorporated under the law of that country;

and the Order may make such provision for all the purposes of this Part or for such purposes as are specified in the Order, and either generally or in relation to such class of cases as are specified in the Order, having regard to the nature and extent of that failure referred to in subsection (1).

(3)   This section applies to literary, dramatic, musical and artistic works, sound recordings and films; and "British works" means works of which the author was a qualifying person at the material time within the meaning of section 154.

(4)   A statutory instrument containing an Order in Council under this section shall be subject to annulment in pursuance of a resolution of either House of Parliament.

[332]

CHAPTER X
MISCELLANEOUS AND GENERAL

Crown and Parliamentary copyright

163   Crown copyright

(1)   Where a work is made by Her Majesty or by an officer or servant of the Crown in the course of his duties—
   (a)   the work qualifies for copyright protection notwithstanding section 153(1) (ordinary requirement as to qualification for copyright protection), and
   (b)   Her Majesty is the first owner of any copyright in the work.

(2)   Copyright in such a work is referred to in this Part as "Crown copyright", notwithstanding that it may be, or have been, assigned to another person.

(3)   Crown copyright in a literary, dramatic, musical or artistic work continues to subsist—
   (a)   until the end of the period of 125 years from the end of the calendar year in which the work was made, or
   (b)   if the work is published commercially before the end of the period of 75 years from the end of the calendar year in which it was made, until the end of the period of 50 years from the end of the calendar year in which it was first so published.

(4)   In the case of a work of joint authorship where one or more but not all of the authors are persons falling within subsection (1), this section applies only in relation to those authors and the copyright subsisting by virtue of their contribution to the work.

(5)   Except as mentioned above, and subject to any express exclusion elsewhere in this Part, the provisions of this Part apply in relation to Crown copyright as to other copyright.

(6)   This section does not apply to work if, or to the extent that, Parliamentary copyright subsists in the work (see sections 165 and 166).

[333]

164   Copyright in Acts and Measures

(1)   Her Majesty is entitled to copyright in every Act of Parliament or Measure of the General Synod of the Church of England.

(2)   The copyright subsists from Royal Assent until the end of the period of 50 years from the end of the calendar year in which Royal Assent was given.

(3)   References in this Part to Crown copyright (except in section 163) include copyright under this section; and, except as mentioned above, the provisions of this Part apply in relation to copyright under this section as to other Crown copyright.

(4)   No other copyright, or right in the nature of copyright, subsists in an Act or Measure.

[334]

165   Parliamentary copyright

(1)   Where a work is made by or under the direction or control of the House of Commons or the House of Lords—

(a) the work qualifies for copyright protection notwithstanding section 153(1) (ordinary requirement as to qualification for copyright protection), and

(b) the House by whom, or under whose direction or control, the work is made is the first owner of any copyright in the work, and if the work is made by or under the direction or control of both Houses, the two Houses are joint first owners of copyright.

(2) Copyright in such a work is referred to in this Part as "Parliamentary copyright", notwithstanding that it may be, or have been, assigned to another person.

(3) Parliamentary copyright in a literary, dramatic, musical or artistic work continues to subsist until the end of the period of 50 years from the end of the calendar year in which the work was made.

(4) For the purposes of this section, works made by or under the direction or control of the House of Commons or the House of Lords include—

(a) any work made by an officer or employee of that House in the course of his duties, and

(b) any sound recording, film, live broadcast or live cable programme of the proceedings of that House;

but a work shall not be regarded as made by or under the direction or control of either House by reason only of its being commissioned by or on behalf of that House.

(5) In the case of a work of joint authorship where one or more but not all of the authors are acting on behalf of, or under the direction or control of, the House of Commons or the House of Lords, this section applies only in relation to those authors and the copyright subsisting by virtue of their contribution to the work.

(6) Except as mentioned above, and subject to any express exclusion elsewhere in this Part, the provisions of this Part apply in relation to Parliamentary copyright as to other copyright.

(7) The provisions of this section also apply, subject to any exceptions or modifications specified by Order in Council, to works made by or under the direction or control of any other legislative body of a country to which this Part extends; and references in this Part to "Parliamentary copyright" shall be construed accordingly.

(8) A statutory instrument containing an Order in Council under subsection (7) shall be subject to annulment in pursuance of a resolution of either House of Parliament.

[335]

166   Copyright in Parliamentary Bills

(1) Copyright in every Bill introduced into Parliament belongs, in accordance with the following provisions, to one or both of the Houses of Parliament.

(2) Copyright in a public Bill belongs in the first instance to the House into which the Bill is introduced, and after the Bill has been carried to the second House to both Houses jointly, and subsists from the time when the text of the Bill is handed in to the House in which it is introduced.

(3) Copyright in a private Bill belongs to both Houses jointly and subsists from the time when a copy of the Bill is first deposited in either House.

(4)   Copyright in a personal Bill belongs in the first instance to the House of Lords, and after the Bill has been carried to the House of Commons to both Houses jointly, and subsists from the time when it is given a First Reading in the House of Lords.

(5)   Copyright under this section ceases—
   (a)   on Royal Assent, or
   (b)   if the Bill does not receive Royal Assent, on the withdrawal or rejection of the Bill or the end of the Session:

Provided that, copyright in a Bill continues to subsist notwithstanding its rejection in any Session by the House of Lords if, by virtue of the Parliament Acts 1911 and 1949, it remains possible for it to be presented for Royal Assent in that Session.

(6)   References in this Part to Parliamentary copyright (except in section 165) include copyright under this section; and, except as mentioned above, the provisions of this Part apply in relation to copyright under this section as to other Parliamentary copyright.

(7)   No other copyright, or right in the nature of copyright, subsists in a Bill after copyright has once subsisted under this section; but without prejudice to the subsequent operation of this section in relation to a Bill which, not having passed in one Session, is reintroduced in a subsequent Session.

[336]

167   Houses of Parliament: supplementary provisions with respect to copyright

(1)   For the purposes of holding, dealing with and enforcing copyright, and in connection with all legal proceedings relating to copyright, each House of Parliament shall be treated as having the legal capacities of a body corporate, which shall not be affected by a prorogation or dissolution.

(2)   The functions of the House of Commons as owner of copyright shall be exercised by the Speaker on behalf of the House; and if so authorised by the Speaker, or in case of a vacancy in the office of Speaker, those functions may be discharged by the Chairman of Ways and Means or a Deputy Chairman.

(3)   For this purpose a person who on the dissolution of Parliament was Speaker of the House of Commons, Chairman of Ways and Means or a Deputy Chairman may continue to act until the corresponding appointment is made in the next Session of Parliament.

(4)   The functions of the House of Lords as owner of copyright shall be exercised by the Clerk of the Parliaments on behalf of the House; and if so authorised by him, or in case of a vacancy in the office of Clerk of the Parliaments, those functions may be discharged by the Clerk Assistant or the Reading Clerk.

(5)   Legal proceedings relating to copyright—
   (a)   shall be brought by or against the House of Commons in the name of "The Speaker of the House of Commons"; and
   (b)   shall be brought by or against the House of Lords in the name of "The Clerk of the Parliaments".

[337]

Interpretation

172 General provisions as to construction

(1)   This Part restates and amends the law of copyright, that is, the provisions of the Copyright Act 1956, as amended.

(2)   A provision of this Part which corresponds to a provision of the previous law shall not be construed as departing from the previous law merely because of a change of expression.

(3)   Decisions under the previous law may be referred to for the purpose of establishing whether a provision of this Part departs from the previous law, or otherwise for establishing the true construction of this Part.

[338]

[172A   Meaning of EEA national and EEA state

(1)   In this Part—
"EEA national" means a national of an EEA state; and
"EEA state" means a state which is a contracting party to the EEA Agreement.

(2)   References in this Part to a person being an EEA national shall be construed in relation to a body corporate as references to its being incorporated under the law of an EEA state.

(3)   The "EEA Agreement" means the Agreement on the European Economic Area signed at Oporto on 2nd May 1992, as adjusted by the Protocol signed at Brussels on 17th March 1993.]

[339]

NOTES
   Commencement: 1 January 1996.
   Inserted by the Duration of Copyright and Rights in Performances Regulations 1995, SI 1995/3297, reg 11(1), subject to transitional provisions and savings specified in regs 12–35 thereof.

173 Construction of references to copyright owner

(1)   Where different persons are (whether in consequence of a partial assignment or otherwise) entitled to different aspects of copyright in a work, the copyright owner for any purpose of this Part is the person who is entitled to the aspect of copyright relevant for that purpose.

(2)   Where copyright (or any aspect of copyright) is owned by more than one person jointly, references in this Part to the copyright owner are to all the owners, so that, in particular, any requirement of the licence of the copyright owner requires the licence of all of them.

[340]

174 Meaning of "educational establishment" and related expressions

(1)   The expression "educational establishment" in a provision of this Part means—
(a)   any school, and
(b)   any other description of educational establishment specified for the purposes of this Part, or that provision, by order of the Secretary of State.

(2)   The Secretary of State may by order provide that the provisions of this Part relating to educational establishments shall apply, with such modifications and

adaptations as may be specified in the order, in relation to teachers who are employed by a local education authority to give instruction elsewhere to pupils who are unable to attend an educational establishment.

(3)   In subsection (1)(a) "school"—

(a)   in relation to England and Wales, has the same meaning as in the Education Act 1944;

(b)   in relation to Scotland, has the same meaning as in the Education (Scotland) Act 1962, except that it includes an approved school within the meaning of the Social Work (Scotland) Act 1968; and

(c)   in relation to Northern Ireland, has the same meaning as in the Education and Libraries (Northern Ireland) Order 1986.

(4)   An order under subsection (1)(b) may specify a description of educational establishment by reference to the instruments from time to time in force under any enactment specified in the order.

(5)   In relation to an educational establishment the expressions "teacher" and "pupil" in this Part include, respectively, any person who gives and any person who receives instruction.

(6)   References in this Part to anything being done "on behalf of" an educational establishment are to its being done for the purposes of that establishment by any person.

(7)   An order under this section shall be made by statutory instrument which shall be subject to annulment in pursuance of a resolution of either House of Parliament.

[341]

175   Meaning of publication and commercial publication

(1)   In this Part "publication", in relation to a work—
(a)   means the issue of copies to the public, and
(b)   includes, in the case of a literary, dramatic, musical or artistic work, making it available to the public by means of an electronic retrieval system;

and related expressions shall be construed accordingly.

(2)   In this Part "commercial publication", in relation to a literary, dramatic, musical or artistic work means—
(a)   issuing copies of the work to the public at a time when copies made in advance of the receipt of orders are generally available to the public, or
(b)   making the work available to the public by means of an electronic retrieval system;

and related expressions shall be construed accordingly.

(3)   In the case of a work of architecture in the form of a building, or an artistic work incorporated in a building, construction of the building shall be treated as equivalent to publication of the work.

(4)   The following do not constitute publication for the purposes of this Part and references to commercial publication shall be construed accordingly—
(a)   in the case of a literary, dramatic or musical work—
(i)   the performance of the work, or
(ii)   the broadcasting of the work or its inclusion in a cable programme service (otherwise than for the purposes of an electronic retrieval system);

(b) in the case of an artistic work—
    (i) the exhibition of the work,
    (ii) the issue to the public of copies of a graphic work representing, or of photographs of, a work of architecture in the form of a building or a model for a building, a sculpture or a work of artistic craftsmanship,
    (iii) the issue to the public of copies of a film including the work, or
    (iv) the broadcasting of the work or its inclusion in a cable programme service (otherwise than for the purposes of an electronic retrieval system);

(c) in the case of a sound recording or film—
    (i) the work being played or shown in public, or
    (ii) the broadcasting of the work or its inclusion in a cable programme service.

(5) References in this Part to publication or commercial publication do not include publication which is merely colourable and not intended to satisfy the reasonable requirements of the public.

(6) No account shall be taken for the purposes of this section of any unauthorised act.

[342]

178 Minor definitions

In this Part—
    "article", in the context of an article in a periodical, includes an item of any description;
    "business" includes a trade or profession;
    "collective work" means—
        (a) a work of joint authorship, or
        (b) a work in which there are distinct contributions by different authors or in which works or parts of works of different authors are incorporated;
    "computer-generated", in relation to a work, means that the work is generated by computer in circumstances such that there is no human author of the work;
    "country" includes any territory;
    "the Crown" includes the Crown in right of Her Majesty's Government in Northern Ireland or in any country outside the United Kingdom to which this Part extends;
    "electronic" means actuated by electric, magnetic, electro-magnetic, electro-chemical or electro-mechanical energy, and "in electronic form" means in a form usable only by electronic means;
    "employed", "employee", "employer" and "employment" refer to employment under a contract of service or of apprenticeship;
    "facsimile copy" includes a copy which is reduced or enlarged in scale;
    "international organisation" means an organisation the members of which include one or more states;
    "judicial proceedings" includes proceedings before any court, tribunal or person having authority to decide any matter affecting a person's legal rights or liabilities;

"parliamentary proceedings" includes proceedings of the Northern Ireland Assembly or of the European Parliament;

"rental" means any arrangement under which a copy of a work is made available—

(a) for payment (in money or money's worth), or

(b) in the course of a business, as part of services or amenities for which payment is made,

on terms that it will or may be returned;

"reprographic copy" and "reprographic copying" refer to copying by means of a reprographic process;

"reprographic process" means a process—

(a) for making facsimile copies, or

(b) involving the use of an appliance for making multiple copies,

and includes, in relation to a work held in electronic form, any copying by electronic means, but does not include the making of a film or sound recording;

"sufficient acknowledgement" means an acknowledgement identifying the work in question by its title or other description, and identifying the author unless—

(a) in the case of a published work, it is published anonymously;

(b) in the case of an unpublished work, it is not possible for a person to ascertain the identity of the author by reasonable inquiry;

"sufficient disclaimer", in relation to an act capable of infringing the right conferred by section 80 (right to object to derogatory treatment of work), means a clear and reasonably prominent indication—

(a) given at the time of the act, and

(b) if the author or director is then identified, appearing along with the identification,

that the work has been subjected to treatment to which the author or director has not consented;

"telecommunications system" means a system for conveying visual images, sounds or other information by electronic means;

"typeface" includes an ornamental motif used in printing;

"unauthorised", as regards anything done in relation to a work, means done otherwise than—

(a) by or with the licence of the copyright owner, or

(b) if copyright does not subsist in the work, by or with the licence of the author or, in a case where section 11(2) would have applied, the author's employer or, in either case, persons, lawfully claiming under him, or

(c) in pursuance of section 48 (copying, etc of certain material by the Crown);

"wireless telegraphy" means the sending of electro-magnetic energy over paths not provided by a material substance constructed or arranged for that purpose;

"writing" includes any form of notation or code, whether by hand or otherwise and regardless of the method by which, or medium in or on which, it is recorded, and "written" shall be construed accordingly.

[343]

PART II
RIGHTS IN PERFORMANCES

Introductory

180 Rights conferred on performers and persons having recording rights

(1)   This Part confers rights—
    (a)   on a performer, by requiring his consent to the exploitation of his performances (see sections 181 to 184), and
    (b)   on a person having recording rights in relation to a performance, in relation to recordings made without his consent or that of the performer (see sections 185 to 188),

and creates offences in relation to dealing with or using illicit recordings and certain other related acts (see sections 198 and 201).

(2)   In this Part—
    "performance" means—
        (a)   a dramatic performance (which includes dance and mime),
        (b)   a musical performance,
        (c)   a reading or recitation of a literary work, or
        (d)   a performance of a variety act or any similar presentation,
        which is, or so far as it is, a live performance given by one or more individuals; and
    "recording", in relation to a performance, means a film or sound recording—
        (a)   made directly from the live performance,
        (b)   made from a broadcast of, or cable programme including, the performance, or
        (c)   made, directly or indirectly, from another recording of the performance.

(3)   The rights conferred by this Part apply in relation to performances taking place before the commencement of this Part; but no act done before commencement, or in pursuance of arrangements made before commencement, shall be regarded as infringing those rights.

(4)   The rights conferred by this Part are independent of—
    (a)   any copyright in, or moral rights relating to, any work performed or any film or sound recording of, or broadcast or cable programme including, the performance, and
    (b)   any other right or obligation arising otherwise than under this Part.

[344]

Performers' rights

181 Qualifying performances

A performance is a qualifying performance for the purposes of the provisions of this Part relating to performers' rights if it is given by a qualifying individual (as defined in section 206) or takes place in a qualifying country (as so defined).

[345]

182   Consent required for recording or live transmission of performance

(1)   A performer's rights are infringed by a person who, without his consent—

    (a)   makes, otherwise than for his private and domestic use, a recording of the whole or any substantial part of a qualifying performance, or

    (b)   broadcasts live, or includes live in a cable programme service, the whole or any substantial part of a qualifying performance.

(2)   In an action for infringement of a performer's rights brought by virtue of this section damages shall not be awarded against a defendant who shows that at the time of the infringement he believed on reasonable grounds that consent had been given.

                                                [346]

183   Infringement of performer's rights by use of recording made without consent

A performer's rights are infringed by a person who, without his consent—

    (a)   shows or plays in public the whole or any substantial part of a qualifying performance, or

    (b)   broadcasts or includes in a cable programme service the whole or any substantial part of a qualifying performance,

by means of a recording which was, and which that person knows or has reason to believe was, made without the performer's consent.

                                                [347]

184   Infringement of performer's rights by importing, possessing or dealing with illicit recording

(1)   A performer's rights are infringed by a person who, without his consent—

    (a)   imports into the United Kingdom otherwise than for his private and domestic use, or

    (b)   in the course of a business possesses, sells or lets for hire, offers or exposes for sale or hire, or distributes,

a recording of a qualifying performance which is, and which that person knows or has reason to believe is, an illicit recording.

(2)   Where in an action for infringement of a performer's rights brought by virtue of this section a defendant shows that the illicit recording was innocently acquired by him or a predecessor in title of his, the only remedy available against him in respect of the infringement is damages not exceeding a reasonable payment in respect of the act complained of.

(3)   In subsection (2) "innocently acquired" means that the person acquiring the recording did not know and had no reason to believe that it was an illicit recording.

                                                [348]

Rights of person having recording rights

185   Exclusive recording contracts and persons having recording rights

(1)   In this Part an "exclusive recording contract" means a contract between a performer and another person under which that person is entitled to the exclusion of all other persons (including the performer) to make recordings of one or more of his performances with a view to their commercial exploitation.

(2)   References in this Part to a "person having recording rights", in relation to a performance, are (subject to subsection (3)) to a person—

    (a)   who is party to and has the benefit of an exclusive recording contract to which the performance is subject, or

    (b)   to whom the benefit of such a contract has been assigned,

and who is a qualifying person.

(3)   If a performance is subject to an exclusive recording contract but the person mentioned in subsection (2) is not a qualifying person, references in this Part to a "person having recording rights" in relation to the performance are to any person—

    (a)   who is licensed by such a person to make recordings of the performance with a view to their commercial exploitation, or

    (b)   to whom the benefit of such a licence has been assigned,

and who is a qualifying person.

(4)   In this section "with a view to commercial exploitation" means with a view to the recordings being sold or let for hire, or shown or played in public.

[349]

186   Consent required for recording of performance subject to exclusive contract

(1)   A person infringes the rights of a person having recording rights in relation to a performance who, without his consent or that of the performer, makes a recording of the whole or any substantial part of the performance, otherwise than for his private and domestic use.

(2)   In an action for infringement of those rights brought by virtue of this section damages shall not be awarded against a defendant who shows that at the time of the infringement he believed on reasonable grounds that consent had been given.

[350]

187   Infringement of recording rights by use of recording made without consent

(1)   A person infringes the rights of a person having recording rights in relation to a performance who, without his consent or, in the case of a qualifying performance, that of the performer—

    (a)   shows or plays in public the whole or any substantial part of the performance, or

    (b)   broadcasts or includes in a cable programme service the whole or any substantial part of the performance,

by means of a recording which was, and which that person knows or has reason to believe was, made without the appropriate consent.

(2)   The reference in subsection (1) to "the appropriate consent" is to the consent of—

    (a)   the performer, or

    (b)   the person who at the time the consent was given had recording rights in relation to the performance (or, if there was more than one such person, of all of them).

[351]

188   Infringement of recording rights by importing, possessing or dealing with illicit recording

(1)   A person infringes the rights of a person having recording rights in relation to a performance who, without his consent or, in the case of a qualifying performance, that of the performer—

(a)   imports into the United Kingdom otherwise than for his private and domestic use, or

(b)   in the course of a business possesses, sells or lets for hire, offers or exposes for sale or hire, or distributes,

a recording of the performance which is, and which that person knows or has reason to believe is, an illicit recording.

(2)   Where in an action for infringement of those rights brought by virtue of this section a defendant shows that the illicit recording was innocently acquired by him or a predecessor in title of his, the only remedy available against him in respect of the infringement is damages not exceeding a reasonable payment in respect of the act complained of.

(3)   In subsection (2) "innocently acquired" means that the person acquiring the recording did not know and had no reason to believe that it was an illicit recording.

[352]

Exceptions to rights conferred

189   Acts permitted notwithstanding rights conferred by this Part

The provisions of Schedule 2 specify acts which may be done notwithstanding the rights conferred by this Part, being acts which correspond broadly to certain of those specified in Chapter III of Part I (acts permitted notwithstanding copyright).

[353]

190   Power of tribunal to give consent on behalf of performer in certain cases

(1)   The Copyright Tribunal may, on the application of a person wishing to make a recording from a previous recording of a performance, give consent in a case where—

(a)   the identity or whereabouts of a performer cannot be ascertained by reasonable inquiry, or

(b)   a performer unreasonably withholds his consent.

(2)   Consent given by the Tribunal has effect as consent of the performer for the purposes of—

(a)   the provisions of this Part relating to performers' rights, and

(b)   section 198(3)(a) (criminal liability: sufficient consent in relation to qualifying performances),

and may be given subject to any conditions specified in the Tribunal's order.

(3)   The Tribunal shall not give consent under subsection (1)(a) except after the service or publication of such notices as may be required by rules made under section 150 (general procedural rules) or as the Tribunal may in any particular case direct.

(4)   The Tribunal shall not give consent under subsection (1)(b) unless satisfied that the performer's reasons for withholding consent do not include the protection of any legitimate interest of his; but it shall be for the performer to show what his reasons are

for withholding consent, and in default of evidence as to his reasons the Tribunal may draw such inferences as it thinks fit.

(5)   In any case the Tribunal shall take into account the following factors—

(a)   whether the original recording was made with the performer's consent and is lawfully in the possession or control of the person proposing to make the further recording;

(b)   whether the making of the further recording is consistent with the obligations of the parties to the arrangements under which, or is otherwise consistent with the purposes for which, the original recording was made.

(6)   Where the Tribunal gives consent under this section it shall, in default of agreement between the applicant and the performer, make such order as it thinks fit as to the payment to be made to the performer in consideration of consent being given.

[354]

Duration and transmission of rights; consent

[191   Duration of rights

(1)   The following provisions have effect with respect to the duration of the rights conferred by this Part.

(2)   The rights conferred by this Part in relation to a performance expire—

(a)   at the end of the period of 50 years from the end of the calendar year in which the performance takes place, or

(b)   if during that period a recording of the performance is released, 50 years from the end of the calendar year in which it is released,

subject as follows.

(3)   For the purposes of subsection (2) a recording is "released" when it is first published, played or shown in public, broadcast or included in a cable programme service; but in determining whether a recording has been released no account shall be taken of any unauthorised act.

(4)   Where a performer is not a national of an EEA state, the duration of the rights conferred by this Part in relation to his performance is that to which the performance is entitled in the country of which he is a national, provided that does not exceed the period which would apply under subsections (2) and (3).

(5)   If or to the extent that the application of subsection (4) would be at variance with an international obligation to which the United Kingdom became subject prior to 29th October 1993, the duration of the rights conferred by this Part shall be as specified in subsections (2) and (3).]

[355]

NOTES

Commencement: 1 January 1996.

Substituted by the Duration of Copyright and Rights in Performances Regulations 1995, SI 1995/3297, reg 10, subject to transitional provisions and savings.

192   Transmission of rights

(1)   The rights conferred by this Part are not assignable or transmissible, except to the extent that performers' rights are transmissible in accordance with the following provisions.

(2)   On the death of a person entitled to performer's rights—

     (a)   the rights pass to such person as he may by testamentary disposition specifically direct, and

     (b)   if or to the extent that there is no such direction, the rights are exercisable by his personal representatives;

and references in this Part to the performer, in the context of the person having performers' rights, shall be construed as references to the person for the time being entitled to exercise those rights.

(3)   Where by virtue of subsection (2)(a) a right becomes exercisable by more than one person, it is exercisable by each of them independently of the other or others.

(4)   The above provisions do not affect section 185(2)(b) or (3)(b), so far as those provisions confer rights under this Part on a person to whom the benefit of a contract or licence is assigned.

(5)   Any damages recovered by personal representatives by virtue of this section in respect of an infringement after a person's death shall devolve as part of his estate as if the right of action had subsisted and been vested in him immediately before his death.

[356]

193   Consent

(1)   Consent for the purposes of this Part may be given in relation to a specific performance, a specified description of performances or performances generally, and may relate to past or future performances.

(2)   A person having recording rights in a performance is bound by any consent given by a person through whom he derives his rights under the exclusive recording contract or licence in question, in the same way as if the consent had been given by him.

(3)   Where a right conferred by this Part passes to another person, any consent binding on the person previously entitled binds the person to whom the right passes in the same way as if the consent had been given by him.

[357]

Remedies for infringement

194   Infringement actionable as breach of statutory duty

An infringement of any of the rights conferred by this Part is actionable by the person entitled to the right as a breach of statutory duty.

[358]

195   Order for delivery up

(1)   Where a person has in his possession, custody or control in the course of a business an illicit recording of a performance, a person having performer's rights or recording rights in relation to the performance under this Part may apply to the court for an order that the recording be delivered up to him or to such other person as the court may direct.

(2)   An application shall not be made after the end of the period specified in section 203; and no order shall be made unless the court also makes, or it appears to the court that there are grounds for making, an order under section 204 (order as to disposal of illicit recording).

(3)   A person to whom a recording is delivered up in pursuance of an order under this section shall, if an order under section 204 is not made, retain it pending the making of an order, or the decision not to make an order, under that section.

(4)   Nothing in this section affects any other power of the court.

[359]

196   Right to seize illicit recordings

(1)   An illicit recording of a performance which is found exposed or otherwise immediately available for sale or hire, and in respect of which a person would be entitled to apply for an order under section 195, may be seized and detained by him or a person authorised by him.

The right to seize and detain is exercisable subject to the following conditions and is subject to any decision of the court under section 204 (order as to disposal of illicit recording).

(2)   Before anything is seized under this section notice of the time and place of the proposed seizure must be given to a local police station.

(3)   A person may for the purpose of exercising the right conferred by this section enter premises to which the public have access but may not seize anything in the possession, custody or control of a person at a permanent or regular place of business of his and may not use any force.

(4)   At the time when anything is seized under this section there shall be left at the place where it was seized a notice in the prescribed form containing the prescribed particulars as to the person by whom or on whose authority the seizure is made and the grounds on which it is made.

(5)   In this section—
     "premises" includes land, buildings, fixed or moveable structures, vehicles, vessels, aircraft and hovercraft; and
     "prescribed" means prescribed by order of the Secretary of State.

(6)   An order of the Secretary of State under this section shall be made by statutory instrument which shall be subject to annulment in pursuance of a resolution of either House of Parliament.

[360]

197   Meaning of "illicit recording"

(1)   In this Part "illicit recording", in relation to a performance, shall be construed in accordance with this section.

(2)   For the purposes of a performer's rights, a recording of the whole or any substantial part of a performance of his is an illicit recording if it is made, otherwise than for private purposes, without his consent.

(3)   For the purposes of the rights of a person having recording rights, a recording of the whole or any substantial part of a performance subject to the exclusive recording contract is an illicit recording if it is made, otherwise than for private purposes, without his consent or that of the performer.

(4)   For the purposes of sections 198 and 199 (offences and orders for delivery up in criminal proceedings), a recording is an illicit recording if it is an illicit recording for the purposes mentioned in subsection (2) or subsection (3).

(5)   In this Part "illicit recording" includes a recording falling to be treated as an illicit recording by virtue of any of the following provisions of Schedule 2—

paragraph 4(3) (recordings made for purposes of instruction or examination),

paragraph 6(2) (recordings made by educational establishments for educational purposes),

paragraph 12(2) (recordings of performance in electronic form retained on transfer of principal recording), or

paragraph 16(3) (recordings made for purposes of broadcast or cable programme),

but otherwise does not include a recording made in accordance with any of the provisions of that Schedule.

(6)   It is immaterial for the purposes of this section where the recording was made.

[361]

Offences

198   Criminal liability for making, dealing with or using illicit recordings

(1)   A person commits an offence who without sufficient consent—

(a)   makes for sale or hire, or

(b)   imports into the United Kingdom otherwise than for his private and domestic use, or

(c)   possesses in the course of a business with a view to committing any act infringing the rights conferred by this Part, or

(d)   in the course of a business—

(i)   sells or lets for hire, or

(ii)   offers or exposes for sale or hire, or

(iii)   distributes,

a recording which is, and which he knows or has reason to believe is, an illicit recording.

(2)   A person commits an offence who causes a recording of a performance made without sufficient consent to be—

(a)   shown or played in public, or

(b)   broadcast or included in a cable programme service,

thereby infringing any of the rights conferred by this Part, if he knows or has reason to believe that those rights are thereby infringed.

(3)   In subsections (1) and (2) "sufficient consent" means—

(a)   in the case of a qualifying performance, the consent of the performer, and

(b)   in the case of a non-qualifying performance subject to an exclusive recording contract—

(i)   for the purposes of subsection (1)(a) (making of recording), the consent of the performer or the person having recording rights, and

(ii)   for the purposes of subsection (1)(b), (c) and (d) and subsection (2) (dealing with or using recording), the consent of the person having recording rights.

The references in this subsection to the person having recording rights are to the person having those rights at the time the consent is given or, if there is more than one such person, to all of them.

(4) No offence is committed under subsection (1) or (2) by the commission of an act which by virtue of any provision of Schedule 2 may be done without infringing the rights conferred by this Part.

(5) A person guilty of an offence under subsection (1)(a), (b) or (d)(iii) is liable—

(a) on summary conviction to imprisonment for a term not exceeding six months or a fine not exceeding the statutory maximum, or both;

(b) on conviction on indictment to a fine or imprisonment for a term not exceeding two years, or both.

(6) A person guilty of any other offence under this section is liable on summary conviction to a fine not exceeding level 5 on the standard scale or imprisonment for a term not exceeding six months, or both.

[362]

[198A Enforcement by local weights and measures authority

(1) It is the duty of every local weights and measures authority to enforce within their area the provisions of section 198.

(2) The following provisions of the Trade Descriptions Act 1968 apply in relation to the enforcement of that section by such an authority as in relation to the enforcement of that Act—

section 27 (power to make test purchases),

section 28 (power to enter premises and inspect and seize goods and documents),

section 29 (obstruction of authorised officers), and

section 33 (compensation for loss, &c of goods seized).

(3) Subsection (1) above does not apply in relation to the enforcement of section 198 in Northern Ireland, but it is the duty of the Department of Economic Development to enforce that section in Northern Ireland.

For that purpose the provisions of the Trade Descriptions Act 1968 specified in subsection (2) apply as if for the references to a local weights and measures authority and any officer of such an authority there were substituted references to that Department and any of its officers.

(4) Any enactment which authorises the disclosure of information for the purpose of facilitating the enforcement of the Trade Descriptions Act 1968 shall apply as if section 198 were contained in that Act and as if the functions of any person in relation to the enforcement of that section were functions under that Act.

(5) Nothing in this section shall be construed as authorising a local weights and measures authority to bring proceedings in Scotland for an offence.]

[363]

NOTES

Commencement: to be appointed.

Inserted by the Criminal Justice and Public Order 1994, s 165(1), (3).

---

199 Order for delivery up in criminal proceedings

(1) The court before which proceedings are brought against a person for an offence under section 198 may, if satisfied that at the time of his arrest or charge he had in his possession, custody or control in the course of a business an illicit recording of a performance, order that it be delivered up to a person having

performers' rights or recording rights in relation to the performance or to such other person as the court may direct.

(2)   For this purpose a person shall be treated as charged with an offence—
   (a)   in England, Wales and Northern Ireland, when he is orally charged or is served with a summons or indictment;
   (b)   in Scotland, when he is cautioned, charged or served with a complaint or indictment.

(3)   An order may be made by the court of its own motion or on the application of the prosecutor (or, in Scotland, the Lord Advocate or procurator-fiscal), and may be made whether or not the person is convicted of the offence, but shall not be made—
   (a)   after the end of the period specified in section 203 (period after which remedy of delivery up not available), or
   (b)   if it appears to the court unlikely that any order will be made under section 204 (order as to disposal of illicit recording).

(4)   An appeal lies from an order made under this section by a magistrates' court—
   (a)   in England and Wales, to the Crown Court, and
   (b)   in Northern Ireland, to the county court;

and in Scotland, where an order has been made under this section, the person from whose possession, custody or control the illicit recording has been removed may, without prejudice to any other form of appeal under any rule of law, appeal against that order in the same manner as against sentence.

(5)   A person to whom an illicit recording is delivered up in pursuance of an order under this section shall retain it pending the making of an order, or the decision not to make an order, under section 204.

(6)   Nothing in this section affects the powers of the court under section 43 of the Powers of Criminal Courts Act 1973, [Part II of the Proceeds of Crime (Scotland) Act 1995] or Article 7 of the Criminal Justice (Northern Ireland) Order 1980 (general provisions as to forfeiture in criminal proceedings).

[364]

NOTES

Sub-s (6): words in square brackets substituted by the Criminal Procedure (Consequential Provisions) (Scotland) Act 1995, ss 4, 5, Sch 3 (see in particular para 16 thereof), Sch 4, para 70(1), (3); the words "Article 7 of the Criminal Justice (Northern Ireland) Order 1980" substituted for the words "Article 11 of the Criminal Justice (Northern Ireland) Order 1994" by the Criminal Justice (Northern Ireland) Order 1994, SI 1994/2795 (NI 15), art 26(1), Sch 2, para 14, as from a day to be appointed.

Qualification for protection and extent

206   Qualifying countries, individuals and persons

(1)   In this Part—
   "qualifying country" means—
      (a)   the United Kingdom,
      (b)   another member State of the European Economic Community, or
      (c)   to the extent that an Order under section 208 so provides, a country designated under that section as enjoying reciprocal protection;
   "qualifying individual" means a citizen or subject of, or an individual resident in, a qualifying country; and

"qualifying person" means a qualifying individual or a body corporate or other body having legal personality which—

(a)   is formed under the law of a part of the United Kingdom or another qualifying country, and

(b)   has in any qualifying country a place of business at which substantial business activity is carried on.

(2)   The reference in the definition of "qualifying individual" to a person's being a citizen or subject of a qualifying country shall be construed—

(a)   in relation to the United Kingdom, as a reference to his being a British citizen, and

(b)   in relation to a colony of the United Kingdom, as a reference to his being a British Dependent Territories' citizen by connection with that colony.

(3)   In determining for the purpose of the definition of "qualifying person" whether substantial business activity is carried on at a place of business in any country, no account shall be taken of dealings in goods which are at all material times outside that country.

[365]

207   Countries to which this Part extends

This Part extends to England and Wales, Scotland and Northern Ireland.

[366]

208   Countries enjoying reciprocal protection

(1)   Her Majesty may by Order in Council designate as enjoying reciprocal protection under this Part—

(a)   a Convention country, or

(b)   a country as to which Her Majesty is satisfied that provision has been or will be made under its law giving adequate protection for British performances.

(2)   A "Convention country" means a country which is a party to a Convention relating to performers' rights to which the United Kingdom is also a party.

(3)   A "British performance" means a performance—

(a)   given by an individual who is a British citizen or resident in the United Kingdom, or

(b)   taking place in the United Kingdom.

(4)   If the law of that country provides adequate protection only for certain descriptions of performance, an Order under subsection (1)(b) designating that country shall contain provision limiting to a corresponding extent the protection afforded by this Part in relation to performances connected with that country.

(5)   The power conferred by subsection (1)(b) is exercisable in relation to any of the Channel Islands, the Isle of Man or any colony of the United Kingdom, as in relation to a foreign country.

(6)   A statutory instrument containing an Order in Council under this section shall be subject to annulment in pursuance of a resolution of either House of Parliament.

[367]

Interpretation

211 Expressions having same meaning as in copyright provisions

(1) The following expressions have the same meaning in this Part as in Part I (copyright)—

broadcast,
business,
cable programme,
cable programme service,
country,
defendant (in Scotland),
delivery up (in Scotland),
[EEA National,]
film,
literary work,
published, and
sound recording.

(2) The provisions of section 6(3) to (5), section 7(5) and 19(4) (supplementary provisions relating to broadcasting and cable programme services) apply for the purposes of this Part, and in relation to an infringement of the rights conferred by this Part, as they apply for the purposes of Part I and in relation to an infringement of copyright.

[368]

NOTES

Sub-s (1): words in square brackets inserted by the Duration of Copyright and Rights in Performances Regulations 1995, SI 1995/3297, reg 11(3), subject to transitional provisions and savings specified in regs 12-35 thereof.

PART VII
MISCELLANEOUS AND GENERAL

Devices designed to circumvent copy-protection

296 Devices designed to circumvent copy-protection

(1) This section applies where copies of a copyright work are issued to the public, by or with the licence of the copyright owner, in an electronic form which is copy-protected.

(2) The person issuing the copies to the public has the same rights against a person who, knowing or having reason to believe that it will be used to make infringing copies—

(a) makes, imports, sells or lets for hire, offers or exposes for sale or hire, or advertises for sale or hire, any device or means specifically designed or adapted to circumvent the form of copy-protection employed, or

(b) publishes information intended to enable or assist persons to circumvent that form of copy-protection,

as a copyright owner has in respect of an infringement of copyright.

[(2A) Where the copies being issued to the public as mentioned in subsection (1) are copies of a computer program, subsection (2) applies as if for the words "or advertises for sale or hire" there were substituted "advertises for sale or hire or possesses in the course of a business".]

(3)   Further, he has the same rights under section 99 or 100 (delivery up or seizure of certain articles) in relation to any such device or means which a person has in his possession, custody or control with the intention that it should be used to make infringing copies of copyright works, as a copyright owner has in relation to an infringing copy.

(4)   References in this section to copy-protection include any device or means intended to prevent or restrict copying of a work or to impair the quality of copies made.

(5)   Expressions used in this section which are defined for the purposes of Part I of this Act (copyright) have the same meaning as in that Part.

(6)   The following provisions apply in relation to proceedings under this section as in relation to proceedings under Part I (copyright)—

   (a)   sections 104 to 106 of this Act (presumptions as to certain matters relating to copyright), and
   (b)   section 72 of the Supreme Court Act 1981, section 15 of the Law Reform (Miscellaneous Provisions) (Scotland) Act 1985 and section 94A of the Judicature (Northern Ireland) Act 1978 (withdrawal of privilege against self-incrimination in certain proceedings relating to intellectual property);

and section 114 of this Act applies, with the necessary modifications, in relation to the disposal of anything delivered up or seized by virtue of subsection (3) above.

[369]

NOTES

Commencement: 1 January 1993 (sub-s (2A)); 1 August 1989 (remainder) (SI 1989/816).

Sub-s (2A): inserted by the Copyright (Computer Programs) Regulations 1992, SI 1992/3233, regs 2, 10, subject to reg 12(2) thereof (agreements entered into before 1 January 1993 to remain unaffected).

[Computer programs

296A   Avoidance of certain terms

(1)   Where a person has the use of a computer program under an agreement, any term or condition in the agreement shall be void in so far as it purports to prohibit or restrict—

   (a)   the making of any back up copy of the program which it is necessary for him to have for the purposes of the agreed use;
   (b)   where the conditions in section 50B(2) are met, the decompiling of the program; or
   (c)   the use of any device or means to observe, study or test the functioning of the program in order to understand the ideas and principles which underlie any element of the program.

(2)   In this section, decompile, in relation to a computer program, has the same meaning as in section 50B.]

[370]

NOTES

Commencement: 1 January 1993.

Inserted, together with the preceding cross heading, by the Copyright (Computer Programs) Regulations 1992, SI 1992/3233, regs 2, 11, subject to reg 12(2) thereof (agreements entered into before 1 January 1993 to remain unaffected).

Provisions for the benefit of the Hospital for Sick Children

301   Provisions for the benefit of the Hospital for Sick Children

The provisions of Schedule 6 have effect for conferring on trustees for the benefit of the Hospital for Sick Children, Great Ormond Street, London, a right to a royalty in respect of the public performance, commercial publication, broadcasting or inclusion in a cable programme service of the play "Peter Pan" by Sir James Matthew Barrie, or of any adaptation of that work, notwithstanding that copyright in the work expired on 31st December 1987.

[371]

306   Short title

This Act may be cited as the Copyright, Designs and Patents Act 1988.

[372]

SCHEDULES

SCHEDULE 2

Section 189

RIGHTS IN PERFORMANCES: PERMITTED ACTS

Introductory

1.—(1)   The provisions of this Schedule specify acts which may be done in relation to a performance or recording notwithstanding the rights conferred by Part II; they relate only to the question of infringement of those rights and do not affect any other right or obligation restricting the doing of any of the specified acts.

(2)   No inference shall be drawn from the description of any act which may by virtue of this Schedule be done without infringing the rights conferred by Part II as to the scope of those rights.

(3)   The provisions of this Schedule are to be construed independently of each other, so that the fact that an act does not fall within one provision does not mean that it is not covered by another provision.

Criticism, reviews and news reporting

2.—(1)   Fair dealing with a performance or recording—
- (a)   for the purpose of criticism or review, of that or another performance or recording, or of a work, or
- (b)   for the purpose of reporting current events,

does not infringe any of the rights conferred by Part II.

(2)   Expressions used in this paragraph have the same meaning as in section 30.

Incidental inclusion of performance or recording

3.—(1)   The rights conferred by Part II are not infringed by the incidental inclusion of a performance or recording in a sound recording, film, broadcast or cable programme.

(2)   Nor are those rights infringed by anything done in relation to copies of, or the playing, showing, broadcasting or inclusion in a cable programme service of, anything whose making was, by virtue of sub-paragraph (1), not an infringement of those rights.

(3) A performance or recording so far as it consists of music, or words spoken or sung with music, shall not be regarded as incidentally included in a sound recording, broadcast or cable programme if it is deliberately included.

(4) Expressions used in this paragraph have the same meaning as in section 31.

Things done for purposes of instruction or examination

4.—(1) The rights conferred by Part II are not infringed by the copying of a recording of a performance in the course of instruction, or of preparation for instruction, in the making of films or film sound-tracks, provided the copying is done by a person giving or receiving instruction.

(2) The rights conferred by Part II are not infringed—

   (a) by the copying of a recording of a performance for the purposes of setting or answering the questions in an examination, or

   (b) by anything done for the purposes of an examination by way of communicating the questions to the candidates.

(3) Where a recording which would otherwise be an illicit recording is made in accordance with this paragraph but is subsequently dealt with, it shall be treated as an illicit recording for the purposes of that dealing, and if that dealing infringes any right conferred by Part II for all subsequent purposes.

For this purpose "dealt with" means sold or let for hire, or offered or exposed for sale or hire.

(4) Expressions used in this paragraph have the same meaning as in section 32.

Playing or showing sound recording, film, broadcast or cable programme at educational establishment

5.—(1) The playing or showing of a sound recording, film, broadcast or cable programme at an educational establishment for the purposes of instruction before an audience consisting of teachers and pupils at the establishment and other persons directly connected with the activities of the establishment is not a playing or showing of a performance in public for the purposes of infringement of the rights conferred by Part II.

(2) A person is not for this purpose directly connected with the activities of the educational establishment simply because he is the parent of a pupil at the establishment.

(3) Expressions used in this paragraph have the same meaning as in section 34 and any provision made under section 174(2) with respect to the application of that section also applies for the purposes of this paragraph.

Recording of broadcasts and cable programmes by educational establishments

6.—(1) A recording of a broadcast or cable programme, or a copy of such a recording, may be made by or on behalf of an educational establishment for the educational purposes of that establishment without thereby infringing any of the rights conferred by Part II in relation to any performance or recording included in it.

(2) Where a recording which would otherwise be an illicit recording is made in accordance with this paragraph but is subsequently dealt with, it shall be treated as an illicit recording for the purposes of that dealing, and if that dealing infringes any right conferred by Part II for all subsequent purposes.

For this purpose "dealt with" means sold or let for hire, or offered or exposed for sale or hire.

(3) Expressions used in this paragraph have the same meaning as in section 35 and any provision made under section 174(2) with respect to the application of that section also applies for the purposes of this paragraph.

Copy of work required to be made as condition of export

7.—(1)   If an article of cultural or historical importance or interest cannot lawfully be exported from the United Kingdom unless a copy of it is made and deposited in an appropriate library or archive, it is not an infringement of any right conferred by Part II to make that copy.

(2)   Expressions used in this paragraph have the same meaning as in section 44.

Parliamentary and judicial proceedings

8.—(1)   The rights conferred by Part II are not infringed by anything done for the purposes of parliamentary or judicial proceedings or for the purpose of reporting such proceedings.

(2)   Expressions used in this paragraph have the same meaning as in section 45.

Royal Commissions and statutory inquiries

9.—(1)   The rights conferred by Part II are not infringed by anything done for the purposes of the proceedings of a Royal Commission or statutory inquiry or for the purpose of reporting any such proceedings held in public.

(2)   Expressions used in this paragraph have the same meaning as in section 46.

Public records

10.—(1)   Material which is comprised in public records within the meaning of the Public Records Act 1958, the Public Records (Scotland) Act 1937 or the Public Records Act (Northern Ireland) 1923 which are open to public inspection in pursuance of that Act, may be copied, and a copy may be supplied to any person, by or with the authority of any officer appointed under that Act, without infringing any right conferred by Part II.

(2)   Expressions used in this paragraph have the same meaning as in section 49.

Acts done under statutory authority

11.—(1)   Where the doing of a particular act is specifically authorised by an Act of Parliament, whenever passed, then, unless the Act provides otherwise, the doing of that act does not infringe the rights conferred by Part II.

(2)   Sub-paragraph (1) applies in relation to an enactment contained in Northern Ireland legislation as it applies to an Act of Parliament.

(3)   Nothing in this paragraph shall be construed as excluding any defence of statutory authority otherwise available under or by virtue of any enactment.

(4)   Expressions used in this paragraph have the same meaning as in section 50.

Transfer of copies of works in electronic form

12.—(1)   This paragraph applies where a recording of a performance in electronic form has been purchased on terms which, expressly or impliedly or by virtue of any rule of law, allow the purchaser to make further recordings in connection with his use of the recording.

(2)   If there are no express terms—
  (a)   prohibiting the transfer of the recording by the purchaser, imposing obligations which continue after a transfer, prohibiting the assignment of any consent or terminating any consent on a transfer, or
  (b)   providing for the terms on which a transferee may do the things which the purchaser was permitted to do,

anything which the purchaser was allowed to do may also be done by a transferee without infringement of the rights conferred by this Part, but any recording made by the purchaser which is not also transferred shall be treated as an illicit recording for all purposes after the transfer.

(3)   The same applies where the original purchased recording is no longer usable and what is transferred is a further copy used in its place.

(4) The above provisions also apply on a subsequent transfer, with the substitution for references in sub-paragraph (2) to the purchaser of references to the subsequent transferor.

(5) This paragraph does not apply in relation to a recording purchased before the commencement of Part II.

(6) Expressions used in this paragraph have the same meaning as in section 56.

Use of recordings of spoken works in certain cases

13.—(1) Where a recording of the reading or recitation of a literary work is made for the purpose—

    (a)   of reporting current events, or

    (b)   of broadcasting or including in a cable programme service the whole or part of the reading or recitation,

it is not an infringement of the rights conferred by Part II to use the recording (or to copy the recording and use the copy) for that purpose, provided the following conditions are met.

(2) The conditions are that—

    (a)   the recording is a direct recording of the reading or recitation and is not taken from a previous recording or from a broadcast or cable programme;

    (b)   the making of the recording was not prohibited by or on behalf of the person giving the reading or recitation;

    (c)   the use made of the recording is not of a kind prohibited by or on behalf of that person before the recording was made; and

    (d)   the use is by or with the authority of a person who is lawfully in possession of the recording.

(3) Expressions used in this paragraph have the same meaning as in section 58.

Recordings of folksongs

14.—(1) A recording of a performance of a song may be made for the purpose of including it in an archive maintained by a designated body without infringing any of the rights conferred by Part II, provided the conditions in sub-paragraph (2) below are met.

(2) The conditions are that—

    (a)   the words are unpublished and of unknown authorship at the time the recording is made,

    (b)   the making of the recording does not infringe any copyright, and

    (c)   its making is not prohibited by any performer.

(3) Copies of a recording made in reliance on sub-paragraph (1) and included in an archive maintained by a designated body may, if the prescribed conditions are met, be made and supplied by the archivist without infringing any of the rights conferred by Part II.

(4) In this paragraph—

    "designated body" means a body designated for the purposes of section 61, and

    "the prescribed conditions" means the conditions prescribed for the purposes of subsection (3) of that section;

and other expressions used in this paragraph have the same meaning as in that section.

Playing of sound recordings for purposes of club, society, etc

15.—(1) It is not an infringement of any right conferred by Part II to play a sound recording as part of the activities of, or for the benefit of, a club, society or other organisation if the following conditions are met.

(2) The conditions are—

    (a)   that the organisation is not established or conducted for profit and its main objects are charitable or are otherwise concerned with the advancement of religion, education or social welfare, and

(b)   that the proceeds of any charge for admission to the place where the recording is to be heard are applied solely for the purposes of the organisation.

(3)   Expressions used in this paragraph have the same meaning as in section 67.

Incidental recording for purposes of broadcast or cable programme

16.—(1)   A person who proposes to broadcast a recording of a performance, or include a recording of a performance in a cable programme service, in circumstances not infringing the rights conferred by Part II shall be treated as having consent for the purposes of that Part for the making of a further recording for the purposes of the broadcast or cable programme.

(2)   That consent is subject to the condition that the further recording—
(a)   shall not be used for any other purpose, and
(b)   shall be destroyed within 28 days of being first used for broadcasting the performance or including it in a cable programme service.

(3)   A recording made in accordance with this paragraph shall be treated as an illicit recording—
(a)   for the purposes of any use in breach of the condition mentioned in sub-paragraph (2)(a), and
(b)   for all purposes after that condition or the condition mentioned in sub-paragraph (2)(b) is broken.

(4)   Expressions used in this paragraph have the same meaning as in section 68.

Recordings for purposes of supervision and control of broadcasts and cable programmes

17.—(1)   The rights conferred by Part II are not infringed by the making or use by the British Broadcasting Corporation, for the purpose of maintaining supervision and control over programmes broadcast by them, of recordings of those programmes.

[(2)   The rights conferred by Part II are not infringed by anything done in pursuance of—
(a)   section 11(1), 95(1), 145(4), (5) or (7), 155(3) or 167(1) of the Broadcasting Act 1990;
(b)   a condition which, by virtue of section 11(2) or 95(2) of that Act, is included in a licence granted under Part I or III of that Act; or
(c)   a direction given under section 109(2) of that Act (power of Radio Authority to require production of recordings etc).

(3)   The rights conferred by Part II are not infringed by—
(a)   the use by the Independent Television Commission or the Radio Authority, in connection with the performance of any of their functions under the Broadcasting Act 1990, of any recording, script or transcript which is provided to them under or by virtue of any provision of that Act; or
(b)   the use by the Broadcasting Complaints Commission or the Broadcasting Standards Council, in connection with any complaint made to them under that Act, of any recording or transcript requested or required to be provided to them, and so provided, under section 145(4) or (7) or section 155(3) of that Act.]

Free public showing or playing of broadcast or cable programme

18.—(1)   The showing or playing in public of a broadcast or cable programme to an audience who have not paid for admission to the place where the broadcast or programme is to be seen or heard does not infringe any right conferred by Part II in relation to a performance or recording included in—
(a)   the broadcast or cable programme, or
(b)   any sound recording or film which is played or shown in public by reception of the broadcast or cable programme.

(2)   The audience shall be treated as having paid for admission to a place—
(a)   if they have paid for admission to a place of which that place forms part; or
(b)   if goods or services are supplied at that place (or a place of which it forms part)—

    (i)   at prices which are substantially attributable to the facilities afforded for seeing or hearing the broadcast or programme, or

    (ii)   at prices exceeeding those usually charged there and which are partly attributable to those facilities.

(3) The following shall not be regarded as having paid for admission to a place—

    (a)   persons admitted as residents or inmates of the place;

    (b)   persons admitted as members of a club or society where the payment is only for membership of the club or society and the provision of facilities for seeing or hearing broadcasts or programmes is only incidental to the main purposes of the club or society.

(4) Where the making of the broadcast or inclusion of the programme in a cable programme service was an infringement of the rights conferred by Part II in relation to a performance or recording, the fact that it was heard or seen in public by the reception of the broadcast or programme shall be taken into account in assessing the damages for that infringement.

(5) Expressions used in this paragraph have the same meaning as in section 72.

Reception and re-transmission of broadcast in cable programme service

19.—(1) This paragraph applies where a broadcast made from a place in the United Kingdom is, by reception and immediate re-transmission, included in a cable programme service.

(2) The rights conferred by Part II in relation to a performance or recording included in the broadcast are not infringed—

    (a)   . . .

    (b)   if and to the extent that the broadcast is made for reception in the area in which the cable programme service is provided;

but where the making of the broadcast was an infringement of those rights, the fact that the broadcast was re-transmitted as a programme in a cable programme service shall be taken into account in assessing the damages for that infringement.

(3) Expressions used in this paragraph have the same meaning as in section 73.

Provision of sub-titled copies of broadcast or cable programme

20.—(1) A designated body may, for the purpose of providing people who are deaf or hard of hearing, or physically or mentally handicapped in other ways, with copies which are sub-titled or otherwise modified for their special needs, make recordings of television broadcasts or cable programmes without infringing any right conferred by Part II in relation to a performance or recording included in the broadcast or cable programme.

(2) In this paragraph "designated body" means a body designated for the purposes of section 74 and other expressions used in this paragraph have the same meaning as in that section.

Recording of broadcast or cable programme for archival purposes

21.—(1) A recording of a broadcast or cable programme of a designated class, or a copy of such a recording, may be made for the purpose of being placed in an archive maintained by a designated body without thereby infringing any right conferred by Part II in relation to a performance or recording included in the broadcast or cable programme.

(2) In this paragraph "designated class" and "designated body" means a class or body designated for the purposes of section 75 and other expressions used in this paragraph have the same meaning as in that section.

[373]

NOTES

    Para 17: sub-paras (2), (3) substituted for sub-paras (2)-(4), as originally enacted, by the Broadcasting Act 1990, s 203(1), Sch 20, para 50(2).

    Para 19: words omitted repealed by the Broadcasting Act 1990, s 203(3), Sch 21.

COUNCIL DIRECTIVE 91/250/EEC

of 14 May 1991

on the legal protection of computer programs

NOTES

Date of publication in OJ: OJ L122, 17.5.91, p 42.

Article 1   Object of protection

1.   In accordance with the provisions of this Directive, Member States shall protect computer programs, by copyright, as literary works within the meaning of the Berne Convention for the Protection of Literary and Artistic Works. For the purposes of this Directive, the term "computer programs" shall include their preparatory design material.

2.   Protection in accordance with this Directive shall apply to the expression in any form of a computer program. Ideas and principles which underlie any element of a computer program, including those which underlie its interfaces, are not protected by copyright under this Directive.

3.   A computer program shall be protected if it is original in the sense that it is the author's own intellectual creation. No other criteria shall be applied to determine its eligibility for protection.

[374]

Article 2   Authorship of computer programs

1.   The author of a computer program shall be the natural person or group of natural persons who has created the program or, where the legislation of the Member State permits, the legal person designated as the rightholder by that legislation. Where collective works are recognised by the legislation of a Member State, the person considered by the legislation of the Member State to have created the work shall be deemed to be its author.

2.   In respect of a computer program created by a group of natural persons jointly, the exclusive rights shall be owned jointly.

3.   Where a computer program is created by an employee in the execution of his duties or following the instructions given by his employer, the employer exclusively shall be entitled to exercise all economic rights in the program so created, unless otherwise provided by contract.

[375]

Article 3   Beneficiaries of protection

Protection shall be granted to all natural or legal persons eligible under national copyright legislation as applied to literary works.

[376]

Article 4   Restricted Acts

Subject to the provisions of Articles 5 and 6, the exclusive rights of the rightholder within the meaning of Article 2, shall include the right to do or to authorise—
       (a) the permanent or temporary reproduction of a computer program by any

means and in any form, in part or in whole. Insofar as loading, displaying, running, transmission or storage of the computer program necessitate such reproduction, such acts shall be subject to authorisation by the rightholder;

(b) the translation, adaptation, arrangement and any other alteration of a computer program and the reproduction of the results thereof, without prejudice to the rights of the person who alters the program;

(c) any form of distribution to the public, including the rental, of the original computer program or of copies thereof. The first sale in the Community of a copy of a program by the rightholder or with his consent shall exhaust the distribution right within the Community of that copy, with the exception of the right to control further rental of the program or a copy thereof.

[377]

Article 5   Exceptions to the restricted acts

1.   In the absence of specific contractual provisions, the acts referred to in Article 4(a) and (b) shall not require authorisation by the rightholder where they are necessary for the use of the computer program by the lawful acquirer in accordance with its intended purpose, including for error correction.

2.   The making of a back-up copy by a person having a right to use the computer program may not be prevented by contract insofar as it is necessary for that use.

3.   The person having a right to use a copy of a computer program shall be entitled, without the authorisation of the rightholder, to observe, study or test the functioning of the program in order to determine the ideas and principles which underlie any element of the program if he does so while performing any of the acts of loading, displaying, running, transmitting or storing the program which he is entitled to do.

[378]

Article 6   Decompilation

1.   The authorisation of the rightholder shall not be required where reproduction of the code and translation of its form within the meaning of Article 4(a) and (b) are indispensable to obtain the information necessary to achieve the interoperability of an independently created computer program with other programs, provided that the following conditions are met—

(a) these acts are performed by the licensee or by another person having a right to use a copy of a program, or on their behalf by a person authorised to do so;

(b) the information necessary to achieve interoperability has not previously been readily available to the persons referred to in subparagraph (a); and

(c) these acts are confined to the parts of the original program which are necessary to achieve interoperability.

2.   The provisions of paragraph 1 shall not permit the information obtained through its application:

(a) to be used for goals other than to achieve the interoperability of the independently created computer program;

(b) to be given to others, except when necessary for the interoperability of the independently created computer program; or

(c) to be used for the development, production or marketing of a computer program substantially similar in its expression, or for any other act which infringes copyright.

3.   In accordance with the provisions of the Berne Convention for the protection of Literary and Artistic Works, the provisions of this Article may not be interpreted in such a way as to allow its application to be used in a manner which unreasonably prejudices the right holder's legitimate interests or conflicts with a normal exploitation of the computer program.

[379]

Article 7   Special measures of protection

1.   Without prejudice to the provisions of Articles 4, 5 and 6, Member States shall provide, in accordance with their national legislation, appropriate remedies against a person committing any of the acts listed in subparagraphs (a), (b) and (c) below—

   (a)   any act of putting into circulation a copy of a computer program knowing, or having reason to believe, that it is an infringing copy;

   (b)   the possession, for commercial purposes, of a copy of a computer program knowing, or having reason to believe, that it is an infringing copy;

   (c)   any act of putting into circulation, or the possession for commercial purposes of, any means the sole intended purpose of which is to facilitate the unauthorised removal or circumvention of any technical device which may have been applied to protect a computer program.

2.   Any infringing copy of a computer program shall be liable to seizure in accordance with the legislation of the Member State concerned.

3.   Member States may provide for the seizure of any means referred to in paragraph 1(c).

[380]

Article 9   Continued application of other legal provisions

1.   The provisions of this Directive shall be without prejudice to any other legal provisions such as those concerning patent rights, trade-marks, unfair competition, trade secrets, protection of semi-conductor products or the law of contract. Any contractual provisions contrary to Article 6 or to the exceptions provided for in Article 5(2) and (3) shall be null and void.

2.   The provisions of this Directive shall apply also to programs created before 1 January 1993 without prejudice to any acts concluded and rights acquired before that date.

[381]

Article 10   Final provisions

1.   Member States shall bring into force the laws, regulations and administrative provisions necessary to comply with this Directive before 1 January 1993.

   When Member States adopt these measures, the latter shall contain a reference to this Directive or shall be accompanied by such reference on the occasion of their official publication. The methods of making such a reference shall be laid down by the Member States.

2.   Member States shall communicate to the Commission the provisions of national law which they adopt in the field governed by this Directive.

[382]

Article 11

This Directive is addressed to the Member States.

[383]

COUNCIL DIRECTIVE 92/100/EEC

of 19 November 1992

on rental right and lending right and on certain rights related to copyright in the field of intellectual property

NOTES

Date of publication in OJ: OJ L346, 27.11.92, p 61.

CHAPTER I
RENTAL AND LENDING RIGHT

Article 1   Object of harmonisation

1.   In accordance with the provisions of this Chapter, Member States shall provide, subject to Article 5, a right to authorise or prohibit the rental and lending of originals and copies of copyright works, and other subject matter as set out in Article 2(1).

2.   For the purposes of this Directive, "rental" means making available for use, for a limited period of time and for direct or indirect economic or commercial advantage.

3.   For the purposes of this Directive, "lending" means making available for use, for a limited period of time and not for direct or indirect economic or commercial advantage, when it is made through establishments which are accessible to the public.

4.   The rights referred to in paragraph 1 shall not be exhausted by any sale or other act of distribution of originals and copies of copyright works and other subject matter as set out in Article 2(1).

[384]

Article 2   Rightholders and subject matter of rental and lending right

1.   The exclusive right to authorise or prohibit rental and lending shall belong—
   — to the author in respect of the original and copies of his work,
   — to the performer in respect of fixations of his performance,
   — to the phonogram producer in respect of his phonograms, and
   — to the producer of the first fixation of a film in respect of the original and copies of his film. For the purposes of this Directive, the term "film" shall designate a cinematographic or audio-visual work or moving images, whether or not accompanied by sound.

2.   For the purposes of this Directive the principal director of a cinematographic or audio-visual work shall be considered as its author or one of its authors. Member States may provide for others to be considered as its co-authors.

3.   This Directive does not cover rental and lending rights in relation to buildings and to works of applied art.

4.   The rights referred to in paragraph 1 may be transferred, assigned or subject to the granting of contractual licences.

5.   Without prejudice to paragraph 7, when a contract concerning film production is concluded, individually or collectively, by performers with a film producer, the performer covered by this contract shall be presumed, subject to contractual clauses to the contrary, to have transferred his rental right, subject to Article 4.

6.   Member States may provide for a similar presumption as set out in paragraph 5 with respect to authors.

7.   Member States may provide that the signing of a contract concluded between a performer and a film producer concerning the production of a film has the effect of authorising rental, provided that such contract provides for an equitable remuneration within the meaning of Article 4 Member States may also provide that this paragraph shall apply *mutatis mutandis* to the rights included in Chapter II.

[385]

Article 3   Rental of computer programs

This Directive shall be without prejudice to Article 4(c) of Council Directive 91/250/EEC of 14 May 1991 on the legal protection of computer programs[1].

[386]

NOTES
   1 OJ L122, 17.5.91, p 42.

Article 4   Unwaivable right to equitable remuneration

1.   Where an author or performer has transferred or assigned his rental right concerning a phonogram or an original or copy of a film to a phonogram or film producer, that author or performer shall retain the right to obtain an equitable remuneration for the rental.

2.   The right to obtain an equitable remuneration for rental cannot be waived by authors or performers.

3.   The administration of this right to obtain an equitable remuneration may be entrusted to collecting societies representing authors or performers.

4.   Member States may regulate whether and to what extent administration by collecting societies of the right to obtain an equitable remuneration may be imposed, as well as the question from whom this remuneration may be claimed or collected.

[387]

Article 5   Derogation from the exclusive public lending right

1.   Member States may derogate from the exclusive right provided for in Article 1 in respect of public lending, provided that at least authors obtain a remuneration for such lending. Member States shall be free to determine this remuneration taking account of their cultural promotion objectives.

2.   When Member States do not apply the exclusive lending right provided for in Article 1 as regards phonograms, films and computer programs, they shall introduce, at least for authors, a remuneration.

3.   Member States may exempt certain categories of establishments from the payment of the remuneration referred to in paragraphs 1 and 2.

4.   The Commission, in co-operation with the Member States, shall draw up before 1 July 1997 a report on public lending in the Community. It shall forward this report to the European Parliament and to the Council.

[388]

CHAPTER II
RIGHTS RELATED TO COPYRIGHT

Article 6   Fixation right

1.   Member States shall provide for performers the exclusive right to authorise or prohibit the fixation of their performances.

2.   Member States shall provide for broadcasting organisations the exclusive right to authorise or prohibit the fixation of their broadcasts, whether these broadcasts are transmitted by wire or over the air, including by cable or satellite.

3.   A cable distributor shall not have the right provided for in paragraph 2 where it merely retransmits by cable the broadcasts of broadcasting organisations.

[389]

Article 7   Reproduction right

1.   Member States shall provide the exclusive right to authorise or prohibit the direct or indirect reproduction—
—   for performers, of fixations of their performances,
—   for phonogram producers, of their phonograms,
—   for producers of the first fixations of films, in respect of the original and copies of their films, and
—   for broadcasting organisations, of fixations of their broadcasts, as set out in Article 6(2).

2.   The reproduction right referred to in paragraph 1 may be transferred, assigned or subject to the granting of contractual licences.

[390]

Article 8   Broadcasting and communication to the public

1.   Member States shall provide for performers the exclusive right to authorise or prohibit the broadcasting by wireless means and the communication to the public of their performances, except where the performance is itself already a broadcast performance or is made from a fixation.

2.   Member States shall provide a right in order to ensure that a single equitable remuneration is paid by the user, if a phonogram published for commercial purposes, or a reproduction of such phonogram, is used for broadcasting by wireless means or for any communication to the public, and to ensure that this remuneration is shared between the relevant performers and phonogram producers. Member States may, in the absence of agreement between the performers and phonogram producers, lay down the conditions as to the sharing of this remuneration between them.

3.   Member States shall provide for broadcasting organisations the exclusive right to authorise or prohibit the rebroadcasting of their broadcasts by wireless means, as well as the communication to the public of their broadcasts if such communication is made in places accessible to the public against payment of an entrance fee.

[391]

Article 9   Distribution right

1.   Member States shall provide—
— for performers, in respect of fixations of their performances,
— for phonogram producers, in respect of their phonograms,
— for producers of the first fixations of films, in respect of the original and copies of their films,
— for broadcasting organisations, in respect of fixations of their broadcast as set out in Article 6(2),

the exclusive right to make available these objects, including copies thereof, to the public by sale or otherwise, hereafter referred to as the "distribution right".

2.   The distribution right shall not be exhausted within the Community in respect of an object as referred to in paragraph 1, except where the first sale in the Community of that object is made by the rightholder or with his consent.

3.   The distribution right shall be without prejudice to the specific provisions of Chapter I, in particular Article 1(4).

4.   The distribution right may be transferred, assigned or subject to the granting of contractual licences.

[392]

Article 10   Limitations to rights

1.   Member States may provide for limitations to the rights referred to in Chapter II in respect of—
(a)   private use;
(b)   use of short excerpts in connection with the reporting of current events;
(c)   ephemeral fixation by a broadcasting organisation by means of its own facilities and for its own broadcasts;
(d)   use solely for the purposes of teaching or scientific research.

2.   Irrespective of paragraph 1, any Member State may provide for the same kinds of limitations with regard to the protection of performers, producers of phonograms, broadcasting organisations and of producers of the first fixations of films, as it provides for in connection with the protection of copyright in literary and artistic works. However, compulsory licences may be provided for only to the extent to which they are compatible with the Rome Convention.

3.   Paragraph 1(a) shall be without prejudice to any existing or future legislation on remuneration for reproduction for private use.

[393]

CHAPTER IV
COMMON PROVISIONS

Article 13   Application in time

1.   This Directive shall apply in respect of all copyright works, performances, phonograms, broadcasts and first fixations of films referred to in this Directive which are, on 1 July 1994, still protected by the legislation of the Member States in the field of copyright and related rights or meet the criteria for protection under the provisions of this Directive on that date.

2.   This Directive shall apply without prejudice to any acts of exploitation performed before 1 July 1994.

3.   Member States may provide that the rightholders are deemed to have given their authorisation to the rental or lending of an object referred to in Article 2(1) which is proven to have been made available to third parties for this purpose or to have been acquired before 1 July 1994. However, in particular where such an object is a digital recording, Member States may provide that rightholders shall have a right to obtain an adequate remuneration for the rental or lending of that object.

4.   Member States need not apply the provisions of Article 2(2) to cinematographic or audio-visual works created before 1 July 1994.

5.   Member States may determine the date as from which the Article 2(2) shall apply, provided that that date is no later than 1 July 1997.

6.   This Directive shall, without prejudice to paragraph 3 and subject to paragraphs 8 and 9, not affect any contracts concluded before the date of its adoption.

7.   Member States may provide, subject to the provisions of paragraphs 8 and 9, that when rightholders who acquire new rights under the national provisions adopted in implementation of this Directive have, before 1 July 1994, given their consent for exploitation, they shall be presumed to have transferred the new exclusive rights.

8.   Member States may determine the date as from which the unwaivable right to an equitable remuneration referred to in Article 4 exists, provided that that date is no later than 1 July 1997.

9.   For contracts concluded before 1 July 1994, the unwaivable right to an equitable remuneration provided for in Article 4 shall apply only where authors or performers or those representing them have submitted a request to that effect before 1 January 1997. In the absence of agreement between rightholders concerning the level of remuneration, Member States may fix the level of equitable remuneration.

[394]

Article 14   Relation between copyright and related rights

Protection of copyright-related rights under this Directive shall leave intact and shall in no way affect the protection of copyright.

[395]

Article 15   Final provisions

1.   Member States shall bring into force the laws, regulations and administrative provisions necessary to comply with this Directive not later than 1 July 1994. They shall forthwith inform the Commission thereof.

When Member States adopt these measures, they shall contain a reference to this Directive or shall be accompanied by such reference at the time of their official publica.ion. The methods of making such a reference shall be laid down by the Member States.

2.   Member States shall communicate to the Commission the main provisions of domestic law which they adopt in the field covered by this Directive.

[396]

Article 16

This Directive is addressed to the Member States.

[397]

COUNCIL DIRECTIVE 93/83/EEC

of 27 September 1993

on the coordination of certain rules concerning copyright and rights related to copyright applicable to satellite broadcasting and cable retransmission

NOTES
Date of publication in OJ: OJ L248, 6.10.93, p 15.

CHAPTER I
DEFINITIONS

Article 1   Definitions

1. For the purpose of this Directive, 'satellite' means any satellite operating on frequency bands which, under telecommunications law, are reserved for the broadcast of signals for reception by the public or which are reserved for closed, point-to-point communication. In the latter case, however, the circumstances in which individual reception of the signals takes place must be comparable to those which apply in the first case.

2—(a) For the purpose of this Directive, "communication to the public by satellite" means the act of introducing, under the control and responsibility of the broadcasting organisation, the programme-carrying signals intended for reception by the public into an uninterrupted chain of communication leading to the satellite and down towards the earth.

(b) The act of communication to the public by satellite occurs solely in the Member State where, under the control and responsibility of the broadcasting organisation, the programme-carrying signals are introduced into an uninterrupted chain of communication leading to the satellite and down towards the earth.

(c) If the programme-carrying signals are encrypted, then there is communication to the public by satellite on condition that the means for decrypting the broadcast are provided to the public by the broadcasting organisation or with its consent.

(d) Where an act of communication to the public by satellite occurs in a non-Community State which does not provide the level of protection provided for under Chapter II,

    (i) if the programme-carrying signals are transmitted to the satellite from an uplink situation situated in a Member State, that act of communication to the public by satellite shall be deemed to have occurred in that Member State and the rights provided for under Chapter II shall be exercisable against the person operating the uplink station; or

    (ii) if there is no use of an uplink station situated in a Member State but a broadcasting organisation established in a Member State has commissioned the act of communication to the public by satellite, that act shall be deemed to have occurred in the Member State in which the broadcasting organisation has its principal establishment in the Community and the rights provided for under Chapter II shall be exercisable against the broadcasting organisation.

3   For the purposes of this Directive, "cable retransmission" means the simultaneous, unaltered and unabridged retransmission by a cable or microwave system for reception by the public of an initial transmission from another Member State, by wire or over the air, including that by satellite, of television or radio programmes intended for reception by the public.

4   For the purposes of this Directive "collecting society" means any organisation which manages or administers copyright or rights related to copyright as its sole purpose or as one of its main purposes.

5   For the purposes of this Directive, the principal director of a cinematographic or audiovisual work shall be considered as its author or one of its authors. Member States may provide for others to be considered as its co-authors.

[398]

CHAPTER II
BROADCASTING OF PROGRAMMES BY SATELLITE

Article 2   Broadcasting right

Member States shall provide an exclusive right for the author to authorise the communication to the public by satellite of copyright works, subject to the provisions set out in this chapter.

[399]

Article 3   Acquisition of broadcasting rights

1   Member States shall ensure that the authorisation referred to in Article 2 may be acquired only by agreement.

2   A Member State may provide that a collective agreement between a collecting society and a broadcasting organisation concerning a given category of works may be extended to rightholders of the same category who are not represented by the collecting society, provided that—
   — the communication to the public by satellite simulcasts a terrestrial broadcast by the same broadcaster, and
   — the unrepresented rightholder shall, at any time, have the possibility of excluding the extension of the collective agreement to his works and of exercising his rights either individually or collectively.

3   Paragraph 2 shall not apply to cinematographic works, including works created by a process analogous to cinematography.

4   Where the law of a Member State provides for the extension of a collective agreement in accordance with the provisions of paragraph 2, that Member State shall inform the Commission which broadcasting organisations are entitled to avail themselves of that law. The Commission shall publish this information in the *Official Journal of the European Communities* (C series).

[400]

Article 4   Rights of performers, phonogram producers and broadcasting organisations

1   For the purposes of communication to the public by satellite, the rights of performers, phonogram producers and broadcasting organisations shall be protected in accordance with the provisions of Articles 6, 7, 8 and 10 of Directive 92/100/EEC.

2   For the purposes of paragraph 1, "broadcasting by wireless means" in Directive 92/100/EEC shall be understood as including communication to the public by satellite.

3   With regard to the exercise of the rights referred to in paragraph 1, Articles 2(7) and 12 of Directive 92/100/EEC shall apply.

[401]

Article 5   Relation between copyright and related rights

Protection of copyright-related rights under this Directive shall leave intact and shall in no way affect the protection of copyright.

[402]

Article 6   Minimum protection

1   Member States may provide for more far-reaching protection for holders of rights related to copyright than that required by Article 8 of Directive 92/100/EEC.

2   In applying paragraph 1 Member States shall observe the definitions contained in Article 1(1) and (2).

[403]

CHAPTER III
CABLE RETRANSMISSION

Article 8   Cable retransmission right

1   Member States shall ensure that when programmes from other Member States are retransmitted by cable in their territory the applicable copyright and related rights are observed and that such retransmission takes place on the basis of individual or collective contractual agreements between copyright owners, holders of related rights and cable operators.

2   Notwithstanding paragraph 1, Member States may retain until 31 December 1997 such statutory licence systems which are in operation or expressly provided for by national law on 31 July 1991.

[404]

Article 9   Exercise of the cable retransmission right

1   Member States shall ensure that the right of copyright owners and holders or related rights to grant or refuse authorisation to a cable operator for a cable retransmission may be exercised only through a collecting society.

2   Where a rightholder has not transferred the management of his rights to a collecting society, the collecting society which manages rights of the same category shall be deemed to be mandated to manage his rights. Where more than one collecting society manages rights of that category, the rightholder shall be free to choose which of those collecting societies is deemed to be mandated to manage his

rights. A rightholder referred to in this paragraph shall have the same rights and obligations resulting from the agreement between the cable operator and the collecting society which is deemed to be mandated to manage his rights as the rightholders who have mandated that collecting society and he shall be able to claim those rights within a period, to be fixed by the Member State concerned, which shall not be shorter than three years from the date of the cable retransmission which includes his work or other protected subject matter.

3   A Member State may provide that, when a right-holder authorises the initial transmission within its territory of a work or other protected subject matter, he shall be deemed to have agreed not to exercise his cable retransmission rights on an individual basis but to exercise them in accordance with the provisions of this Directive.

[405]

Article 10   Exercise of the cable retransmission right by broadcasting organisations

Member States shall ensure that Article 9 does not apply to the rights exercised by a broadcasting organisation in respect of its own transmission, irrespective of whether the rights concerned are its own or have been transferred to it by other copyright owners and/or holders of related rights.

[406]

CHAPTER IV
GENERAL PROVISIONS

Article 13   Collective administration of rights

This Directive shall be without prejudice to the regulation of the activities of collecting societies by the Member States.

[407]

Article 14   Final provisions

1   Member States shall bring into force the laws, regulations and administrative provisions necessary to comply with this Directive before 1 January 1995. They shall immediately inform the Commission thereof.

When Member States adopt these measures, the latter shall contain a reference to this Directive or shall be accompanied by such reference at the time of their official publication. The methods of making such a reference shall be laid down by the Member States.

2   Member States shall communicate to the Commission the provisions of national law which they adopt in the field covered by this Directive.

3   Not later than 1 January 2000, the Commission shall submit to the European Parliament, the Council and the Economic and Social Committee a report on the application of this Directive and, if necessary, make further proposals to adapt it to developments in the audio and audiovisual sector.

[408]

Article 15

This Directive is addressed to the Member States.

[409]

COUNCIL DIRECTIVE 93/98/EEC

of 29 October 1993

harmonising the term of protection of copyright and certain related rights

NOTES

Date of publication in OJ: OJ L290, 24.11.93, p 9.

Article 1   Duration of authors' rights

1.   The rights of an author of a literary or artistic work within the meaning of Article 2 of the Berne Convention shall run for the life of the author and for 70 years after his death, irrespective of the date when the work is lawfully made available to the public.

2.   In the case of a work of joint authorship the term referred to in paragraph 1 shall be calculated from the death of the last surviving author.

3.   In the case of anonymous or pseudonymous works, the term of protection shall run for seventy years after the work is lawfully made available to the public. However, when the pseudonym adopted by the author leaves no doubt as to his identity, or if the author discloses his identity during the period referred to in the first sentence, the term of protection applicable shall be that laid down in paragraph 1.

4.   Where a Member State provides for particular provisions on copyright in respect of collective works or for a legal person to be designated as the rightholder, the term of protection shall be calculated according to the provisions of paragraph 3, except if the natural persons who have created the work as such are identified as such in the versions of the work which are made available to the public. This paragraph is without prejudice to the rights of identified authors whose identifiable contributions are included in such works, to which contributions paragraph 1 or 2 shall apply.

5.   Where a work is published in volumes, parts, instalments, issues or episodes and the term of protection runs from the time when the work was lawfully made available to the public, the term of protection shall run for each such item separately.

6.   In the case of works for which the term of protection is not calculated from the death of the author or authors and which have not been lawfully made available to the public within seventy years from their creation, the protection shall terminate.

[410]

Article 2   Cinematographic or audiovisual works

1.   The principal director of a cinematographic or audiovisual work shall be considered as its author or one of its authors. Member States shall be free to designate other co-authors.

2.   The term of protection of cinematographic or audiovisual works shall expire 70 years after the death of the last of the following persons to survive, whether or not these persons are designated as co-authors: the principal director, the author of the screenplay, the author of the dialogue and the composer of music specifically created for use in the cinematographic or audiovisual work.

[411]

Article 3   Duration of related rights

1.   The rights of performers shall expire 50 years after the date of the performance. However, if a fixation of the performance is lawfully published or lawfully communicated to the public within this period, the rights shall expire 50 years from the date of the first such publication or the first such communication to the public, whichever is the earlier.

2.   The rights of producers of phonograms shall expire 50 years after the fixation is made. However, if the phonogram is lawfully published or lawfully communicated to the public during this period, the rights shall expire 50 years from the date of the first such publication or the first such communication to the public, whichever is the earlier.

3.   The rights of producers of the first fixation of a film shall expire 50 years after the fixation is made. However, if the film is lawfully published or lawfully communicated to the public during this period, the rights shall expire 50 years from the date of the first such publication or the first such communication to the public, whichever is the earlier. The term "film" shall designate a cinematographic or audio-visual work or moving images, whether or not accompanied by sound.

4.   The rights of broadcasting organisations shall expire 50 years after the first transmission of a broadcast, whether this broadcast is transmitted by wire or over the air, including by cable or satellite.

[412]

Article 4   Protection of previously unpublished works

Any person who, after the expiry of copyright protection, for the first time lawfully publishes or lawfully communicates to the public a previously unpublished work, shall benefit from a protection equivalent to the economic rights of the author. The term of protection of such rights shall be 25 years from the time when the work was first lawfully published or lawfully communicated to the public.

[413]

Article 5   Critical and scientific publications

Member States may protect critical and scientific publications of works which have come into the public domain. The maximum term of protection of such rights shall be 30 years from the time when the publication was first lawfully published.

[414]

Article 6   Protection of photographs

Photographs which are original in the sense that they are the author's own intellectual creation shall be protected in accordance with Article 1. No other criteria shall be applied to determine their eligibility for protection. Member States may provide for the protection of other photographs.

[415]

Article 7   Protection *vis-à-vis* third countries

1.   Where the country of origin of a work, within the meaning of the Berne Convention, is a third country, and the author of the work is not a Community national, the term of protection granted by the Member States shall expire on the date of expiry of the protection granted in the country of origin of the work, but may not exceed the term laid down in Article 1.

2. The terms of protection laid down in Article 3 shall also apply in the case of rightholders who are not Community nationals, provided Member States grant them protection. However, without prejudice to the international obligations of the Member States, the term of protection granted by Member States shall expire no later than the date of expiry of the protection granted in the country of which the rightholder is a national and may not exceed the term laid down in Article 3.

3. Member States which, at the date of adoption of this Directive, in particular pursuant to their international obligations, granted a longer term of protection than that which would result from the provisions, referred to in paragraphs 1 and 2 may maintain this protection until the conclusion of international agreements on the term of protection by copyright or related rights.

[416]

Article 8   Calculation of terms

The terms laid down in this Directive are calculated from the first day of January of the year following the event which gives rise to them.

[417]

Article 9   Moral rights

This Directive shall be without prejudice to the provisions of the Member States regulating moral rights.

[418]

Article 10   Application in time

1. Where a term of protection, which is longer than the corresponding term provided for by this Directive, is already running in a Member State on the date referred to in Article 13(1), this Directive shall not have the effect of shortening that term of protection in that Member State.

2. The terms of protection provided for in this Directive shall apply to all works and subject matter which are protected in at least one Member State, on the date referred to in Article 13(1), pursuant to national provisions on copyright or related rights or which meet the criteria for protection under Directive 92/100/EEC.

3. This Directive shall be without prejudice to any acts of exploitation performed before the date referred to in Article 13(1). Member States shall adopt the necessary provisions to protect in particular acquired rights of third parties.

4. Member States need not apply the provisions of Article 2(1) to cinematographic or audiovisual works created before 1 July 1994.

5. Member States may determine the date as from which Article 2(1) shall apply, provided that date is no later than 1 July 1997.

[419]

Article 12   Notification procedure

Member States shall immediately notify the Commission of any governmental plan to grant new related rights, including the basic reasons for their introduction and the term of protection envisaged.

[420]

Article 13   General provisions

1.   Member States shall bring into force the laws, regulations and administrative provisions necessary to comply with Articles 1 to 11 of this Directive before 1 July 1995.

When Member States adopt these provisions, they shall contain a reference to this Directive or shall be accompanied by such reference at the time of their official publication. The methods of making such a reference shall be laid down by the Member States.

Member States shall communicate to the Commission the texts of the provisions of national law which they adopt in the field governed by this Directive.

2.   Member States shall apply Article 12 from the date of notification of this Directive.

[421]

Article 14

This Directive is addressed to the Member States.

[422]

COUNCIL DIRECTIVE 96/9/EEC

of 11 March 1996

on the legal protection of databases

NOTES
    Date of publication in OJ: OJ L77, 27.3.96, p 20.

CHAPTER I
SCOPE

Article 1   Scope

1.   This Directive concerns the legal protection of databases in any form.

2.   For the purposes of this Directive, "database" shall mean a collection of independent works, data or other materials arranged in a systematic or methodical way and individually accessible by electronic or other means.

3.   Protection under this Directive shall not apply to computer programs used in the making or operation of databases accessible by electronic means.

Article 2   Limitations on the scope

This Directive shall apply without prejudice to Community provisions relating to—
    (a)   the legal protection of computer programs;
    (b)   rental right, lending right and certain rights related to copyright in the field of intellectual property;
    (c)   the term of protection of copyright and certain related rights.

[423]

CHAPTER II
COPYRIGHT

Article 3   Object of protection

1.   In accordance with this Directive, databases which, by reason of the selection or arrangement of their contents, constitute the author's own intellectual creation shall be protected as such by copyright. No other criteria shall be applied to determine their eligibility for that protection.

2.   The copyright protection of databases provided for by this Directive shall not extend to their contents and shall be without prejudice to any rights subsisting in those contents themselves.

Article 4   Database authorship

1.   The author of a database shall be the natural person or group of natural persons who created the base or, where the legislation of the Member States so permits, the legal person designated as the rightholder by that legislation.

2.   Where collective works are recognised by the legislation of a Member State, the economic rights shall be owned by the person holding the copyright.

3.   In respect of a database created by a group of natural persons jointly, the exclusive rights shall be owned jointly.

Article 5   Restricted acts

In respect of the expression of the database which is protectable by copyright, the author of a database shall have the exclusive right to carry out or to authorise—
  (a) temporary or permanent reproduction by any means and in any form, in whole or in part;
  (b) translation, adaptation, arrangement and any other alteration;
  (c) any form of distribution to the public of the database or of copies thereof. The first sale in the Community of a copy of the database by the rightholder or with his consent shall exhaust the right to control resale of that copy within the Community;
  (d) any communication, display or performance to the public;
  (e) any reproduction, distribution, communication, display or performance to the public of the results of the acts referred to in (b).

Article 6   Exceptions to restricted acts

1.   The performance by the lawful user of a database or of a copy thereof of any of the acts listed in Article 5 which is necessary for the purposes of access to the contents of the databases and normal use of the contents by the lawful user shall not require the authorisation of the author of the database. Where the lawful user is authorised to use only part of the database, this provision shall apply only to that part.

2.   Member States shall have the option of providing for limitations on the rights set out in Article 5 in the following cases—
  (a) in the case of reproduction for private purposes of a non-electronic database;
  (b) where there is use for the sole purpose of illustration for teaching or scientific research, as long as the source is indicated and to the extent justified by the non-commercial purpose to be achieved;

(c) where there is use for the purposes of public security of for the purposes of an administrative or judicial procedure;

(d) where other exceptions to copyright which are traditionally authorised under national law are involved, without prejudice to points (a), (b) and (c).

3.   In accordance with the Berne Convention for the protection of Literary and Artistic Works, this Article may not be interpreted in such a way as to allow its application to be used in a manner which unreasonably prejudices the rightholder's legitimate interests or conflicts with normal exploitation of the database.

[424]

CHAPTER III
SUI GENERIS RIGHT

Article 7   Object of protection

1.   Member States shall provide for a right for the maker of a database which shows that there has been qualitatively and/or quantitatively a substantial investment in either the obtaining, verification or presentation of the contents to prevent extraction and/or re-utilisation of the whole or of a substantial part, evaluated qualitatively and/or quantitatively, of the contents of that database.

2.   For the purposes of this Chapter—

(a) "extraction" shall mean the permanent or temporary transfer of all or a substantial part of the contents of a database to another medium by any means or in any form;

(b) "re-utilisation" shall mean any form of making available to the public all or a substantial part of the contents of a database by the distribution of copies, by renting, by on-line or other forms of transmission. The first sale of a copy of a database within the Community by the rightholder or with his consent shall exhaust the right to control resale of that copy within the Community;

Public lending is not an act of extraction or re-utilisation.

3.   The right referred to in paragraph 1 may be transferred, assigned or granted under contractual licence.

4.   The right provided for in paragraph 1 shall apply irrespective of the eligibility of that database for protection by copyright or by other rights. Moreover, it shall apply irrespective of eligibility of the contents of that database for protection by copyright or by other rights. Protection of databases under the right provided for in paragraph 1 shall be without prejudice to rights existing in respect of their contents.

5.   The repeated and systematic extraction and/or re-utilisation of insubstantial parts of the contents of the database implying acts which conflict with a normal exploitation of that database or which unreasonably prejudice the legitimate interests of the maker of the database shall not be permitted.

Article 8   Rights and obligations of lawful users

1.   The maker of a database which is made available to the public in whatever manner may not prevent a lawful user of the database from extracting and/or re-utilising insubstantial parts of its contents, evaluated qualitatively and/or

quantitatively, for any purposes whatsoever. Where the lawful user is authorised to extract and/or re-utilise only part of the database, this paragraph shall apply only to that part.

2.   A lawful user of a database which is made available to the public in whatever manner may not perform acts which conflict with normal exploitation of the database or unreasonably prejudice the legitimate interests of the maker of the database.

3.   A lawful user of a database which is made available to the public in any manner may not cause prejudice to the holder of a copyright or related right in respect of the works or subject matter contained in the database.

Article 9   Exceptions to the *sui generis* right

Member States may stipulate that lawful users of a database which is made available to the public in whatever manner may, without the authorisation of its maker, extract or re-utilise a substantial part of its contents—

    (a)   in the case of extraction for private purposes of the contents of a non-electronic database;

    (b)   in the case of extraction for the purposes of illustration for teaching or scientific research, as long as the source is indicated and to the extent justified by the non-commercial purpose to be achieved;

    (c)   in the case of extraction and/or re-utilisation for the purposes of public security or an administrative or judicial procedure.

Article 10   Term of protection

1.   The right provided for in Article 7 shall run from the date of completion of the making of the database. It shall expire fifteen years from the first of January of the year following the date of completion.

2.   In the case of a database which is made available to the public in whatever manner before expiry of the period provided for in paragraph 1, the term of protection by that right shall expire fifteen years from the first of January of the year following the date when the database was first made available to the public.

3.   Any substantial change, evaluated qualitatively or quantitatively, to the contents of a database, including any substantial change resulting from the accumulation of successive additions, deletions or alterations, which would result in the database being considered to be a substantial new investment, evaluated qualitatively or quantitatively, shall qualify the database resulting from that investment for its own term of protection.

Article 11   Beneficiaries of protection under the *sui generis* right

1.   The right provided for in Article 7 shall apply to database whose makers or rightholders are nationals of a Member State or who have their habitual residence in the territory of the Community.

2.   Paragraph 1 shall also apply to companies and firms formed in accordance with the law of a Member State and having their registered office, central administration or principal place of business within the Community; however, where such a company or firm has only its registered office in the territory of the Community, its operations must be genuinely linked on an ongoing basis with the economy of a Member State.

3.   Agreements extending the right provided for in Article 7 to databases made in third countries and falling outside the provisions of paragraphs 1 and 2 shall be concluded by the Council acting on a proposal from the Commission. The term of any protection extended to databases by virtue of that procedure shall not exceed that available pursuant to Article 10.

[425]

CHAPTER IV
COMMON PROVISIONS

Article 12   Remedies

Member States shall provide appropriate remedies in respect of infringements of the rights provided for in this Directive.

Article 13   Continued application of other legal provisions

This Directive shall be without prejudice to provisions concerning in particular copyright, rights related to copyright or any other rights or obligations subsisting in the data, works or other materials incorporated into a database, patent rights, trade marks, design rights, the protection of national treasures, laws on restrictive practices and unfair competition, trade secrets, security, confidentiality, data protection and privacy, access to public documents, and the law of contract.

Article 14   Application over time

1.   Protection pursuant to this Directive as regards copyright shall also be available in respect of databases created prior to the date referred to Article 16(1) which on that date fulfil the requirements laid down in this Directive as regards copyright protection of databases.

2.   Notwithstanding paragraph 1, where a database protected under copyright arrangements in a Member State on the date of publication of this Directive does not fulfil the eligibility criteria for copyright protection laid down in Article 3(1), this Directive shall not result in any curtailing in that Member State of the remaining term of protection afforded under those arrangements.

3.   Protection pursuant to the provisions of this Directive as regards the right provided for in Article 7 shall also be available in respect of databases the making of which was completed not more than fifteen years prior to the date referred to in Article 16(1) and which on that date fulfil the requirements laid down in Article 7.

4.   The protection provided for in paragraphs 1 and 3 shall be without prejudice to any acts concluded and rights acquired before the date referred to in those paragraphs.

5.   In the case of a database the making of which was completed not more than fifteen years prior to the date referred to in Article 16(1), the term of protection by the right provided for in Article 7 shall expire fifteen years from the first of January following that date.

Article 15   Binding nature of certain provisions

Any contractual provision contrary to Articles 6(1) and 8 shall be null and void.

Article 16   Final provisions

1.   Member States shall bring into force the laws, regulations and administrative provisions necessary to comply with this Directive before 1 January 1998.

When Member States adopt these provisions, they shall contain a reference to this Directive or shall be accompanied by such reference on the occasion of their official publication. The methods of making such reference shall be laid down by Member States.

2.   Member States shall communicate to the Commission the text of the provisions of domestic law which they adopt in the field governed by this Directive.

3.   Not later than at the end of the third year after the date referred to in paragraph 1, and every three years thereafter, the Commission shall submit to the European Parliament, the Council and the Economic and Social Committee a report on the application of this Directive, in which, *inter alia,* on the basis of specific information supplied by the Member States, it shall examine in particular the application of the *sui generis* right, including Articles 8 and 9, and shall verify especially whether the application of this right has led to abuse of a dominant position or other interference with free competition which would justify appropriate measures being taken, including the establishment of non-voluntary licensing arrangements. Where necessary, it shall submit proposals for adjustment of this Directive in line with developments in the area of databases.

Article 17

This Directive is addressed to the Member States.

[426]

COPYRIGHT (INDUSTRIAL PROCESS AND EXCLUDED ARTICLES) (NO 2) ORDER 1989

(SI 1989/1070)

NOTES

Made: 26 June 1989.

Authority: Copyright, Designs and Patents Act 1988, s 52(4).

1   This Order may be cited as the Copyright (Industrial Process and Excluded Articles) (No 2) Order 1989 and shall come into force on 1st August 1989

[427]

2   An article is to be regarded for the purposes of section 52 of the Act (limitation of copyright protection for design derived from artistic work) as made by an industrial process if—

(a)   it is one of more than fifty articles which—

    (i)   all fall to be treated for the purposes of Part I of the Act as copies of a particular artistic work, but

    (ii)   do not all together constitute a single set of articles as defined in section 44(1) of the Registered Designs Act 1949; or

(b)   it consists of goods manufactured in lengths or pieces, not being hand-made goods.

[428]

3—(1)   There are excluded from the operation of section 52 of the Act—

(a)   works of sculpture, other than casts or models used or intended to be used as models or patterns to be multiplied by any industrial process;

(b)   wall plaques, medals and medallions; and

(c)   printed matter primarily of a literary or artistic character, including book jackets, calendars, certificates, coupons, dress-making patterns, greetings cards, labels, leaflets, maps, plans, playing cards, postcards, stamps, trade advertisements, trade forms and cards, transfers and similar articles.

(2)   Nothing in article 2 of this Order shall be taken to limit the meaning of "industrial process" in paragraph (1)(a) of this article.

[429]–[500]

PART IV
DESIGNS

REGISTERED DESIGNS ACT 1949

(c 88)

An Act to consolidate certain enactments relating to registered designs

[16 December 1949]

NOTES

Trade marks and registered trade marks: note that references to trade marks and registered trade marks within the meaning of the Trade Marks Act 1938 shall, unless the context otherwise requires, be construed after the commencement of the Trade Marks Act 1994 as references to trade marks and registered trade marks within the meaning of that Act. See the Trade Marks Act 1994, s 102(1), Sch 4, para 1.

Registrable designs and proceedings for registration

[1   Designs registrable under Act

(1) In this Act "design" means features of shape, configuration, pattern or ornament applied to an article by any industrial process, being features which in the finished article appeal to and are judged by the eye, but does not include—

    (a) a method or principle of construction, or

    (b) features of shape or configuration of an article which—

        (i) are dictated solely by the function which the article has to perform, or

        (ii) are dependent upon the appearance of another article of which the article is intended by the author of the design to form an integral part.

(2) A design which is new may, upon application by the person claiming to be the proprietor, be registered under this Act in respect of any article, or set of articles, specified in the application.

(3) A design shall not be registered in respect of an article if the appearance of the article is not material, that is, if aesthetic considerations are not normally taken into account to a material extent by persons acquiring or using articles of that description, and would not be so taken into account if the design were to be applied to the article.

(4) A design shall not be regarded as new for the purposes of this Act if it is the same as a design—

    (a) registered in respect of the same or any other article in pursuance of a prior application, or

    (b) published in the United Kingdom in respect of the same or any other article before the date of the application,

or if it differs from such a design only in immaterial details or in features which are variants commonly used in the trade.

This subsection has effect subject to the provisions of sections 4, 6 and 16 of this Act.

(5) The Secretary of State may by rules provide for excluding from registration under this Act designs for such articles of a primarily literary or artistic character as the Secretary of State thinks fit.

[(6) A design shall not be registered if it consists of or contains a controlled representation within the meaning of the Olympic Symbol etc (Protection) Act 1995 unless it appears to the registrar—

(a) that the application is made by the person for the time being appointed under section 1(2) of the Olympic Symbol etc (Protection) Act 1995 (power of Secretary of State to appoint a person as the proprietor of the Olympics association right), or

(b) that consent has been given by or on behalf of the person mentioned in paragraph (a) of this subsection.]]

[501]

NOTES

Substituted by the Copyright, Designs and Patents Act 1988, s 265(1), except in relation to applications for registration before 1 August 1989.

Sub-s (6): added by the Olympic Symbol etc (Protection) Act 1995, s 13(1), (3), with effect in relation to applications for registration made on or after 20 September 1995.

2   Proprietorship of designs

[(1)   The author of a design shall be treated for the purposes of this Act as the original proprietor of the design, subject to the following provisions.

(1A)   Where a design is created in pursuance of a commission for money or money's worth, the person commissioning the design shall be treated as the original proprietor of the design.

(1B)   Where, in a case not falling within subsection (1A), a design is created by an employee in the course of his employment, his employer shall be treated as the original proprietor of the design.]

(2)   Where a design, or the right to apply a design to any article, becomes vested, whether by assignment, transmission or operation of law, in any person other than the original proprietor, either alone or jointly with the original proprietor, that other person, or as the case may be the original proprietor and that other person, shall be treated for the purposes of this Act as the proprietor of the design or as the proprietor of the design in relation to that article.

[(3)   In this Act the "author" of a design means the person who creates it.

(4)   In the case of a design generated by computer in circumstances such that there is no human author, the person by whom the arrangements necessary for the creation of the design are made shall be taken to be the author.]

[502]

NOTES

Sub-ss (1)–(1B): substituted for sub-s (1) as originally enacted by the Copyright, Designs and Patents Act 1988, s 267(2), except in relation to applications for registration before 1 August 1989.

Sub-ss (3), (4): added by the Copyright, Designs and Patents Act 1988, s 267(3), except in relation to applications for registration before 1 August 1989.

3   Proceedings for registration

(1)   An application for the registration of a design shall be made in the prescribed form and shall be filed at the Patent Office in the prescribed manner.

[(2)   An application for the registration of a design in which design right subsists shall not be entertained unless made by the person claiming to be the design right owner.

(3)   For the purpose of deciding whether a design is new, the registrar may make such searches, if any, as he thinks fit.

(4)   The registrar may, in such cases as may be prescribed, direct that for the purpose of deciding whether a design is new an application shall be treated as made on a date earlier or later than that on which it was in fact made.

(5)   The registrar may refuse an application for the registration of a design or may register the design in pursuance of the application subject to such modifications, if any, as he thinks fit; and a design when registered shall be registered as of the date on which the application was made or is treated as having been made.

(6)   An application which, owing to any default or neglect on the part of the applicant, has not been completed so as to enable registration to be effected within such time as may be prescribed shall be deemed to be abandoned.

(7)   An appeal lies from any decision of the registrar under this section.]

[503]

NOTES

     Sub-ss (2)–(7): substituted for sub-ss (2)–(6), as originally enacted, by the Copyright, Designs and Patents Act 1988, s 272, Sch 3, para 1.

---

4   Registration of same design in respect of other articles, etc

(1)   Where the registered proprietor of a design registered in respect of any article makes an application—

     (a)   for registration in respect of one or more other articles, of the registered design, or

     (b)   for registration in respect of the same or one or more other articles, of a design consisting of the registered design with modifications or variations not sufficient to alter the character or substantially to affect the identity thereof,

the application shall not be refused and the registration made on that application shall not be invalidated by reason only of the previous registration or publication of the registered design:

[Provided that the right in a design registered by virtue of this section shall not extend beyond the end of the period, and any extended period, for which the right subsists in the original registered design].

(2)   Where any person makes an application for the registration of a design in respect of any article and either—

     (a)   that design has been previously registered by another person in respect of some other article; or

     (b)   the design to which the application relates consists of a design previously registered by another person in respect of the same or some other article with modifications or variations not sufficient to alter the character or substantially to affect the identity thereof,

then, if at any time while the application is pending the applicant becomes the registered proprietor of the design previously registered, the foregoing provisions of this section shall apply as if at the time of making the application the applicant had been the registered proprietor of that design.

[504]

NOTES

     Sub-s (1): words in square brackets substituted by the Copyright, Designs and Patents Act 1988, s 272, Sch 3, para 2.

5 Provisions for secrecy of certain designs

(1) Where, either before or after the commencement of this Act, an application for the registration of a design has been made, and it appears to the registrar that the design is one of a class notified to him by [the Secretary of State] as relevant for defence purposes, he may give directions for prohibiting or restricting the publication of information with respect to the design, or the communication of such information to any person or class of persons specified in the directions.

[(2) The Secretary of State shall by rules make provision for securing that where such directions are given—

(a) the representation or specimen of the design, and

(b) any evidence filed in support of the applicant's contention that the appearance of an article is material (for the purposes of section 1(3) of this Act),

shall not be open to public inspection at the Patent Office during the continuance in force of the directions.]

(3) Where the registrar gives any such directions as aforesaid, he shall give notice of the application and of the directions to [the Secretary of State], and thereupon the following provisions shall have effect, that is to say:—

(a) [the Secretary of State] shall, upon receipt of such notice, consider whether the publication of the design would be prejudicial to the defence of the realm and unless a notice under paragraph (c) of this subsection has previously been given by that authority to the registrar, shall reconsider that question before the expiration of nine months from the date of filing of the application for registration of the design and at least once in every subsequent year;

(b) for the purpose aforesaid, [the Secretary of State] may, at any time after the design has been registered or, with the consent of the applicant, at any time before the design has been registered, inspect the representation or specimen of the design[, or any such evidence as is mentioned in subsection (2)(b) above,] filed in pursuance of the application;

(c) if upon consideration of the design at any time it appears to [the Secretary of State] that the publication of the design would not, or would no longer, be prejudicial to the defence of the realm, [he] shall give notice to the registrar to that effect;

(d) on the receipt of any such notice the registrar shall revoke the directions and may, subject to such conditions, if any, as he thinks fit, extend the time for doing anything required or authorised to be done by or under this Act in connection with the application or registration, whether or not that time has previously expired.

(4) No person resident in the United Kingdom shall, except under the authority of a written permit granted by or on behalf of the registrar, make or cause to be made any application outside the United Kingdom for the registration of a design of any class prescribed for the purposes of this subsection unless—

(a) an application for registration of the same design has been made in the United Kingdom not less than six weeks before the application outside the United Kingdom; and

(b) either no directions have been given under subsection (1) of this section in relation to the application in the United Kingdom or all such directions have been revoked:

Provided that this subsection shall not apply in relation to a design for which an application for protection has first been filed in a country outside the United Kingdom by a person resident outside the United Kingdom.

(5)   . . .

NOTES

Sub-s (1): words in square brackets substituted by the Copyright, Designs and Patents Act 1988, s 272, Sch 3, para 3.

Sub-s (2): substituted by the Copyright, Designs and Patents Act 1988, s 272, Sch 3, para 3.

Sub-s (3): first words in square brackets substituted and second words in square brackets inserted by the Copyright, Designs and Patents Act 1988, s 272, Sch 3, para 3.

6   Provisions as to confidential disclosure, etc

(1)   An application for the registration of a design shall not be refused, and the registration of a design shall not be invalidated, by reason only of—

- (a) the disclosure of the design by the proprietor to any other person in such circumstances as would make it contrary to good faith for that other person to use or publish the design;
- (b) the disclosure of the design in breach of good faith by any person other than the proprietor of the design; or
- (c) in the case of a new or original textile design intended for registration, the acceptance of a first and confidential order for goods bearing the design.

(2)   An application for the registration of a design shall not be refused and the registration of a design shall not be invalidated by reason only—

- (a) that a representation of the design, or any article to which the design has been applied, has been displayed, with the consent of the proprietor of the design, at an exhibition [certified by the Secretary of State] for the purposes of this subsection;
- (b) that after any such display as aforesaid, and during the period of the exhibition, a representation of the design or any such article as aforesaid has been displayed by any person without the consent of the proprietor; or
- (c) that a representation of the design has been published in consequence of any such display as is mentioned in paragraph (a) of this subsection,

if the application for registration of the design is made not later than six months after the opening of the exhibition.

(3)   An application for the registration of a design shall not be refused, and the registration of a design shall not be invalidated, by reason only of the communication of the design by the proprietor thereof to a Government department or to any person authorised by a Government department to consider the merits of the design, or of anything done in consequence of such a communication.

[(4)   Where an application is made by or with the consent of the owner of copyright in an artistic work for the registration of a corresponding design, the design shall not be treated for the purposes of this Act as being other than new by reason only of any use previously made of the artistic work, subject to subsection (5).

(5)   Subsection (4) does not apply if the previous use consisted of or included the sale, letting for hire or offer or exposure for sale or hire of articles to which had been applied industrially—

(a) the design in question, or

(b) a design differing from it only in immaterial details or in features which are variants commonly used in the trade,

and that previous use was made by or with the consent of the copyright owner.

(6) The Secretary of State may make provision by rules as to the circumstances in which a design is to be regarded for the purposes of this section as "applied industrially" to articles, or any description of articles.]

[506]

NOTES

Sub-s (2): words in square brackets substituted by the Copyright, Designs and Patents Act 1988, s 272, Sch 3, para 4.

Sub-ss (4)–(6): substituted for sub-ss (4), (5) (as added by the Copyright Act 1956, s 44(1)) by the Copyright, Designs and Patents Act 1988, s 272, Sch 3, para 4.

Effect of registration, etc

[7   Right given by registration

(1)   The registration of a design under this Act gives the registered proprietor the exclusive right—

(a) to make or import—

(i) for sale or hire, or

(ii) for use for the purposes of a trade or business, or

(b) to sell, hire or offer or expose for sale or hire,

an article in respect of which the design is registered and to which that design or a design not substantially different from it has been applied.

(2)   The right in the registered design is infringed by a person who without the licence of the registered proprietor does anything which by virtue of subsection (1) is the exclusive right of the proprietor.

(3)   The right in the registered design is also infringed by a person who without the licence of the registered proprietor makes anything for enabling any such article to be made, in the United Kingdom or elsewhere, as mentioned in subsection (1).

(4)   The right in the registered design is also infringed by a person who without the licence of the registered proprietor—

(a) does anything in relation to a kit that would be an infringement if done in relation to the assembled article (see subsection (1)), or

(b) makes anything for enabling a kit to be made or assembled, in the United Kingdom or elsewhere, if the assembled article would be such an article as is mentioned in subsection (1);

and for this purpose a "kit" means a complete or substantially complete set of components intended to be assembled into an article.

(5)   No proceedings shall be taken in respect of an infringement committed before the date on which the certificate of registration of the design under this Act is granted.

(6)   The right in a registered design is not infringed by the reproduction of a feature of the design which, by virtue of section 1(1)(b), is left out of account in determining whether the design is registrable.]

[507]

NOTES

Substituted by the Copyright, Designs and Patents Act 1988, s 268, except in relation to designs registered in pursuance of applications made before 1 August 1989.

[8   Duration of right in registered design

(1)   The right in a registered design subsists in the first instance for a period of five years from the date of the registration of the design.

(2)   The period for which the right subsists may be extended for a second, third, fourth and fifth period of five years, by applying to the registrar for an extension and paying the prescribed renewal fee.

(3)   If the first, second, third or fourth period expires without such application and payment being made, the right shall cease to have effect; and the registrar shall, in accordance with rules made by the Secretary of State, notify the proprietor of that fact.

(4)   If during the period of six months immediately following the end of that period an application for extension is made and the prescribed renewal fee and any prescribed additional fee is paid, the right shall be treated as if it had never expired, with the result that—

(a)   anything done under or in relation to the right during that further period shall be treated as valid,

(b)   an act which would have constituted an infringement of the right if it had not expired shall be treated as an infringement, and

(c)   an act which would have constituted use of the design for the services of the Crown if the right had not expired shall be treated as such use.

(5)   Where it is shown that a registered design—

(a)   was at the time it was registered a corresponding design in relation to an artistic work in which copyright subsists, and

(b)   by reason of a previous use of that work would not have been registrable but for section 6(4) of this Act (registration despite certain prior applications of design),

the right in the registered design expires when the copyright in that work expires, if that is earlier than the time at which it would otherwise expire, and it may not thereafter be renewed.

(6)   The above provisions have effect subject to the proviso to section 4(1) (registration of same design in respect of other articles, &c) [and, in the case of the right of the Secretary of State in any design forming part of the British mercantile marine uniform registered under this Act, to that right's subsisting so long as the design remains on the register].]

[508]

NOTES

Substituted together with ss 8A, 8B, for s 8 as originally enacted by the Copyright, Designs and Patents Act 1988, s 269, except in relation to designs registered in pursuance of applications made before 1 August 1989.

Sub-s (6): words in square brackets added by the Merchant Shipping Act 1995, s 314(2), Sch 13, para 26.

[8A   Restoration of lapsed right in design

(1)   Where the right in a registered design has expired by reason of a failure to extend, in accordance with section 8(2) or (4), the period for which the right subsists,

an application for the restoration of the right in the design may be made to the registrar within the prescribed period.

(2)   The application may be made by the person who was the registered proprietor of the design or by any other person who would have been entitled to the right in the design if it had not expired; and where the design was held by two or more persons jointly, the application may, with the leave of the registrar, be made by one or more of them without joining the others.

(3)   Notice of the application shall be published by the registrar in the prescribed manner.

(4)   If the registrar is satisfied that the proprietor took reasonable care to see that the period for which the right subsisted was extended in accordance with section 8(2) or (4), he shall, on payment of any unpaid renewal fee and any prescribed additional fee, order the restoration of the right in the design.

(5)   The order may be made subject to such conditions as the registrar thinks fit, and if the proprietor of the design does not comply with any condition the registrar may revoke the order and give such consequential directions as he thinks fit.

(6)   Rules altering the period prescribed for the purposes of subsection (1) may contain such transitional provisions and savings as appear to the Secretary of State to be necessary or expedient.]

[509]

NOTES
Substituted together with ss 8, 8B, for s 8 as originally enacted by the Copyright, Designs and Patents Act 1988, s 269, except in relation to designs registered in pursuance of applications made before 1 August 1989.

[8B   Effect of order for restoration of right

(1)   The effect of an order under section 8A for the restoration of the right in a registered design is as follows.

(2)   Anything done under or in relation to the right during the period between expiry and restoration shall be treated as valid.

(3)   Anything done during that period which would have constituted an infringement if the right had not expired shall be treated as an infringement—
  (a)   if done at a time when it was possible for an application for extension to be made under section 8(4); or
  (b)   if it was a continuation or repetition of an earlier infringing act.

(4)   If, after it was no longer possible for such an application for extension to be made and before publication of notice of the application for restoration, a person—
  (a)   began in good faith to do an act which would have constituted an infringement of the right in the design if it had not expired, or
  (b)   made in good faith effective and serious preparations to do such an act,

he has the right to continue to do the act or, as the case may be, to do the act, notwithstanding the restoration of the right in the design; but this does not extend to granting a licence to another person to do the act.

(5)   If the act was done, or the preparations were made, in the course of a business, the person entitled to the right conferred by subsection (4) may—
  (a)   authorise the doing of that act by any partners of his for the time being in that business, and

(b) assign that right, or transmit it on death (or in the case of a body corporate on its dissolution), to any person who acquires that part of the business in the course of which the act was done or the preparations were made.

(6) Where an article is disposed of to another in exercise of the rights conferred by subsection (4) or subsection (5), that other and any person claiming through him may deal with the article in the same way as if it had been disposed of by the registered proprietor of the design.

(7) The above provisions apply in relation to the use of a registered design for the services of the Crown as they apply in relation to infringement of the right in the design.]

[510]

NOTES

Substituted together with ss 8, 8A, for s 8 as originally enacted by the Copyright, Designs and Patents Act 1988, s 269, except in relation to designs registered in pursuance of applications made before 1 August 1989.

9   Exemption of innocent infringer from liability for damages

(1) In proceedings for the infringement of [the right in a registered design] damages shall not be awarded against a defendant who proves that at the date of the infringement he was not aware, and had no reasonable ground for supposing, that the design was registered; and a person shall not be deemed to have been aware or to have had reasonable grounds for supposing as aforesaid by reason only of the marking of an article with the word "registered" or any abbreviation thereof, or any word or words expressing or implying that the design applied to the article has been registered, unless the number of the design accompanied the word or words or the abbreviation in question.

(2) Nothing in this section shall affect the power of the court to grant an injunction in any proceedings for infringement of [the right in a registered design].

[511]

NOTES

Sub-ss (1), (2): words in square brackets substituted by the Copyright, Designs and Patents Act 1988, s 272, Sch 3, para 5.

10   Compulsory licence in respect of registered design

(1) At any time after a design has been registered any person interested may apply to the registrar for the grant of a compulsory licence in respect of the design on the ground that the design is not applied in the United Kingdom by any industrial process or means to the article in respect of which it is registered to such an extent as is reasonable in the circumstances of the case; and the registrar may make such order on the application as he thinks fit.

(2) An order for the grant of a licence shall, without prejudice to any other method of enforcement, have effect as if it were a deed executed by the registered proprietor and all other necessary parties, granting a licence in accordance with the order.

(3) No order shall be made under this section which would be at variance with any treaty, convention, arrangement or engagement applying to the United Kingdom and any convention country.

(4) An appeal shall lie from any order of the registrar under this section.

[512]

11 Cancellation of registration

(1) The registrar may, upon a request made in the prescribed manner by the registered proprietor, cancel the registration of a design.

(2) At any time after a design has been registered any person interested may apply to the registrar for the cancellation of the registration of the design on the ground that the design was not, at the date of the registration thereof, new . . . , or on any other ground on which the registrar could have refused to register the design; and the registrar may make such order on the application as he thinks fit.

[(3) At any time after a design has been registered, any person interested may apply to the registrar for the cancellation of the registration on the ground that—
    (a) the design was at the time it was registered a corresponding design in relation to an artistic work in which copyright subsisted, and
    (b) the right in the registered design has expired in accordance with section 8(4) of this Act (expiry of right in registered design on expiry of copyright in artistic work);

and the registrar may make such order on the application as he thinks fit.

(4) A cancellation under this section takes effect—
    (a) in the case of cancellation under subsection (1), from the date of the registrar's decision,
    (b) in the case of cancellation under subsection (2), from the date of registration,
    (c) in the case of cancellation under subsection (3), from the date on which the right in the registered design expired,

or, in any case, from such other date as the registrar may direct.

(5) An appeal lies from any order of the registrar under this section.]

[513]

NOTES

Sub-s (2): words omitted repealed by the Copyright, Designs and Patents Act 1988, ss 272, 303(2), Sch 3, para 6, Sch 8.

Sub-ss (3)–(5): substituted for sub-s (2A) (as inserted by the Copyright Act 1956, s 44(3)) and sub-s (3), by the Copyright, Designs and Patents Act 1988, s 272, Sch 3, para 6.

[11A Powers exercisable for protection of the public interest

(1) Where a report of the Monopolies and Mergers Commission has been laid before Parliament containing conclusions to the effect—
    (a) on a monopoly reference, that a monopoly situation exists and facts found by the Commission operate or may be expected to operate against the public interest,
    (b) on a merger reference, that a merger situation qualifying for investigation has been created and the creation of the situation, or particular elements in or consequences of it specified in the report, operate or may be expected to operate against the public interest,
    (c) on a competition reference, that a person was engaged in an anti-competitive practice which operated or may be expected to operate against the public interest, or
    (d) on a reference under section 11 of the Competition Act 1980 (reference of public bodies and certain other persons), that a person is pursuing a course of conduct which operates against the public interest,

the appropriate Minister or Ministers may apply to the registrar to take action under this section.

(2)   Before making an application the appropriate Minister or Ministers shall publish, in such a manner as he or they think appropriate, a notice describing the nature of the proposed application and shall consider any representations which may be made within 30 days of such publication by persons whose interests appear to him or them to be affected.

(3)   If on an application under this section it appears to the registrar that the matters specified in the Commission's report as being those which in the Commission's opinion operate or operated or may be expected to operate against the public interest include—

(a)   conditions in licences granted in respect of a registered design by its proprietor restricting the use of the design by the licensee or the right of the proprietor to grant other licences, or

(b)   a refusal by the proprietor of a registered design to grant licences on reasonable terms,

he may by order cancel or modify any such condition or may, instead or in addition, make an entry in the register to the effect that licences in respect of the design are to be available as of right.

(4)   The terms of a licence available by virtue of this section shall, in default of agreement, be settled by the registrar on an application by the person requiring the licence; and terms so settled shall authorise the licensee to do everything which would be an infringement of the right in the registered design in the absence of a licence.

(5)   Where the terms of a licence are settled by the registrar the licence has effect from the date on which the application to him was made.

(6)   An appeal lies from any order of the registrar under this section.

(7)   In this section "the appropriate Minister or Ministers" means the Minister or Ministers to whom the report of the Monopolies and Mergers Commission was made.]

[514]

NOTES
Inserted by the Copyright, Designs and Patents Act 1988, s 270.

[11B   Undertaking to take licence of right in infringement proceedings

(1)   If in proceedings for infringement of the right in a registered design in respect of which a licence is available as of right under section 11A of this Act the defendant undertakes to take a licence on such terms as may be agreed or, in default of agreement, settled by the registrar under that section—

(a)   no injunction shall be granted against him, and

(b)   the amount recoverable against him by way of damages or on an account of profits shall not exceed double the amount which would have been payable by him as licensee if such a licence on those terms had been granted before the earliest infringement.

(2)   An undertaking may be given at any time before final order in the proceedings, without any admission of liability.

(3)   Nothing in this section affects the remedies available in respect of an infringement committed before licences of right were available.]

[515]

NOTES
Inserted by the Copyright, Designs and Patents Act 1988, s 270.

12   Use for services of Crown

The provisions of the First Schedule to this Act shall have effect with respect to the use of registered designs for the services of the Crown and the rights of third parties in respect of such use.

[516]

Legal proceedings and Appeals

26   Remedy for groundless threats of infringement proceedings

(1)   Where any person (whether entitled to or interested in a registered design or an application for registration of a design or not) by circulars, advertisements or otherwise threatens any other person with proceedings for infringement of [the right in a registered design], any person aggrieved thereby may bring an action against him for any such relief as is mentioned in the next following subsection.

(2)   Unless in any action brought by virtue of this section the defendant proves that the acts in respect of which proceedings were threatened constitute or, if done, would constitute, an infringement of [the right in a registered design] the registration of which is not shown by the plaintiff to be invalid, the plaintiff shall be entitled to the following relief, that is to say—
  (a)   a declaration to the effect that the threats are unjustifiable;
  (b)   an injunction against the continuance of the threats; and
  (c)   such damages, if any, as he has sustained thereby.

[(2A) Proceedings may not be brought under this section in respect of a threat to bring proceedings for an infringement alleged to consist of the making or importing of anything.]

(3)   For the avoidance of doubt it is hereby declared that a mere notification that a design is registered does not constitute a threat of proceedings within the meaning of this section.

[517]

NOTES
Sub-ss (1), (2): words in square brackets substituted by the Copyright, Designs and Patents Act 1988, s 272, Sch 3, para 15.
Sub-s (2A): inserted by the Copyright, Designs and Patents Act 1988, s 272, Sch 3, para 15.

Offences

33   Offences under s 5

(1)   If any person fails to comply with any direction given under section five of this Act or makes or causes to be made an application for the registration of a design in contravention of that section, he shall be guilty of an offence and liable—
  [(a)   on conviction on indictment to imprisonment for a term not exceeding two years or a fine, or both;

(b) on summary conviction to imprisonment for a term not exceeding six months or a fine not exceeding the statutory maximum, or both.]

(2)   . . .

[518]

NOTES

Sub-s (1): words in square brackets substituted by the Copyright, Designs and Patents Act 1988, s 272, Sch 3, para 22, except in relation to offences committed before 1 August 1989.

Sub-s (2): repealed by the Copyright, Designs and Patents Act 1988, ss 272, 303(2), Sch 3, para 22, Sch 8, except in relation to offences committed before 1 August 1989.

34   Falsification of register, etc

If any person makes or causes to be made a false entry in the register of designs, or a writing falsely purporting to be a copy of an entry in that register, or produces or tenders or causes to be produced or tendered in evidence any such writing, knowing the entry or writing to be false, he [shall be guilty of an offence and liable—

(a) on conviction on indictment to imprisonment for a term not exceeding two years or a fine, or both;

(b) on summary conviction to imprisonment for a term not exceeding six months or a fine not exceeding the statutory maximum, or both].

[519]

NOTES

Words in square brackets substituted by the Copyright, Designs and Patents Act 1988, s 272, Sch 3, para 23, except in relation to offences committed before 1 August 1989.

35   Fine for falsely representing a design as registered

(1)   If any person falsely represents that a design applied to any article sold by him is registered in respect of that article, he shall be liable on summary conviction to a fine not exceeding [level 3 on the standard scale]; and for the purposes of this provision a person who sells an article having stamped, engraved or impressed thereon or otherwise applied thereto the word "registered", or any other word expressing or implying that the design applied to the article is registered, shall be deemed to represent that the design applied to the article is registered in respect of the article.

(2)   If any person, after [the right in a registered design] has expired, marks any article to which the design has been applied with the word "registered", or any word or words implying that there is a [subsisting right in the design under this Act], or causes any such article to be so marked, he shall be liable on summary conviction [to a fine not exceeding level 1 on the standard scale].

[520]

NOTES

Sub-s (1): words in square brackets substituted by the Copyright, Designs and Patents Act 1988, s 272, Sch 3, para 24, except in relation to offences committed before 1 August 1989.

Sub-s (2): words in square brackets substituted by the Copyright, Designs and Patents Act 1988, s 272, Sch 3, para 24.

[35A   Offence by body corporate: liability of officers

(1)   Where an offence under this Act committed by a body corporate is proved to have been committed with the consent or connivance of a director, manager, secretary or other similar officer of the body, or a person purporting to act in any such capacity, he as well as the body corporate is guilty of the offence and liable to be

proceeded against and punished accordingly.

(2)   In relation to a body corporate whose affairs are managed by its members "director" means a member of the body corporate.]

[521]

NOTES
Inserted by the Copyright, Designs and Patents Act 1988, s 272, Sch 3, para 25, except in relation to offences committed before 1 August 1989.

Supplemental

43   Savings

(1)   Nothing in this Act shall be construed as authorising or requiring the registrar to register a design the use of which would, in his opinion, be contrary to law or morality.

(2)   Nothing in this Act shall affect the right of the Crown or of any person deriving title directly or indirectly from the Crown to sell or use articles forfeited under the laws relating to customs or excise.

[522]

44   Interpretation

(1)   In this Act, except where the context otherwise requires, the following expressions have the meanings hereby respectively assigned by them, that is to say—
["Appeal Tribunal" means the Appeal Tribunal constituted and acting in accordance with section 28 of this Act as amended by the Administration of Justice Act 1969];
"article" means any article of manufacture and includes any part of an article if that part is made and sold separately;
["artistic work" has the same meaning as in [Part I of the Copyright, Designs and Patents Act 1988];]
"assignee" includes the personal representative of a deceased assignee, and references to the assignee of any person include references to the assignee of the personal representative or assignee of that person;
["author" in relation to a design, has the meaning given by section 2(3) and (4);]

. . . . .

["corresponding design"[, in relation to an artistic work, means a design which if applied to an article would produce something which would be treated for the purposes of Part I of the Copyright, Designs and Patents Act 1988 as a copy of that work;]]
["the court" shall be construed in accordance with section 27 of this Act;]
"design" has the meaning assigned to it by [section 1(1) of this Act];
["employee", "employment" and "employer" refer to employment under a contract of service or of apprenticeship;]

. . . . .

"prescribed" means prescribed by rules made by [the Secretary of State] under this Act;
"proprietor" has the meaning assigned to it by section two of this Act;
"registered proprietor" means the person or persons for the time being entered in the register of designs as proprietor of the design;

"registrar" means the Comptroller-General of Patents Designs and Trade Marks;

"set of articles" means a number of articles of the same general character ordinarily on sale or intended to be used together, to each of which the same design, or the same design with modifications or variations not sufficient to alter the character or substantially to affect the identity thereof, is applied.

(2)   Any reference in this Act to an article in respect of which a design is registered shall, in the case of a design registered in respect of a set of articles, be construed as a reference to any article of that set.

(3)   Any question arising under this Act whether a number of articles constitute a set of articles shall be determined by the registrar; and notwithstanding anything in this Act any determination of the registrar under this subsection shall be final.

(4)   For the purposes of subsection (1) of section fourteen and of section sixteen of this Act, the expression "personal representative", in relation to a deceased person, includes the legal representative of the deceased appointed in any country outside the United Kingdom.

[523]

NOTES

Sub-s (1): definition "Appeal Tribunal" substituted by the Administration of Justice Act 1969, s 35(1), Sch 1; definitions "artistic work" and "corresponding design" inserted by the Copyright Act 1956, s 44(5), words in square brackets therein substituted by the Copyright, Designs and Patents Act 1988, s 272, Sch 3, para 31; definitions "author", "employee", "employment" and "employer" inserted by the Copyright, Designs and Patents Act 1988, s 272, Sch 3, para 31; definition "the court" substituted by the Copyright, Designs and Patents Act 1988, s 272, Sch 3, para 31; in definitions "design" and "prescribed" words in square brackets substituted by the Copyright, Designs and Patents Act 1988, s 272, Sch 3, para 31; definitions "copyright" and "journal" repealed by the Copyright, Designs and Patents Act 1988, ss 272, 303(2), Sch 3, para 31, Sch 8.

49   Short title and commencement

(1)   This Act may be cited as the Registered Designs Act 1949.

(2)   This Act shall come into operation on the first day of January, nineteen hundred and fifty, immediately after the coming into operation of the Patents and Designs Act 1949.

[524]

COPYRIGHT, DESIGNS AND PATENTS ACT 1988

(c 48)

An Act to restate the law of copyright, with amendments; to make fresh provision as to the rights of performers and others in performances; to confer a design right in original designs; to amend the Registered Designs Act 1949; to make provision with respect to patent agents and trade mark agents; to confer patents and designs jurisdiction on certain county courts; to amend the law of patents; to make provision with respect to devices designed to circumvent copy-protection of works in electronic form; to make fresh provision penalising the fraudulent reception of transmissions; to make the fraudulent application or use of a trade mark an offence; to make provision for the benefit of the Hospital for Sick Children, Great Ormond Street, London; to enable financial assistance to be given to certain international bodies; and for connected purposes

[15 November 1988]

NOTES

Trade marks and registered trade marks: note that references to trade marks and registered trade marks within the meaning of the Trade Marks Act 1938 shall, unless the context otherwise requires, be construed after the commencement of the Trade Marks Act 1994 as references to trade marks and registered trade marks within the meaning of that Act. See the Trade Marks Act 1994, s 102(1), Sch 4, para 1.

PART III
DESIGN RIGHT

NOTES

Modified in relation to semiconductor topographies by the Design Right (Semiconductor Topographies) Regulations 1989, SI 1989/1100, at paras **[554]**–**[563]**.

CHAPTER I
DESIGN RIGHT IN ORIGINAL DESIGNS

Introductory

213   Design right

(1)   Design right is a property right which subsists in accordance with this Part in an original design.

(2)   In this Part "design" means the design of any aspect of the shape or configuration (whether internal or external) of the whole or part of an article.

(3)   Design right does not subsist in—
    (a)   a method or principle of construction,
    (b)   features of shape or configuration of an article which—
        (i)   enable the article to be connected to, or placed in, around or against, another article so that either article may perform its function, or
        (ii)   are dependent upon the appearance of another article of which the article is intended by the designer to form an integral part, or
    (c)   surface decoration.

(4)   A design is not "original" for the purposes of this Part if it is commonplace in the design field in question at the time of its creation.

(5)   Design right subsists in a design only if the design qualifies for design right protection by reference to—
    (a)   the designer or the person by whom the design was commissioned or the designer employed (see sections 218 and 219), or
    (b)   the person by whom and country in which articles made to the design were first marketed (see section 220),

or in accordance with any Order under section 221 (power to make further provision with respect to qualification).

[(5A) Design right does not subsist in a design which consists of or contains a controlled representation within the meaning of the Olympic Symbol etc (Protection) Act 1995.]

(6)   Design right does not subsist unless and until the design has been recorded in a design document or an article has been made to the design.

(7)   Design right does not subsist in a design which was so recorded, or to which an article was made, before the commencement of this Part.

[525]

NOTES

Sub-s (5A): inserted by the Olympic Symbol etc (Protection) Act 1995, s 14, with effect in relation to designs created on or after 20 September 1995.

214   The designer

(1)   In this Part the "designer", in relation to a design, means the person who creates it.

(2)   In the case of a computer-generated design the person by whom the arrangements necessary for the creation of the design are undertaken shall be taken to be the designer.

[526]

215   Ownership of design right

(1)   The designer is the first owner of any design right in a design which is not created in pursuance of a commission or in the course of employment.

(2)   Where a design is created in pursuance of a commission, the person commissioning the design is the first owner of any design right in it.

(3)   Where, in a case not falling within subsection (2) a design is created by an employee in the course of his employment, his employer is the first owner of any design right in the design.

(4)   If a design qualifies for design right protection by virtue of section 220 (qualification by reference to first marketing of articles made to the design), the above rules do not apply and the person by whom the articles in question are marketed is the first owner of the design right.

[527]

216   Duration of design right

(1)   Design right expires—
   (a) fifteen years from the end of the calendar year in which the design was first recorded in a design document or an article was first made to the design, whichever first occurred, or
   (b) if articles made to the design are made available for sale or hire within five years from the end of that calendar year, ten years from the end of the calendar year in which that first occurred.

(2)   The reference in subsection (1) to articles being made available for sale or hire is to their being made so available anywhere in the world by or with the licence of the design right owner.

[528]

Qualification for design right protection

217 Qualifying individuals and qualifying persons

(1)   In this Part—

"qualifying individual" means a citizen or subject of, or an individual habitually resident in, a qualifying country; and

"qualifying person" means a qualifying individual or a body corporate or other body having legal personality which—

(a)   is formed under the law of a part of the United Kingdom or another qualifying country, and

(b)   has in any qualifying country a place of business at which substantial business activity is carried on.

(2)   References in this Part to a qualifying person include the Crown and the government of any other qualifying country.

(3)   In this section "qualifying country" means—

(a)   the United Kingdom,

(b)   a country to which this Part extends by virtue of an Order under section 255,

(c)   another member State of the European Economic Community, or

(d)   to the extent that an Order under section 256 so provides, a country designated under that section as enjoying reciprocal protection.

(4)   The reference in the definition of "qualifying individual" to a person's being a citizen or subject of a qualifying country shall be construed—

(a)   in relation to the United Kingdom, as a reference to his being a British citizen, and

(b)   in relation to a colony of the United Kingdom, as a reference to his being a British Dependent Territories' citizen by connection with that colony.

(5)   In determining for the purpose of the definition of "qualifying person" whether substantial business activity is carried on at a place of business in any country, no account shall be taken of dealings in goods which are at all material times outside that country.

[529]

218 Qualification by reference to designer

(1)   This section applies to a design which is not created in pursuance of a commission or in the course of employment.

(2)   A design to which this section applies qualifies for design right protection if the designer is a qualifying individual or, in the case of a computer-generated design, a qualifying person.

(3)   A joint design to which this section applies qualifies for design right protection if any of the designers is a qualifying individual or, as the case may be, a qualifying person.

(4)   Where a joint design qualifies for design right protection under this section, only those designers who are qualifying individuals or qualifying persons are entitled to design right under section 215(1) (first ownership of design right: entitlement of designer).

[530]

219   Qualification by reference to commissioner or employer

(1)   A design qualifies for design right protection if it is created in pursuance of a commission from, or in the course of employment with, a qualifying person.

(2)   In the case of a joint commission or joint employment a design qualifies for design right protection if any of the commissioners or employers is a qualifying person.

(3)   Where a design which is jointly commissioned or created in the course of joint employment qualifies for design right protection under this section, only those commissioners or employers who are qualifying persons are entitled to design right under section 215(2) or (3) (first ownership of design right: entitlement of commissioner or employer).

[531]

220   Qualification by reference to first marketing

(1)   A design which does not qualify for design right protection under section 218 or 219 (qualification by reference to designer, commissioner or employer) qualifies for design right protection if the first marketing of articles made to the design—

    (a)   is by a qualifying person who is exclusively authorised to put such articles on the market in the United Kingdom, and

    (b)   takes place in the United Kingdom, another country to which this Part extends by virtue of an Order under section 255, or another member State of the European Economic Community.

(2)   If the first marketing of articles made to the design is done jointly by two or more persons, the design qualifies for design right protection if any of those persons meets the requirements specified in subsection (1)(a).

(3)   In such a case only the persons who meet those requirements are entitled to design right under section 215(4) (first ownership of design right: entitlement of first marketer of articles made to the design).

(4)   In subsection (1)(a) "exclusively authorised" refers—

    (a)   to authorisation by the person who would have been first owner of design right as designer, commissioner of the design or employer of the designer if he had been a qualifying person, or by a person lawfully claiming under such a person, and

    (b)   to exclusivity capable of being enforced by legal proceedings in the United Kingdom.

[532]

221   Power to make further provision as to qualification

(1)   Her Majesty may, with a view to fulfilling an international obligation of the United Kingdom, by Order in Council provide that a design qualifies for design right protection if such requirements as are specified in the Order are met.

(2)   An Order may make different provision for different descriptions of design or article; and may make such consequential modifications of the operation of section 215 (ownership of design right) and sections 218 to 220 (other means of qualification) as appear to Her Majesty to be appropriate.

(3)   A statutory instrument containing an Order in Council under this section shall be subject to annulment in pursuance of a resolution of either House of Parliament.

[533]

Dealings with design right

222 Assignment and licences

(1) Design right is transmissible by assignment, by testamentary disposition or by operation of law, as personal or moveable property.

(2) An assignment or other transmission of design right may be partial, that is, limited so as to apply—

    (a) to one or more, but not all, of the things the design right owner has the exclusive right to do;

    (b) to part, but not the whole, of the period for which the right is to subsist.

(3) An assignment of design right is not effective unless it is in writing signed by or on behalf of the assignor.

(4) A licence granted by the owner of design right is binding on every successor in title to his interest in the right, except a purchaser in good faith for valuable consideration and without notice (actual or constructive) of the licence or a person deriving title from such a purchaser; and references in this Part to doing anything with, or without, the licence of the design right owner shall be construed accordingly.

[534]

223 Prospective ownership of design right

(1) Where by an agreement made in relation to future design right, and signed by or on behalf of the prospective owner of the design right, the prospective owner purports to assign the future design right (wholly or partially) to another person, then if, on the right coming into existence, the assignee or another person claiming under him would be entitled as against all other persons to require the right to be vested in him, the right shall vest in him by virtue of this section.

(2) In this section—

    "future design right" means design right which will or may come into existence in respect of a future design or class of designs or on the occurrence of a future event; and

    "prospective owner" shall be construed accordingly, and includes a person who is prospectively entitled to design right by virtue of such an agreement as is mentioned in subsection (1).

(3) A licence granted by a prospective owner of design right is binding on every successor in title to his interest (or prospective interest) in the right, except a purchaser in good faith for valuable consideration and without notice (actual or constructive) of the licence or a person deriving title from such a purchaser; and references in this Part to doing anything with, or without, the licence of the design right owner shall be construed accordingly.

[535]

224 Assignment of right in registered design presumed to carry with it design right

Where a design consisting of a design in which design right subsists is registered under the Registered Designs Act 1949 and the proprietor of the registered design is also the design right owner, an assignment of the right in the registered design shall be taken to be also an assignment of the design right, unless a contrary intention appears.

[536]

225   Exclusive licences

(1)   In this Part an "exclusive licence" means a licence in writing signed by or on behalf of the design right owner authorising the licensee to the exclusion of all other persons, including the person granting the licence, to exercise a right which would otherwise be exercisable exclusively by the design right owner.

(2)   The licensee under an exclusive licence has the same rights against any successor in title who is bound by the licence as he has against the person granting the licence.

[537]

CHAPTER II
RIGHTS OF DESIGN RIGHT OWNER AND REMEDIES

Infringement of design right

226   Primary infringement of design right

(1)   The owner of design right in a design has the exclusive right to reproduce the design for commercial purposes—
   (a)   by making articles to that design, or
   (b)   by making a design document recording the design for the purpose of enabling such articles to be made.

(2)   Reproduction of a design by making articles to the design means copying the design so as to produce articles exactly or substantially to that design, and references in this Part to making articles to a design shall be construed accordingly.

(3)   Design right is infringed by a person who without the licence of the design right owner does, or authorises another to do, anything which by virtue of this section is the exclusive right of the design right owner.

(4)   For the purposes of this section reproduction may be direct or indirect, and it is immaterial whether any intervening acts themselves infringe the design right.

(5)   This section has effect subject to the provisions of Chapter III (exceptions to rights of design right owner).

[538]

227   Secondary infringement: importing or dealing with infringing article

(1)   Design right is infringed by a person who, without the licence of the design right owner—
   (a)   imports into the United Kingdom for commercial purposes, or
   (b)   has in his possession for commercial purposes, or
   (c)   sells, lets for hire, or offers or exposes for sale or hire, in the course of a business,

an article which is, and which he knows or has reason to believe is, an infringing article.

(2)   This section has effect subject to the provisions of Chapter III (exceptions to rights of design right owner).

[539]

228 Meaning of "infringing article"

(1)   In this Part "infringing article", in relation to a design, shall be construed in accordance with this section.

(2)   An article is an infringing article if its making to that design was an infringement of design right in the design.

(3)   An article is also an infringing article if—

    (a)   it has been or is proposed to be imported into the United Kingdom, and

    (b)   its making to that design in the United Kingdom would have been an infringement of design right in the design or a breach of an exclusive licence agreement relating to the design.

(4)   Where it is shown that an article is made to a design in which design right subsists or has subsisted at any time, it shall be presumed until the contrary is proved that the article was made at a time when design right subsisted.

(5)   Nothing in subsection (3) shall be construed as applying to an article which may lawfully be imported into the United Kingdom by virtue of any enforceable Community right within the meaning of section 2(1) of the European Communities Act 1972.

(6)   The expression "infringing article" does not include a design document, notwithstanding that its making was or would have been an infringement of design right.

[540]

Remedies for infringement

229 Rights and remedies of design right owner

(1)   An infringement of design right is actionable by the design right owner.

(2)   In an action for infringement of design right all such relief by way of damages, injunctions, accounts or otherwise is available to the plaintiff as is available in respect of the infringement of any other property right.

(3)   The court may in an action for infringement of design right, having regard to all the circumstances and in particular to—

    (a)   the flagrancy of the infringement, and

    (b)   any benefit accruing to the defendant by reason of the infringement,

award such additional damages as the justice of the case may require.

(4)   This section has effect subject to section 233 (innocent infringement).

[541]

230 Order for delivery up

(1)   Where a person—

    (a)   has in his possession, custody or control for commercial purposes an infringing article, or

    (b)   has in his possession, custody or control anything specifically designed or adapted for making articles to a particular design, knowing or having reason to believe that it has been or is to be used to make an infringing article, the owner of the design right in the design in question may apply to the court for an order that the infringing article or other thing be delivered up to him or to such other person as the court may direct.

(2)   An application shall not be made after the end of the period specified in the following provisions of this section; and no order shall be made unless the court also makes, or it appears to the court that there are grounds for making, an order under section 231 (order as to disposal of infringing article, &c).

(3)   An application for an order under this section may not be made after the end of the period of six years from the date on which the article or thing in question was made, subject to subsection (4).

(4)   If during the whole or any part of that period the design right owner—
   (a)   is under a disability, or
   (b)   is prevented by fraud or concealment from discovering the facts entitling him to apply for an order,

an application may be made at any time before the end of the period of six years from the date on which he ceased to be under a disability or, as the case may be, could with reasonable diligence have discovered those facts.

(5)   In subsection (4) "disability"—
   (a)   in England and Wales, has the same meaning as in the Limitation Act 1980;
   (b)   in Scotland, means legal disability within the meaning of the Prescription and Limitation (Scotland) Act 1973;
   (c)   in Northern Ireland, has the same meaning as in the Statute of Limitations (Northern Ireland) 1958.

(6)   A person to whom an infringing article or other thing is delivered up in pursuance of an order under this section shall, if an order under section 231 is not made, retain it pending the making of an order, or the decision not to make an order, under that section.

(7)   Nothing in this section affects any other power of the court.

[542]

231   Order as to disposal of infringing articles, etc

(1)   An application may be made to the court for an order that an infringing article or other thing delivered up in pursuance of an order under section 230 shall be—
   (a)   forfeited to the design right owner, or
   (b)   destroyed or otherwise dealt with as the court may think fit,

or for a decision that no such order should be made.

(2)   In considering what order (if any) should be made, the court shall consider whether other remedies available in an action for infringement of design right would be adequate to compensate the design right owner and to protect his interests.

(3)   Provision shall be made by rules of court as to the service of notice on persons having an interest in the article or other thing, and any such person is entitled—
   (a)   to appear in proceedings for an order under this section, whether or not he was served with notice, and
   (b)   to appeal against any order made, whether or not he appeared;

and an order shall not take effect until the end of the period within which notice of an appeal may be given or, if before the end of that period notice of appeal is duly given, until the final determination or abandonment of the proceedings on the appeal.

(4)   Where there is more than one person interested in an article or other thing, the court shall make such order as it thinks just and may (in particular) direct that the thing be sold, or otherwise dealt with, and the proceeds divided.

(5)   If the court decides that no order should be made under this section, the person in whose possession, custody or control the article or other thing was before being delivered up or seized is entitled to its return.

(6)   References in this section to a person having an interest in an article or other thing include any person in whose favour an order could be made in respect of it under this section or under section 114 or 204 of this Act or [section 93 of the Trade Marks Act 1994] (which make similar provision in relation to infringement of copyright, rights in performances and trade marks).

[543]

NOTES
    Sub-s (6): words in square brackets substituted by the Trade Marks Act 1994, s 102(1), Sch 4, para 7(2).

232   Jurisdiction of county court and sheriff court

(1)   In England, Wales and Northern Ireland a county court may entertain proceedings under—
    section 230 (order for delivery up of infringing article, etc),
    section 231 (order as to disposal of infringing article, etc), or
    section 235(5) (application by exclusive licensee having concurrent rights),

[save that, in Northern Ireland, a county court may entertain such proceedings only] where the value of the infringing articles and other things in question does not exceed the county court limit for actions in tort.

(2)   In Scotland proceedings for an order under any of those provisions may be brought in the sheriff court.

(3)   Nothing in this section shall be construed as affecting the jurisdiction of the High Court or, in Scotland, the Court of Session.

[544]

NOTES
    Sub-s (1): words in square brackets inserted by the High Court and County Courts Jurisdiction Order 1991, SI 1991/724, art 2(8), Schedule, Pt I.

233   Innocent infringement

(1)   Where in an action for infringement of design right brought by virtue of section 226 (primary infringement) it is shown that at the time of the infringement the defendant did not know, and had no reason to believe, that design right subsisted in the design to which the action relates, the plaintiff is not entitled to damages against him, but without prejudice to any other remedy.

(2)   Where in an action for infringement of design right brought by virtue of section 227 (secondary infringement) a defendant shows that the infringing article was innocently acquired by him or a predecessor in title of his, the only remedy available against him in respect of the infringement is damages not exceeding a reasonable royalty in respect of the act complained of.

(3)   In subsection (2) "innocently acquired" means that the person acquiring the article did not know and had no reason to believe that it was an infringing article.

[545]

234   Rights and remedies of exclusive licensee

(1)   An exclusive licensee has, except against the design right owner, the same rights and remedies in respect of matters occurring after the grant of the licence as if the licence had been an assignment.

(2)   His rights and remedies are concurrent with those of the design right owner; and references in the relevant provisions of this Part to the design right owner shall be construed accordingly.

(3)   In an action brought by an exclusive licensee by virtue of this section a defendant may avail himself of any defence which would have been available to him if the action had been brought by the design right owner.

[546]

235   Exercise of concurrent rights

(1)   Where an action for infringement of design right brought by the design right owner or an exclusive licensee relates (wholly or partly) to an infringement in respect of which they have concurrent rights of action, the design right owner or, as the case may be, the exclusive licensee may not, without the leave of the court, proceed with the action unless the other is either joined as a plaintiff or added as a defendant.

(2)   A design right owner or exclusive licensee who is added as a defendant in pursuance of subsection (1) is not liable for any costs in the action unless he takes part in the proceedings.

(3)   The above provisions do not affect the granting of interlocutory relief on the application of the design right owner or an exclusive licensee.

(4)   Where an action for infringement of design right is brought which relates (wholly or partly) to an infringement in respect of which the design right owner and an exclusive licensee have concurrent rights of action—
- (a)   the court shall, in assessing damages, take into account—
  - (i)   the terms of the licence, and
  - (ii)   any pecuniary remedy already awarded or available to either of them in respect of the infringement;
- (b)   no account of profits shall be directed if an award of damages has been made, or an account of profits has been directed, in favour of the other of them in respect of the infringement; and
- (c)   the court shall if an account of profits is directed apportion the profits between them as the court considers just, subject to any agreement between them;

and these provisions apply whether or not the design right owner and the exclusive licensee are both parties to the action.

(5)   The design right owner shall notify any exclusive licensee having concurrent rights before applying for an order under section 230 (order for delivery up of infringing article, etc); and the court may on the application of the licensee make such order under that section as it thinks fit having regard to the terms of the licence.

[547]

CHAPTER III
EXCEPTIONS TO RIGHTS OF DESIGN RIGHT OWNERS

Infringement of copyright

236   Infringement of copyright

Where copyright subsists in a work which consists of or includes a design in which design right subsists, it is not an infringement of design right in the design to do anything which is an infringement of the copyright in that work.

[548]

CHAPTER V
MISCELLANEOUS AND GENERAL

Miscellaneous

253   Remedy for groundless threats of infringement proceedings

(1)   Where a person threatens another person with proceedings for infringement of design right, a person aggrieved by the threats may bring an action against him claiming—

    (a)   a declaration to the effect that the threats are unjustifiable;

    (b)   an injunction against the continuance of the threats;

    (c)   damages in respect of any loss which he has sustained by the threats.

(2)   If the plaintiff proves that the threats were made and that he is a person aggrieved by them, he is entitled to the relief claimed unless the defendant shows that the acts in respect of which proceedings were threatened did constitute, or if done would have constituted, an infringement of the design right concerned.

(3)   Proceedings may not be brought under this section in respect of a threat to bring proceedings for an infringement alleged to consist of making or importing anything.

(4)   Mere notification that a design is protected by design right does not constitute a threat of proceedings for the purposes of this section.

[549]

Interpretation

258   Construction of references to design right owner

(1)   Where different persons are (whether in consequence of a partial assignment or otherwise) entitled to different aspects of design right in a work, the design right owner for any purpose of this Part is the person who is entitled to the right in the respect relevant for that purpose.

(2)   Where design right (or any aspect of design right) is owned by more than one person jointly, references in this Part to the design right owner are to all the owners, so that, in particular, any requirement of the licence of the design right owner requires the licence of all of them.

[550]

259   Joint designs

(1)   In this Part a "joint design" means a design produced by the collaboration of two or more designers in which the contribution of each is not distinct from that of the other or others.

(2)   References in this Part to the designer of a design shall, except as otherwise provided, be construed in relation to a joint design as references to all the designers of the design.

[551]

260   Application of provisions to articles in kit form

(1)   The provisions of this Part apply in relation to a kit, that is, a complete or substantially complete set of components intended to be assembled into an article, as they apply in relation to the assembled article.

(2)   Subsection (1) does not affect the question whether design right subsists in any aspect of the design of the components of a kit as opposed to the design of the assembled article.

[552]

263   Minor definitions

(1)   In this Part—
> "British design" means a design which qualifies for design right protection by reason of a connection with the United Kingdom of the designer or the person by whom the design is commissioned or the designer is employed;
> "business" includes a trade or profession;
> "commission" means a commission for money or money's worth;
> "the comptroller" means the Comptroller-General of Patents, Designs and Trade Marks;
> "computer-generated", in relation to a design, means that the design is generated by computer in circumstances such that there is no human designer,
> "country" includes any territory;
> "the Crown" includes the Crown in right of Her Majesty's Government in Northern Ireland;
> "design document" means any record of a design, whether in the form of a drawing, a written description, a photograph, data stored in a computer or otherwise;
> "employee", "employment" and "employer" refer to employment under a contract of service or of apprenticeship;
> "government department" includes a Northern Ireland department.

(2)   References in this Part to "marketing", in relation to an article, are to its being sold or let for hire, or offered or exposed for sale or hire, in the course of a business, and related expressions shall be construed accordingly; but no account shall be taken for the purposes of this Part of marketing which is merely colourable and not intended to satisfy the reasonable requirements of the public.

(3)   References in this Part to an act being done in relation to an article for "commercial purposes" are to its being done with a view to the article in question being sold or hired in the course of a business.

[553]

DESIGN RIGHT (SEMICONDUCTOR TOPOGRAPHIES) REGULATIONS 1989

(SI 1989/1100)

1   Citation and commencement

These Regulations may be cited as the Design Right (Semiconductor Topographies) Regulations 1989 and shall come into force on 1st August 1989.

[554]

2   Interpretation

(1)   In these Regulations—
    "the Act" means the Copyright, Designs and Patents Act 1988;
    "semiconductor product" means an article the purpose, or one of the purposes, of which is the performance of an electronic function and which consists of two or more layers, at least one of which is composed of semiconducting material and in or upon one or more of which is fixed a pattern appertaining to that or another function; and
    "semiconductor topography" means a design within the meaning of section 213(2) of the Act which is a design of either of the following—
      (a)   the pattern fixed, or intended to be fixed, in or upon—
        (i)   a layer of a semiconductor product, or
        (ii)   a layer of material in the course of and for the purpose of the manufacture of a semiconductor product, or
      (b)   the arrangement of the patterns fixed, or intended to be fixed, in or upon the layers of a semiconductor product in relation to one another.

(2) Except where the context otherwise requires, these Regulations shall be construed as one with Part III of the Act (design right).

[555]

3   Application of Copyright, Designs and Patents Act 1988, Part III

In its application to a design which is a semiconductor topography, Part III of the Act shall have effect subject to regulations 4 to 9 below.

[556]

4   Qualification

(1)   Section 213(5) of the Act has effect subject to paragraphs (2) to (4) below.

(2)   Part III of the Act has effect as if for section 217 of the Act there was substituted the following—

    "**217** (1)   In this Part—
      "qualifying individual" means a citizen or subject of, or an individual habitually resident in, a qualifying country; and
      "qualifying person" means—
        (a)   a qualifying individual,
        (b)   a body corporate or other body having legal personality which has in any qualifying country or in Gibraltar a place of business at which substantial business activity is carried on, or

(c)   a person who falls within one of the additional classes set out in Part I of the Schedule to the Design Right (Semiconductor Topographies) Regulations 1989.

(2)   References in this Part to a qualifying person include the Crown and the government of any other qualifying country.

(3)   In this section "qualifying country" means—
    (a)   the United Kingdom, or
    (b)   another member State of the European Economic Community.

(4)   The reference in the definition of "qualifying individual" to a person's being a citizen or subject of a qualifying country shall be construed in relation to the United Kingdom as a reference to his being a British citizen.

(5)   In determining for the purpose of the definition of "qualifying person" whether substantial business activity is carried on at a place of business in any country, no account shall be taken of dealings in goods which are at all material times outside that country.".

(3)   Where a semiconductor topography is created in pursuance of a commission or in the course of employment and the designer of the topography is, by virtue of section 215 of the Act (as substituted by regulation 5 below), the first owner of design right in that topography, section 219 of the Act does not apply and section 218(2) to (4) of the Act shall apply to the topography as if it had not been created in pursuance of a commission or in the course of employment.

(4)   Section 220 of the Act has effect subject to regulation 7 below and as if for subsection (1) there was substituted the following—

"**220** (1)   A design which does not qualify for design right protection under section 218 or 219 (as modified by regulation 4(3) of the Design Right (Semiconductor Topographies) Regulations 1989) or under the said regulation 4(3) qualifies for design right protection if the first marketing of articles made to the design—
    (a)   is by a qualifying person who is exclusively authorised to put such articles on the market in every member State of the European Economic Community, and
    (b)   takes place within the territory of any member State.";

and subsection (4) of section 220 accordingly has effect as if the words "in the United Kingdom" were omitted.

[557]

5   Ownership of design right

Part III of the Act has effect as if for section 215 of the Act there was substituted the following—

"**215** (1)   The designer is the first owner of any design right in a design which is not created in pursuance of a commission or in the course of employment.

(2)   Where a design is created in pursuance of a commission, the person commissioning the design is the first owner of any design right in it subject to any agreement in writing to the contrary.

(3)   Where, in a case not falling within subsection (2) a design is created by an employee in the course of his employment, his employer is the first owner of any design right in the design subject to any agreement in writing to the contrary.

(4)   If a design qualifies for design right protection by virtue of section 220 (as modified by regulation 4(4) of the Design Right (Semiconductor Topographies) Regulations 1989), the above rules do not apply and, subject to regulation 7 of the said Regulations, the person by whom the articles in question are marketed is the first owner of the design right.".

[558]

6   Duration of design right

(1)   Part III of the Act has effect as if for section 216 of the Act there was substituted the following—

"**216** The design right in a semiconductor topography expires—
  (a)   ten years from the end of the calendar year in which the topography or articles made to the topography were first made available for sale or hire anywhere in the world by or with the licence of the design right owner, or
  (b)   if neither the topography nor articles made to the topography are so made available within a period of fifteen years commencing with the earlier of the time when the topography was first recorded in a design document or the time when an article was first made to the topography, at the end of that period.".

(2)   Subsection (2) of section 263 of the Act has effect as if the words "or a semiconductor topography" were inserted after the words "in relation to an article".

(3)   The substitute provision set out in paragraph (1) above has effect subject to regulation 7 below.

[559]

7   Confidential information

In determining, for the purposes of section 215(4), 216 or 220 of the Act (as modified by these Regulations), whether there has been any marketing, or anything has been made available for sale or hire, no account shall be taken of any sale or hire, or any offer or exposure for sale or hire, which is subject to an obligation of confidence in respect of information about the semiconductor topography in question unless either—
  (a)   the article or semiconductor topography sold or hired or offered or exposed for sale or hire has been sold or hired on a previous occasion (whether or not subject to an obligation of confidence), or
  (b)   the obligation is imposed at the behest of the Crown, or of the government of any country outside the United Kingdom, for the protection of security in connection with the production of arms, munitions or war material.

[560]

8   Infringement

(1)   Section 226 of the Act has effect as if for subsection (1) there was substituted the following—

"**226** (1)   Subject to subsection (1A), the owner of design right in a design has the exclusive right to reproduce the design—
  (a)   by making articles to that design, or
  (b)   by making a design document recording the design for the purpose of enabling such articles to be made.

(1A) Subsection (1) does not apply to—

    (a) the reproduction of a design privately for non-commercial aims; or

    (b) the reproduction of a design for the purpose of analysing or evaluating the design or analysing, evaluating or teaching the concepts, processes, systems or techniques embodied in it.".

(2) Section 227 of the Act does not apply if the article in question has previously been sold or hired within—

    (a) the United Kingdom by or with the licence of the owner of design right in the semiconductor topography in question, or

    (b) the territory of any other member State of the European Economic Community or the territory of Gibraltar by or with the consent of the person for the time being entitled to import it into or sell or hire it within that territory.

(3) Section 228(6) of the Act does not apply.

(4) It is not an infringement of design right in a semiconductor topography to—

    (a) create another original semiconductor topography as a result of an analysis or evaluation of the first topography or of the concepts, processes, systems or techniques embodied in it, or

    (b) reproduce that other topography.

(5) Anything which would be an infringement of the design right in a semiconductor topography if done in relation to the topography as a whole is an infringement of the design right in the topography if done in relation to a substantial part of the topography.

[561]

9 Licences of right

Section 237 of the Act does not apply.

[562]

10 Revocation and transitional provisions

(1) . . .

(2) Sub-paragraph (1) of paragraph 19 of Schedule 1 to the Act shall not apply in respect of a semiconductor topography created between 7th November 1987 and 31st July 1989.

(3) In its application to copyright in a semiconductor topography created before 7th November 1987, sub-paragraph (2) of the said paragraph 19 shall have effect as if the reference to sections 237 to 239 were a reference to sections 238 and 239; and sub-paragraph (3) of that paragraph accordingly shall not apply to such copyright.

[563]–[700]

PART V
TRADE MARKS

TRADE MARKS ACT 1994

(c 26)

An Act to make new provision for registered trade marks, implementing Council Directive No 89/104/EEC of 21st December 1988 to approximate the laws of the Member States relating to trade marks; to make provision in connection with Council Regulation (EC) No 40/94 of 20th December 1993 on the Community trade mark; to give effect to the Madrid Protocol Relating to the International Registration of Marks of 27th June 1989, and to certain provisions of the Paris Convention for the Protection of Industrial Property of 20th March 1883, as revised and amended; and for connected purposes

[21 July 1994]

PART I
REGISTERED TRADE MARKS

Introductory

1 Trade Marks

(1)   In this Act a "trade mark" means any sign capable of being represented graphically which is capable of distinguishing goods or services of one undertaking from those of other undertakings.

A trade mark may, in particular, consist of words (including personal names), designs, letters, numerals or the shape of goods or their packaging.

(2)   References in this Act to a trade mark include, unless the context otherwise requires, references to a collective mark (see section 49) or certification mark (see section 50).

[701]

2 Registered trade marks

(1)   A registered trade mark is a property right obtained by the registration of the trade mark under this Act and the proprietor of a registered trade mark has the rights and remedies provided by this Act.

(2)   No proceedings lie to prevent or recover damages for the infringement of an unregistered trade mark as such; but nothing in this Act affects the law relating to passing off.

[702]

Grounds for refusal of registration

3 Absolute grounds for refusal of registration

(1)   The following shall not be registered—
    (a) signs which do not satisfy the requirements of section 1(1),
    (b) trade marks which are devoid of any distinctive character,
    (c) trade marks which consist exclusively of signs or indications which may serve, in trade, to designate the kind, quality, quantity, intended purpose, value, geographical origin, the time of production of goods or of rendering of services, or other characteristics of goods or services,

    (d)   trade marks which consist exclusively of signs or indications which have become customary in the current language or in the bona fide and established practices of the trade:

Provided that, a trade mark shall not be refused registration by virtue of paragraph (b), (c) or (d) above if, before the date of application for registration, it has in fact acquired a distinctive character as a result of the use made of it.

(2)   A sign shall not be registered as a trade mark if it consists exclusively of—
    (a)   the shape which results from the nature of the goods themselves,
    (b)   the shape of goods which is necessary to obtain a technical result, or
    (c)   the shape which gives substantial value to the goods.

(3)   A trade mark shall not be registered if it is—
    (a)   contrary to public policy or to accepted principles of morality, or
    (b)   of such a nature as to deceive the public (for instance as to the nature, quality or geographical origin of the goods or service).

(4)   A trade mark shall not be registered if or to the extent that its use is prohibited in the United Kingdom by any enactment or rule of law or by any provision of Community law.

(5)   A trade mark shall not be registered in the cases specified, or referred to, in section 4 (specially protected emblems).

(6)   A trade mark shall not be registered if or to the extent that the application is made in bad faith.

[703]

4   Specially protected emblems

(1)   A trade mark which consists of or contains—
    (a)   the Royal arms, or any of the principal armorial bearings of the Royal arms, or any insignia or device so nearly resembling the Royal arms or any such armorial bearing as to be likely to be mistaken for them or it,
    (b)   a representation of the Royal crown or any of the Royal flags,
    (c)   a representation of Her Majesty or any member of the Royal family, or any colourable imitation thereof, or
    (d)   words, letters or devices likely to lead persons to think that the applicant either has or recently has had Royal patronage or authorisation,

shall not be registered unless it appears to the registrar that consent has been given by or on behalf of Her Majesty or, as the case may be, the relevant member of the Royal family.

(2)   A trade mark which consists of or contains a representation of—
    (a)   the national flag of the United Kingdom (commonly known as the Union Jack), or
    (b)   the flag of England, Wales, Scotland, Northern Ireland or the Isle of Man,

shall not be registered if it appears to the registrar that the use of the trade mark would be misleading or grossly offensive.

Provision may be made by rules identifying the flags to which paragraph (b) applies.

(3)   A trade mark shall not be registered in the cases specified in—
    section 57 (national emblems, &c of Convention countries), or
    section 58 (emblems, &c of certain international organisations).

(4)   Provision may be made by rules prohibiting in such cases as may be prescribed the registration of a trade mark which consists of or contains—

(a)   arms to which a person is entitled by virtue of a grant of arms by the Crown, or

(b)   insignia so nearly resembling such arms as to be likely to be mistaken for them,

unless it appears to the registrar that consent has been given by or on behalf of that person.

Where such a mark is registered, nothing in this Act shall be construed as authorising its use in any way contrary to the laws of arms.

[(5)   A trade mark which consists of or contains a controlled representation within the meaning of the Olympic Symbol etc (Protection) Act 1995 shall not be registered unless it appears to the registrar—

(a)   that the application is made by the person for the time being appointed under section 1(2) of the Olympic Symbol etc (Protection) Act 1995 (power of Secretary of State to appoint a person as the proprietor of the Olympics association right), or

(b)   that consent has been given by or on behalf of the person mentioned in paragraph (a) above.]

                                                                                   [704]

NOTES

Sub-s (5): added by the Olympic Symbol etc (Protection) Act 1995, s 13(2), (3), with effect in relation to applications for registration made on or after 20 September 1995.

5   Relative grounds for refusal of registration

(1)   A trade mark shall not be registered if it is identical with an earlier trade mark and the goods or services for which the trade mark is applied for are identical with the goods or services for which the earlier trade mark is protected.

(2)   A trade mark shall not be registered if because—

(a)   it is identical with an earlier trade mark and is to be registered for goods or services similar to those for which the earlier trade mark is protected, or

(b)   it is similar to an earlier trade mark and is to be registered for goods or services identical with or similar to those for which the earlier trade mark is protected,

there exists a likelihood of confusion on the part of the public, which includes the likelihood of association with the earlier trade mark.

(3)   A trade mark which—

(a)   is identical with or similar to an earlier trade mark, and

(b)   is to be registered for goods or services which are not similar to those for which the earlier trade mark is protected,

shall not be registered if, or to the extent that, the earlier trade mark has a reputation in the United Kingdom (or, in the case of a Community trade mark, in the European Community) and the use of the later mark without due cause would take unfair advantage of, or be detrimental to, the distinctive character or the repute of the earlier trade mark.

(4)   A trade mark shall not be registered if, or to the extent that, its use in the United Kingdom is liable to be prevented—

(a) by virtue of any rule of law (in particular, the law of passing off) protecting an unregistered trade mark or other sign used in the course of trade, or

(b) by virtue of an earlier right other than those referred to in subsections (1) to (3) or paragraph (a) above, in particular by virtue of the law of copyright, design right or registered designs.

A person thus entitled to prevent the use of a trade mark is referred to in this Act as the proprietor of an "earlier right" in relation to the trade mark.

(5) Nothing in this section prevents the registration of a trade mark where the proprietor of the earlier trade mark or other earlier right consents to the registration.

[705]

6   Meaning of "earlier trade mark"

(1) In this Act an "earlier trade mark" means—

(a) a registered trade mark, international trade mark (UK) or Community trade mark which has a date of application for registration earlier than that of the trade mark in question, taking account (where appropriate) of the priorities claimed in respect of the trade marks,

(b) a Community trade mark which has a valid claim to seniority from an earlier registered trade mark or international trade mark (UK), or

(c) a trade mark which, at the date of application for registration of the trade mark in question or (where appropriate) of the priority claimed in respect of the application, was entitled to protection under the Paris Convention as a well known trade mark.

(2) References in this Act to an earlier trade mark include a trade mark in respect of which an application for registration has been made and which, if registered, would be an earlier trade mark by virtue of subsection 1(a) or (b), subject to its being so registered.

(3) A trade mark within subsection (1)(a) or (b) whose registration expires shall continue to be taken into account in determining the registrability of a later mark for a period of one year after the expiry unless the registrar is satisfied that there was no bona fide use of the mark during the two years immediately preceding the expiry.

[706]

7   Raising of relative grounds in case of honest concurrent use

(1) This section applies where on an application for the registration of a trade mark it appears to the registrar—

(a) that there is an earlier trade mark in relation to which the conditions set out in section 5(1), (2) or (3) obtain, or

(b) that there is an earlier right in relation to which the condition set out in section 5(4) is satisfied,

but the applicant shows to the satisfaction of the registrar that there has been honest concurrent use of the trade mark for which registration is sought.

(2) In that case the registrar shall not refuse the application by reason of the earlier trade mark or other earlier right unless objection on that ground is raised in opposition proceedings by the proprietor of that earlier trade mark or other earlier right.

(3)   For the purposes of this section "honest concurrent use" means such use in the United Kingdom, by the applicant or with his consent, as would formerly have amounted to honest concurrent use for the purposes of section 12(2) of the Trade Marks Act 1938.

(4)   Nothing in this section affects—
  (a)   the refusal of registration on the grounds mentioned in section 3 (absolute grounds for refusal), or
  (b)   the making of an application for a declaration of invalidity under section 47(2) (application on relative grounds where no consent to registration).

(5)   This section does not apply when there is an order in force under section 8 below.

[707]

8   Power to require that relative grounds be raised in opposition proceedings

(1)   The Secretary of State may by order provide that in any case a trade mark shall not be refused registration on a ground mentioned in section 5 (relative grounds for refusal) unless objection on that ground is raised in opposition proceedings by the proprietor of the earlier trade mark or other earlier right.

(2)   The order may make such consequential provision as appears to the Secretary of State appropriate—
  (a)   with respect to the carrying out by the registrar of searches of earlier trade marks, and
  (b)   as to the persons by whom an application for a declaration of invalidity may be made on the grounds specified in section 47(2) (relative grounds).

(3)   An order making such provision as is mentioned in subsection (2)(a) may direct that so much of section 37 (examination of application) as requires a search to be carried out shall cease to have effect.

(4)   An order making such provision as is mentioned in subsection (2)(b) may provide that so much of section 47(3) as provides that any person may make an application for a declaration of invalidity shall have effect subject to the provisions of the order.

(5)   An order under this section shall be made by statutory instrument, and no order shall be made unless a draft of it has been laid before and approved by a resolution of each House of Parliament.

No such draft of an order making such provision as is mentioned in subsection (1) shall be laid before Parliament until after the end of the period of ten years beginning with the day on which applications for Community trade marks may first be filed in pursuance of the Community Trade Mark Regulation.

(6)   An order under this section may contain such transitional provisions as appear to the Secretary of State to be appropriate.

[708]

Effects of registered trade mark

9   Rights conferred by registered trade mark

(1)   The proprietor of a registered trade mark has exclusive rights in the trade mark which are infringed by use of the trade mark in the United Kingdom without his consent.

The acts amounting to infringement, if done without the consent of the proprietor, are specified in section 10.

(2)   References in this Act to the infringement of a registered trade mark are to any such infringement of the rights of the proprietor.

(3)   The rights of the proprietor have effect from the date of registration (which in accordance with section 40(3) is the date of filing of the application for registration):

Provided that—
(a)   no infringement proceedings may be begun before the date on which the trade mark is in fact registered; and
(b)   no offence under section 92 (unauthorised use of trade mark, &c in relation to goods) is committed by anything done before the date of publication of the registration.

[709]

10   Infringement of registered trade mark

(1)   A person infringes a registered trade mark if he uses in the course of trade a sign which is identical with the trade mark in relation to goods or services which are identical with those for which it is registered.

(2)   A person infringes a registered trade mark if he uses in the course of trade a sign where because—
(a)   the sign is identical with the trade mark and is used in relation to goods or services similar to those for which the trade mark is registered, or
(b)   the sign is similar to the trade mark and is used in relation to goods or services identical with or similar to those for which the trade mark is registered,

there exists a likelihood of confusion on the part of the public, which includes the likelihood of association with the trade mark.

(3)   A person infringes a registered trade mark if he uses in the course of trade a sign which—
(a)   is identical with or similar to the trade mark, and
(b)   is used in relation to goods or services which are not similar to those for which the trade mark is registered,

where the trade mark has a reputation in the United Kingdom and the use of the sign, being without due cause, takes unfair advantage of, or is detrimental to, the distinctive character or the repute of the trade mark.

(4)   For the purposes of this section a person uses a sign if, in particular, he—
(a)   affixes it to goods or the packaging thereof;
(b)   offers or exposes goods for sale, puts them on the market or stocks them for those purposes under the sign, or offers or supplies services under the sign;
(c)   imports or exports goods under the sign; or
(d)   uses the sign on business papers or in advertising.

(5)   A person who applies a registered trade mark to material intended to be used for labelling or packaging goods, as a business paper, or for advertising goods or services, shall be treated as a party to any use of the material which infringes the registered trade mark if when he applied the mark he knew or had reason to believe that the application of the mark was not duly authorised by the proprietor or a licensee.

(6)   Nothing in the preceding provisions of this section shall be construed as preventing the use of a registered trade mark by any person for the purpose of identifying goods or services as those of the proprietor or a licensee.

But any such use otherwise than in accordance with honest practices in industrial or commercial matters shall be treated as infringing the registered trade mark if the use without due cause takes unfair advantage of, or is detrimental to, the distinctive character or repute of the trade mark.

[710]

11   Limits on effect of registered trade mark

(1)   A registered trade mark is not infringed by the use of another registered trade mark in relation to goods or services for which the latter is registered (but see section 47(6) (effect of declaration of invalidity of registration)).

(2)   A registered trade mark is not infringed by—
    (a)   the use by a person of his own name or address,
    (b)   the use of indications concerning the kind, quality, quantity, intended purpose, value, geographical origin, the time of production of goods or of rendering of services, or other characteristics of goods or services, or
    (c)   the use of the trade mark where it is necessary to indicate the intended purpose of a product or service (in particular, as accessories or spare parts),

provided the use is in accordance with honest practices in industrial or commercial matters.

(3)   A registered trade mark is not infringed by the use in the course of trade in a particular locality of an earlier right which applies only in that locality.

For this purpose an "earlier right" means an unregistered trade mark or other sign continuously used in relation to goods or services by a person or a predecessor in title of his from a date prior to whichever is the earlier of—
    (a)   the use of the first-mentioned trade mark in relation to those goods or services by the proprietor or a predecessor in title of his, or
    (b)   the registration of the first-mentioned trade mark in respect of those goods or services in the name of the proprietor or a predecessor in title of his;

and an earlier right shall be regarded as applying in a locality if, or to the extent that, its use in that locality is protected by virtue of any rule of law (in particular, the law of passing off).

[711]

12   Exhaustion of rights conferred by registered trade mark

(1)   A registered trade mark is not infringed by the use of the trade mark in relation to goods which have been put on the market in the European Economic Area under that trade mark by the proprietor or with his consent.

(2)   Subsection (1) does not apply where there exist legitimate reasons for the proprietor to oppose further dealings in the goods (in particular, where the condition of the goods has been changed or impaired after they have been put on the market).

[712]

13   Registration subject to disclaimer or limitation

(1)   An applicant for registration of a trade mark, or the proprietor of a registered trade mark, may—

    (a)   disclaim any right to the exclusive use of any specified element of the trade mark, or

    (b)   agree that the rights conferred by the registration shall be subject to a specified territorial or other limitation;

and where the registration of a trade mark is subject to a disclaimer or limitation, the rights conferred by section 9 (rights conferred by registered trade mark) are restricted accordingly.

(2)   Provision shall be made by rules as to the publication and entry in the register of a disclaimer or limitation.

[713]

Infringement proceedings

14   Action for infringement

(1)   An infringement of a registered trade mark is actionable by the proprietor of the trade mark.

(2)   In an action for infringement all such relief by way of damages, injunctions, accounts or otherwise is available to him as is available in respect of the infringement of any other property right.

[714]

15   Order for erasure, &c of offending sign

(1)   Where a person is found to have infringed a registered trade mark, the court may make an order requiring him—

    (a)   to cause the offending sign to be erased, removed or obliterated from any infringing goods, material or articles in his possession, custody or control, or

    (b)   if it is not reasonably practicable for the offending sign to be erased, removed or obliterated, to secure the destruction of the infringing goods, material or articles in question.

(2)   If an order under subsection (1) is not complied with, or it appears to the court likely that such an order would not be complied with, the court may order that the infringing goods, material or articles be delivered to such person as the court may direct for erasure, removal or obliteration of the sign, or for destruction, as the case may be.

[715]

16   Order for delivery up of infringing goods, material or articles

(1)   The proprietor of a registered trade mark may apply to the court for an order for the delivery up to him, or such other person as the court may direct, of any infringing goods, material or articles which a person has in his possession, custody or control in the course of a business.

(2)   An application shall not be made after the end of the period specified in section 18 (period after which remedy of delivery up not available); and no order shall be made unless the court also makes, or it appears to the court that there are grounds for making, an order under section 19 (order as to disposal of infringing goods, &c).

(3)   A person to whom any infringing goods, material or articles are delivered up in pursuance of an order under this section shall, if an order under section 19 is not made, retain them pending the making of an order, or the decision not to make an order, under that section.

(4)   Nothing in this section affects any other power of the court.

[716]

17   Meaning of "infringing goods, material or articles"

(1)   In this Act the expressions "infringing goods", "infringing material" and "infringing articles" shall be construed as follows.

(2)   Goods are "infringing goods", in relation to a registered trade mark, if they or their packaging bear a sign identical or similar to that mark and—

    (a)   the application of the sign to the goods or their packaging was an infringement of the registered trade mark, or

    (b)   the goods are proposed to be imported into the United Kingdom and the application of the sign in the United Kingdom to them or their packaging would be an infringement of the registered trade mark, or

    (c)   the sign has otherwise been used in relation to the goods in such a way as to infringe the registered trade mark.

(3)   Nothing in subsection (2) shall be construed as affecting the importation of goods which may lawfully be imported into the United Kingdom by virtue of an enforceable Community right.

(4)   Material is "infringing material", in relation to a registered trade mark if it bears a sign identical or similar to that mark and either—

    (a)   it is used for labelling or packaging goods, as a business paper, or for advertising goods or services, in such a way as to infringe the registered trade mark, or

    (b)   it is intended to be so used and such use would infringe the registered trade mark.

(5)   "Infringing articles", in relation to a registered trade mark, means articles—

    (a)   which are specifically designed or adapted for making copies of a sign identical or similar to that mark, and

    (b)   which a person has in his possession, custody or control, knowing or having reason to believe that they have been or are to be used to produce infringing goods or material.

[717]

18   Period after which remedy of delivery up not available

(1)   An application for an order under section 16 (order for delivery up of infringing goods, material or articles) may not be made after the end of the period of six years from—

    (a)   in the case of infringing goods, the date on which the trade mark was applied to the goods or their packaging,

    (b)   in the case of infringing material, the date on which the trade mark was applied to the material, or

    (c)   in the case of infringing articles, the date on which they were made,

except as mentioned in the following provisions.

(2)   If during the whole or part of that period the proprietor of the registered trade mark—

    (a)   is under a disability, or

    (b)   is prevented by fraud or concealment from discovering the facts entitling him to apply for an order,

an application may be made at any time before the end of the period of six years from the date on which he ceased to be under a disability or, as the case may be, could with reasonable diligence have discovered those facts.

(3)   In subsection (2) "disability"—

    (a)   in England and Wales, has the same meaning as in the Limitation Act 1980;

    (b)   in Scotland, means legal disability within the meaning of the Prescription and Limitation (Scotland) Act 1973;

    (c)   in Northern Ireland, has the same meaning as in the Limitation (Northern Ireland) Order 1989.

[718]

19   Order as to disposal of infringing goods, material or articles

(1)   Where infringing goods, material or articles have been delivered up in pursuance of an order under section 16, an application may be made to the court—

    (a)   for an order that they be destroyed or forfeited to such person as the court may think fit, or

    (b)   for a decision that no such order should be made.

(2)   In considering what order (if any) should be made, the court shall consider whether other remedies available in an action for infringement of the registered trade mark would be adequate to compensate the proprietor and any licensee and protect their interests.

(3)   Provision shall be made by rules of court as to the service of notice on persons having an interest in the goods, material or articles, and any such person is entitled—

    (a)   to appear in proceedings for an order under this section, whether or not he was served with notice, and

    (b)   to appeal against any order made, whether or not he appeared;

and an order shall not take effect until the end of the period within which notice of an appeal may be given or, if before the end of that period notice of appeal is duly given, until the final determination or abandonment of the proceedings on the appeal.

(4)   Where there is more than one person interested in the goods, material or articles, the court shall make such order as it thinks just.

(5)   If the court decides that no order should be made under this section, the person in whose possession, custody or control the goods, material or articles were before being delivered up is entitled to their return.

(6)   References in this section to a person having an interest in goods, material or articles include any person in whose favour an order could be made under this section or under section 114, 204 or 231 of the Copyright, Designs and Patents Act 1988 (which make similar provision in relation to infringement of copyright, rights in performances and design right).

[719]

21   Remedy for groundless threats of infringement proceedings

(1)   Where a person threatens another with proceedings for infringement of a registered trade mark other than—

    (a)   the application of the mark to goods or their packaging,

    (b)   the importation of goods to which, or to the packaging of which, the mark has been applied, or

    (c)   the supply of services under the mark,

any person aggrieved may bring proceedings for relief under this section.

(2)   The relief which may be applied for is any of the following—

    (a)   a declaration that the threats are unjustifiable,

    (b)   an injunction against the continuance of the threats,

    (c)   damages in respect of any loss he has sustained by the threats;

and the plaintiff is entitled to such relief unless the defendant shows that the acts in respect of which proceedings were threatened constitute (or if done would constitute) an infringement of the registered trade mark concerned.

(3)   If that is shown by the defendant, the plaintiff is nevertheless entitled to relief if he shows that the registration of the trade mark is invalid or liable to be revoked in a relevant respect.

(4)   The mere notification that a trade mark is registered, or that an application for registration has been made, does not constitute a threat of proceedings for the purposes of this section.

[720]

Registered trade mark as object of property

22   Nature of registered trade mark

A registered trade mark is personal property (in Scotland, incorporeal moveable property).

[721]

23   Co-ownership of registered trade mark

(1)   Where a registered trade mark is granted to two or more persons jointly, each of them is entitled, subject to any agreement to the contrary, to an equal undivided share in the registered trade mark.

(2)   The following provisions apply where two or more persons are co-proprietors of a registered trade mark, by virtue of subsection (1) or otherwise.

(3)   Subject to any agreement to the contrary, each co-proprietor is entitled, by himself or his agents, to do for his own benefit and without the consent of or the need to account to the other or others, any act which would otherwise amount to an infringement of the registered trade mark.

(4)   One co-proprietor may not without the consent of the other or others—

    (a)   grant a licence to use the registered trade mark, or

    (b)   assign or charge his share in the registered trade mark (or, in Scotland, cause or permit security to be granted over it).

(5)   Infringement proceedings may be brought by any co-proprietor, but he may not, without the leave of the court, proceed with the action unless the other, or each of the others, is either joined as a plaintiff or added as a defendant.

A co-proprietor who is thus added as a defendant shall not be made liable for any costs in the action unless he takes part in the proceedings.

Nothing in this subsection affects the granting of interlocutory relief on the application of a single co-proprietor.

(6)   Nothing in this section affects the mutual rights and obligations of trustees or personal representatives, or their rights and obligations as such.

[722]

24   Assignment, &c of registered trade mark

(1)   A registered trade mark is transmissible by assignment, testamentary disposition or operation of law in the same way as other personal or moveable property.

It is so transmissible either in connection with the goodwill of a business or independently.

(2)   An assignment or other transmission of a registered trade mark may be partial, that is, limited so as to apply—
  (a)   in relation to some but not all of the goods or services for which the trade mark is registered, or
  (b)   in relation to use of the trade mark in a particular manner or a particular locality.

(3)   An assignment of a registered trade mark, or an assent relating to a registered trade mark, is not effective unless it is in writing signed by or on behalf of the assignor or, as the case may be, a personal representative.

Except in Scotland, this requirement may be satisfied in a case where the assignor or personal representative is a body corporate by the affixing of its seal.

(4)   The above provisions apply to assignment by way of security as in relation to any other assignment.

(5)   A registered trade mark may be the subject of a charge (in Scotland, security) in the same way as other personal or moveable property.

(6)   Nothing in this Act shall be construed as affecting the assignment or other transmission of an unregistered trade mark as part of the goodwill of a business.

[723]

25   Registration of transactions affecting registered trade mark

(1)   On application being made to the registrar by—
  (a)   a person claiming to be entitled to an interest in or under a registered trade mark by virtue of a registrable transaction, or
  (b)   any other person claiming to be affected by such a transaction,

the prescribed particulars of the transaction shall be entered in the register.

(2)   The following are registrable transactions—
  (a)   an assignment of a registered trade mark or any right in it;
  (b)   the grant of a licence under a registered trade mark;
  (c)   the granting of any security interest (whether fixed or floating) over a registered trade mark or any right in or under it;
  (d)   the making by personal representatives of an assent in relation to a registered trade mark or any right in or under it;

    (e)   an order of a court or other competent authority transferring a registered trade mark or any right in or under it.

(3)   Until an application has been made for registration of the prescribed particulars of a registrable transaction—

    (a)   the transaction is ineffective as against a person acquiring a conflicting interest in or under the registered trade mark in ignorance of it, and

    (b)   a person claiming to be a licensee by virtue of the transaction does not have the protection of section 30 or 31 (rights and remedies of licensee in relation to infringement).

(4)   Where a person becomes the proprietor or a licensee of a registered trade mark by virtue of a registrable transaction, then unless—

    (a)   an application for registration of the prescribed particulars of the transaction is made before the end of the period of six months beginning with its date, or

    (b)   the court is satisfied that it was not practicable for such an application to be made before the end of that period and that an application was made as soon as practicable thereafter,

he is not entitled to damages or an account of profits in respect of any infringement of the registered trade mark occurring after the date of the transaction and before the prescribed particulars of the transaction are registered.

(5)   Provision may be made by rules as to—

    (a)   the amendment of registered particulars relating to a licence so as to reflect any alteration of the terms of the licence, and

    (b)   the removal of such particulars from the register—

        (i)   where it appears from the registered particulars that the licence was granted for a fixed period and that period has expired, or

        (ii)   where no such period is indicated and, after such period as may be prescribed, the registrar has notified the parties of his intention to remove the particulars from the register.

(6)   Provision may also be made by rules as to the amendment or removal from the register of particulars relating to a security interest on the application of, or with the consent of, the person entitled to the benefit of that interest.

[724]

26   Trusts and equities

(1)   No notice of any trust (express, implied or constructive) shall be entered in the register; and the registrar shall not be affected by any such notice.

(2)   Subject to the provisions of this Act, equities (in Scotland, rights) in respect of a registered trade mark may be enforced in like manner as in respect of other personal or moveable property.

[725]

27   Application for registration of trade mark as an object of property

(1)   The provisions of sections 22 to 26 (which relate to a registered trade mark as an object of property) apply, with the necessary modifications, in relation to an application for the registration of a trade mark as in relation to a registered trade mark.

(2)   In section 23 (co-ownership of registered trade mark) as it applies in relation to an application for registration the reference in subsection (1) to the granting of the registration shall be construed as a reference to the making of the application.

(3)   In section 25 (registration of transactions affecting registered trade marks) as it applies in relation to a transaction affecting an application for the registration of a trade mark, the references to the entry of particulars in the register, and to the making of an application to register particulars, shall be construed as references to the giving of notice to the registrar of those particulars.

[726]

Licensing

28   Licensing of registered trade mark

(1)   A licence to use a registered trade mark may be general or limited.

    A limited licence may, in particular, apply—

    (a)   in relation to some but not all of the goods or services for which the trade mark is registered, or

    (b)   in relation to use of the trade mark in a particular manner or a particular locality.

(2)   A licence is not effective unless it is in writing signed by or on behalf of the grantor.

    Except in Scotland, this requirement may be satisfied in a case where the grantor is a body corporate by the affixing of its seal.

(3)   Unless the licence provides otherwise, it is binding on a successor in title to the grantor's interest.

    References in this Act to doing anything with, or without, the consent of the proprietor of a registered trade mark shall be construed accordingly.

(4)   Where the licence so provides, a sub-licence may be granted by the licensee; and references in this Act to a licence or licensee include a sub-licence or sub-licensee.

[727]

29   Exclusive licenses

(1)   In this Act an "exclusive licence" means a licence (whether general or limited) authorising the licensee to the exclusion of all other persons, including the person granting the licence, to use a registered trade mark in the manner authorised by the licence.

    The expression "exclusive licensee" shall be construed accordingly.

(2)   An exclusive licensee has the same rights against a successor in title who is bound by the licence as he has against the person granting the licence.

[728]

30   General provisions as to rights of licensees in case of infringement

(1)   This section has effect with respect to the rights of a licensee in relation to infringement of a registered trade mark.

The provisions of this section do not apply where or to the extent that, by virtue of section 31(1) below (exclusive licensee having rights and remedies of assignee), the licensee has a right to bring proceedings in his own name.

(2) A licensee is entitled, unless his licence, or any licence through which his interest is derived, provides otherwise, to call on the proprietor of the registered trade mark to take infringement proceedings in respect of any matter which affects his interests.

(3) If the proprietor—
   (a) refuses to do so, or
   (b) fails to do so within two months after being called upon,

the licensee may bring the proceedings in his own name as if he were the proprietor.

(4) Where infringement proceedings are brought by a licensee by virtue of this section, the licensee may not, without the leave of the court, proceed with the action unless the proprietor is either joined as a plaintiff or added as a defendant.

This does not affect the granting of interlocutory relief on an application by a licensee alone.

(5) A proprietor who is added as a defendant as mentioned in subsection (4) shall not be made liable for any costs in the action unless he takes part in the proceedings.

(6) In infringement proceedings brought by the proprietor of a registered trade mark any loss suffered or likely to be suffered by licensees shall be taken into account; and the court may give such directions as it thinks fit as to the extent to which the plaintiff is to hold the proceeds of any pecuniary remedy on behalf of licensees.

(7) The provisions of this section apply in relation to an exclusive licensee if or to the extent that he has, by virtue of section 31(1), the rights and remedies of an assignee as if he were the proprietor of the registered trade mark.

[729]

31 Exclusive licensee having rights and remedies of assignee

(1) An exclusive licence may provide that the licensee shall have, to such extent as may be provided by the licence, the same rights and remedies in respect of matters occurring after the grant of the licence as if the licence had been an assignment.

Where or to the extent that such provision is made, the licensee is entitled, subject to the provisions of the licence and to the following provisions of this section, to bring infringement proceedings, against any person other than the proprietor, in his own name.

(2) Any such rights and remedies of an exclusive licensee are concurrent with those of the proprietor of the registered trade mark; and references to the proprietor of a registered trade mark in the provisions of this Act relating to infringement shall be construed accordingly.

(3) In an action brought by an exclusive licensee by virtue of this section a defendant may avail himself of any defence which would have been available to him if the action had been brought by the proprietor of the registered trade mark.

(4)   Where proceedings for infringement of a registered trade mark brought by the proprietor or an exclusive licensee relate wholly or partly to an infringement in respect of which they have concurrent rights of action, the proprietor or, as the case may be, the exclusive licensee may not, without the leave of the court, proceed with the action unless the other is either joined as a plaintiff or added as a defendant.

This does not affect the granting of interlocutory relief on an application by a proprietor or exclusive licensee alone.

(5)   A person who is added as a defendant as mentioned in subsection (4) shall not be made liable for any costs in the action unless he takes part in the proceedings.

(6)   Where an action for infringement of a registered trade mark is brought which relates wholly or partly to an infringement in respect of which the proprietor and an exclusive licensee have or had concurrent rights of action—

  (a)   the court shall in assessing damages take into account—
    (i)   the terms of the licence, and
    (ii) any pecuniary remedy already awarded or available to either of them in respect of the infringement;
  (b)   no account of profits shall be directed if an award of damages has been made, or an account of profits has been directed, in favour of the other of them in respect of the infringement; and
  (c)   the court shall if an account of profits is directed apportion the profits between them as the court considers just, subject to any agreement between them.

The provisions of this subsection apply whether or not the proprietor and the exclusive licensee are both parties to the action; and if they are not both parties the court may give such directions as it thinks fit as to the extent to which the party to the proceedings is to hold the proceeds of any pecuniary remedy on behalf of the other.

(7)   The proprietor of a registered trade mark shall notify any exclusive licensee who has a concurrent right of action before applying for an order under section 16 (order for delivery up); and the court may on the application of the licensee make such order under that section as it thinks fit having regard to the terms of the licence.

(8)   The provisions of subsections (4) to (7) above have effect subject to any agreement to the contrary between the exclusive licensee and the proprietor.

[730]

Application for registered trade mark

32   Application for registration

(1)   An application for registration of a trade mark shall be made to the registrar.

(2)   The application shall contain—
  (a)   a request for registration of a trade mark,
  (b)   the name and address of the applicant,
  (c)   a statement of the goods or services in relation to which it is sought to register the trade mark, and
  (d)   a representation of the trade mark.

(3)   The application shall state that the trade mark is being used, by the applicant or with his consent, in relation to those goods or services, or that he has a bona fide intention that it should be so used.

(4)   The application shall be subject to the payment of the application fee and such class fees as may be appropriate.

[731]

33   Date of filing

(1)   The date of filing of an application for registration of a trade mark is the date on which documents containing everything required by section 32(2) are furnished to the registrar by the applicant.

If the documents are furnished on different days, the date of filing is the last of those days.

(2)   References in this Act to the date of application for registration are to the date of filing of the application.

[732]

34   Classification of trade marks

(1)   Goods and services shall be classified for the purposes of the registration of trade marks according to a prescribed system of classification.

(2)   Any question arising as to the class within which any goods or services fall shall be determined by the registrar, whose decision shall be final.

[733]

Priority

35   Claim to priority of Convention application

(1)   A person who has duly filed an application for protection of a trade mark in a Convention country (a "Convention application"), or his successor in title, has a right to priority, for the purposes of registering the same trade mark under this Act for some or all of the same goods or services, for a period of six months from the date of filing of the first such application.

(2)   If the application for registration under this Act is made within that six-month period—
  (a)   the relevant date for the purposes of establishing which rights take precedence shall be the date of filing of the first Convention application, and
  (b)   the registrability of the trade mark shall not be affected by any use of the mark in the United Kingdom in the period between that date and the date of the application under this Act.

(3)   Any filing which in a Convention country is equivalent to a regular national filing, under its domestic legislation or an international agreement, shall be treated as giving rise to the right of priority.

A "regular national filing" means a filing which is adequate to establish the date on which the application was filed in that country, whatever may be the subsequent fate of the application.

(4)   A subsequent application concerning the same subject as the first Convention application, filed in the same Convention country, shall be considered the first Convention application (of which the filing date is the starting date of the period of priority), if at the time of the subsequent application—

(a) the previous application has been withdrawn, abandoned or refused, without having been laid open to public inspection and without leaving any rights outstanding, and

(b) it has not yet served as a basis for claiming a right of priority.

The previous application may not thereafter serve as a basis for claiming a right of priority.

(5) Provision may be made by rules as to the manner of claiming a right to priority on the basis of a Convention application.

(6) A right to priority arising as a result of a Convention application may be assigned or otherwise transmitted, either with the application or independently.

The reference in subsection (1) to the applicant's "successor in title" shall be construed accordingly.

[734]

36 Claim to priority from other relevant overseas application

(1) Her Majesty may by Order in Council make provision for conferring on a person who has duly filed an application for protection of a trade mark in—

(a) any of the Channel Islands or a colony, or

(b) a country or territory in relation to which Her Majesty's Government in the United Kingdom have entered into a treaty, convention, arrangement or engagement for the reciprocal protection of trade marks,

a right to priority, for the purpose of registering the same trade mark under this Act for some or all of the same goods or services, for a specified period from the date of filing of that application.

(2) An Order in Council under this section may make provision corresponding to that made by section 35 in relation to Convention countries or such other provision as appears to Her Majesty to be appropriate.

(3) A statutory instrument containing an Order in Council under this section shall be subject to annulment in pursuance of a resolution of either House of Parliament.

[735]

Registration procedure

37 Examination of application

(1) The registrar shall examine whether an application for registration of a trade mark satisfies the requirements of this Act (including any requirements imposed by rules).

(2) For that purpose he shall carry out a search, to such extent as he considers necessary, of earlier trade marks.

(3) If it appears to the registrar that the requirements for registration are not met, he shall inform the applicant and give him an opportunity, within such period as the registrar may specify, to make representations or to amend the application.

(4) If the applicant fails to satisfy the registrar that those requirements are met, or to amend the application so as to meet them, or fails to respond before the end of the specified period, the registrar shall refuse to accept the application.

(5)   If it appears to the registrar that the requirements for registration are met, he shall accept the application.

[736]

38   Publication, opposition proceedings and observations

(1)   When an application for registration has been accepted, the registrar shall cause the application to be published in the prescribed manner.

(2)   Any person may, within the prescribed time from the date of the publication of the application, give notice to the registrar of opposition to the registration.

The notice shall be given in writing in the prescribed manner, and shall include a statement of the grounds of opposition.

(3)   Where an application has been published, any person may, at any time before the registration of the trade mark, make observations in writing to the registrar as to whether the trade mark should be registered; and the registrar shall inform the applicant of any such observations.

A person who makes observations does not thereby become a party to the proceedings on the application.

[737]

39   Withdrawal, restriction or amendment of application

(1)   The applicant may at any time withdraw his application or restrict the goods or services covered by the application.

If the application has been published, the withdrawal or restriction shall also be published.

(2)   In other respects, an application may be amended, at the request of the applicant, only by correcting—
    (a)   the name or address of the applicant,
    (b)   errors of wording or of copying, or
    (c)   obvious mistakes,

and then only where the correction does not substantially affect the identity of the trade mark or extend the goods or services covered by the application.

(3)   Provision shall be made by rules for the publication of any amendment which affects the representation of the trade mark, or the goods or services covered by the application, and for the making of objections by any person claiming to be affected by it.

[738]

40   Registration

(1)   Where an application has been accepted and—
    (a)   no notice of opposition is given within the period referred to in section 38(2), or—
    (b)   all opposition proceedings are withdrawn or decided in favour of the applicant,

the registrar shall register the trade mark, unless it appears to him having regard to matters coming to his notice since he accepted the application that it was accepted in error.

(2)   A trade mark shall not be registered unless any fee prescribed for the registration is paid within the prescribed period.

If the fee is not paid within that period, the application shall be deemed to be withdrawn.

(3)   A trade mark when registered shall be registered as of the date of filing of the application for registration; and that date shall be deemed for the purposes of this Act to be the date of registration.

(4)   On the registration of a trade mark the registrar shall publish the registration in the prescribed manner and issue to the applicant a certificate of registration.

[739]

41   Registration: supplementary provisions

(1)   Provision may be made by rules as to—
  (a)   the division of an application for the registration of a trade mark into several applications;
  (b)   the merging of separate applications or registrations;
  (c)   the registration of a series of trade marks.

(2)   A series of trade marks means a number of trade marks which resemble each other as to their material particulars and differ only as to matters of a non-distinctive character not substantially affecting the identity of the trade mark.

(3)   Rules under this section may include provision as to—
  (a)   the circumstances in which, and conditions subject to which, division, merger or registration of a series is permitted, and
  (b)   the purposes for which an application to which the rules apply is to be treated as a single application and those for which it is to be treated as a number of separate applications.

[740]

Duration, renewal and alteration of registered trade mark

42   Duration of registration

(1)   A trade mark shall be registered for a period of ten years from the date of registration.

(2)   Registration may be renewed in accordance with section 43 for further periods of ten years.

[741]

43   Renewal of registration

(1)   The registration of a trade mark may be renewed at the request of the proprietor, subject to payment of a renewal fee.

(2)   Provision shall be made by rules for the registrar to inform the proprietor of a registered trade mark, before the expiry of the registration, of the date of expiry and the manner in which the registration may be renewed.

(3)   A request for renewal must be made, and the renewal fee paid, before the expiry of the registration.

Failing this, the request may be made and the fee paid within such further period (of not less than six months) as may be prescribed, in which case an additional renewal fee must also be paid within that period.

(4)   Renewal shall take effect from the expiry of the previous registration.

(5)   If the registration is not renewed in accordance with the above provisions, the registrar shall remove the trade mark from the register.

Provision may be made by rules for the restoration of the registration of a trade mark which has been removed from the register, subject to such conditions (if any) as may be prescribed.

(6)   The renewal or restoration of the registration of a trade mark shall be published in the prescribed manner.

[742]

44   Alteration of registered trade mark

(1)   A registered trade mark shall not be altered in the register, during the period of registration or on renewal.

(2)   Nevertheless, the registrar may, at the request of the proprietor, allow the alteration of a registered trade mark where the mark includes the proprietor's name or address and the alteration is limited to alteration of that name or address and does not substantially affect the identity of the mark.

(3)   Provision shall be made by rules for the publication of any such alteration and the making of objections by any person claiming to be affected by it.

[743]

Surrender, revocation and invalidity

45   Surrender of registered trade mark

(1)   A registered trade mark may be surrendered by the proprietor in respect of some or all of the goods or services for which it is registered.

(2)   Provision may be made by rules—
    (a)   as to the manner and effect of a surrender, and
    (b)   for protecting the interests of other persons having a right in the registered trade mark.

[744]

46   Revocation of registration

(1)   The registration of a trade mark may be revoked on any of the following grounds—
    (a)   that within the period of five years following the date of completion of the registration procedure it has not been put to genuine use in the United Kingdom, by the proprietor or with his consent, in relation to the goods or services for which it is registered, and there are no proper reasons for non-use;
    (b)   that such use has been suspended for an uninterrupted period of five years, and there are no proper reasons for non-use;
    (c)   that, in consequence of acts or inactivity of the proprietor, it has become the common name in the trade for a product or service for which it is registered;

(d) that in consequence of the use made of it by the proprietor or with his consent in relation to the goods or services for which it is registered, it is liable to mislead the public, particularly as to the nature, quality or geographical origin of those goods or services.

(2) For the purposes of subsection (1) use of a trade mark includes use in a form differing in elements which do not alter the distinctive character of the mark in the form in which it was registered, and use in the United Kingdom includes affixing the trade mark to goods or to the packaging of goods in the United Kingdom solely for export purposes.

(3) The registration of a trade mark shall not be revoked on the ground mentioned in subsection (1)(a) or (b) if such use as is referred to in that paragraph is commenced or resumed after the expiry of the five year period and before the application for revocation is made:

Provided that, any such commencement or resumption of use after the expiry of the five year period but within the period of three months before the making of the application shall be disregarded unless preparations for the commencement or resumption began before the proprietor became aware that the application might be made.

(4) An application for revocation may be made by any person, and may be made either to the registrar or to the court, except that—

(a) if proceedings concerning the trade mark in question are pending in the court, the application must be made to the court; and

(b) if in any other case the application is made to the registrar, he may at any stage of the proceedings refer the application to the court.

(5) Where grounds for revocation exist in respect of only some of the goods or services for which the trade mark is registered, revocation shall relate to those goods or services only.

(6) Where the registration of a trade mark is revoked to any extent, the rights of the proprietor shall be deemed to have ceased to that extent as from—

(a) the date of the application for revocation, or

(b) if the registrar or court is satisfied that the grounds for revocation existed at an earlier date, that date.

[745]

47   Grounds for invalidity of registration

(1) The registration of a trade mark may be declared invalid on the ground that the trade mark was registered in breach of section 3 or any of the provisions referred to in that section (absolute grounds for refusal of registration).

Where the trade mark was registered in breach of subsection (1)(b), (c) or (d) of that section, it shall not be declared invalid if, in consequence of the use which has been made of it, it has after registration acquired a distinctive character in relation to the goods or services for which it is registered.

(2) The registration of a trade mark may be declared invalid on the ground—

(a) that there is an earlier trade mark in relation to which the conditions set out in section 5(1), (2) or (3) obtain, or

(b) that there is an earlier right in relation to which the condition set out in section 5(4) is satisfied, unless the proprietor of that earlier trade mark or other earlier right has consented to the registration.

(3)   An application for a declaration of invalidity may be made by any person, and may be made either to the registrar or to the court, except that—

    (a)   if proceedings concerning the trade mark in question are pending in the court, the application must be made to the court; and

    (b)   if in any other case the application is made to the registrar, he may at any stage of the proceedings refer the application to the court.

(4)   In the case of bad faith in the registration of a trade mark, the registrar himself may apply to the court for a declaration of the invalidity of the registration.

(5)   Where the grounds of invalidity exist in respect of only some of the goods or services for which the trade mark is registered, the trade mark shall be declared invalid as regards those goods or services only.

(6)   Where the registration of a trade mark is declared invalid to any extent, the registration shall to that extent be deemed never to have been made:

    Provided that this shall not affect transactions past and closed.

[746]

48   Effect of acquiescence

(1)   Where the proprietor of an earlier trade mark or other earlier right has acquiesced for a continuous period of five years in the use of a registered trade mark in the United Kingdom, being aware of that use, there shall cease to be any entitlement on the basis of that earlier trade mark or other right—

    (a)   to apply for a declaration that the registration of the later trade mark is invalid, or

    (b)   to oppose the use of the later trade mark in relation to the goods or services in relation to which it has been so used,

unless the registration of the later trade mark was applied for in bad faith.

(2)   Where subsection (1) applies, the proprietor of the later trade mark is not entitled to oppose the use of the earlier trade mark or, as the case may be, the exploitation of the earlier right, notwithstanding that the earlier trade mark or right may no longer be invoked against his later trade mark.

[747]

Collective marks

49   Collective marks

(1)   A collective mark is a mark distinguishing the goods or services of members of the association which is the proprietor of the mark from those of other undertakings.

(2)   The provisions of this Act apply to collective marks subject to the provisions of Schedule 1.

[748]

Certification marks

50   Certification marks

(1)   A certification mark is a mark indicating that the goods or services in connection with which it is used are certified by the proprietor of the mark in respect of origin, material, mode of manufacture of goods or performance of services, quality, accuracy or other characteristics.

(2)   The provisions of this Act apply to certification marks subject to the provisions of Schedule 2.

[749]

PART II
COMMUNITY TRADE MARKS AND INTERNATIONAL MATTERS

Community trade marks

51   Meaning of "Community trade mark"

In this Act—

     "Community trade mark" has the meaning given by Article 1(1) of the Community Trade Mark Regulation; and

     "the Community Trade Mark Regulation" means Council Regulation (EC) No 40/94 of 20th December 1993 on the Community trade mark.

[750]

52   Power to make provision in connection with Community Trade Mark Regulation

(1)   The Secretary of State may by regulations make such provision as he considers appropriate in connection with the operation of the Community Trade Mark Regulation.

(2)   Provision may, in particular, be made with respect to—

     (a)   the making of applications for Community trade marks by way of the Patent Office;

     (b)   the procedures for determining a posteriori the invalidity, or liability to revocation, of the registration of a trade mark from which a Community trade mark claims seniority;

     (c)   the conversion of a Community trade mark, or an application for a Community trade mark, into an application for registration under this Act;

     (d)   the designation of courts in the United Kingdom having jurisdiction over proceedings arising out of the Community Trade Mark Regulation.

(3)   Without prejudice to the generality of subsection (1), provision may be made by regulations under this section—

     (a)   applying in relation to a Community trade mark the provisions of—

         (i)   section 21 (remedy for groundless threats of infringement proceedings);

         (ii)   sections 89 to 91 (importation of infringing goods, material or articles); and

         (iii)   sections 92, 93, 95 and 96 (offences); and

(b) making in relation to the list of professional representatives maintained in pursuance of Article 89 of the Community Trade Mark Regulation, and persons on that list, provision corresponding to that made by, or capable of being made under, sections 84 to 88 in relation to the register of trade mark agents and registered trade mark agents.

(4) Regulations under this section shall be made by statutory instrument which shall be subject to annulment in pursuance of a resolution of either House of Parliament.

[751]

The Madrid Protocol: international registration

53   The Madrid Protocol

In this Act—

"the Madrid Protocol" means the Protocol relating to the Madrid Agreement concerning the International Registration of Marks, adopted at Madrid on 27th June 1989;

"the International Bureau" has the meaning given by Article 2(1) of that Protocol; and

"international trade mark (UK)" means a trade mark which is entitled to protection in the United Kingdom under that Protocol.

[752]

54   Power to make provision giving effect to Madrid Protocol

(1) The Secretary of State may by order make such provision as he thinks fit for giving effect in the United Kingdom to the provisions of the Madrid Protocol.

(2) Provision may, in particular, be made with respect to—
   (a) the making of applications for international registrations by way of the Patent Office as office of origin;
   (b) the procedures to be followed where the basic United Kingdom application or registration fails or ceases to be in force;
   (c) the procedures to be followed where the Patent Office receives from the International Bureau a request for extension of protection to the United Kingdom;
   (d) the effects of a successful request for extension of protection to the United Kingdom;
   (e) the transformation of an application for an international registration, or an international registration, into a national application for registration;
   (f) the communication of information to the International Bureau;
   (g) the payment of fees and amounts prescribed in respect of applications for international registrations, extensions of protection and renewals.

(3) Without prejudice to the generality of subsection (1), provision may be made by regulations under this section applying in relation to an international trade mark (UK) the provisions of—
   (a) section 21 (remedy for groundless threats of infringement proceedings);
   (b) sections 89 to 91 (importation of infringing goods, material or articles); and
   (c) sections 92, 93, 95 and 96 (offences).

(4) An order under this section shall be made by statutory instrument which shall be subject to annulment in pursuance of a resolution of either House of Parliament.

[753]

The Paris Convention: supplementary provisions

55 The Paris Convention

(1) In this Act—

    (a) "the Paris Convention" means the Paris Convention for the Protection of Industrial Property of March 20th 1883, as revised or amended from time to time, and

    (b) a "Convention country" means a country, other than the United Kingdom, which is a party to that Convention.

(2) The Secretary of State may by order make such amendments of this Act, and rules made under this Act, as appear to him appropriate in consequence of any revision or amendment of the Paris Convention after the passing of this Act.

(3) Any such order shall be made by statutory instrument which shall be subject to annulment in pursuance of a resolution of either House of Parliament.

[754]

56 Protection of well-known trade marks: Article 6bis

(1) References in this Act to a trade mark which is entitled to protection under the Paris Convention as a well known trade mark are to a mark which is well-known in the United Kingdom as being the mark of a person who—

    (a) is a national of a Convention country, or

    (b) is domiciled in, or has a real and effective industrial or commercial establishment in, a Convention country,

whether or not that person carries on business, or has any goodwill, in the United Kingdom.

References to the proprietor of such a mark shall be construed accordingly.

(2) The proprietor of a trade mark which is entitled to protection under the Paris Convention as a well known trade mark is entitled to restrain by injunction the use in the United Kingdom of a trade mark which, or the essential part of which, is identical or similar to his mark, in relation to identical or similar goods or services, where the use is likely to cause confusion.

This right is subject to section 48 (effect of acquiescence by proprietor of earlier trade mark).

(3) Nothing in subsection (2) affects the continuation of any bona fide use of a trade mark begun before the commencement of this section.

[755]

PART III
ADMINISTRATIVE AND OTHER SUPPLEMENTARY PROVISIONS

Importation of infringing goods, material or articles

89 Infringing goods, material or articles may be treated as prohibited goods

(1) The proprietor of a registered trade mark, or a licensee, may give notice in writing to the Commissioners of Customs and Excise—

    (a) that he is the proprietor or, as the case may be, a licensee of the registered trade mark,

    (b) that, at a time and place specified in the notice, goods which are, in relation to that registered trade mark, infringing goods, material or articles are expected to arrive in the United Kingdom—

        (i) from outside the European Economic Area, or

        (ii) from within that Area but not having been entered for free circulation, and

    (c) that he requests the Commissioners to treat them as prohibited goods.

(2)   When a notice is in force under this section the importation of the goods to which the notice relates, otherwise than by a person for his private and domestic use, is prohibited; but a person is not by reason of the prohibition liable to any penalty other than forfeiture of the goods.

[(3) This section does not apply to goods entered, or expected to be entered, for free circulation, export, re-export or for a suspensive procedure in respect of which an application may be made under Article 3(1) of Council Regulation (EC) No 3295/94 laying down measures to prohibit the release for free circulation, export, re-export or entry for a suspensive procedure of counterfeit and pirated goods.]

                                                                                      [756]

NOTES

Sub-s (3): substituted by the Trade Marks (EC Measures Relating to Counterfeit Goods) Regulations 1995, SI 1995/1444, reg 2 with effect from 1 July 1995.

90   Power of Commissioners of Customs and Excise to make regulations

(1)   The Commissioners of Customs and Excise may make regulations prescribing the form in which notice is to be given under section 89 and requiring a person giving notice—

    (a) to furnish the Commissioners with such evidence as may be specified in the regulations, either on giving notice or when the goods are imported, or at both those times, and

    (b) to comply with such other conditions as may be specified in the regulations.

(2)   The regulations may, in particular, require a person giving such a notice—

    (a) to pay such fees in respect of the notice as may be specified by the regulations;

    (b) to give such security as may be so specified in respect of any liability or expense which the Commissioners may incur in consequence of the notice by reason of the detention of any goods or anything done to goods detained;

    (c) to indemnify the Commissioners against any such liability or expense, whether security has been given or not.

(3)   The regulations may make different provision as respects different classes of case to which they apply and may include such incidental and supplementary provisions as the Commissioners consider expedient.

(4)   Regulations under this section shall be made by statutory instrument which shall be subject to annulment in pursuance of a resolution of either House of Parliament.

(5)   Section 17 of the Customs and Excise Management Act 1979 (general provisions as to Commissioners' receipts) applies to fees paid in pursuance of regulations under this section as to receipts under the enactments relating to customs and excise.

                                                                                                 [757]

91 Power of Commissioners of Customs and Excise to disclose information

Where information relating to infringing goods, material or articles has been obtained by the Commissioners of Customs and Excise for the purposes of, or in connection with, the exercise of their functions in relation to imported goods, the Commissioners may authorise the disclosure of that information for the purpose of facilitating the exercise by any person of any function in connection with the investigation or prosecution of an offence under section 92 below (unauthorised use of trade mark, &c in relation to goods) or under the Trade Descriptions Act 1968.

[758]

Offences

92 Unauthorised use of trade mark, &c in relation to goods

(1)   A person commits an offence who with a view to gain for himself or another, or with intent to cause loss to another, and without the consent of the proprietor—
   (a) applies to goods or their packaging a sign identical to, or likely to be mistaken for, a registered trade mark, or
   (b) sells or lets for hire, offers or exposes for sale or hire or distributes goods which bear, or the packaging of which bears, such a sign, or
   (c) has in his possession, custody or control in the course of a business any such goods with a view to the doing of anything, by himself or another, which would be an offence under paragraph (b).

(2)   A person commits an offence who with a view to gain for himself or another, or with intent to cause loss to another, and without the consent of the proprietor—
   (a) applies a sign identical to, or likely to be mistaken for, a registered trade mark to material intended to be used—
      (i)   for labelling or packaging goods,
      (ii) as a business paper in relation to goods, or
      (iii) for advertising goods, or
   (b) uses in the course of a business material bearing such a sign for labelling or packaging goods, as a business paper in relation to goods, or for advertising goods, or
   (c) has in his possession, custody or control in the course of a business any such material with a view to the doing of anything, by himself or another, which would be an offence under paragraph (b).

(3)   A person commits an offence who with a view to gain for himself or another, or with intent to cause loss to another, and without the consent of the proprietor—
   (a) makes an article specifically designed or adapted for making copies of a sign identical to, or likely to be mistaken for, a registered trade mark, or
   (b) has such an article in his possession, custody or control in the course of a business,

knowing or having reason to believe that it has been, or is to be, used to produce goods, or material for labelling or packaging goods, as a business paper in relation to goods, or for advertising goods.

(4)   A person does not commit an offence under this section unless—
   (a) the goods are goods in respect of which the trade mark is registered, or
   (b) the trade mark has a reputation in the United Kingdom and the use of the sign takes or would take unfair advantage of, or is or would be detrimental to, the distinctive character or the repute of the trade mark.

(5)   It is a defence for a person charged with an offence under this section to show that he believed on reasonable grounds that the use of the sign in the manner in which it was used, or was to be used, was not an infringement of the registered trade mark.

(6)   A person guilty of an offence under this section is liable—

   (a)   on summary conviction to imprisonment for a term not exceeding six months or a fine not exceeding the statutory maximum, or both;

   (b)   on conviction on indictment to a fine or imprisonment for a term not exceeding ten years, or both.

[759]

Forfeiture of counterfeit goods, &c

97   Forfeiture: England and Wales or Northern Ireland

(1)   In England and Wales or Northern Ireland where there has come into the possession of any person in connection with the investigation or prosecution of a relevant offence—

   (a)   goods which, or the packaging of which, bears a sign identical to or likely to be mistaken for a registered trade mark,

   (b)   material bearing such a sign and intended to be used for labelling or packaging goods, as a business paper in relation to goods, or for advertising goods, or

   (c)   articles specifically designed or adapted for making copies of such a sign,

that person may apply under this section for an order for the forfeiture of the goods, material or articles.

(2)   An application under this section may be made—

   (a)   where proceedings have been brought in any court for a relevant offence relating to some or all of the goods, material or articles, to that court;

   (b)   where no application for the forfeiture of the goods, material or articles has been made under paragraph (a), by way of complaint to a magistrates' court.

(3)   On an application under this section the court shall make an order for the forfeiture of any goods, material or articles only if it is satisfied that a relevant offence has been committed in relation to the goods, material or articles.

(4)   A court may infer for the purposes of this section that such an offence has been committed in relation to any goods, material or articles if it is satisfied that such an offence has been committed in relation to goods, material or articles which are representative of them (whether by reason of being of the same design or part of the same consignment or batch or otherwise).

(5)   Any person aggrieved by an order made under this section by a magistrates' court, or by a decision of such a court not to make such an order, may appeal against that order or decision—

   (a)   in England and Wales, to the Crown Court;

   (b)   in Northern Ireland, to the county court;

and an order so made may contain such provision as appears to the court to be appropriate for delaying the coming into force of the order pending the making and determination of any appeal (including any application under section 111 of the Magistrates' Courts Act 1980 or Article 146 of the Magistrates' Courts (Northern Ireland) Order 1981 (statement of case)).

(6)   Subject to subsection (7), where any goods, material or articles are forfeited under this section they shall be destroyed in accordance with such directions as the court may give.

(7)   On making an order under this section the court may, if it considers it appropriate to do so, direct that the goods, material or articles to which the order relates shall (instead of being destroyed) be released, to such person as the court may specify, on condition that that person—

    (a)   causes the offending sign to be erased, removed or obliterated and

    (b)   complies with any order to pay costs which has been made against him in the proceedings for the order for forfeiture.

(8)   For the purposes of this section a "relevant offence" means an offence under section 92 above (unauthorised use of trade mark, &c in relation to goods) or under the Trade Descriptions Act 1968 or any offence involving dishonesty or deception.

[760]

PART IV
MISCELLANEOUS AND GENERAL PROVISIONS

Interpretation

103   Minor definitions

(1)   In this Act—

"business" includes a trade or profession;

"director", in relation to a body corporate whose affairs are managed by its members, means any member of the body;

"infringement proceedings", in relation to a registered trade mark, includes proceedings under section 16 (order for delivery up of infringing goods, &c);

"publish" means make available to the public, and references to publication—

    (a)   in relation to an application for registration, are to publication under section 38(1), and

    (b)   in relation to registration, are to publication under section 40(4);

"statutory provisions" includes provisions of subordinate legislation within the meaning of the Interpretation Act 1978;

"trade" includes any business or profession.

(2)   References in this Act to use (or any particular description of use) of a trade mark, or of a sign identical with, similar to, or likely to be mistaken for a trade mark, include use (or that description of use) otherwise than by means of a graphic representation.

(3)   References in this Act to a Community instrument include references to any instrument amending or replacing that instrument.

[761]

Other general provisions

108   Extent

(1)   This Act extends to England and Wales, Scotland and Northern Ireland.

(2)   . . .

[762]

NOTES

Sub-s (2): not relevant to this work.

109 Commencement

(1) The provisions of this Act come into force on such day as the Secretary of State may appoint by order made by statutory instrument.

Different days may be appointed for different provisons and different purposes.

(2) . . .

[763]

NOTES

Sub-s (2): not relevant to this work.

Order under this section. The Trade Marks Act 1994 (Commencement) Order 1994, SI 1994/2550, brought all the provisions of this Act into force on 31 October 1994, subject to the exceptions mentioned below, and provides that for the purposes of sub-s (2) above that date shall be the date of commencement in respect of the references to commencement in Schs 3, 4. The exceptions referred to are as follows—

(i) ss 4(4), 13(2), 25(1), (5), (6), 34(1), 35(5), 38(1), (2), 39(3), 40(4), 41(1), (3), 43(2), (3), (5), (6), 44(3), 45(2), 63(2), (3), 64(4), 65(1), (3)–(5), 66(2), 67(1), (2), 68(1), (3), 69, 76(1), 78, 79, 80(3), 81, 82, 88, Sch 1, paras 6(2), 7(2), and Sch 3, paras 10(2), 11(2), 12, 14(5), as read (except in the case of s 78 and Sch 3, paras 10(2), 14(5)) with s 78(1)(a) or (b), or both, as appropriate, came into force on 29 September 1994 for the purpose only of enabling the making of rules thereunder by the Secretary of State expressed to come into force on 31 October 1994;

(ii) ss 66(1) and 80(1), (3) came into force on 29 September 1994 for the purpose of enabling the registrar to excercise his powers thereunder with effect from 31 October 1994;

(iii) s 90 came into force on 29 September 1994 for the purpose only of enabling the making of regulations thereunder by the Commissioners of Customs and Excise expressed to come into force on 31 October 1994.

110 Short title

(1) This Act may be cited as the Trade Marks Act 1994.

[764]

SCHEDULES

SCHEDULE 1

Section 49

COLLECTIVE MARKS

General

1.—The provisions of this Act apply to collective marks subject to the following provisions.

Signs of which a collective mark may consist

2.—In relation to a collective mark the reference in section 1(1) (signs of which a trade mark may consist) to distinguishing goods or services of one undertaking from those of other undertakings shall be construed as a reference to distinguishing goods or services of members of the association which is the proprietor of the mark from those of other undertakings.

Indication of geographical origin

3.—(1) Notwithstanding section 3(1)(c), a collective mark may be registered which consists of signs or indications which may serve, in trade, to designate the geographical origin of the goods or services.

(2) However, the proprietor of such a mark is not entitled to prohibit the use of the signs or indications in accordance with honest practices in industrial or commercial matters (in particular, by a person who is entitled to use a geographical name).

Mark not to be misleading as to character or significance

4.—(1) A collective mark shall not be registered if the public is liable to be misled as regards the character or significance of the mark, in particular if it is likely to be taken to be something other than a collective mark.

(2) The registrar may accordingly require that a mark in respect of which application is made for registration include some indication that it is a collective mark.

Notwithstanding section 39(2), an application may be amended so as to comply with any such requirement.

Regulations governing use of collective mark

5.—(1) An applicant for registration of a collective mark must file with the registrar regulations governing the use of the mark.

(2) The regulations must specify the persons authorised to use the mark, the conditions of membership of the association and, where they exist, the conditions of use of the mark, including any sanctions against misuse.

Further requirements with which the regulations have to comply may be imposed by rules.

Infringement: rights of authorised users

11.—The following provisions apply in relation to an authorised user of a registered collective mark as in relation to a licensee of a trade mark—
- (a) section 10(5) (definition of infringement: unauthorised application of mark to certain material);
- (b) section 19(2) (order as to disposal of infringing goods, material or articles: adequacy of other remedies);
- (c) section 89 (prohibition of importation of infringing goods, material or articles: request to Commissioners of Customs and Excise).

12.—(1) The following provisions (which correspond to the provisions of section 30 (general provisions as to rights of licensees in case of infringement)) have effect as regards the rights of an authorised user in relation to infringement of a registered collective mark.

(2) An authorised user is entitled, subject to any agreement to the contrary between him and the proprietor, to call on the proprietor to take infringement proceedings in respect of any matter which affects his interests.

(3) If the proprietor—
- (a) refuses to do so, or
- (b) fails to do so within two months after being called upon,

the authorised user may bring the proceedings in his own name as if he were the proprietor.

(4) Where infringement proceedings are brought by virtue of this paragraph, the authorised user may not, without the leave of the court, proceed with the action unless the proprietor is either joined as a plaintiff or added as a defendant.

This does not affect the granting of interlocutory relief on an application by an authorised user alone.

(5) A proprietor who is added as a defendant as mentioned in sub-paragraph (4) shall not be made liable for any costs in the action unless he takes part in the proceedings.

(6) In infringement proceedings brought by the proprietor of a registered collective mark any loss suffered or likely to be suffered by authorised users shall be taken into account; and the court may give such directions as it thinks fit as to the extent to which the plaintiff is to hold the proceeds of any pecuniary remedy on behalf of such users.

Grounds for revocation of registration

13.—Apart from the grounds of revocation provided for in section 46, the registration of a collective mark may be revoked on the ground—

(a) that the manner in which the mark has been used by the proprietor has caused it to become liable to mislead the public in the manner referred to in paragraph 4(1), or

(b) that the proprietor has failed to observe, or to secure the observance of, the regulations governing the use of the mark, or

(c) that an amendment of the regulations has been made so that the regulations—

    (i) no longer comply with paragraph 5(2) and any further conditions imposed by rules, or

    (ii) are contrary to public policy or to accepted principles of morality.

Grounds for invalidity of registration

14.—Apart from the grounds of invalidity provided for in section 47, the registration of a collective mark may be declared invalid on the ground that the mark was registered in breach of the provisions of paragraph 4(1) or 6(1).

[765]

SCHEDULE 2

Section 50

CERTIFICATION MARKS

General

1.—The provisions of this Act apply to certification marks subject to the following provisions.

Signs of which a certification mark may consist

2.—In relation to a certification mark the reference in section 1(1) (signs of which a trade mark may consist) to distinguishing goods or services of one undertaking from those of other undertakings shall be construed as a reference to distinguishing goods or services which are certified from those which are not.

Indication of geographical origin

3.—(1) Notwithstanding section 3(1)(c), a certification mark may be registered which consists of signs or indications which may serve, in trade, to designate the geographical origin of the goods or services.

(2) However, the proprietor of such a mark is not entitled to prohibit the use of the signs or indications in accordance with honest practices in industrial or commercial matters (in particular, by a person who is entitled to use a geographical name).

Nature of proprietor's business

4.—A certification mark shall not be registered if the proprietor carries on a business involving the supply of goods or services of the kind certified.

Mark not to be misleading as to character or significance

5.—(1) A certification mark shall not be registered if the public is liable to be misled as regards the character or significance of the mark, in particular if it is likely to be taken to be something other than a certification mark.

(2) The registrar may accordingly require that a mark in respect of which application is made for registration include some indication that it is a certification mark.

Notwithstanding section 39(2), an application may be amended so as to comply with any such requirement.

Regulations governing use of certification mark

6.—(1)   An applicant for registration of a certification mark must file with the registrar regulations governing the use of the mark.

(2)   The regulations must indicate who is authorised to use the mark, the characteristics to be certified by the mark, how the certifying body is to test those characteristics and to supervise the use of the mark, the fees (if any) to be paid in connection with the operation of the mark and the procedures for resolving disputes.

Further requirements with which the regulations have to comply may be imposed by rules.

Consent to assignment of registered certification mark

12.—The assignment or other transmission of a registered certification mark is not effective without the consent of the registrar.

Infringement: rights of authorised users

13.—The following provisions apply in relation to an authorised user of a registered certification mark as in relation to a licensee of a trade mark—

    (a)   section 10(5) (definition of infringement: unauthorised application of mark to certain material);
    (b)   section 19(2) (order as to disposal of infringing goods, material or articles: adequacy of other remedies);
    (c)   section 89 (prohibition of importation of infringing goods, material or articles: request to Commissioners of Customs and Excise).

14.—In infringement proceedings brought by the proprietor of a registered certification mark any loss suffered or likely to be suffered by authorised users shall be taken into account; and the court may give such directions as it thinks fit as to the extent to which the plaintiff is to hold the proceeds of any pecuniary remedy on behalf of such users.

Grounds for revocation of registration

15.—Apart from the grounds of revocation provided for in section 46, the registration of a certification mark may be revoked on the ground—

    (a)   that the proprietor has begun to carry on such a business as is mentioned in paragraph 4,
    (b)   that the manner in which the mark has been used by the proprietor has caused it to become liable to mislead the public in the manner referred to in paragraph 5(1),
    (c)   that the proprietor has failed to observe, or to secure the observance of, the regulations governing the use of the mark,
    (d)   that an amendment of the regulations has been made so that the regulations—
       (i)   no longer comply with paragraph 6(2) and any further conditions imposed by rules, or
       (ii)   are contrary to public policy or to accepted principles of morality, or
    (e)   that the proprietor is no longer competent to certify the goods or services for which the mark is registered.

Grounds for invalidity of registration

16.—Apart from the grounds of invalidity provided for in section 47, the registration of a certification mark may be declared invalid on the ground that the mark was registered in breach of the provisions of paragraph 4, 5(1) or 7(1).

TRADE MARKS RULES 1994

(SI 1994/2583)

NOTES
Made: 5 October 1994.
Authority: Trade Marks Act 1994, ss 4(4), 13(2), 25(1), (5), (6), 34(1), 35(5), 38(1), (2), 39(3), 40(4), 41(1), (3), 43(2), (3), (5), (6), 44(3), 45(2), 63(2), (3), 64(4), 65, 66(2), 67(1), (2), 68(1), (3), 69, 76(1), 78, 80(3), 81, 82, 88, Sch 1, para 6(2), Sch 2, para 7(2), Sch 3, paras 10(2), 11(2), 12, 14(5).

SCHEDULE 4
CLASSIFICATION OF GOODS AND SERVICES
Rule 7(2)

GOODS

Class 1. Chemicals used in industry, science and photography, as well as in agriculture, horticulture and forestry; unprocessed artificial resins, unprocessed plastics; manures; fire extinguishing compositions; tempering and soldering preparations; chemical substances for preserving foodstuffs; tanning substances; adhesives used in industry.

Class 2. Paints, varnishes, lacquers; preservatives against rust and against deterioration of wood; colorants; mordants; raw natural resins; metals in foil and powder form for painters, decorators, printers and artists.

Class 3. Bleaching preparations and other substances for laundry use; cleaning, polishing, scouring and abrasive preparations; soaps; perfumery, essential oils, cosmetics, hair lotions; dentifrices.

Class 4. Industrial oils and greases; lubricants; dust absorbing, wetting and binding compositions; fuels (including motor spirit) and illuminants; candles, wicks.

Class 5. Pharmaceutical, veterinary and sanitary preparations; dietetic substances adapted for medical use, food for babies; plasters, materials for dressings; material for stopping teeth, dental wax; disinfectants; preparations for destroying vermin; fungicides, herbicides.

Class 6. Common metals and their alloys; metal building materials; transportable buildings of metal; materials of metal for railway tracks; non-electric cables and wires of common metal; ironmongery, small items of metal hardware; pipes and tubes of metal; safes; goods of common metal not included in other classes; ores.

Class 7. Machines and machine tools; motors and engines (except for land vehicles); machine coupling and transmission components (except for land vehicles); agricultural implements; incubators for eggs.

Class 8. Hand tools and implements (hand operated); cutlery; side arms; razors.

Class 9. Scientific, nautical, surveying, electric, photographic, cinematographic, optical, weighing, measuring, signalling, checking (supervision), life-saving and teaching apparatus and instruments; apparatus for recording, transmission or reproduction of sound or images; magnetic data carriers, recording discs; automatic vending machines and mechanisms for coin-operated apparatus; cash registers, calculating machines, data processing equipment and computers; fire-extinguishing apparatus.

Class 10. Surgical, medical, dental and veterinary apparatus and instruments, artificial limbs, eyes and teeth; orthopaedic articles; suture materials.

Class 11. Apparatus for lighting, heating, steam generating, cooking, refrigerating, drying, ventilating, water supply and sanitary purposes.

Class 12. Vehicles; apparatus for locomotion by land, air or water.

Class 13. Firearms; ammunition and projectiles; explosives; fireworks.

Class 14. Precious metals and their alloys and goods in precious metals or coated therewith, not included in other classes; jewellery, precious stones; horological and chronometric instruments.

Class 15. Musical instruments.

Class 16. Paper, cardboard and goods made from these materials, not included in other classes; printed matter; bookbinding material; photographs; stationery; adhesives for stationery or household purposes; artists' materials; paint brushes; typewriters and office requisites (except furniture); instructional and teaching material (except apparatus); plastic materials for packaging (not included in other classes); playing cards; printers' type; printing blocks.

Class 17. Rubber, gutta-percha, gum, asbestos, mica and goods made from these materials and not included in other classes; plastics in extruded form for use in manufacture; packing, stopping and insulating materials; flexible pipes, not of metal.

Class 18. Leather and imitations of leather, and goods made of these materials and not included in other classes; animal skins, hides; trunks and travelling bags; umbrellas, parasols and walking sticks; whips, harness and saddlery.

Class 19. Building materials (non-metallic); non-metallic rigid pipes for building; asphalt, pitch and bitumen; non-metallic transportable buildings; monuments, not of metal.

Class 20. Furniture, mirrors, picture frames; goods (not included in other classes) of wood, cork, reed, cane, wicker, horn, bone, ivory, whalebone, shell, amber, mother-of-pearl, meerschaum and substitutes for all these materials, or of plastics.

Class 21. Household or kitchen utensils and containers (not of precious metal or coated therewith); combs and sponges; brushes (except paint brushes); brush-making materials; articles for cleaning purposes; steelwool; unworked or semi-worked glass (except glass used in building); glassware, porcelain and earthenware not included in other classes.

Class 22. Ropes, string, nets, tents, awnings, tarpaulins, sails, sacks and bags (not included in other classes); padding and stuffing materials (except of rubber or plastics); raw fibrous textile materials.

Class 23. Yarns and threads, for textile use.

Class 24. Textiles and textile goods, not included in other classes; bed and table covers.

Class 25. Clothing, footwear, headgear.

Class 26. Lace and embroidery, ribbons and braid; buttons, hooks and eyes, pins and needles; artificial flowers.

Class 27. Carpets, rugs, mats and matting, linoleum and other materials for covering existing floors; wall hangings (non-textile).

Class 28. Games and playthings; gymnastic and sporting articles not included in other classes; decorations for Christmas trees.

Class 29. Meat, fish, poultry and game; meat extracts; preserved, dried and cooked fruits and vegetables; jellies, jams, fruit sauces; eggs, milk and milk products; edible oils and fats.

Class 30. Coffee, tea, cocoa, sugar, rice, tapioca, sago, artificial coffee; flour and preparations made from cereals, bread, pastry and confectionery, ices; honey, treacle; yeast, baking-powder; salt, mustard; vinegar, sauces (condiments); spices; ice.

Class 31. Agricultural, horticultural and forestry products and grains not included in other classes; live animals; fresh fruits and vegetables; seeds, natural plants and flowers; foodstuffs for animals, malt.

Class 32. Beers; mineral and aerated waters and other non-alcoholic drinks; fruit drinks and fruit juices; syrups and other preparations for making beverages.

Class 33. Alcoholic beverages (except beers).

Class 34. Tobacco; smokers' articles; matches.

[767]

SERVICES

Class 35. Advertising; business management; business administration; office functions.

Class 36. Insurance; financial affairs; monetary affairs; real estate affairs.

Class 37. Building construction; repair; installation services.

Class 38. Telecommunications.

Class 39. Transport; packaging and storage of goods; travel arrangement.

Class 40. Treatment of materials.

Class 41. Education; providing of training; entertainment; sporting and cultural activities.

Class 42. Providing of food and drink; temporary accommodation; medical, hygienic and beauty care; veterinary and agricultural services; legal services; scientific and industrial research; computer programming; services that cannot be placed in other classes.

[768]

COUNCIL REGULATION (EEC) 40/94

of 20 December 1993

on the Community trade mark

NOTES
    Date of publication in OJ: OJ L11, 14.1.94, p 1.

TITLE I
GENERAL PROVISIONS

Article 1   Community trade mark

1.   A trade mark for goods or services which is registered in accordance with the conditions contained in this Regulation and in the manner herein provided is hereinafter referred to as a "Community trade mark".

2.   A Community trade mark shall have a unitary character. It shall have equal effect throughout the Community: it shall not be registered, transferred or surrendered or be the subject of a decision revoking the rights of the proprietor or declaring it invalid, nor shall its use be prohibited, save in respect of the whole Community. This principle shall apply unless otherwise provided in this Regulation.

[769]

Article 2   Office

An Office for Harmonisation in the Internal Market (trade marks and designs), hereinafter referred to as "the Office", is hereby established.

[770]

Article 3   Capacity to act

For the purpose of implementing this Regulation, companies or firms and other legal bodies shall be regarded as legal persons if, under the terms of the law governing them, they have the capacity in their own name to have rights and obligations of all kinds, to make contracts or accomplish other legal acts and to sue and be sued.

[771]

TITLE II
THE LAW RELATING TO TRADE MARKS

SECTION 1
DEFINITION OF A COMMUNITY TRADE MARK
OBTAINING A COMMUNITY TRADE MARK

Article 4   Signs of which a Community trade mark may consist

A Community trade mark may consist of any signs capable of being represented graphically, particularly words, including personal names, designs, letters, numerals, the shape of goods or of their packaging, provided that such signs are capable of distinguishing the goods or services of one undertaking from those of other undertakings.

[772]

Article 5   Persons who can be proprietors of Community trade marks

1.   The following natural or legal persons, including authorities established under public law, may be proprietors of Community trade marks—

    (a)   nationals of the Member States; or

    (b)   nationals of other States which are parties to the Paris Convention for the protection of industrial property, hereinafter referred to as "the Paris Convention"; or

    (c)   nationals of States which are not parties to the Paris Convention who are domiciled or have their seat or who have real and effective industrial or commercial establishments within the territory of the Community or of a State which is party to the Paris Convention; or

    (d)   nationals, other than those referred to under subparagraph (c), of any State which is not party to the Paris Convention and which, according to published findings, accords to nationals of all the Member States the same protection for trade marks as it accords to its own nationals and, if nationals of the Member States are required to prove registration in the country of origin, recognises the registration of Community trade marks as such proof.

2.   With respect to the application of paragraph 1, stateless persons as defined by Article 1 of the Convention relating to the Status of Stateless Persons signed at New York on 28 September 1954, and refugees as defined by Article 1 of the Convention relating to the Status of Refugees signed at Geneva on 28 July 1951 and modified by the Protocol relating to the Status of Refugees signed at New York on 31 January 1967, shall be regarded as nationals of the country in which they have their habitual residence.

3.   Persons who are nationals of a State covered by paragraph 1(d) must prove that the trade mark for which an application for a Community trade mark has been submitted is registered in the State of origin, unless, according to published findings, the trade marks of nationals of the Member States are registered in the State of origin in question without proof of prior registration as a Community trade mark or as a national trade mark in a Member State.

[773]

Article 6   Means whereby a Community trade mark is obtained

A Community trade mark shall be obtained by registration.

[774]

Article 7   Absolute grounds for refusal

1.   The following shall not be registered—
   (a)   signs which do not conform to the requirements of Article 4;
   (b)   trade marks which are devoid of any distinctive character;
   (c)   trade marks which consist exclusively of signs or indications which may serve, in trade, to designate the kind, quality, quantity, intended purpose, value, geographical origin or the time of production of the goods or of rendering of the service, or other characteristics of the goods or service;
   (d)   trade marks which consist exclusively of signs or indications which have become customary in the current language or in the bona fide and established practices of the trade;
   (e)   signs which consist exclusively of—
      (i)   the shape which results from the nature of the goods themselves; or
      (ii) the shape of goods which is necessary to obtain a technical result; or
      (iii) the shape which gives substantial value to the goods;
   (f)   trade marks which are contrary to public policy or to accepted principles of morality;
   (g)   trade marks which are of such a nature as to deceive the public, for instance as to the nature, quality or geographical origin of the goods or service;
   (h)   trade marks which have not been authorised by the competent authorities and are to be refused pursuant to Article 6ter of the Paris Convention;
   (i)   trade marks which include badges, emblems or escutcheons other than those covered by Article 6ter of the Paris Convention and which are of particular public interest, unless the consent of the appropriate authorities to their registration has been given.

2.   Paragraph 1 shall apply notwithstanding that the grounds of non-registrability obtain in only part of the Community.

3.   Paragraph 1(b), (c) and (d) shall not apply if the trade mark has become distinctive in relation to the goods or services for which registration is requested in consequence of the use which has been made of it.

[775]

Article 8   Relative grounds for refusal

1.   Upon opposition by the proprietor of an earlier trade mark, the trade mark applied for shall not be registered—

(a) if it is identical with the earlier trade mark and the goods or services for which registration is applied for are identical with the goods or services for which the earlier trade mark is protected;

(b) if because of its identity with or similarity to the earlier trade mark and the identity or similarity of the goods or services covered by the trade marks there exists a likelihood of confusion on the part of the public in the territory in which the earlier trade mark is protected; the likelihood of confusion includes the likelihood of association with the earlier trade mark.

2.   For the purposes of paragraph 1, "Earlier trade marks" means—

(a) trade marks of the following kinds with a date of application for registration which is earlier than the date of application for registration of the Community trade mark, taking account, where appropriate, of the priorities claimed in respect of those trade marks—

   (i) Community trade marks;

   (ii) trade marks registered in a Member State, or, in the case of Belgium, the Netherlands or Luxembourg, at the Benelux Trade Mark Office;

   (iii) trade marks registered under international arrangements which have effect in a Member State;

(b) applications for the trade marks referred to in subparagraph (a), subject to their registration;

(c) trade marks which, on the date of application for registration of the Community trade mark, or, where appropriate, of the priority claimed in respect of the application for registration of the Community trade mark, are well known in a Member State, in the sense in which the words "well known" are used in Article 6bis of the Paris Convention.

3.   Upon opposition by the proprietor of the trade mark, a trade mark shall not be registered where an agent or representative of the proprietor of the trade mark applies for registration thereof in his own name without the proprietor"s consent, unless the agent or representative justifies his action.

4.   Upon opposition by the proprietor of a non-registered trade mark or of another sign used in the course of trade of more than mere local significance, the trade mark applied for shall not be registered where and to the extent that, pursuant to the law of the Member State governing that sign,

(a) rights to that sign were acquired prior to the date of application for registration of the Community trade mark, or the date of the priority claimed for the application for registration of the Community trade mark;

(b) that sign confers on its proprietor the right to prohibit the use of a subsequent trade mark.

5.   Furthermore, upon opposition by the proprietor of an earlier trade mark within the meaning of paragraph 2, the trade mark applied for shall not be registered where it is identical with or similar to the earlier trade mark and is to be registered for goods or services which are not similar to those for which the earlier trade mark is registered, where in the case of an earlier Community trade mark the trade mark has a reputation in the Community and, in the case of an earlier national trade mark, the trade mark has a reputation in the Member State concerned and where the use without due cause of the trade mark applied for would take unfair advantage of, or be detrimental to, the distinctive character or the repute of the earlier trade mark.

SECTION 2
EFFECTS OF COMMUNITY TRADE MARKS

Article 9   Rights conferred by a Community trade mark

1.   A Community trade mark shall confer on the proprietor exclusive rights therein. The proprietor shall be entitled to prevent all third parties not having his consent from using in the course of trade—

    (a)   any sign which is identical with the Community trade mark in relation to goods or services which are identical with those for which the Community trade mark is registered;

    (b)   any sign where, because of its identity with or similarity to the Community trade mark and the identity or similarity of the goods or services covered by the Community trade mark and the sign, there exists a likelihood of confusion on the part of the public; the likelihood of confusion includes the likelihood of association between the sign and the trade mark;

    (c)   any sign which is identical with or similar to the Community trade mark in relation to goods or services which are not similar to those for which the Community trade mark is registered, where the latter has a reputation in the Community and where use of that sign without due cause takes unfair advantage of, or is detrimental to, the distinctive character or the repute of the Community trade mark.

2.   The following, inter alia, may be prohibited under paragraph 1—

    (a)   affixing the sign to the goods or to the packaging thereof;

    (b)   offering the goods, putting them on the market or stocking them for these purposes under that sign, or offering or supplying services thereunder;

    (c)   importing or exporting the goods under that sign;

    (d)   using the sign on business papers and in advertising.

3.   The rights conferred by a Community trade mark shall prevail against third parties from the date of publication of registration of the trade mark. Reasonable compensation may, however, be claimed in respect of matters arising after the date of publication of a Community trade mark application, which matters would, after publication of the registration of the trade mark, be prohibited by virtue of that publication. The court seized of the case may not decide upon the merits of the case until the registration has been published.

[777]

Article 12   Limitation of the effects of a Community trade mark

A Community trade mark shall not entitle the proprietor to prohibit a third party from using in the course of trade—

    (a)   his own name or address;

    (b)   indications concerning the kind, quality, quantity, intended purpose, value, geographical origin, the time of production of the goods or of rendering of the service, or other characteristics of the goods or service;

    (c)   the trade mark where it is necessary to indicate the intended purpose of a product or service, in particular as accessories or spare parts,

provided he uses them in accordance with honest practices in industrial or commercial matters.

[778]

Article 13   Exhaustion of the rights conferred by a Community trade mark

1.   A Community trade mark shall not entitle the proprietor to prohibit its use in relation to goods which have been put on the market in the Community under that trade mark by the proprietor or with his consent.

2.   Paragraph 1 shall not apply where there exist legitimate reasons for the proprietor to oppose further commercialisation of the goods, especially where the condition of the goods is changed or impaired after they have been put on the market.

[779]

Article 14   Complementary application of national law relating to infringement

1.   The effects of Community trade marks shall be governed solely by the provisions of this Regulation. In other respects, infringement of a Community trade mark shall be governed by the national law relating to infringement of a national trade mark in accordance with the provisions of Title X.

2.   This Regulation shall not prevent actions concerning a Community trade mark being brought under the law of Member States relating in particular to civil liability and unfair competition.

3.   The rules of procedure to be applied shall be determined in accordance with the provisions of Title X.

[780]

SECTION 3
USE OF COMMUNITY TRADE MARKS

Article 15   Use of Community trade marks

1.   If, within a period of five years following registration, the proprietor has not put the Community trade mark to genuine use in the Community in connection with the goods or services in respect of which it is registered, or if such use has been suspended during an uninterrupted period of five years, the Community trade mark shall be subject to the sanctions provided for in this Regulation, unless there are proper reasons for non-use.

2.   The following shall also constitute use within the meaning of paragraph 1—
    (a)   use of the Community trade mark in a form differing in elements which do not alter the distinctive character of the mark in the form in which it was registered;
    (b)   affixing of the Community trade mark to goods or to the packaging thereof in the Community solely for export purposes.

3.   Use of the Community trade mark with the consent of the proprietor shall be deemed to constitute use by the proprietor.

[781]

SECTION 4
COMMUNITY TRADE MARKS AS OBJECTS OF PROPERTY

Article 16   Dealing with Community trade marks as national trade marks

1.   Unless Articles 17 to 24 provide otherwise, a Community trade mark as an object of property shall be dealt with in its entirety, and for the whole area of the Community, as a national trade mark registered in the Member State in which, according to the Register of Community trade marks,
   - (a) the proprietor has his seat or his domicile on the relevant date; or
   - (b) where subparagraph (a) does not apply, the proprietor has an establishment on the relevant date.

2.   In cases which are not provided for by paragraph 1, the Member State referred to in that paragraph shall be the Member State in which the seat of the Office is situated.

3.   If two or more persons are mentioned in the Register of Community trade marks as joint proprietors, paragraph 1 shall apply to the joint proprietor first mentioned; failing this, it shall apply to the subsequent joint proprietors in the order in which they are mentioned. Where paragraph 1 does not apply to any of the joint proprietors, paragraph 2 shall apply.

[782]

Article 17   Transfer

1.   A Community trade mark may be transferred, separately from any transfer of the undertaking in respect of some or all of the goods or services for which it is registered.

2.   A transfer of the whole of the undertaking shall include the transfer of the Community trade mark except where, in accordance with the law governing the transfer, there is agreement to the contrary or circumstances clearly dictate otherwise. This provision shall apply to the contractual obligation to transfer the undertaking.

3.   Without prejudice to paragraph 2, an assignment of the Community trade mark shall be made in writing and shall require the signature of the parties to the contract, except when it is a result of a judgment; otherwise it shall be void.

4.   Where it is clear from the transfer documents that because of the transfer the Community trade mark is likely to mislead the public concerning the nature, quality or geographical origin of the goods or services in respect of which it is registered, the Office shall not register the transfer unless the successor agrees to limit registration of the Community trade mark to goods or services in respect of which it is not likely to mislead.

5.   On request of one of the parties a transfer shall be entered in the Register and published.

6.   As long as the transfer has not been entered in the Register, the successor in title may not invoke the rights arising from the registration of the Community trade mark.

7.   Where there are time limits to be observed vis-à-vis the Office, the successor in title may make the corresponding statements to the Office once the request for registration of the transfer has been received by the Office.

8.   All documents which require notification to the proprietor of the Community trade mark in accordance with Article 77 shall be addressed to the person registered as proprietor.

[783]

Article 18   Transfer of a trade mark registered in the name of an agent

Where a Community trade mark is registered in the name of the agent or representative of a person who is the proprietor of that trade mark, without the proprietor's authorisation, the latter shall be entitled to demand the assignment in his favour of the said registration, unless such agent or representative justifies his action.

[784]

Article 22   Licensing

1.   A Community trade mark may be licensed for some or all of the goods or services for which it is registered and for the whole or part of the Community. A licence may be exclusive or non-exclusive.

2.   The proprietor of a Community trade mark may invoke the rights conferred by that trade mark against a licensee who contravenes any provision in his licensing contract with regard to its duration, the form covered by the registration in which the trade mark may be used, the scope of the goods or services for which the licence is granted, the territory in which the trade mark may be affixed, or the quality of the goods manufactured or of the services provided by the licensee.

3.   Without prejudice to the provisions of the licensing contract, the licensee may bring proceedings for infringement of a Community trade mark only if its proprietor consents thereto. However, the holder of an exclusive licence may bring such proceedings if the proprietor of the trade mark, after formal notice, does not himself bring infringement proceedings within an appropriate period.

4.   A licensee shall, for the purpose of obtaining compensation for damage suffered by him, be entitled to intervene in infringement proceedings brought by the proprietor of the Community trade mark.

5.   On request of one of the parties the grant or transfer of a licence in respect of a Community trade mark shall be entered in the Register and published.

[785]

Article 23   Effects *vis-à-vis* third parties

1.   Legal acts referred to in Article 17, 19 and 22 concerning a Community trade mark shall only have effects vis-à-vis third parties in all the Member States after entry in the Register. Nevertheless, such an act, before it is so entered, shall have effect vis-à-vis third parties who have acquired rights in the trade mark after the date of that act but who knew of the act at the date on which the rights were acquired.

2.   Paragraph 1 shall not apply in the case of a person who acquires the Community trade mark or a right concerning the Community trade mark by way of transfer of the whole of the undertaking or by any other universal succession.

3.   The effects vis-à-vis third parties of the legal acts referred to in Article 20 shall be governed by the law of the Member State determined in accordance with Article 16.

4.   Until such time as common rules for the Member States in the field of bankruptcy enter into force, the effects vis-à-vis third parties of bankruptcy or like proceedings shall be governed by the law of the Member State in which such proceedings are first brought within the meaning of national law or of conventions applicable in this field.

[786]

Article 24   The application for a Community trade mark as an object of property

Articles 16 to 23 shall apply to applications for Community trade marks.

[787]

TITLE III
APPLICATION FOR COMMUNITY TRADE MARKS

SECTION 1
FILING OF APPLICATIONS AND THE CONDITIONS WHICH GOVERN THEM

Article 25   Filing of applications

1.   An application for a Community trade mark shall be filed, at the choice of the applicant,
  (a)   at the Office; or
  (b)   at the central industrial property office of a Member State or at the Benelux Trade Mark Office.

   An application filed in this way shall have the same effect as if it had been filed on the same date at the Office.

2.   Where the application is filed at the central industrial property office of a Member State or at the Benelux Trade Mark Office, that office shall take all steps to forward the application to the Office within two weeks after filing. It may charge the applicant a fee which shall not exceed the administrative costs of receiving and forwarding the application.

3.   Applications referred to in paragraph 2 which reach the Office more than one month after filing shall be deemed withdrawn.

4.   Ten years after the entry into force of this Regulation, the Commission shall draw up a report on the operation of the system of filing applications for Community trade marks, together with any proposals for modifying this system.

[788]

Article 26   Conditions with which applications must comply

1.   An application for a Community trade mark shall contain—
  (a)   a request for the registration of a Community trade mark;
  (b)   information identifying the applicant;
  (c)   a list of the goods or services in respect of which the registration is requested;
  (d)   a representation of the trade mark.

2.   The application for a Community trade mark shall be subject to the payment of the application fee and, when appropriate, of one or more class fees.

3.   An application for a Community trade mark must comply with the conditions laid down in the implementing Regulation referred to in Article 140.

[789]

Article 27   Date of filing

The date of filing of a Community trade mark application shall be the date on which documents containing the information specified in Article 26(1) are filed with the Office by the applicant or, if the application has been filed with the central office of a Member State or with the Benelux Trade Mark Office, with that office, subject to payment of the application fee within a period of one month of filing the abovementioned documents.

[790]

Article 28   Classification

Goods and services in respect of which Community trade marks are applied for shall be classified in conformity with the system of classification specified in the Implementing Regulation.

[791]

SECTION 2
PRIORITY

Article 29   Right of priority

1.   A person who has duly filed an application for a trade mark in or for any State party to the Paris Convention, or his successors in title, shall enjoy, for the purpose of filing a Community trade mark application for the same trade mark in respect of goods or services which are identical with or contained within those for which the application has been filed, a right of priority during a period of six months from the date of filing of the first application.

2.   Every filing that is equivalent to a regular national filing under the national law of the State where it was made or under bilateral or multilateral agreements shall be recognised as giving rise to a right of priority.

3.   By a regular national filing is meant any filing that is sufficient to establish the date on which the application was filed, whatever may be the outcome of the application.

4.   A subsequent application for a trade mark which was the subject of a previous first application in respect of the same goods or services, and which is filed in or in respect of the same State shall be considered as the first application for the purposes of determining priority, provided that, at the date of filing of the subsequent application, the previous application has been withdrawn, abandoned or refused, without being open to public inspection and without leaving any rights outstanding, and has not served as a basis for claiming a right of priority. The previous application may not thereafter serve as a basis for claiming a right of priority.

5.   If the first filing has been made in a State which is not a party to the Paris Convention, paragraphs 1 to 4 shall apply only in so far as that State, according to published findings, grants, on the basis of a first filing made at the Office and subject to conditions equivalent to those laid down in this Regulation, a right of priority having equivalent effect.

[792]

Article 30   Claiming priorite

An applicant desiring to take advantage of the priority of a previous application shall file a declaration of priority and a copy of the previous application. If the language of the latter is not one of the languages of the Office, the applicant shall file a translation of the previous application in one of those languages.

[793]

Article 31   Effect of priority right

The right of priority shall have the effect that the date of priority shall count as the date of filing of the Community trade mark application for the purposes of establishing which rights take precedence.

[794]

Article 32   Equivalence of Community filing with national filing

A Community trade mark application which has been accorded a date of filing shall, in the Member States, be equivalent to a regular national filing, where appropriate with the priority claimed for the Community trade mark application.

[795]

SECTION 4
CLAIMING THE SENIORITY OF A NATIONAL TRADE MARK

Article 34   Claiming the seniority of a national trade mark

1.   The proprietor of an earlier trade mark registered in a Member State, including a trade mark registered in the Benelux countries, or registered under international arrangements having effect in a Member State, who applies for an identical trade mark for registration as a Community trade mark for goods or services which are identical with or contained within those for which the earlier trade mark has been registered, may claim for the Community trade mark the seniority of the earlier trade mark in respect of the Member State in or for which it is registered.

2.   Seniority shall have the sole effect under this Regulation that, where the proprietor of the Community trade mark surrenders the earlier trade mark or allows it to lapse, he shall be deemed to continue to have the same rights as he would have had if the earlier trade mark had continued to be registered.

3.   The seniority claimed for the Community trade mark shall lapse if the earlier trade mark the seniority of which is claimed is declared to have been revoked or to be invalid or if it is surrendered prior to the registration of the Community trade mark.

[796]

Article 35   Claiming seniority after registration of the Community trade mark

1.   The proprietor of a Community trade mark who is the proprietor of an earlier identical trade mark registered in a Member State, including a trade mark registered in the Benelux countries, or of a trade mark registered under

international arrangements having effect in a Member State, for identical goods or services, may claim the seniority of the earlier trade mark in respect of the Member State in or for which it is registered.

2.   Article 34(2) and (3) shall apply.

[797]

TITLE V
DURATION, RENEWAL AND ALTERATION OF COMMUNITY TRADE MARKS

Article 46   Duration of registration

Community trade marks shall be registered for a period of ten years from the date of filing of the application. Registration may be renewed in accordance with Article 47 for further periods of ten years.

[798]

Article 47   Renewal

1.   Registration of the Community trade mark shall be renewed at the request of the proprietor of the trade mark or any person expressly authorised by him, provided that the fees have been paid.

2.   The Office shall inform the proprietor of the Community trade mark, and any person having a registered right in respect of the Community trade mark, of the expire of the registration in good time before the said expiry. Failure to give such information shall not involve the responsibility of the Office.

3.   The request for renewal shall be submitted within a period of six months ending on the last day of the month in which protection ends. The fees shall also be paid within this period. Failing this, the request may be submitted and the fees paid within a further period of six months following the day referred to in the first sentence, provided that an additional fee is paid within this further period.

4.   Where the request is submitted or the fees paid in respect of only some of the goods or services for which the Community trade mark is registered, registration shall be renewed for those goods or services only.

5.   Renewal shall take effect from the day following the date on which the existing registration expires. The renewal shall be registered.

[799]

Article 48   Alteration

1.   The Community trade mark shall not be altered in the register during the period of registration or on renewal thereof.

2.   Nevertheless, where the Community trade mark includes the name and address of the proprietor, any alteration thereof not substantially affecting the identity of the trade mark as originally registered may be registered at the request of the proprietor.

3.   The publication of the registration of the alteration shall contain a representation of the Community trade mark as altered. Third parties whose rights may be affected by the alteration may challenge the registration thereof within a period of three months following publication.

[800]

TITLE VI
SURRENDER, REVOCATION AND INVALIDITY

SECTION 1
SURRENDER

Article 49   Surrender

1.   A Community trade mark may be surrendered in respect of some or all of the goods or services for which it is registered.

2.   The surrender shall be declared to the Office in writing by the proprietor of the trade mark. It shall not have effect until it has been entered in the Register.

3.   Surrender shall be entered only with the agreement of the proprietor of a right entered in the Register. If a licence has been registered, surrender shall only be entered in the Register if the proprietor of the trade mark proves that he has informed the licensee of his intention to surrender; this entry shall be made on expiry of the period prescribed by the Implementing Regulation.

[801]

SECTION 2
GROUNDS FOR REVOCATION

Article 50   Grounds for revocation

1.   The rights of the proprietor of the Community trade mark shall be declared to be revoked on application to the Office or on the basis of a counterclaim infringement proceedings—

    (a) if, within a continuous period of five years, the trade mark has not been put to genuine use in the Community in connection with the goods or services in respect of which it is registered, and there are no proper reasons for non-use; however, no person may claim that the proprietor's rights in a Community trade mark should be revoked where, during the interval between expiry of the five-year period and filing of the application or counterclaim, genuine use of the trade mark has been started or resumed; the commencement or resumption of use within a period of three months preceding the filing of the application or counterclaim which began at the earliest on expiry of the continuous period of five years of non-use shall, however, be disregarded where preparations for the commencement or resumption occur only after the proprietor becomes aware that the application or counterclaim may be filed;

    (b) if, in consequence of acts or inactivity of the proprietor, the trade mark has become the common name in the trade for a product or service in respect of which it is registered;

    (c) if, in consequence of the use made of it by the proprietor of the trade mark or with his consent in respect of the goods or services for which it is registered, the trade mark is liable to mislead the public, particularly as to the nature, quality or geographical origin of those goods or services;

    (d) if the proprietor of the trade mark no longer satisfies the conditions laid down by Article 5.

2.   Where the grounds for revocation of rights exist in respect of only some of
the goods or services for which the Community trade mark is registered, the rights
of the proprietor shall be declared to be revoked in respect of those goods or
services only.

[802]

SECTION 3
GROUNDS FOR INVALIDITY

Article 51   Absolute grounds for invalidity

1.   A Community trade mark shall be declared invalid on application to the Office
or on the basis of a counterclaim in infringement proceedings—
   (a)   where the Community trade mark has been registered in breach of the
         provisions of Article 5 or of Article 7;
   (b)   where the applicant was acting in bad faith when he filed the application
         for the trade mark.

2.   Where the Community trade mark has been registered in breach of the
provisions of Article 7(1) (b), (c) or (d), it may nevertheless not be declared invalid
if, in consequence of the use which has been made of it, it has after registration
acquired a distinctive character in relation to the goods or services for which it is
registered.

3.   Where the ground for invalidity exists in respect of only some of the goods or
services for which the Community trade mark is registered, the trade mark shall be
declared invalid as regards those goods or services only.

[803]

Article 52   Relative grounds for invalidity

1.   A Community trade mark shall be declared invalid on application to the Office
or on the basis of a counterclaim in infringement proceedings—
   (a)   where there is an earlier trade mark as referred to in Article 8(2) and the
         conditions set out in paragraph 1 or paragraph 5 of that Article are
         fulfilled;
   (b)   where there is a trade mark as referred to in Article 8(3) and the conditions
         set out in that paragraph are fulfilled;
   (c)   where there is an earlier right as referred to in Article 8(4) and the
         conditions set out in that paragraph are fulfilled.

2.   A Community trade mark shall also be declared invalid on application to the
Office or on the basis of a counterclaim in infringement proceedings where the use of
such trade mark may be prohibited pursuant to the national law governing the
protection of any other earlier right and in particular—
   (a)   a right to a name;
   (b)   a right of personal portrayal;
   (c)   a copyright;
   (d)   an industrial property right.

3.   A Community trade mark may not be declared invalid where the proprietor
of a right referred to in paragraphs 1 or 2 consents expressly to the registration of
the Community trade mark before submission of the application for a declaration
of invalidity or the counterclaim.

4.   Where the proprietor of one of the rights referred to in paragraphs 1 or 2 has previously applied for a declaration that a Community trade mark is invalid or made a counterclaim in infringement proceedings, he may not submit a new application for a declaration of invalidity or lodge a counterclaim on the basis of another of the said rights which he could have invoked in support of his first application or counterclaim.

5.   Article 51(3) shall apply.

[804]

Article 53   Limitation in consequence of acquiescence

1.   Where the proprietor of a Community trade mark has acquiesced, for a period of five successive years, in the use of a later Community trade mark in the Community while being aware of such use, he shall no longer be entitled on the basis of the earlier trade mark either to apply for a declaration that the later trade mark is invalid or to oppose the use of the later trade mark in respect of the goods or services for which the later trade mark has been used, unless registration of the later Community trade mark was applied for in bad faith.

2.   Where the proprietor of an earlier national trade mark as referred to in Article 8(2) or of another earlier sign referred to in Article 8(4) has acquiesced, for a period of five successive years, in the use of a later Community trade mark in the Member State in which the earlier trade mark or the other earlier sign is protected while being aware of such use, he shall no longer be entitled on the basis of the earlier trade mark or of the other earlier sign either to apply for a declaration that the later trade mark is invalid or to oppose the use of the later trade mark in respect of the goods or services for which the later trade mark has been used, unless registration of the later Community trade mark was applied for in bad faith.

3.   In the cases referred to in paragraphs 1 and 2, the proprietor of a later Community trade mark shall not be entitled to oppose the use of the earlier right, even though that right may no longer be invoked against the later Community trade mark.

[805]

SECTION 4
CONSEQUENCES OF REVOCATION AND INVALIDITY

Article 54   Consequences of revocation and invalidity

1.   The Community trade mark shall be deemed not to have had, as from the date of the application for revocation or of the counterclaim, the effects specified in this Regulation, to the extent that the rights of the proprietor have been revoked. An earlier date, on which one of the grounds for revocation occurred, may be fixed in the decision at the request of one of the parties.

2.   The Community trade mark shall be deemed not to have had, as from the outset, the effects specified in this Regulation, to the extent that the trade mark has been declared invalid.

3.   Subject to the national provisions relating either to claims for compensation for damage caused by negligence or lack of good faith on the part of the proprietor of the trade mark, or to unjust enrichment, the retroactive effect of revocation or invalidity of the trade mark shall not affect—

    (a)   any decision on infringement which has acquired the authority of a final decision and been enforced prior to the revocation or invalidity decision;

(b) any contract concluded prior to the revocation or invalidity decision, in so far as it has been performed before that decision; however, repayment, to an extent justified by the circumstances, of sums paid under the relevant contract, may be claimed on grounds of equity.

[806]

TITLE VIII
COMMUNITY COLLECTIVE MARKS

Article 64   Community collective marks

1.   A Community collective mark shall be a Community trade mark which is described as such when the mark is applied for and is capable of distinguishing the goods or services of the members of the association which is the proprietor of the mark from those of other undertakings. Associations of manufacturers, producers, suppliers of services, or traders which, under the terms of the law governing them, have the capacity in their own name to have rights and obligations of all kinds, to make contracts or accomplish other legal acts and to sue and be sued, as well as legal persons governed by public law, may apply for Community collective marks.

2.   In derogation from Article 7(1)(c), signs or indications which may serve, in trade, to designate the geographical origin of the goods or services may constitute Community collective marks within the meaning of paragraph 1. A collective mark shall not entitle the proprietor to prohibit a third party from using in the course of trade such signs or indications, provided he uses them in accordance with honest practices in industrial or commercial matters; in particular, such a mark may not be invoked against a third party who is entitled to use a geographical name.

3.   The provisions of this Regulation shall apply to Community collective marks, unless Articles 65 to 72 provide otherwise.

[807]

Article 65   Regulations governing use of the mark

1.   An applicant for a Community collective mark must submit regulations governing its use within the period prescribed.

2.   The regulations governing use shall specify the persons authorised to use the mark, the conditions of membership of the association and, where they exist, the conditions of use of the mark including sanctions. The regulations governing use of a mark referred to in Article 64(2) must authorise any person whose goods or services originate in the geographical area concerned to become a member of the association which is the proprietor of the mark.

[808]

Article 66   Refusal of the application

1.   In addition to the grounds for refusal of a Community trade mark application provided for in Articles 36 and 38, an application for a Community collective mark shall be refused where the provisions of Article 64 or 65 are not satisfied, or where the regulations governing use are contrary to public policy or to awaited principles of morality.

2.   An application for a Community collective mark shall also be refused if the public is liable to be misled as regards the character or the significance of the mark, in particular if it is likely to be taken to be something other than a collective mark.

3.   An application shall not be refused if the applicant, as a result of amendment of the regulations governing use, meets the requirements of paragraphs 1 and 2.

[809]

Article 67   Observations by third parties

Apart from the cases mentioned in Article 41, any person, group or body referred to in that Article may submit to the Office written observations based on the particular grounds on which the application for a Community collective mark should be refused under the terms of Article 66.

[810]

Article 68   Use of marks

Use of a Community collective mark by any person who has authority to use it shall satisfy the requirements of this Regulation, provided that the other conditions which this Regulation imposes with regard to the use of Community trade marks are fulfilled.

[811]

Article 69   Amendment of the regulations governing use of the mark

1.   The proprietor of a Community collective mark must submit to the Office any amended regulations governing use.

2.   The amendment shall not be mentioned in the Register if the amended regulations do not satisfy the requirements of Article 65 or involve one of the grounds for refusal referred to in Article 66.

3.   Article 67 shall apply to amended regulations governing use.

4.   For the purposes of applying this Regulation, amendments to the regulations governing use shall take effect only from the date of entry of the mention of the amendment in the Register.

[812]

Article 70   Persons who are entitled to bring an action for infringement

1.   The provisions of Article 22(3) and (4) concerning the rights of licensees shall apply to every person who has authority to use a Community collective mark.

2.   The proprietor of a Community collective mark shall be entitled to claim compensation on behalf of persons who have authority to use the mark where they have sustained damage in consequence of unauthorised use of the mark.

[813]

Article 71   Grounds for revocation

Apart from the grounds for revocation provided for in Article 50, the rights of the proprietor of a Community collective mark shall be revoked on application to the Office or on the basis of a counterclaim in infringement proceedings, if—
    (a) the proprietor does not take reasonable steps to prevent the mark being
         used in a manner incompatible with the conditions of use, where these

exist, laid down in the regulations governing use, amendments to which have, where appropriate, been mentioned in the Register;

(b) the manner in which the mark has been used by the proprietor has caused it to become liable to mislead the public in the manner referred to in Article 66(2);

(c) an amendment to the regulations governing use of the mark has been mentioned in the Register in breach of the provisions of Article 69(2), unless the proprietor of the mark, by further amending the regulations governing use, complies with the requirements of those provisions.

[814]

Article 72   Grounds for invalidity

Apart from the grounds for invalidity provided for in Articles 51 and 52, a Community collective mark which is registered in breach of the provisions of Article 66 shall be declared invalid on application to the Office or on the basis of a counterclaim in infringement proceedings, unless the proprietor of the mark, by amending the regulations governing use, complies with the requirements of those provisions.

[815]

TITLE XIII
FINAL PROVISIONS

Article 140   Community implementing provisions

1.   The rules implementing this Regulation shall be adopted in an Implementing Regulation.

2.   In addition to the fees provided for in the preceding Articles, fees shall be charged, in accordance with the detailed rules of application laid down in the Implementing Regulation, in the cases listed below—

     1.   alteration of the representation of a Community trade mark;
     2.   late payment of the registration fee;
     3.   issue of a copy of the certificate of registration;
     4.   registration of the transfer of a Community trade mark;
     5.   registration of a licence or another right in respect of a Community trade mark;
     6.   registration of a licence or another right in respect of an application for a Community trade mark;
     7.   cancellation of the registration of a licence or another right;
     8.   alteration of a registered Community trade mark;
     9.   issue of an extract from the Register;
     10.   inspection of the files;
     11.   issue of copies of file documents;
     12.   issue of certified copies of the application;
     13.   communication of information in a file;
     14.   review of the determination of the procedural costs to be refunded.

3.   The Implementing Regulation and the rules of procedure of the Boards of Appeal shall be adopted and amended in accordance with the procedure laid down in Article 141.

[816]

Article 141   Establishment of a committee and procedure for the adoption of implementing regulations

1.   The Commission shall be assisted by a Committee on Fees, Implementation Rules and the Procedure of the Boards of Appeal of the Office for Harmonisation in the Internal Market (trade marks and designs), which shall be composed of representatives of the Member States and chaired by a representative of the Commission.

2.   The representative of the Commission shall submit to the Committee a draft of the measures to be taken. The Committee shall deliver its opinion on the draft within a time limit which the chairman may lay down according to the urgency of the matter. The opinion shall be delivered by the majority laid down in Article 148(2) of the Treaty in the case of decisions which the Council is required to adopt on a proposal from the Commission. The votes of the representatives of the Member States within the Committee shall be weighted in the manner set out in that Article. The chairman shall not vote.

The Commission shall adopt the measures envisaged if they are in accordance with the opinion of the Committee.

If the measures envisaged are not in accordance with the opinion of the Committee, or if no opinion is delivered, the Commission shall, without delay, submit to the Council a proposal relating to the measures to be taken. The Council shall act by a qualified majority.

If, on the expiry of a period of three months from the date of referral to the Council, the Council has not acted, the proposed measures shall be adopted by the Commission, save where the Council has decided against the measures by a simple majority.

[817]

Article 142   Compatibility with other Community legal provisions

This Regulation shall not affect Council Regulation (EEC) No 2081/92 on the protection of geographical indications and designations of origin for agricultural products and foodstuffs[1] of 14 July 1992, and in particular Article 14 thereof.

[818]

NOTES

   1   OJ L208, 24.7.92, p 1.

Article 143   Entry into force

1.   This Regulation shall enter into force on the 60th day following that of its publication in the Official Journal of the European Communities.

2.   The Member States shall within three years following entry into force of this Regulation take the necessary measures for the purpose of implementing Articles 91 and 110 hereof and shall forthwith inform the Commission of those measures.

3.   Applications for Community trade marks may be filed at the Office from the date fixed by the Administrative Board on the recommendation of the President of the Office.

4.   Applications for Community trade marks filed within three months before the date referred to in paragraph 3 shall be deemed to have been filed on that date.

This Regulation shall be binding in its entirety and directly applicable in all Member States.

[819]

Statement by the Council and the Commission on the seat of the Office for Harmonisation in the Internal Market (trade marks and designs)

"In adopting the Regulation on the Community Trade Mark, the Council and the Commission note—

— that the representatives of the Governments of the Member States, meeting at Head of State and Government level on 29 October 1993, decided that the Office for Harmonisation in the Internal Market (trade marks and designs) should have its seat in Spain, in a town to be determined by the Spanish Government;

— that the Spanish Government has designated Alicante as the seat of the Office."

[820]

PART VI
MISCELLANEOUS

PRACTICE DIRECTION
(MAREVA AND ANTON PILLER ORDERS: NEW FORMS)

(28 July 1994)

[1994] 4 All ER 52, [1994] 1 WLR 1233.

(1)   The granting of a Mareva injunction or Anton Piller order is a matter for the discretion of the judge hearing the application. However, it is desirable that a consistent approach should in general be adopted in relation to the form and carrying out of such orders, since they represent serious restrictions on the rights of those persons subjected to them imposed after hearing only the applicant's case on an ex parte application. This practice direction sets out guidelines for the assistance of judges and those who apply for these orders.

(2)   Attached to this practice direction are new standard forms of the following orders: annex 1, Anton Piller order; annex 2, worldwide Mareva injunction; and annex 3, Mareva injunction limited to assets within the jurisdiction. These forms, inevitably, are complicated, but their language and layout are intended to make it easier for persons served with these orders to understand what they mean. These forms of order should be used save to the extent that the judge hearing a particular application considers there is a good reason for adopting a different form.

(3)   The following matters should be borne in mind in relation to an ex parte application for any of these orders.

(A)   *On an application for either a Mareva or an Anton Piller order*

1.   Where practicable the papers to be used on the application should be lodged with the judge at least two hours before the hearing.

2.   An applicant should be required, in an appropriate case, to support his cross-undertaking in damages by a payment into court or the provision of a bond by an insurance company. Alternatively, the judge may order a payment by way of such security to the applicant's solicitor to be held by the solicitor as an officer of the court pending further order.

3.   So far as practicable, any application for the discharge or variation of the order should be dealt with effectively on the return date.

(B)   *On an application for an Anton Piller order*

1.   (a) As suggested in *Universal Thermosensors Ltd v Hibben* [1992] 3 All ER 257 at 276, [1992] 1 WLR 840 at 861 the specimen order provides for it to be served by a supervising solicitor and carried out in his presence and under his supervision. The supervising solicitor should be an experienced solicitor, having some familiarity with the operation of Anton Piller orders, who is not a member or employee of the firm acting for the applicant. The evidence in support of the application should include the identity and experience of the proposed supervising solicitor. (b) If in any particular case the judge does not think it appropriate to provide for the order to be served by a supervising solicitor, his reasons should be expressed in the order itself.

2.   Where the premises are likely to be occupied by an unaccompanied woman and the supervising solicitor is a man, at least one of the persons attending on the service of the order should be a woman: see para 2(3) of the standard form of order and footnote b.

3.   Where the nature of the items removed under the order makes this appropriate, the applicant should be required to insure them: see Sch 3, footnote e of the standard form.

4.   The applicant should undertake not to inform any third party of the proceedings until after the return date: see Sch 3, para 6.

5.   In future, applications in the Queen's Bench Division will no longer be heard by the judge in chambers. In both Chancery and Queen's Bench Divisions, whenever practicable, applications will be listed before a judge in such a manner as to ensure that he has sufficient time to read and consider the papers in advance.

6.   On circuit, applications will be listed before a High Court judge or a Circuit Judge, sitting as a judge of the High Court specially designated by the Presiding Judge to hear such applications.

(4)   If an Anton Piller order or Mareva injunction is discharged on the return date, the judge should always consider whether it is appropriate that he should assess damages at once and direct immediate payment by the applicant.

(5)   This practice direction applies to all Divisions of the High Court.

By direction of the Lord Chief Justice, Lord Taylor, with the concurrence of the President of the Family Division, Sir Stephen Brown, and the Vice-Chancellor, Sir Donald Nicholls.

Annex 1

[Heading]

Order to allow entry and search of premises

IMPORTANT:

NOTICE TO THE DEFENDANT

(1)   This order orders you to allow the persons mentioned below to enter the premises described in the order and to search for, examine and remove or copy the articles specified in the order. This part of the order is subject to restrictions. The order also requires you to hand over any of the articles which are under your control and to provide information to the plaintiff's solicitors, and prohibits you from doing certain acts. You should read the terms of the order very carefully. You are advised to consult a solicitor as soon as possible.

(2)   Before you the defendant or the person appearing to be in control of the premises allow anybody onto the premises to carry out this order you are entitled to have the solicitor who serves you with this order explain to you what it means in every day language.

(3)   You are entitled to insist that there is nobody [or nobody except Mr ...] present who could gain commercially from anything he might read or see on your premises.

(4)   You are entitled to refuse to permit entry before 9.30 am or after 5.30 pm or at all on Saturday and Sunday.

(5)   You are entitled to seek legal advice, and to ask the Court to vary or discharge this order, provided you do so at once, and provided that meanwhile you permit the supervising solicitor (who is a solicitor acting independently of the plaintiff) and the plaintiff's solicitor to enter, but not start to search: see para 3.

(6) If you ... the defendant disobey this order you will be guilty of contempt of Court and may be [sent to prison or] fined or your assets seized. (Delete the words "sent to prison" in the case of a corporate defendant. This notice is not a substitute for the indorsement of a penal notice.)

THE ORDER

An application was made today [date] by counsel [or solicitors] for ... the plaintiff to Mr Justice [...]. Mr Justice [...] heard the application and read the affidavits listed in Sch 6 at the end of this order.

As a result of the application IT IS ORDERED by Mr Justice [...] that:

Entry and search of premises and vehicles on the premises

1.   (1) The defendant must allow Mr/Mrs/Miss ... : ("the supervising solicitor"), together with Mr ... a solicitor of the Supreme Court, and a partner in the firm of the plaintiff's solicitors ... and up to ... other persons being [their capacity] accompanying them, to enter the premises mentioned in Sch 1 to this order and any vehicles on the premises so that they can search for, inspect, photograph or photocopy, and deliver into the safekeeping of the plaintiff's solicitors all the documents and articles which are listed in Sch 2 to this order ("the listed items") or which Mr ... believes to be listed items. The defendant must allow those persons to remain on the premises until the search is complete, and if necessary to re-enter the premises on the same or the following day in order to complete the search.

(2) This order must be complied with either by the defendant himself or by a responsible employee of the defendant or by the person appearing to be in control of the premises.

(3) This order requires the defendant or his employee or the person appearing to be in control of the premises to permit entry to the premises immediately the order is served upon him, except as stated in para 3 below.

Restrictions on the service and carrying out of para 1 of this order

2.   Paragraph 1 of this order is subject to the following restrictions.

(1) This order may only be served between 9.30 am and 5.30 pm on a weekday.

(2) This order may not be carried out at the same time as any police search warrant.

(3) This order must be served by the supervising solicitor, and para 1 of the order must be carried out in his presence and under his supervision. [At least one of the persons accompanying him as provided by para 1 of this order shall be a woman.] (The words in square brackets are to be included in a case where the premises are likely to be occupied by an unaccompanied woman and the superivising solicitor is a man.)

(4) This order does not require the person served with the order to allow anyone [or anyone except Mr ...] who could gain commercially from anything he might read or see on the premises if the person served with the order objects.

(5) No item may be removed from the premises until a list of the items to be removed has been prepared, and a copy of the list has been supplied to the person served with the order, and he has been given a reasonable opportunity to check the list.

(6) The premises must not be searched, and items must not be removed from them, except in the presence of the defendant or a person appearing to be a responsible employee of the defendant.

(7) If the supervising solicitor is satisfied that full compliance with sub-para (5) or (6) above is impracticable, he may permit the search to proceed and items to be removed without compliance with the impracticable requirements.

Obtaining legal advice and applying to the court

3. Before permitting entry to the premises by any person other than the Supervising Officer and the plaintiff's solicitors, the defendant or other person appearing to be in control of the premises may seek legal advice, and apply to the Court to vary or discharge this order, provided he does so at once. While this is being done, he may refuse entry to the premises by any other person, and may refuse to permit the search to begin, for a short time (not to exceed two hours, unless the supervising solicitor agrees to a longer period).

Delivery of listed items and computer print-outs

4. (1) The defendant must immediately hand over to the plaintiff's solicitors any of the listed items which are in his possession or under his control.

(2) If any of the listed items exists only in computer readable form, the defendant must immediately give the plaintiff's solicitors effective access to the computers, with all necessary passwords, to enable them to be searched, and cause the listed items to be printed out. A print-out of the items must be given to the plaintiff's solicitors or displayed on the computer screen so that they can be read and copied. All reasonable steps shall be taken by the plaintiff to ensure that no damage is done to any computer or data. The plaintiff and his representatives may not themselves search the defendant's computers unless they have sufficient expertise to do so without damaging the defendant's system.

Disclosure of information by the defendant

5. (1) The defendant must immediately inform the plaintiff's solicitors: (a) where all the listed items are; and (b) so far as he is aware: (i) the name and address of everyone who has supplied him, or offered to supply him, with listed items; (ii) the name and address of everyone to whom he has supplied, or offered to supply, listed items; and (iii) full details of the dates and quantities of every such supply and offer.

(2) Within . . . days after being served with this order the defendant must prepare and swear an affidavit confirming the above information.

Prohibited acts

6. (1) Except for the purpose of obtaining legal advice, the defendant must not directly or indirectly inform anyone of these proceedings or of the contents of this order, or warn anyone that proceedings have been or may be brought against him by the plaintiff until [. . .] (The date to be inserted here should be the return date or, if sooner, seven days from the date of the order.)

(2) [Insert any negative injunctions.]

EFFECT OF THIS ORDER

1) A defendant who is an individual who is ordered not to do something must not do it himself or in any other way. He must not do it through others acting on his behalf or on his instructions or with his encouragement.

2) A defendant which is a corporation and which is ordered not to do something must not do it itself or by its directors officers employees or agents or in any other way.

UNDERTAKINGS

The plaintiff, the plaintiff's solicitors and the supervising solicitor gave to the court the undertakings contained in Schs 3, 4 and 5 respectively to this order.

DURATION OF THIS ORDER

Paragraph 6(2) of this order will remain in force up to and including [: :19] (which is "the return date"), unless before then it is varied or discharged by a further order of the court. (The date should be the earliest practicable return date.) The application in which this order is made shall come back to the court for further hearing on the return date.

VARIATION OR DISCHARGE OF THIS ORDER

The defendant (or anyone notified of this order) may apply to the court at any time to vary or discharge this order (or so much of it as affects that person), but anyone wishing to do so must first inform the plaintiff's solicitors.

NAME AND ADDRESS OF PLAINTIFF'S SOLICITORS

The plaintiff's solicitors are: [Name, address and telephone numbers both in and out of office hours.]

[INTERPRETATION OF THIS ORDER]

1) In this order "he" "him" or "his" include "she" or "her" and "it" or "its".

2) Where there are two or more defendants then (unless the context indicates differently) (a) references to "the defendants" means both or all of them; (b) an order requiring "the defendants" to do or not to do anything requires each defendant to do or not to do it; (c) a requirement relating to service of this order, or of any legal proceedings, on "the defendants" means on each of them; and (d) any other requirement that something shall be done to or in the presence of "the defendants" means to or in the presence of one of them.]

SCHEDULE 1

The Premises

SCHEDULE 2

The listed items

SCHEDULE 3

Undertakings given by the plaintiff

1) If the court later finds that this order or carrying it out has caused loss to the defendant, and decides that the defendant should be compensated for that loss, the plaintiff will comply with any order the court may make.

[2] As soon as practicable to issue a writ of summons [in the form of the draft writ produced to the court] [claiming appropriate relief.]]

3) To [swear and file an affidavit] [cause an affidavit to be sworn and filed] [substantially in the terms of the draft produced to the court] [confirming the substance of what was said to the court by the plaintiff's counsel/solicitors.]

4) To serve on the defendant at the same time as this order is served upon him (i) the writ (ii) a notice of motion/summons for ... 19 and (iii) copies of the affidavits and copiable exhibits containing the evidence relied on by the plaintiff. [Copies of the confidential exhibits need not be served, but they must be made available for inspection by or on behalf of the defendant in the presence of the plaintiff's solicitors while the order is carried out. Afterwards they must be provided to a solicitor representing the defendant who gives a written undertaking not to

permit the defendant to see them or copies of them except in his presence and not to permit the defendant to make or take away any note or record of the exhibits.]

5) To serve on the defendant a copy of the supervising solicitor's report on the carrying out of this order as soon as it is received and to produce a copy of the report to the Court.

6) Not, without the leave of the court, to use any information or documents obtained as a result of carrying out this order except for the purposes of these proceedings or to inform anyone else of these proceedings until after the return date.

[7)] (In appropriate cases an undertaking to insure the items removed from the premises shall be included.)

SCHEDULE 4

Undertakings given by the plaintiff's solicitors.

1)   To answer at once to the best of their ability any question whether a particular item is a listed item.

2)   To return the originals of all documents obtained as a result of this order (except original documents which belong to the plaintiff) as soon as possible and in any event within two working days of their removal.

3)   While ownership of any item obtained as a result of this order is in dispute, to deliver the article into the keeping of solicitors acting for the defendant within two working days from receiving a written undertaking by them to retain the article in safe keeping and to produce it to the court when required.

4)   To retain in their own safe keeping all other items obtained as a result of this order until the Court directs otherwise.

SCHEDULE 5

Undertakings given by the supervising solicitor

1)   To offer to explain to the person served with the order its meaning and effect fairly and in everyday language, and to inform him of his right to seek legal advice and apply to vary or discharge the order as mentioned in para 3 of the order.

2)   To make and provide to the plaintiff's solicitors a written report on the carrying out of the order.

SCHEDULE 6

Affidavits

The judge read the following affidavits before making this order:

1) ...

2) ...

Annex 2

[Heading]

Injunction prohibiting disposal of assets worldwide

IMPORTANT

NOTICE TO THE DEFENDANT

(1)   This order prohibits you from dealing with your assets up to the amount stated. The order is subject to the exceptions at the end of the order. You should read it all carefully. You are advised to consult a solicitor as soon as possible. You have a right to ask the court to vary or discharge this order.

(2) If you disobey this order you will be guilty of contempt of court and may be [sent to prison or] fined or your assets may be seized. (Delete the words "sent to prison" in the case of a corporate defendant. This notice is not a substitute for the indorsement of a penal notice.)

THE ORDER

An application was made today [date] by counsel for [or solicitors] for ... the plaintiff to Mr Justice [...]. Mr Justice [...] heard the application and read the affidavits listed in Sch 2 at the end of this order.

As a result of the application IT IS ORDERED by Mr Justice [...] that:

1. *Disposal of assets*

1)   The defendant must not (i) remove from England and Wales any of his assets which are in England and Wales whether in his own name or not and whether solely or jointly owned up to the value of £ ... or (ii) in any way dispose of or deal with or diminish the value of any of his assets whether they are in or outside England or Wales whether in his own name or not and whether solely or jointly owned up to the same value. This prohibition includes the following assets in particular: (a) the property known as ... or the net sale money after payment of any mortgages if it has been sold; (b) the property and assets of the defendant's business known as ... (or carried on at ...) or the sale money if any of them have been sold; and (c) any money in the accounts numbered ... at ...

2)   If the total unincumbered value of the defendant's assets in England and Wales exceeds £ ... the defendant may remove any of those assets from England and Wales or may dispose of or deal with them so long as the total unincumbered value of his assets still in England and Wales remains above £ .... If the total unincumbered value of the defendant's assets in England and Wales does not exceed £ ..., the defendant must not remove any of those assets from England and Wales and must not dispose of or deal with any of them, but if he has other assets outside England and Wales the defendant may dispose of or deal with those assets so long as the total unincumbered value of all his assets whether in or outside England and Wales remains above £ ...

2. *Disclosure of information*

1)   The defendant must inform the plaintiff in writing at once of all his assets whether in or outside England and Wales and whether in his own name or not and whether solely or jointly owned, giving the value, location and details of all such assets.

2)   The information must be confirmed in an affidavit which must be served on the plaintiff's solicitors within days after this order has been served on the defendant.

EXCEPTIONS TO THIS ORDER

1)   This order does not prohibit the defendant from spending £ ... a week towards his ordinary living expenses [and £ ... a week towards his ordinary and proper business expenses] and also £ ... a week [or a reasonable sum] on legal advice and representation. But before spending any money the defendant must tell the plaintiff's solicitors where the money is to come from.

[2]   This order does not prohibit the defendant from dealing with or disposing of any of his assets in the ordinary and proper course of business.]

3)   The defendant may agree with the plaintiff's solicitors that the above spending limits should be increased or that this order should be varied in any other respect but any such agreement must be in writing.

EFFECT OF THIS ORDER

1) A defendant who is an individual who is ordered not to do something must not do it himself or in any other way. He must not do it through others acting on his behalf or on his instructions or with his encouragement.

2) A defendant which is a corporation and which is ordered not to do something must not do it itself or by its directors officers employees or agents or in any other way.

THIRD PARTIES

1) *Effect of this order.* It is a contempt of court for any person notified of this order knowingly to assist in or permit a breach of the order. Any person doing so may be sent to prison, fined, or have his assets seized.

2) *Effect of this order outside England and Wales.* The terms of this order do not affect or concern anyone outside the jurisdiction of this court until it is declared enforceable or is enforced by a court in the relevant country and then they are to affect him only to the extent they have been declared enforceable or have been enforced UNLESS such person is: (a) a person to whom this order is addressed or an officer or an agent appointed by power of attorney of such a person; or (b) a person who is subject to the jurisdiction of this Court and (i) has been given written notice of this order at his residence or place of business within the jurisdiction of this Court and (ii) is able to prevent acts or omissions outside the jurisdiction of this Court which constitute or assist in a breach of the terms of this order.

3) *Set off by banks.* This injunction does not prevent any bank from exercising any right of set off it may have in respect of any facility which it gave to the defendant before it was notified of the order.

4) *Withdrawals by the defendant.* No bank need inquire as to the application or proposed application of any money withdrawn by the defendant if the withdrawal appears to be permitted by this order.

[SERVICE OUT OF THE JURISDICTION AND SUBSTITUTED SERVICE

1) The plaintiff may serve the writ of summons on the defendant at ... by ...

2) If the defendant wishes to defend the action he must acknowledge service within ... days of being served with the writ of summons.]

UNDERTAKINGS

The plaintiff gives to the court the undertakings set out in Sch 1 to this order.

DURATION OF THIS ORDER

This order will remain in force up to and including : :19 ("the return date"), unless before then it is varied or discharged by a further order of the court. (The date should be the earliest practicable return date.) The application in which this order is made shall come back to the court for further hearing on the return date.

VARIATION OR DISCHARGE OF THIS ORDER

The defendant (or anyone notified of this order) may apply to the court at any time to vary or discharge this order (or so much of it as affects that person), but anyone wishing to do so must first inform the plaintiff's solicitors.

NAME AND ADDRESS OF PLAINTIFF'S SOLICITORS

The plaintiff's solicitors are:

[Name, address and telephone numbers both in and out of office hours].

[INTERPRETATION OF THIS ORDER]

1)   In this order "he" "him" or "his" include "she" or "her" and "it" or "its".

2)   Where there are two or more defendants then (unless the context indicates differently) (a) references to "the defendants" means both or all of them; (b) an order requiring "the defendants" to do or not to do anything requires each defendant to do or not to do it; (c) a requirement relating to the service of this order, or of any legal proceedings, on "the defendants" means on each of them.]

SCHEDULE 1

Undertakings given to the court by the plaintiff

1)   If the court later finds that this order has caused loss to the defendant, and decides that the defendant should be compensated for that loss, the plaintiff will comply with any order the court may make.

2)   As soon as practicable the plaintiff will [issue and] serve on the defendant [a] [the] writ of summons [in the form of the draft writ produced to the court] [claiming appropriate relief] together with this order.

3)   The plaintiff will cause an affidavit to be sworn and filed [substantially in the terms of the draft affidavit produced to the court] [confirming the substance of what was said to the court by the plaintiff's counsel/solicitors].

4)   As soon as practicable the plaintiff will serve on the defendant a [notice of motion] [summons] for the return date together with a copy of the affidavits and exhibits containing the evidence relied on by the plaintiff.

5)   Anyone notified of this order will be given a copy of it by the plaintiff's solicitors.

6)   The plaintiff will pay the reasonable costs of anyone other than the defendant which have been incurred as a result of this order including the costs of ascertaining whether that person holds any of the defendant's assets and that if the court later finds that this order has caused such a person loss, and decides that the person should be compensated for that loss, the plaintiff will comply with any order the court may make.

[7)   The plaintiff will not without the leave of the court begin proceedings against the defendant in any other jurisdiction or use information obtained as a result of an order of the court in this jurisdiction for the purpose of civil or criminal proceedings in any other jurisdiction.

8)   The plaintiff will not without the leave of the court seek to enforce this order in any country outside England and Wales [or seek an order of a similar nature including orders conferring a charge or other security against the defendant or the defendant's assets].]

SCHEDULE 2

Affidavits

The judge read the following affidavits before making this order:

1) ...

2) ...

Annex 3

[Heading]

Injunction prohibiting disposal of assets in England and Wales

IMPORTANT

NOTICE TO THE DEFENDANT

(1)   This order prohibits you from dealing with your assets up to the amount stated. The order is subject to the exceptions at the end of the order. You should read it all carefully. You are advised to consult a solicitor as soon as possible. You have a right to ask the court to vary or discharge this order.

(2)   If you disobey this order you will be guilty of contempt of court and may be [sent to prison or] fined or your assets may be seized. (Delete the words "sent to prison" in the case of a corporate defendant. This notice is not a substitute for the indorsement of a penal notice.)

THE ORDER

An application was made today [date] by counsel [or solicitors] for ... the plaintiff to Mr Justice [...]. Mr Justice [...] heard the application and read the affidavits listed in Sch 2 to this order.

As a result of the application IT IS ORDERED by Mr Justice [...] that:

1.   *Disposal of assets*

1)   The defendant must not remove from England and Wales or in any way dispose of or deal with or diminish the value of any of his assets which are in England and Wales whether in his own name or not and whether solely or jointly owned up to the value of £ .... This prohibition includes the following assets in particular: (a) the property known as ... or the net sale money after payment of any mortgages if it has been sold; (b) the property and assets of the defendant's business known as ... (or carried on at ...) or the sale money if any of them have been sold; and (c) any money in the accounts numbered ... at ...

2)   If the total unincumbered value of the defendant's assets in England and Wales exceeds £ ..., the defendant may remove any of those assets from England and Wales or may dispose of or deal with them so long as the total unincumbered value of his assets still in England and Wales remains above £ ...

2.   *Disclosure of information*

1)   The defendant must inform the plaintiff in writing at once of all his assets in England and Wales whether in his own name or not and whether solely or jointly owned, giving the value, location and details of all such assets. The information must be confirmed in an affidavit which must be served on the plaintiff's solicitors within days after this order has been served on the defendant.

EXCEPTIONS TO THIS ORDER

1)   This order does not prohibit the defendant from spending £ ... a week towards his ordinary living expenses [and £ ... a week towards his ordinary and proper business expenses] and also £ ... a week [or a reasonable sum] on legal advice and representation. But before spending any money the defendant must tell the plaintiff's solicitors where the money is to come from.

[2)   This order does not prohibit the defendant from dealing with or disposing of any of his assets in the ordinary and proper course of business.]

3)   The defendant may agree with the plaintiff's solicitors that the above spending limits should be increased or that this order should be varied in any other respect but any such agreement must be in writing.

EFFECT OF THIS ORDER
1)   A defendant who is an individual who is ordered not to do something must not do it himself or in any other way. He must not do it through others acting on his behalf or on his instructions or with his encouragement.

2)   A defendant which is a corporation and which is ordered not to do something must not do it itself or by its directors officers employees or agents or in any other way.

THIRD PARTIES
1)   *Effect of this order.* It is a contempt of court for any person notified of this order knowingly to assist in or permit a breach of the order. Any person doing so may be sent to prison, fined, or have his assets seized.

2)   *Set off by banks.* This injunction does not prevent any bank from exercising any right of set off it may have in respect of any facility which it gave to the defendant before it was notified of the order.

3)   *Withdrawals by the defendant.* No bank need inquire as to the application or proposed application of any money withdrawn by the defendant if the withdrawal appears to be permitted by this order.

[SERVICE OUT OF THE JURISDICTION AND SUBSTITUTED SERVICE
1)   The plaintiff may serve the writ of summons on the defendant at … by …

2)   If the defendant wishes to defend the action he must acknowledge service within … days of being served with the writ of summons.]

UNDERTAKINGS
The plaintiff gives to the court the undertakings set out in Sch 1 to this order.

DURATION OF THIS ORDER
This order will remain in force up to and including : :19   ("the return date") unless before then it is varied or discharged by a further order of the court. (The date should be the earliest practicable return date.) The application in which this order is made shall come back to the court for further hearing on the return date.

VARIATION OR DISCHARGE OF THIS ORDER
The defendant (or anyone notified of this order) may apply to the court at any time to vary or discharge this order (or so much of it as affects that person), but anyone wishing to do so must first inform the plaintiff's solicitors.

NAME AND ADDRESS OF PLAINTIFF'S SOLICITORS
The plaintiff's solicitors are:

[Name, address and telephone numbers both in and out of office hours].

[INTERPRETATION OF THIS ORDER
1)   In this order "he" "him" or "his" include "she" or "her" and "it" or "its".

2)   Where there are two or more defendants then (unless otherwise stated) (a) references to "the defendants" mean both or all of them; (b) an order requiring

"the defendants" to do or not to do anything requires each defendant to do or not to do it; and (c) a requirement relating to service of this order or of any legal proceedings on "the defendants" means on each of them.]

SCHEDULE 1

Undertakings given to the court by the plaintiff

1) If the court later finds that this order has caused loss to the defendant, and decides that the defendant should be compensated for that loss, the plaintiff will comply with any order the court may make.

2) As soon as practicable the plaintiff will [issue and] serve on the defendant [a] [the] writ of summons [in the form of the draft writ produced to the court] [claiming appropriate relief] together with this order.

3) The plaintiff will cause an affidavit to be sworn and filed [substantially in the terms of the draft affidavit produced to the court] [confirming the substance of what was said to the court by the plaintiff's counsel/solicitors].

4) As soon as practicable the plaintiff will serve on the defendant a [notice of motion] [summons] for the return date together with a copy of the affidavits and exhibits containing the evidence relied on by the plaintiff.

5) Anyone notified of this order will be given a copy of it by the plaintiff's solicitors.

6) The plaintiff will pay the reasonable costs of anyone other than the defendant which have been incurred as a result of this order including the costs of ascertaining whether that person holds any of the defendant's assets and that if the court later finds that this order has caused such person loss, and decides that such person should be compensated for that loss, the plaintiff will comply with any order the court may make.

SCHEDULE 2

Affidavits

The judge read the following affidavits before making this order:

1) ...

2) ...

INDEX

References are to paragraph number